PRAISE FOR TAMAR ADLER'S *AN EVERLASTING MEAL*

"Beautifully intimate, approaching cooking as a narrative that begins not with a list of ingredients or a tutorial on cutting an onion, but with a way of thinking. . . . Tamar is one of the great writers I know—her prose is exquisitely crafted, beautiful and clear-eyed and open, in the thoughtful spirit of M. F. K. Fisher. This is a book to sink into and read deeply."

—Alice Waters, from the Foreword

"Lessons so right and so eloquent that I think of them as homilies."

—Corby Kummer, *The New York Times Book Review*

"Tamar Adler has written the best book on 'cooking with economy and grace' that I have read since M. F. K. Fisher."

—Michael Pollan

"Reads less like a cookbook than like a recipe for a delicious life."

—*New York* magazine

"A book about how to live a good life: take the long view, give to others, learn from everything you do, and always, always, always mindfully enjoy what you are doing and what you've done. The fact you'll learn to be a great cook is just a bonus."

—Forbes.com

"Adler proves herself an adept essayist in this discourse on instinctive home cooking. Though highly personal, it's much less a food memoir than a kind of cooking tao."

—*The Atlanta Journal-Constitution*

"Simultaneously meditative and practical, about how to appreciate and use what you have and how to prepare it appropriately with a minimum of fuss, space, equipment, or waste."

—*The Austin Chronicle*

"Like having a cooking teacher whispering suggestions in your ear. . . . Mindfulness, I'm discovering through this terrific book, can be delicious."

—Novella Carpenter, author of *Farm City*

"Adler's terrific book wisely presents itself as a series of how-tos with the suggestion that it's not only possible to do all these things but, in fact, a pleasure. An Everlasting Meal provides the very best kind of lesson, that there is real joy to be had in eating, and eating well."

—Dan Barber, chef/co-owner of Blue Hill and Blue Hill at Stone Barns

PRAISE FOR TAMAR ADLER'S *SOMETHING OLD, SOMETHING NEW*

"Tamar Adler is a curious magpie, skillfully collecting culinary ephemera from across the ages and weaving them into an unimaginably beautiful nest. Step inside. You'll find yourself comforted and inspired by the writing and the food, both equally sensible and elegant."
—Samin Nosrat, author of
Salt, Fat, Acid, Heat

"A lovely and literary cookbook . . . handsome and witty and personal, full of glimpses into Adler's life."
—Vogue.com

"Adler is a peaceable cook, and a pragmatic one. . . . Her economizing ethos shines in her new book."
—*The Washington Post*

"A personal, nostalgic journey inspiring the rediscovery of classics . . . as much about the writing as it is about the cooking."
—Jenny Rosenstrach,
The New York Times Book Review

"Adler has a curious intelligence and technical command to back up a thoughtful approach. . . . Any cook looking to exercise and enhance creativity will find in Adler a worthy muse."
—*Booklist*

"Adler's beautiful, reflective prose provides history and insight into each dish. Adler shows how nostalgic, old school dishes can taste current when remade with a modern sensibility."
—*Publishers Weekly*

"Tamar Adler is more than a wonderful food writer—she is a wonderful writer. She delves into these past and forgotten recipes with the spirit of an adventurer and a sleuth, and while writing about food, she is always secretly writing about something else—a love of life, eternal values, industry, thrift, friendship, the unknown. Her books—written with a charmingly loose confidence and care—feel timeless."
—Sheila Heti, author of *Pure Colour*

"I treasure Something Old, Something New for the writing, which is as suave and fun to read as M. F. K. Fisher. Adler is the best kind of kitchen companion, someone whose warm and witty voice I want to carry with me as I cook."
—Bee Wilson, author of *Consider the Fork*

THE
EVERLASTING MEAL
COOKBOOK
LEFTOVERS A–Z

TAMAR ADLER

ILLUSTRATIONS BY
CAITLIN WINNER

SCRIBNER

NEW YORK LONDON TORONTO SYDNEY NEW DELHI

SCRIBNER

An Imprint of Simon & Schuster, Inc.

1230 Avenue of the Americas

New York, NY 10020

Copyright © 2023 by Tamar Adler

Illustrations copyright © 2023 by Caitlin Winner

The essay at the beginning of Chapter 13 was originally published in a different form in *The New York Times Magazine* in 2016.

Recipes reprinted unchanged with permission from Deborah Madison: Basic Galette Dough and Cheese Soufflé

Recipes reprinted unchanged with permission from *Just One Cookbook*: Tempura Dipping Sauce, Chicken Katsudon, and Teriyaki Sauce

All rights reserved, including the right to reproduce this book or portions thereof in any form whatsoever. For information, address Scribner Subsidiary Rights Department, 1230 Avenue of the Americas, New York, NY 10020.

First Scribner hardcover edition March 2023

SCRIBNER and design are registered trademarks of The Gale Group, Inc., used under license by Simon & Schuster, Inc., the publisher of this work.

For information about special discounts for bulk purchases, please contact Simon & Schuster Special Sales at 1-866-506-1949 or business@simonandschuster.com.

The Simon & Schuster Speakers Bureau can bring authors to your live event. For more information or to book an event, contact the Simon & Schuster Speakers Bureau at 1-866-248-3049 or visit our website at www.simonspeakers.com.

Interior design by Alvaro Villanueva, Bookish Design

Manufactured in the United States of America

10 9 8 7 6 5 4 3 2

Library of Congress Cataloging-in-Publication Data has been applied for.

ISBN 978-1-4767-9966-7

ISBN 978-1-4767-9969-8 (ebook)

To Louis and Peter,
and for savers of short string

A man was cleaning the attic of an old home in New England and he found a box which was full of tiny pieces of string. On the lid of the box there was an inscription in an old hand: "String too short to be saved."

—*Donald Hall*, String Too Short to Be Saved

CONTENTS

INTRODUCTION

This book contains most of what I know about cooking, spread among recipes for making much with odds and ends.

I feel about leftovers as I do about empty restaurants and unkempt gardens. I love them because they are unloved. I know this isn't a universal sentiment. But I imagine that other people also look at the dried out slice of bread whose companion tasted so good this morning, or at the end of a pot of soup or rice and *wish* they could love them, and believe that they could, if any could taste as good again. That is what I fantasized about while I wrote this book.

This is a leftovers encyclopedia, organized by leftover ingredient. A friend suggested I call it *How to Cook Everything . . . Again*, because that is the information it contains. The vegetable chapter has hundreds of ideas for leftover vegetables and their stems and leaves. The fruit chapter has recipes for overripe and underripe fruit and its peels and pits. The beans and rice chapter is what to make of pots of beans and rice. And so on. My definitions are broad, including foods that are not strictly "leftover." The writer Richard Olney, half of whose recipes in *Simple French Food* rely on stale bread, wrote that "the wild things of nature" were the economic ally of leftovers. This is sound. Like leftovers, foraged foods are free. I've included edible weeds and mushrooms where I knew what to do with them.

I've left entries in the terms that come first to my mind. A recipe using leftover mashed potatoes will be found under "Mashed potatoes" rather than "Potatoes, mashed." Leftover "candied yams" are listed as such. In the case of eggs–where I somewhat religiously consider the egg itself before how it assembles itself in the pot or pan, I list "Eggs, poached" and "Eggs, scrambled." When an ingredient or dish entered my life in a language other than English, I used its native language.

There is a paradox in writing recipes for this style of cooking. To provide directions for turning leftover mashed potatoes into crisp, fried cakes, I had to posit an *amount* of leftover mashed potatoes. How else to succinctly say how much flour to add and how much fat to fry them in? But the amount of leftover mashed potatoes you need is the amount you have. This is true in general and certainly for every recipe in this book. It is one of the inalienable rewards of treating old and leftover food as food, and you must claim it. I've included a logical if arbitrary amount of mashed potatoes (and so on) throughout. You can read and note the ratios in the recipes and about how much flour you need for what is in your bowl, and how much fat, and how many cakes it will make, and make decisions accordingly.

All cooking really requires is perception, practice, and patience. (This alliteration is galling but so were the synonyms.) Most other inputs are distractions. The chef Edna Lewis used to say that she *listened* to know when a cake was done. I've never heard a cake finishing, but I listen for eggs clattering around in a pot, and water burning off sauteing greens when they go from a light hiccup to a hard fry. These sounds are as good as a timer going off, and they are better for learning. This is even truer of smell. We have intricate noses, evolved over millions of years to ensure our survival. We smell some things better than bloodhounds do. We receive little reassurance that we bloodhounds can trust our senses to say food has gone bad. This is in part due to the preeminence in what exists of a collective American consciousness of expiration dates—which are not in fact expiration dates. (Nor are sell-by dates or best-by dates.) Most of the time, we *can* trust our senses. Our meticulous olfactory instruments are also at work when water boils and greens begin to fry. I've used standard time estimates in most of these recipes, in addition to saying what you should listen and smell for, so you know how long it will be until dinner is ready. Please let your observations remain the arbiter. Only you know if a thing is "done" or "good." And you know it through your eyes and ears and nose and mouth.

I yearn to repeat on every page that ½ tsp of salt is a good starting point for seasoning anything but the water in a boiling pot–which demands a small handful. And to measure the ½ tsp into your hand so it eventually becomes your personal measuring device. I want to counsel you that frying–which I love–is not for the faint of heart. It hurts, even if you do it perfectly. Little beads of oil spring up and burn your forearms, not to mention what they do to your stovetop. But your skin and stovetop are fast to recover, and you're not doing anything wrong even if it is a little painful and a little messy. The way you are doing it is the one you'll learn from. If I were standing beside you, I would tell you to change nothing, but how close your hand is to the oil (it should be closer) and how much you're worrying. I've tried to include this sort of advice throughout. But sometimes I simply say to add ½ tsp of salt. And sometimes I just instruct you to fry.

In my attempt to be comprehensive, I have often been eccentric–how many suggestions does one really need for leftover aillade? There is no excuse for there being three entries for certain ingredients and one–or none–for others. I grew up with a Middle Eastern father. We ate pita and hummus and pickles. I cooked at Chez Panisse, where the food was unpretentious and garlicky. These facts have imprinted on my repertoire and my preferences. They have been inescapable in the selection of these entries.

If you've never felt tenderly toward leftovers, it may still be of interest that thousands of culinary delicacies rely on using what seems useless. They include ribollita and French onion soup, bouillabaisse, minestrone, arancini, rice pudding, fried rice, cider vinegar, and dumplings and bone broth and, and, and. All of those and more are products of the ancient happy marriage of economy and pleasure. That so much good food is born of this abiding coupling is simply not *said* often enough. But it is true. I find that truth not only practical but holy.

It is mostly women who have devised the methods in these recipes: more mothers than childless, more poor than rich. Where I remember how I first read of a recipe or tasted a dish, I've included a credit. Where there is no credit, this note should serve to emphasize that everything comes from somewhere. I only claim participation in the history of feeding.

This book is my best attempt at a compendium of what to do with what you have–with your string too short to be saved. So once again, I boldly suggest that by having saved what's left of an earlier meal, you are already cooking another one. And I offer you these pages as a companion while you continue on from where you are.

THINGS YOU NEED TO COOK
AN EVERLASTING MEAL

FAT: Fat is a great diplomat, skilled at smoothing transitions from one day to the next. I use olive oil promiscuously for all cooking but frying, and for general drizzling. I use grapeseed or peanut oil for frying. I use sesame oil where recipes call for it, because it is too fervently nutty to be replicated, though I've substituted the oil that rises to the top of a jar of tahini or peanut butter. Vegetable oil is neutral enough for everything. I love butter and ghee, and I cook with both, but I let myself run out of ghee first, because it is clarified butter and can be made by very slowly melting butter then straining out the milk solids.

SALT: I mostly use kosher salt, but I can adjust. After a few mishaps—oversalted pasta and oversalted eggs and a brief mea culpa—I recalibrate my pinches to whatever kind is around. Sea salt is also good. Iodized is fine if that's what you have. I use flaky salt for sprinkling over at the end. It contributes specialness to simple things, which makes it worth the fuss.

ACID: A sprinkle of acid often all it takes to brighten up what dimmed overnight. I like plain distilled white vinegar, red wine vinegar, white wine vinegar, apple cider vinegar, and rice vinegar and use them all with little differentiation. I go through phases of buying lemons and limes and phases of not buying them. During the *not* phases I use one of the vinegars above, and we survive, even thrive.

HERBS OR CRUNCHY THINGS: Parsley, cilantro, mint, toasted bread crumbs, toasted nuts, fried shallots, or any other green leaf or bit of toasted seed cheers up anything leftover or plain via a combination of distraction and magnetism.

SPICE: Chile flakes, pickled chiles, chili sauce, garlic-chili sauce, chili crisp, kosho, and the other piquant amendments on which nature and culture have conspired, are indispensable to remaking and transforming odds and ends.

AN ALLIUM: This can be a clove of garlic or a few scallions or half a shallot or onion or leek. They all supply some of the same round rich sweetness.

PICKLES: Olives, capers, anchovies, kimchi, pickles, and all other salty, preserved things, are as reliable as parsley and bread crumbs and nuts for transforming simple or left-over food.

COOKING TOOLS: It is good to have a sharp chef's knife and a serrated knife, to keep from blunting your sharp one on bread. I always need at least one large pot, big enough to boil two pounds of pasta, with a lid. A large heavy-bottomed saucepan is vital for cooking greens and other vegetables that start voluminous then shrink. At least one 12-inch skillet, nonstick or cast iron, makes frittatas easier. A small pot keeps you from having to heat up a big one when it's just you. I turn regularly to one to two sheet pans or cookie sheets, a big colander, a handheld sieve for scooping things out of the boiling pot, a mortar and pestle, a peeler, a whisk, tongs, wooden spoons, plus various metals ones that have outlived some of the wooden ones. I have a blender *and* a food processor. If I had to choose, I would probably choose the food processor, but no one has asked me to.

A VERY BRIEF MANIFESTO TO COVER ANYTHING I'VE LEFT OUT: If a kitchen tool helps, and you love it, keep and it and use it until it is worn out. If you wonder whether you *need* a certain knife or pot or anything else that vows to change your cooking and your life, consider restraint. A sharp knife, regardless of its size, will cut almost anything. Even the thinnest tin pot will boil and braise and fry. Each new thing we buy to help us cook will need to go somewhere when we are done with it. So the best counsel I have is to go about your cooking, only adding *things* if there's no more creative way of resolving the issue.

USEFUL CONVERSIONS

There are **3 TEASPOONS** in **1 TABLESPOON**

There are **16 TABLESPOONS** in **1 CUP**

1 LIME produces about **1½ TABLESPOONS JUICE**

1 LEMON produces about **3 TABLESPOONS JUICE**

1 LEMON produces about **1 TABLESPOON GRATED ZEST**

1 LIME produces about **2 TEASPOONS GRATED ZEST**

1 ORANGE produces **2–3 TABLESPOONS GRATED ZEST**

1 INCH OF FRESH GINGER produces about **1 TABLESPOON CHOPPED**

1 MEDIUM CLOVE GARLIC is **BETWEEN 1 HEAPING TEASPOON AND 1 TABLESPOON**, and the range is fine

1 MEDIUM ONION (chopped) is about **1 CUP**

1 MEDIUM FENNEL BULB (chopped) is **1½–2 CUPS**, and the range is fine

1 MEDIUM CARROT (chopped) is about **½ CUP**

1 STALK CELERY produces about **½ CUP SLICED** and **⅓ CUP CHOPPED**

1 POUND GROUND MEAT is about **2 CUPS RAW** and **1½ CUPS COOKED**

1 CUP COOKED MEAT (chopped) is a little over **10½ OUNCES**

1 CUP ALL-PURPOSE FLOUR weighs about **120 GRAMS**

1 CUP SUGAR weighs about **200 GRAMS**

1 CUP BUTTER weighs about **227 GRAMS**

1 CUP SOURDOUGH STARTER discard weighs about **226 GRAMS**

VEGETABLE OIL can be replaced by **BUTTER** at a **1:1 RATIO** in baking

HOW TO EAT WELL
Vegetables

Who wants to eat a good supper should eat
a weed of every kind.

—*A Tuscan saying, via Patience Gray*

A vegetable that has basked in hot heat with good fat is more useful to the home cook than one left raw. This is as true of the most baroque broccoli Romanesco as it is of the lowliest butternut. Once vegetables are cooked, there can be an herby roasted vegetable salad one day, a soup another, a fried rice dish a third, and so on, with only minimal adjustments in between.

Two rewarding ways to turn vegetables from raw to cooked are: 1) Roast them: Set the oven to 400°F. Trim off anything wilted. Wash what's left, cut it into 1- to 2-inch pieces of about equal volume, place them in a bowl, drizzle them heavily with olive oil and sprinkle liberally with salt, then tip them onto a sheet pan, careful to leave a little breathing room among and between. Add a drizzle of water, a whole clove of garlic and/or a branch of rosemary, if you have, and roast them until they are browned and caramelized. Or 2) Boil them: Set a large pot of water on the stove. Bring it to a boil, then add salt by hand, tasting it by tapping the surface with the tip of your finger or by dipping in a shallow spoon, as you go. If you taste water, add more salt. Continue until it approaches the saltiness of a pleasantly salted sea. When it does, you have a seasoned medium for cooking, and you can begin, boiling vegetables in batches by type, checking for the doneness of each batch with a sharp knife and a taste, removing with a handheld sieve or tongs to a waiting tray, and drizzling with olive oil. In most cases, following one of those directions in advance of a vegetable aging—or as soon as possible after aging has begun—will save a vegetable and a trip to the store. And it will furnish the category of vegetables-ready-to-be-used.

To make the most of vegetables-ready-to-be-used, and therefore all leftover vegetables, it helps to acquaint yourself with the most pleasurable temperature for eating anything: room temperature. When you are cold, there's nothing as good as hot broth, and when you're hot, only ice water provides real relief. But when it's plain daily hunger you're addressing, the ambient temperature of a room is most flattering to ingredients.

Treat any you've stored away like wine or cheese, letting them sit out and breathe a bit, so their oils and fibers slacken on their own. This will let you taste the flavors you took the care to store, rather than the effects of storage.

Cooking ingredients prolongs their lives, which is why the prescription for a fading vegetable is the same as for a fresh one: Cook it. If a vegetable is raw but seems left over because it has begun to yellow and droop, it has already begun to be cooked by time. Now pick up where entropy left off. Pare off anything gray or unnerving. Slice what's left across its grain and cook it thoroughly, to a lovely Italian consistency. Or add it to cooking minestrone or to a stew, where droopiness is to be expected.

Vegetables that are left over because they were sliced yesterday are most helped by being added to. Slice another zucchini to add to the sliced half that wasn't grilled, giving you enough to roast for dinner. This works especially well when you pack your own lunch for work. If you have a little sliced tomato left, slice some mozzarella, store the two together in a lunch container, and you'll have Caprese at your desk tomorrow.

As with weeds like dandelion and wild sorrel and nettles, whose edibility resides in the eye of their beholder, vegetables' stems and peels and leaves are useful ingredients when allowed to be. Tough ribs and stems must be thinly sliced across, but then can be cooked along with everything else, or saved and used as cooking greens. Peels can be fried. Leafy tops do a miraculous imitation of herbs. You do not have to eat weeds—though they merit sampling. But seeing vegetables' stems and peels and leaves and tired vegetables and leftover vegetables for what they *are* rather than what they are not paves the way more reliably for a good supper than would a narrower perspective.

Here are some fundamental vegetable techniques:

TO PREPARE GARLIC

Cut each clove in half and peel it. If you have time, remove the green germ in the middle to avoid bitterness. Slice off the root end, and proceed.

MIREPOIX

Finely chop onion, carrot, celery or fennel in a ratio of 2:1:1. For example: 1 cup onion, ½ cup each of the other two. Cook in olive oil over medium-low heat, salting immediately, until tender. Freezes well, raw or cooked.

PUERTO RICAN SOFRITO

2 medium onions (chopped), 1 cup (16–20) peeled cloves garlic, 3 cups chopped mostly sweet or hot sweet peppers, 3–4 whole tomatoes (fresh or canned), 1 bunch cilantro (stems and leaves).

In a food processor, combine the onions and garlic and pulse. Add the peppers, tomatoes, and cilantro and puree to fairly smooth. Cook in olive oil over medium-low heat, salting immediately, until tender. Freezes well, raw or cooked.

FRIED SHALLOTS

4–5 shallots, neutral oil (peanut, grapeseed, or vegetable).

Thinly slice the shallots into rounds. In a heavy-bottomed pot or saucepan, combine the shallots and enough oil to cover them by about 1 inch. Place the pot over high heat and slowly bring the oil to a bubble. Cook, stirring constantly, until they are just golden, about 10 min. Strain, reserving the oil (which you can now label "shallot oil" and use to make things extra delicious and shallot-y) and drain on a paper towel until cool.

And here are adaptable vegetable recipes:

ALMOST ANY VEGETABLE PASTA

Salt, 1 head broccoli (or cauliflower, broccoli Romanesco, cabbage, peas, or any other vegetable you want to boil), olive oil, 1 lb short pasta (orecchiette or penne), Parmesan cheese.

Bring a large pot of water to a boil. Salt it to taste like pleasant seawater. Cut the core and stem from the broccoli (or so on) and slice very finely and include, or reserve for another use. Cut the remainder into florets or pieces, 2–3 inches each. Boil in batches until perfectly tender and easily pierced by a sharp knife. Retrieve with a sieve and set in a big bowl. Drizzle heavily with olive oil. Add the pasta to the same pot and cook it. Remove it directly to the bowl of vegetables, drizzle with more olive oil, shower heavily with Parmesan, mix well, taste, adjust, and eat.

This can be made with roasted vegetables rather than boiled. You will be deprived of the satisfaction of using a single pot of water to make a full meal, but you will still have a good dinner. Cut your vegetable into small florets or other uniform pieces, drizzle heavily with olive oil, salt amply, add a little water, and then roast at 400°F until toasty and tender and caramelized. Mix with the pasta, top with Parmesan, toasted bread crumbs, and parsley, and eat.

ANY VEGETABLE MASH

3 tbsp butter, 1 clove garlic (chopped or sliced), ⅛ tsp salt plus to taste, ½–1 tsp white wine (optional), 2 cups leftover cooked vegetables (squash, root vegetables, broccoli, cauliflower), ¼ cup heavy cream. *Optional seasoning*: a scrape of lemon zest, cinnamon, or nutmeg, a few pounded green coriander seeds.

Heat a small pot. Add the butter, then the garlic and salt, and cook until it softens, 30 sec–1 min, adding a sprinkle of water if it threatens to brown. Add wine (if using), then the vegetables and cream and simmer for 5 min. Add any optional seasonings that seem enticing. Puree or smash to smooth. Taste for salt and adjust. Eat as you would mashed potatoes.

ANY VEGETABLE MINESTRA

3 tbsp butter or olive oil plus for serving, ½ onion (sliced or chopped), 1 clove garlic, ½ tsp salt plus to taste, 2–3 sprigs thyme or rosemary, 2 cups combined chopped vegetables (cooked or raw or a combination. Or some peels and some stems and cores—anything works, as long as it is chopped neatly), 4 cups any cooking liquid or a combination (left from vegetable cooking, bean cooking, farro cooking, or Savory Stock/Broth, p. 247), 1 cup cooked starches (optional; beans, rice, small pasta), and toppings (optional; olive tapenade, parsley oil, or other herb oil).

Heat a soup pot. Add the butter or olive oil, onion, garlic, and salt and cook until tender, 5–10 min, then add the herbs, vegetables, and liquid. Simmer for 15–20 min, add any cooked starches, and simmer for 5 min. Taste for salt and adjust. Eat drizzled copiously with olive oil and any other toppings.

ANY VEGETABLE POTAGE

3 tbsp butter or olive oil plus for serving, ½ onion (sliced or chopped), 1 clove garlic, ½ tsp salt plus to taste, 1 sprig thyme or rosemary or other herb, leftover vegetables (squash, root vegetables, sweet potatoes, leeks, broccoli, cauliflower), an equal quantity water or stock.

Heat a soup pot. Add the butter or olive oil, onion, garlic, and salt and cook until tender, 5–10 min, then add the herbs, vegetables, and liquid. Simmer for 15–20 min and puree in batches, blending more solids than liquid, because it's easier to add liquid than to remove it. Combine in a pot before eating. Taste and add leftover liquid if you want. Taste for salt and adjust. Good with crisp croutons on top.

ANY VEGETABLE SABZI

2–3 tbsp neutral oil (peanut, grapeseed, or olive) or ghee, ½ tsp cumin seeds, ½ tbsp chopped garlic, ½ tbsp minced fresh ginger, 1 onion (finely chopped), 1 fresh green chile (chopped), ½ tsp salt plus to taste, ¼ tsp ground turmeric, 1 tsp garam masala, ½ tsp ground coriander, ½–1 tsp ground chile powder, a scrape of hing (asafoetida), 3 cups left-over cooked vegetables (squash, root vegetables, broccoli, cauliflower, cabbage, eggplant, green beans) in bite-size pieces, 1 canned or fresh tomato (chopped), 1 tsp kasuri methi (fenugreek leaves), 2 tbsp chopped cilantro, rice, or flatbread for serving.

Heat a large, heavy-bottomed sauté pan. Add the oil or ghee, then cumin seeds. Once they've sizzled and become aromatic, add the garlic and ginger, then the onion, green chile, and salt. Sauté until the onion begins to soften, about 2 min. Add the turmeric, garam masala, coriander, chile powder, and hing. Add the cooked vegetables, then the tomato and kasuri methi and cook until the tomato has broken down, about 5 min, adding a bit of water or oil if needed. Taste for salt and adjust. Add the cilantro, and eat with hot rice or warm flat bread.

ANY VEGETABLE SALAD

2 cups leftover cooked chopped vegetables (squash, root vegetables, broccoli, cauli-flower), ¼ cup almonds (chopped), ¼ onion of any color or a shallot (sliced lengthwise into very thin half-moons), ½ tsp salt plus to taste, 1 tbsp vinegar or more to taste, ½ tsp Dijon mustard, 2 tbsp olive oil or to taste, ¼ cup roughly chopped parsley or mint, ¼ cup chopped greens (optional; turnip greens, carrot tops, radish tops, or mustard greens), a squeeze of lemon.

Heat the oven to 400°F. Allow the vegetables to come to room temperature. Set the al-monds on a sheet pan and lightly toast in the oven, 5–10 min. Remove from the pan. In a big bowl, combine the onion or shallot, salt, vinegar, and mustard and let sit for 10 min. Mix well. Add the vegetables, olive oil, then almonds and mix well. Add the herbs and greens (if using). Taste for salt and adjust. Add a squeeze of lemon juice before eating.

ANY VEGETABLE CURRY

3 tbsp neutral oil (peanut, grapeseed, or olive), ½ onion (medium-diced), ½ tsp salt plus to taste, ½ tsp ground spices (roughly equal parts ground turmeric, ground cardamom, and ground cumin), 1 fresh chile (minced) or ½ tsp chile flakes, ½ cup cooked chickpeas or black-eyed peas, ½–1 (14-oz) can coconut milk, 1 cup other liquid (stock, vegetable cooking liquid, bean broth, farro liquid, water), 2–3 pieces lemon or lime peel (removed with a peeler), 1 tsp fish sauce (optional), 2 cups leftover cooked vegetables, ½ cup toasted peanuts (chopped), fresh lemon or lime juice, fresh herb leaves (mint, basil, or cilantro), freshly cooked rice for serving.

Heat a large, heavy-bottomed sauté pan. Add the oil, onion, and salt and cook until tender, 5–10 min. Add the spices and chile. Once the spices are fragrant, add the chickpeas or black-eyed peas, coconut milk, liquid, and citrus peel. Cook, stirring occasionally, at just below a simmer for about 30 min. Add the fish sauce (if using). Add the vegetables and peanuts and cook for 15 min over low heat. Taste for salt and spiciness and adjust. Add lemon or lime juice to taste. Top with herbs and eat with hot rice.

ANY VEGETABLE THAI-STYLE CURRY

Two (14-oz) cans coconut milk (3–4 cups), 3 tbsp red or green Thai curry paste, 3–6 cups combined leftover vegetables (cooked or raw, cut into 1- to 2-inch pieces), 1–2 chiles (optional; chopped), 6–7 makrut lime leaves, ¼ cup fish sauce, a handful of Thai basil and/or cilantro (optional), freshly cooked rice for serving.

Heat a large, heavy-bottomed sauté pan, then add ¼ cup of the coconut milk and the curry paste and stir to dissolve the curry paste, 1–2 min. Add the remaining coconut milk and 1½ cups water, stir to combine, then add all of the vegetables and the chiles (if using). Bring to a boil, then reduce to a simmer and cook until all the vegetables are nearly tender, about 10 min. If you're using sturdier vegetables and they take longer, add a little pour of water if needed to keep everything bubbling along. Add the lime leaves and continue cooking until the vegetables are completely tender, another 5–7 min. Add the fish sauce and simmer for 1 min or so, then taste and adjust if needed. Add the fresh herbs (if using) and eat with hot rice.

BY-MISTAKE-UNDERCOOKED WINTER VEGETABLE SALAD

2 tbsp olive oil, 1 crisp green or red apple (cut into ½-inch cubes), 2 shallots or ¼ red onion (very thinly sliced), ½ cup ½-inch-diced fennel, 1 cup diced undercooked winter vegetable (squash, turnip, carrot, or parsnip), 1½ tbsp red or white wine vinegar, ¼ tsp salt plus to taste, ½ tsp walnut or olive oil, 4 cups torn escarole or very finely sliced stemmed kale.

Heat a pan over medium heat. Add the olive oil, then add the apple, shallots or onion, and fennel and cook until they've begun to get tender, about 5 min. Add the undercooked vegetable, stir to combine, increase the heat to medium-high, add the vinegar and salt, and cook for another 30 sec to 1 min. Remove from the heat. Add the walnut or olive oil, stir through, taste for salt and adjust. Arrange the greens on a plate and tip the vegetables onto it, piling a little as you do.

HERB TEA

Bring water to a boil, pour it over clean herbs, still on the stem, let sit for 5 min, and drink, adding honey or sugar if you like.

ACORN SQUASH, COOKED

It is enduringly frustrating to have the first entry in a book refer you elsewhere. It is the fault of squash, which is nearly universally replaceable with other squash, regardless of the type. This fact is suboptimal from a searching perspective but optimal from a culinary one: Leftovers of cooked squashes can be thanked for their endurance and mutability, and then used in the Any Vegetable Mash (p. 8), Any Vegetable Minestra (p. 8), Any Vegetable Potage (p. 8), Any Vegetable Sabzi (p. 9), Any Vegetable Salad (p. 9), Any Vegetable Curry (p. 9), or Any Vegetable Thai-Style Curry (p. 10). Or, scoop leftover acorn squash out of its shell into a mixing bowl, smash it with a bit of salt and olive oil, and spread it, cold, on toasted bread rubbed with a garlic clove, with olive oil and grated Parmesan and black pepper adorning it all. If cold smashed squash doesn't appeal, warm it in a little pot with a sprinkle of water, stirring so it doesn't burn, and then proceed. Leftover acorn squash is also a warming addition to Risotto (p. 206). Or, it can be scooped, roughly cubed, and warmed up with lunchtime beans into something not nameable but filling and good.

ACORN SQUASH PEEL

What to do with a squash peel depends on the squash. Acorn squash peels are hard, and find their way to my compost bucket. Same with butternut. Honeynut and delicata peels can be eaten along with their flesh. Whether you eat kabocha peel is a personal choice. Summer squash peels should mostly be eaten with their flesh, except for cucuzza, which grows as big as a French horn and whose skin is immutably tough.

ALFALFA SPROUTS, WILTED

TOFU SMASH (*5 min*)
½ block extra-firm tofu, 1 scallion (minced), ¼ cup chopped celery, 1 tbsp mayonnaise, 1 tsp salt plus to taste, lots of freshly ground black pepper, a small handful of alfalfa sprouts.

In a bowl, smash the tofu with a fork to a fine crumble. Add the scallion, celery, mayonnaise, salt, and black pepper. Mix well. Add the sprouts and mix to combine. Taste for salt and adjust. Good on its own or on lettuce leaves or in a sandwich.

GARDEN EGG TACO (*5–10 min*)
1 boiled egg, 1–2 tbsp olive oil, a small handful of alfalfa sprouts, salt, feshly ground black pepper, a warmed tortilla, hot sauce (optional).

In a bowl, smash the egg with a fork into uneven pieces. Heat a small pan. Add the oil, then the egg, sprouts, a sprinkle of salt, and a good deal of black pepper. Stir to warm and fry, about 30 sec. Tip the contents of the pan directly onto the tortilla. Add hot sauce if you want!

ALOO GOBI

ALOO GOBI SOUP (*15–20 min*)
1 tbsp ghee or butter or coconut oil, 1 tsp amchur powder or grated zest of 1 lime, 1 tsp ground turmeric, 1 can coconut milk, 1 cup aloo gobi, 1¼ tsp salt plus to taste. *Optional additions:* cooked rice, cilantro, and/or spinach, and moong dal.

Heat a small pot. Add the ghee. Add amchur (but not lime zest, if you are using) and turmeric and let sizzle 20 sec or so. Add the coconut milk, aloo gobi, 1 cup water, the salt, and lime zest (if using) and simmer for 15 min. Taste for salt and adjust. Eat as is, or puree to a creamy soup.

A scoop of cooked rice is also good stirred in at the end, as is a handful of chopped cilantro, or a handful of fresh spinach or all three. For an even heartier version, add a little cooked moong dal. (Adapted from Spice Chronicles website)

ALOO GOBI SAMOSAS (*1½ hr*)
Samosa Dough (p. 350), salt, 1 cup aloo gobi, peanut or grapeseed oil for frying.

Make the samosa dough, then set aside to rest for 30–40 min. Add salt to taste to the leftover aloo gobi. It should be highly seasoned. Knead the dough. Divide it into 8 pieces, covering the dough you're not using. Roll each ball into an oval then divide it in half horizontally. Holding a piece in your hand, apply water to the straight edge, then form into a cone. Fill with about 1 tbsp filling.

Wet the rim, then pinch to seal. Continue with the remaining dough, keeping the finished samosas covered as you work. In a small, deep pot, heat 3–4 inches of oil to 325°F. Fry 2–3 samosas at a time for 10–12 min over low heat, then increase the heat slightly and continue cooking until crisp and golden, another 5 min. Good with any chutney. (Adapted from Cook with Manali website)

ALOO GOBI GRILLED CHEESE *(15 min)*
Softened butter, 2 slices sandwich bread, ¼ cup aloo gobi, thinly sliced or grated cheddar cheese, chopped cilantro, sauerkraut (or kimchi or curtido), cilantro chutney (optional).

Butter the bread on both sides. Spread with the aloo gobi, smashing it as you do. Top with cheddar, then the remaining ingredients. Cook as you do a grilled cheese, griddling each side until golden brown and flipping, cooking until the cheese has melted.

AMARANTH

Amaranth is one of the many wild greens that can be discarded as a weed or cooked in a hot pan with garlic and olive oil for a spinach stand-in. If you have it growing in your yard, wash it well and cook it as in *Greens (p. 45)*.

ANISE HYSSOP, WILTED

Anise hyssop, even wilted, makes good Herb Tea (p. 10).

ARTICHOKES, COOKED

ARTICHOKES AND BEANS WITH AIOLI *(20 min)*
1 or 2 artichokes, 1-2 cups cooked beans with their cooking liquid, 1 sprig rosemary or savory, salt, olive oil to taste, Aioli (p. 395).

If they are baby artichokes, cut them into wedges. If they are big, remove the leaves and eat them as you putter, a cook's treat. Scoop out the hairy choke with a fork or a grapefruit spoon (my mother's trick) and cut the heart and stem into wedges or chunks. In a small pot, combine the artichokes with the beans, rosemary, and a little bean cooking liquid and bring to a simmer. Taste for salt and adjust. Eat warm, heavily dolloped with aioli.

ARTICHOKE LIQUID FROM BRAISING ARTICHOKES

IMPROVED POTATOES (*10–20 min*)
Potatoes, artichoke braising liquid, salt, olive oil plus for drizzling.

If you steamed or fried artichokes, this doesn't apply, and your artichoke alone must suffice. But if you went through the nail-stinging ordeal of trimming and turning and choking your artichokes, you will have braised them. Then, you will have artichoke braising liquid, which has been enriched by the salt, olive oil, herbs, and garlic you added. It is also, more importantly, a potent concentrate of the deep metallic thrill of artichoke. Cut potatoes of any kind, from Idaho to Magic Molly, into large chunks of uniform size and put them into a pot. Add the artichoke braising liquid. If you don't have enough to cover them, add water to make up the difference. Taste the liquid to make sure it tastes like a broth of which you would gladly take another sip, and add salt or water or a drizzle of olive oil as needed. Bring to a boil, then reduce to a simmer and cook until the potatoes are completely tender. These are perfect.

ARTICHOKES, CANNED

AN ODDLY GOOD SCRAMBLE (*5–10 min*)
2–3 eggs (whisked), ¼ tsp salt plus to taste, 2 tbsp butter or oil, 3 canned artichoke hearts (rinsed and wedged), a pinch of chopped parsley or Herbes de Provence, freshly ground black pepper.

In a bowl, whisk the eggs and salt. Heat a small nonstick or regular frying pan, add half the butter or oil, then add the artichoke wedges. Cook over medium heat until just beginning to brown, then turn and brown their second sides. Remove to a bowl and sprinkle with herbs. Return the pan to the heat. Add the remaining fat, then the eggs, then artichokes, and scramble softly, adding black pepper at the end.

ARUGULA, WILTED

Cull any leaves that have liquified, then thinly slice what's left. Treat this as parsley, sprinkling it over pasta or stirring it into a sauce or a cooking vegetable or pot of beans. Or combine whatever amount you have with an equal quantity of chopped toasted nuts and sprinkle it over cooked eggs, or grilled or poached meat or fish, or beans or pasta.

Or use it instead of half the basil in Basil Pesto (p. 394) for a pesto with a bitter edge. If you find the edge unpleasantly bitter, next time use less arugula and more basil or parsley.

See also Greens (p. 45).

ASPARAGUS, COOKED

Cooked asparagus is delicious quickly cut up and eaten on hot rice, or chopped more finely and stirred into risotto at the end of its cooking. Asparagus is also good in Fried Rice (p. 205), in Any Vegetable Potage (p. 8), Almost Any Vegetable Pasta (p. 7), Any Vegetable Minestra (p. 8), or instead of Swiss chard stems in Swiss Chard Stem Gratin (p. 89). Or it can be used instead of asparagus bottoms in Simplest Asparagus Soup (p. 15), Asparagus Stock (p. 16), or Asparagus-and-Fill-in-the-Grains (p. 16).

ASPARAGUS BOTTOMS

SIMPLEST ASPARAGUS SOUP *(25 min)*
Asparagus bottoms from 1 bunch, 2 cups strong chicken stock (achieved by boiling weak chicken stock for 30 min), salt, 1 tbsp butter.

Cut off only the most impossibly hard white bottoms of the asparagus. In a pot, combine the reamining not-as-tough bottoms with the chicken stock and bring to a boil. Lower to a simmer and cook until the asparagus is totally tender, 15–20 min. Remove from the heat, taste for salt, and adjust. Add the butter, blend in a blender until completely smooth and frothy, even if it takes a few min. Pour it through a sieve if it's not entirely smooth. Eat at any temperature.

ASPARAGUS STOCK (*20 min*)

The subtle flavor of asparagus stock makes a worthy contribution if you plan on making asparagus risotto or asparagus soup. In a medium pot, combine the bottoms from 1 bunch of asparagus with 3–4 cups water to cover. Add 1–2 onion skins, a sprig of thyme, and a few peppercorns. Bring to a boil, reduce to a simmer, cook 20 min, and strain. When you begin your next asparagus recipe, use asparagus stock.

ASPARAGUS-AND-FILL-IN-THE-GRAINS (*40 min*)

Asparagus bottoms from 1 bunch, 1–2 Parmesan or Pecorino Romano rinds, 1 bay leaf, salt, 1 cup grain (farro, barley, rice, etc.), olive oil, lemon juice. *Optional additions:* leftover cooked greens, leftover cooked beans, chopped fresh basil and/or spinach.

Cut off only the most impossibly hard white bottoms of the asparagus. Slice the remaining not-as-tough bottoms into thin rounds. In a pot, combine them with the cheese rinds, bay leaf, and the right amount of water for your chosen grain and bring to a boil. Lower to a simmer and cook until the asparagus is totally tender, 10–15 min. Remove the cheese rinds and bay leaf. Pour into a measuring cup and add any additional liquid needed. Taste for salt and adjust. Return the pot to the stove, add the grains and asparagus bottoms in liquid, and cook according to the grain's directions. When cooked, stir in any add-ins, then cover and let sit for 10 min. Drizzle with olive oil, add a few drops of lemon juice, and eat.

AVOCADO, OVERRIPE

A version of a wonderful Hanoian breakfast smoothie can be reasonably approximated with avocado that's full of stringy fibers and too ripe to be used for anything else.

SORT OF SINH TO BO/VIETNAMESE BREAKFAST SMOOTHIE (*5 min*)

¼–½ avocado (only the darkest brown bits removed), 1 cup ice cubes or crushed ice, ⅓ cup sweetened condensed milk, whole milk (optional).

In a blender, combine all the ingredients and blend to smooth. If it's too thick for your taste, add some milk and blend again. This is one of the world's perfect breakfasts.

AVOCADO PITS AND PEELS

DUSTY ROSE CLOTH OR EASTER EGG DYE (*2 days, but mostly waiting*)
Clean the pits and peels and store them in an airtight container until you have 2–3 avocados' worth. Fill a pot with several quarts of water. Add the pits and peels to the pot. Bring to a boil, then reduce to a simmer. Simmer until the water is dark maroon, 30–40 min. To dye clothing, dampen any once-white linen or cotton. Add to the pot and stir with a long spoon. Let sit on very low heat 1–2 hr, adding water if needed, then remove the pot from the heat and let the clothing soak overnight. The following day, remove, wash very well in cool water, and hang to dry. To use as Easter Egg Dye, proceed as above, but without leaving the pot sitting on low heat.

BASIL STEMS

Though I was taught in restaurant kitchens to discard everything but basil's fragrant leaves, I've learned at home that any soft stems and even basil seeds can be included in Basil Pesto (p. 394). Harder stems can be made into Herb Tea (p. 10). If you're dealing with old, wilting basil, pick through and compost any blackened leaves and include the remaining green ones in the next thing you cook.

BEAN SPROUTS, WILTED

This can be made with sprouts that are fresh and spry, too.

BEAN SPROUT BANCHAN (*35 min*)
½ tsp salt plus to taste, 1 tsp sugar, 2½ tsp soy sauce, 1 tsp sesame oil, 2 tbsp neutral oil, 3 cloves garlic (minced), 2 scallions (sliced), ¾–1 lb wilted bean sprouts.

In a small bowl, combine the salt, sugar, soy sauce, and sesame oil. In a large skillet, heat the oil and sauté the garlic until it just turns golden. Add the scallions, stir, then add the bean sprouts and cook over high heat for about 1 min. Add the sauce mixture and cook 2–3 min. Taste for salt and adjust, then remove from the heat. Leave at room temperature until ready to eat, ideally at least 30 min. (Adapted from Omnivore's Cookbook website)

BEETS, COOKED

VINEGARED BEETS (*15 min*)
Beets, vinegar (red wine, white wine, or rice), salt, olive oil, sugar (optional).

Wedge or cube cooked, peeled beets. In a bowl, heavily drizzle them with vinegar until easy to stir with a spoon, then lightly salt. Let sit for 10 min. Taste for salt and acid. If over-enthusiasm prevailed and they taste acidic, strain the beets into another bowl and reserve the vinegar for a Basic Vinaigrette (p. 376). If they are sweet and lightly acidic, proceed. Drizzle the beets with olive oil. Taste and adjust, adding sugar or salt if needed. Eat as an appetizer, or add to a Citrus Avocado Salad (p. 439). These are also wonderful in a composed salad, where they can stay separate and ruby and not stain everything. Or, further dice and mix them into yogurt with a sprinkle of masala spice mixture for a gaudy pink raita, good on rice or flatbread or boiled potatoes, or in a vegetable soup or stew.

BEET GREENS, COOKED

Cooked beet greens present the recipe writer with a quandary similar to that of cooked squash. They are endlessly adaptable. Here is a lengthy and still incomplete list of ways leftover beet greens can be used. Use them in Beans and Greens and Egg (p. 212), Ribollita (p. 178), Fast Ribollita (p. 179), Bean and Salami Soup (p. 213), Farro Soup (p. 225), Pan-Fried Farro (p. 224), Greens Gratin (p. 46), Greens Frittata (p. 46), Greens Sandwich and Toast (p. 47), Greens Pesto (p. 47), Greener Greens and Beans (p. 47), Greens Risotto (p. 47), Italian Creamed Greens (p. 48).

See also Greens (p. 45).

BEET GREENS, RAW

BOILED BEET GREENS WITH AIOLI *(20 min)*

Beet greens are a vegetable top nonpareil. Bring a pot of water to a boil. Salt it to taste like pleasant seawater. Wash the greens well in several changes of cold water. Boil them whole until just tender. Remove to a plate to cool. Make Aioli (p. 395) or combine a clove of chopped garlic, pounded into a paste with a little salt, with purchased mayonnaise. Eat the two together, in whatever ratio you like.

SAUTÉED BEET GREENS *(15 min)*

Garlic, beet greens, peanut oil, salt.

Slice or chop 1 clove garlic per bunch of beet greens. Thinly slice the stems and slice the leafy parts into wide ribbons. Wash the greens well in several changes of cold water. Heat a big pan. Add a bit more oil than you're inclined to, about 3 tbsp per bunch, then add the garlic and a pinch of salt, reduce the heat, and cook until beginning to soften, about 30 sec. Add the beet greens without drying, including the clean water that clings to them. Cook over high heat, stirring repeatedly and well, until completely wilted and tender and a little oily, up to 10–12 min. Taste for salt and adjust. These are delicious, especially in sandwiches or on toast.

BEETS, OLD

If your old beets are still fleshier than raisins, they should be quickly rinsed and then tightly fit, whole, into a roasting pan, with enough water added to fill a corner of the pan when you tilt it, then covered with foil and roasted in a 400°F oven until they are easily pierced with a sharp knife. Peel them with a small hand towel and then cut and taste them. Now you have roasted beets. Vinegar them as in Vinegared Beets (p. 18), adding a sprinkle of sugar if they taste starchy, or use in the Camino Sauerkraut Beet Soup (p. 441). If they have fully desiccated, compost is the only recourse.

BOK CHOY, COOKED

Leftover bok choy lends itself particularly well to soups. Chop and warm it in any broth, then add rice or wheat noodles and season the soup with salt or fish sauce and vinegar, add a leftover half of a boiled egg and any bits of leftover meat or fish, and eat.

BROCCOLI, COOKED

Leftover broccoli can be used so many ways I am tempted to just type the symbol for infinity. As long as the broccoli was well-cooked the first time, the product of your next-day decisions will be good. If you notice, upon retrieving it, that your leftover broccoli seems underseasoned or undercooked, add a bit more salt and a bit more time to its next phase. Use it in the Almost Any Vegetable Pasta (p. 7), Any Vegetable Mash (p. 8), Any Vegetable Minestra (p. 8), Any Vegetable Potage (p. 8), Any Vegetable Sabzi (p. 9), Any Vegetable Salad (p. 9), Any Vegetable Curry (p. 9), or Any Vegetable Thai-Style Curry (p. 10). Leftover broccoli is also delicious in a Greens Gratin (p. 46), or Greens Frittata (p. 46). Or it can be added to Ribollita (p. 178), or Minestrone (p. 210), or Fried Rice (p. 205), or Fried Beans and Rice (p. 214). And like any other cooked vegetable, leftover broccoli can be further chopped, mixed with more olive oil and perhaps some fresh parsley, and spread copiously on garlic-rubbed toast. Or make:

HOT TOASTY BROCCOLI (*30–40 min*)
½ onion (sliced lengthwise into thin half-moons), 2 chopped anchovy fillets (optional), 2 tbsp olive oil or butter, 2 cups chopped cooked broccoli, 1 tbsp chopped fresh herbs (mint, parsley, basil, or any combination), toasted bread crumbs (see p. 176).

Heat a skillet. Add the oil or butter, onion, and anchovies (if using) and cook until the onion is nearly tender, 5–10 min. Heat the oven to 400°F. Lightly oil or butter a gratin dish or baking dish. Mix the chopped broccoli with the onion and herbs. Spread the mixture into the prepared dish and bake until hot and bubbling, about 20 min. Top with bread crumbs to cover well and bake until the bread crumbs are lightly browned, another 5–10 min.

BROCCOLI STEMS AND LEAVES

GARLICKY STEM AND CORE PESTO *(20 min)*

¼ cup olive oil, 2 small cloves garlic (chopped), ¼ tsp salt, 2 cups chopped broccoli stems (or stems and cores from other brassicas, such as cauliflower, cabbage, etc.).

Heat a small pot. Add the olive oil, garlic, and salt and cook until the garlic begins to soften, about 30 sec. Add the chopped stems (and cores) and enough water to cover by half. Simmer, adding water if needed, until the vegetables are easily pierced with a knife, about 15 min. Scoop out the vegetables, transfer to a blender, and puree to completely smooth, only adding as much liquid as you need to blend and reserving the rest for future needs. This is delicious on toast, or eaten as a side dish like mashed potatoes, or as a pasta sauce, with lots of freshly grated Parmesan cheese, plus some reserved cooking liquid added.

A variation is to use heavy cream instead of all or some of the water when you cook the stems and cores.

BROCCOLI, OLD

ITALIAN GREENS *(30 min)*

3 packed cups any combined chopped greens (as old and fibrous as you want or have, including radish and carrot tops), 1 head yellowing broccoli (chopped), ¼ cup olive oil plus to taste, 3 cloves garlic (chopped), ½ tsp salt plus to taste, ¾–1½ cups liquid (broth, stock, or water).

Wash the greens and broccoli very well in cold water. Heat a pan. Add the oil, garlic, and salt, and cook until beginning to soften, 30 sec–1 min. Add the greens. Cook about 5 min, then add the broccoli and broth and cook, partially covered, over medium heat, until completely mushy, tasting for salt and adjusting, and adding more olive oil if you like. These greens are comforting and simple and can be finished with a few drops of lemon juice and eaten on their own, or spread onto grilled or toasted bread, or tossed with pasta, or eaten with fried or poached eggs, or, or, or . . .

BROCCOLI COOKING WATER

Boiling vegetables is a straightforward technique that offers the dual advantages of seasoning vegetables and producing broth. For a brief review: Salt the water well and taste it to ensure it has nearly the saltiness of the sea. Refrain from overcrowding, letting any vegetable you add have ample room to jump and jiggle. Boil vegetables from greenest to starchiest, forgiving the little green bits that adhere to your final vegetables. Once boiled vegetables have been amply drizzled with olive oil, they are ready to be eaten or stored away. Then, the question is what to do with the liquid that remains. First is to taste it again. It has had further impressions made on it. Some water has turned to steam. Sip from a spoon and pay close attention to what your primitive broth tastes like. If it's too salty, add water until it tastes good again. Now you have broccoli stock for making broccoli soup or broccoli risotto, or for boiling rice you'll eat with the broccoli on top, sprinkled with furikake and squeezed with lemon. If you had boiled potatoes, some of the liquid might have been used to mash them. And so on. Any vegetable cooking water other than cabbage is good in minestrone.

BRUSSELS SPROUTS, COOKED

Cooked Brussels sprouts should be finely sliced and then added to Bread Salad (p. 181), where they add an earthy greenness. If the Brussels sprouts were boiled or underroasted, first crisp them: finely slice them, sizzle them in hot olive oil until they begin to caramelize, and *then* add them to the bread salad. Or sprinkle them on top of anything, from meat to eggs to pasta to soup to rice.

BUTTERNUT SQUASH, COOKED

Use leftover butternut squash in the Any Vegetable Mash (p. 8), Any Vegetable Minestra (p. 8), Any Vegetable Potage (p. 8), Any Vegetable Sabzi (p. 9), Any Vegetable Salad (p. 9), Any Vegetable Curry (p. 9), or Any Vegetable Thai-Style Curry (p. 10). Leftover butternut squash is also delicious smashed with olive oil and eaten on grilled or toasted bread, or cubed and warmed up with lunchtime beans. It is worth noting that leftover cooked squash is also a wonderful snack all on its own, given 20 min at room temperature before eating.

CABBAGE

I have only one really useful thing to say about cabbage: You may find yourself with forgotten or neglected or graying cabbage—which you could call "dubious cabbage," except that it is you who are dubious, not the cabbage. But cabbage that has actually gone bad is a rarer breed than the passenger pigeon. Cabbage is one of the longest lasting vegetables humans grow. Protected from oxygen in a cool environment, it will stay good for months. I don't use "good" figuratively. I mean that the cabbage will *taste* good—as long as it's trimmed attentively and seasoned and cooked well. If cabbage starts to gray at its root or along its cut edge, remove what has grayed with a sharp knife. Do the same with the outer leaves that have grayed or wilted conspicuously, along with anything else about which you are dubious. Eventually, you'll get to a clean crisp part. That is where your cabbage for today begins. There are no recipes in this book for "cabbage, old," or "cabbage, wilted," but just for "cabbage" since cabbage is what you have.

THE BEST COLESLAW *(40 min)*
1 shallot (thinly sliced), 2 tbsp lemon juice (or wine vinegar or rice vinegar), 1 tsp salt plus to taste, ½ tsp maple syrup or sugar, ½ cup mayonnaise, ½–1 carrot (julienned or just very thinly sliced), ½ large head cabbage (thinly sliced), up to a bunch cilantro (chopped).

In a large bowl, combine the shallot, lemon juice, and 1 tsp salt. Let sit 20 min. Add the maple syrup or sugar, mayonnaise, carrot, and cabbage and mix well. Let sit 10 min, then taste for salt and adjust.

CABBAGE-CELERY SLAW *(30 min)*
2 stalks celery, ¼ large head cabbage (thinly sliced), 2 tsp distilled white vinegar plus to taste, ½ tsp salt plus to taste, ¼–½ cup sour cream, ¼ cup mayonnaise.

Thinly slice the celery on the diagonal so you have longish, thin strips. In a large bowl, combine the celery, cabbage, vinegar, and ½ tsp salt. Let sit 10 min. Stir in the sour cream and mayonnaise and let sit another 10 min. Taste for salt and adjust. If you don't have time to wait, don't!

CABBAGE, COOKED

Leftover cooked cabbage is delicious combined with a vinaigrette and toasted nuts. Use in the Any Vegetable Salad (p. 9) especially with toasted croutons (see p. 176). It is also wonderful in a Frittata (p. 140) with 1 cup celery leaves added, or added to Fried Rice (p. 205), Pan-Fried Farro (p. 224), or Savory Miso Rice Stew (p. 255). Or make:

CABBAGE PIEROGIS *(45 min)*
Pierogi Dough (p. 350), 1½ cups sliced or julienned cooked cabbage, ½–1 cup grated sharp cheddar cheese (to taste), ¼ tsp salt plus to taste, freshly ground black pepper, melted butter for serving.

Make the pierogi dough. In a bowl, mix together the cabbage, cheddar, salt, and black pepper. Taste for salt and adjust. Scantly fill pierogi dough rounds with 1½ tsp each. In a large pot of boiling water, add a few at a time, removing when they've floated for 30 seconds or so. Serve drizzled with melted butter.

CABBAGE FARRO SALAD *(10 min)*
2 cups cooked farro, 1 cup sliced or julienned roasted cabbage, 2 tbsp lemon juice, 1 tsp capers (drained), olive oil, ½–1 tsp Calabrian chiles (or chili paste, chili oil, or dash of chile flakes), ¼ cup toasted almonds, salt, ½–1 cup shaved Pecorino Romano or Parmesan cheese.

In a large bowl, combine the farro, cabbage, lemon juice, capers, olive oil to taste, chiles, and almonds. Taste for salt and adjust. Serve topped with the cheese.
     A variation is to add ¼ cup very finely sliced celery.

CABBAGE PASTA *(20 min)*
Salt, 2–3 tbsp olive oil, 2 cloves garlic (sliced), 2–3 anchovy fillets, ½ tsp chile flakes, 1 cup chopped cooked cabbage, ½ lb pasta (any shape), a squeeze of lemon, 1 cup freshly grated Parmesan or Pecorino Romano cheese plus to taste, 2 tbsp chopped parsley, 2 tbsp toasted bread crumbs (see p. 176).

Heat a pan large enough to hold the pasta. Add the olive oil, garlic, anchovies, chile flakes, and a tiny pinch of salt. Cook over medium-low heat, stirring, until the garlic has begun to soften and the anchovies have broken down, 1–2 min. Add the cabbage, mix through, then remove from the heat. In a large pot of boiling water salted to taste like pleasant seawater, cook the pasta.

Reserve ½ cup pasta water just before draining. Add the pasta and pasta water to the pan and return to medium-low heat, stirring, until combined and glossy. Taste for doneness and salt and continue cooking until done. Add a squeeze of lemon, then the cheese, and mix well. Top with the parsley and bread crumbs and eat.

CABBAGE, OUTER LEAVES

Slice outer cabbage leaves and begin their cooking before the rest of the cabbage, so the toughest bits get a head start. Or thinly slice and sauté outer leaves with other cooking greens, taking note of their toughness and making sure that everything gets as much cooking as it needs. Or thinly slice and add them to Any Vegetable Minestra (p. 8) or Lemony Vegetable Soup (p. 49) or Minestrone (p. 210). Cabbage leaves also make excellent wrappers. Cook them as whole leaves in boiling water, then drain and stuff them with any meat or vegetable dumpling filling and steam until just cooked. Eat on rice, dipped in black vinegar and soy and ginger. Or wrap boiled cabbage leaves around finely chopped shrimp and scallions and ginger and lemon zest and steam them. Or wrap boiled leaves around cooked rice and herbs and let it simmer a bit in braising liquid or tomato sauce for house-stuffed cabbage.

CABBAGE CORE

The core of a cabbage can be thinly sliced and cooked in a pot with a bit of butter and broth or water. Or it can be thinly sliced and included in a soup, or it can be used in the Garlicky Stem and Core Pesto (p. 21).

CANDIED YAMS

YAM BREAD PUDDING *(1 hr)*
4 tbsp (½ stick) butter, 2 cups cubed stale white or rustic bread or biscuits, 2 cups heavy cream, 2 eggs, ½ cup sugar, 1 tsp vanilla extract, 1–1¼ cups candied yams.

Heat the oven to 350°F. Use some of the butter to grease a large baking dish, then melt the rest. In a bowl, pour the cream over the bread or biscuits and let sit until completely absorbed, about 15 min. In a large bowl, beat together the eggs and sugar. Add the vanilla and melted butter. Add the bread and candied yams to the egg-butter mixture. Pour into the prepared baking dish and bake until completely cooked through and set, with a slightly browned top, about 45 min. Good with ice cream.

Or substitute candied yams for the sweet potato in Sweet Potato Scones (p. 87) or Sweet Potato Muffins (p. 88), taking care to decrease either recipe's sugar, since candied yams are already sweet.

CAPONATA

CAPONATA PASTA (*20 min*)
4 tbsp olive oil, 1 cup chopped fresh or canned tomatoes, 2–3 tbsp capers (drained), 1 cup caponata, salt, ½ lb short pasta (rigatoni, mezze maniche, orecchiette, gemelli, or fusilli), 1 cup julienned or chopped arugula, ½ cup freshly grated Parmesan cheese plus for serving.

Heat a pan large enough to hold the pasta. Add 2 tbsp of the olive oil, the tomatoes, and capers. Cook over medium heat for 5 min. Stir in the caponata and reduce to the lowest heat. In a large pot of boiling water salted to taste like pleasant seawater, cook the pasta. Reserve ¼ cup pasta water just before draining. Add the pasta and pasta water to the pan along with the remaining olive oil, the arugula, and half the cheese, and stir to combine. Serve topped with the remaining cheese, plus passing more if you like.

CARAMELIZED ONIONS

Caramelized onions are alchemical, like pickled chiles and anchovies and olives and herbs. Spoon leftovers, hot or cold, onto crisp toast for onion bruschetta. Or add them to leftover pizza for a Provençal pizza. Add them to an omelet or frittata or sandwich or soup, or warm them and scatter them over any meat or tofu dish for overall improvement. Or make:

ONION-ANCHOVY PASTA *(15–20 min)*

2 tbsp olive oil plus to taste, 1 cup caramelized onions, 4–6 anchovy fillets, 1 lb pasta, salt, a handful of chopped parsley, toasted bread crumbs (see p. 176).

Heat a pan large enough to hold the pasta. Add the olive oil, then caramelized onions, then the anchovy fillets, crushing and mixing them with the onions. In a large pot of boiling water salted to taste like pleasant seawater, cook the pasta. Reserve ½ cup pasta water just before draining. Add the drained pasta directly to the pan, along with a pour of the pasta water, mixing well, and adding more water if needed. Taste for salt and adjust. Stir in the parsley. Top each serving with toasted bread crumbs.

ONION SOUP *(20 min)*

1 tbsp olive oil plus for the bread, 1 tbsp butter, 1 cup caramelized onions, ½ tsp all-purpose flour, ½ tbsp sherry or white wine, 2 cups beef or other stock, 1–3 thick slices stale bread, 1 clove garlic (halved), parsley (optional), freshly ground black pepper.

Heat a soup pot. Add the oil and butter, then the caramelized onions and 2–3 tbsp water. When they're warm, stir in the flour. Add the sherry or wine and cook until you can't smell the alcohol, 20–30 sec. Add the stock. Simmer for 15 min. Grill or toast the stale bread. Rub each slice with garlic, then drizzle with olive oil. Place a garlic toast in the bottom of each bowl and ladle the soup, hot, over each one. Top with chopped parsley (if using) and black pepper.

CARROTS, COOKED

Leftover cooked carrots are remarkably versatile. Use in the Any Vegetable Mash (p. 8), Any Vegetable Minestra (p. 8), Any Vegetable Potage (p. 8), Any Vegetable Sabzi (p. 9), Any Vegetable Salad (p. 9), or Any Vegetable Curry (p. 9). Or add whatever amount you have to the Best Grain or Bean Salad (p. 206), mixing them through before adding the vinaigrette.

CARROT PEELS

These are surprisingly good.

FRIED ONIONS BUT CARROTS *(5 min)*
Oil for deep-frying (peanut, grapeseed, or vegetable), carrot peels, salt, optional seasoning (chaat masala, cumin, cayenne, za'atar).

In a small pot, heat a few inches of oil to 350°–365°F. Add the carrot peels by the handful, cooking until they just stop sizzling (it's not very long). Remove to a paper towel or cooking rack. Sprinkle with salt and any other spice you like. Use in place of fried onions or shallots in dishes like mujadara, or over salads, or on any rice, or over a soup. These don't store very long, but the oil for frying can be reused and the procedure produces a lot of savory crispness.

Carrot peels are also good in any stock or broth. Or wash and finely mince them and include them in the Any Vegetable Minestra (p. 8) or any other soup that would willingly host carrot. Chopped peels can also make up some of the grated carrot in Carrot Coconut Almond Muffins (p. 29).

CARROT TOPS

CARROT TOP PESTO *(5–10 min)*
2 cloves garlic (peeled), 3 tbsp pine nuts or walnuts (toasted or raw), ½ tsp salt plus to taste, 3 cups chopped carrot tops (tender stems included), 1 cup parsley leaves (chopped), ½ cup freshly grated Parmesan cheese, ⅓ cup olive oil.

In a food processor or blender, pulse the garlic, nuts, and salt. Add the carrot tops and parsley, pulse to combine, then add the Parmesan and olive oil and blend. Use to sauce pasta or anywhere you would use basil pesto.

This next recipe demands a comical number of ingredients other than carrot tops. But it doesn't taste like itself when made without carrot tops, fitting it firmly in the "carrot top" category.

SPRING SHRIMP AND RICE CAKE STIR-FRY *(25–30 min)*

½ tsp salt plus to taste, ½ pack Chinese or Korean rice cakes, 2–3 tbsp neutral cooking oil (peanut or grapeseed), 1 tbsp thinly sliced fresh ginger, 1 heaping tbsp shrimp paste, 10–12 ramps or scallions (sliced, white and green parts separated), 1 shallot (sliced; or ¼ onion sliced, or another 5 scallions, green and white sliced together), 5 stalks green garlic (white parts only, chopped) or 2 cloves garlic (minced), 1 bunch asparagus (trimmed and sliced on the diagonal) or kohlrabi (peeled and cut into batons), 1–2 tbsp soy sauce, 1 lb peeled shrimp, 3 stalks celery (cut on the diagonal into ½-inch slices), a handful of dried whole chiles like chiles de árbol (broken in half) or 1 tsp–1 tbsp chile flakes, 2 tbsp Chinese cooking wine, 1–2 tbsp cornstarch dissolved in ¼ cup Chinese cooking wine, 3 cups chopped carrot tops.

In a pot of salted boiling water, cook the rice cakes until swollen and tender and then drain and set aside. Heat a large pan. Add the oil, then the ginger, shrimp paste, ramp or scallion whites, shallot, and garlic. Add the ½ tsp salt and stir. Add the asparagus, rice cakes, a sprinkle of water, and the soy sauce. Cook over medium heat, stirring occasionally, about 2 min. Add the shrimp, celery, chiles, and cooking wine. Increase the heat and cook, stirring, until things seem quite hot and beginning to brown, another 30 sec. Add the ramp greens and dissolved cornstarch. Stir through. Add the carrot tops, taste for salt, adjust, and serve.

The leafy ends of carrot tops are also good additions to other cooking greens, or in Ribollita (p. 178), or as an herb in the Best Grain or Bean Salad (p. 206) or in Minestrone (p. 210).

CARROTS, HUGE

CARROT COCONUT ALMOND MUFFINS *(30 min)*

Butter for the muffin tin, 2 cups almond flour (or another nut flour), ¾ tsp salt, 1 tsp baking soda, ¾ tsp ground cinnamon, ½ cup unsweetened shredded coconut, 3 large eggs, ½ cup olive oil, ⅓ cup maple syrup, 1 cup grated peeled carrot (about 1 huge carrot).

Heat the oven to 350°F. Butter a muffin tin. In a bowl, combine the nut flour, salt, baking soda, cinnamon, and coconut. In a separate bowl, whisk the eggs, oil, maple syrup, and grated carrot. Stir the egg mixture into the nut mixture.

Spoon the batter into the prepared muffin tin and bake until set and a skewer emerges clean, 20–22 min. These freeze very well.

CAULIFLOWER, COOKED

Leftover cauliflower is as useful as cooked asparagus and cooked broccoli. Use it in the Any Vegetable Mash (p. 8), Any Vegetable Minestra (p. 8), Any Vegetable Potage (p. 8), Any Vegetable Sabzi (p. 9), Any Vegetable Salad (p. 9), Any Vegetable Curry (p. 9), Any Vegetable Thai-Style Curry (p. 10), or instead of broccoli in the Hot Toasty Broccoli (p. 20). Or add to Fried Rice (p. 205) or Minestrone (p. 210) or Pan-Fried Farro (p. 224). Or make:

CAULIFLOWER PASTA *(15 min)*
3 tbsp olive oil, salt, 2 cloves garlic (sliced), sprinkle of chile flakes (optional), 1–3 cups cooked cauliflower, 1 lb short pasta (ziti or rigatoni), 1 tbsp butter, ¼–½ cup chopped parsley leaves or a combination of parsley and mint, grated zest of 1 lemon, a squeeze of lemon juice, ½–1 cup toasted bread crumbs (see p. 176), ¼ cup toasted pine nuts or walnuts (optional).

Heat a pan large enough to hold all the pasta. Add the olive oil, garlic, a tiny pinch of salt, and chile flakes (if using). Cook until the garlic is softened, about 30 sec. Add the cauliflower to warm, breaking it up with a spoon. In a large pot of boiling water salted to taste like pleasant seawater, cook the pasta. Reserve ¼ cup pasta water just before draining. Add the pasta water and simmer to reduce to almost glossy. Add the pasta, then butter, herbs, lemon zest, and lemon juice. Top copiously with bread crumbs and nuts (if using).

CAULIFLOWER LEAVES

Cauliflower leaves can be sliced thinly, across their fibers, then boiled or roasted, or sautéed along with the florets. Or they can be sliced and added to the Any Vegetable Sabzi (p. 9), Swiss Chard Stem Gratin (p. 89), or Minestrone (p. 210). Or they can be treated like cooking greens and sautéed in hot fat with garlic and sprinkles of water until tender.

CAULIFLOWER STEM AND CORE

Include the cauliflower stem and core in the Garlicky Stem and Core Pesto (p. 21).

CAULIFLOWER, OLD

CHEESY CAULIFLOWER (*50 min*)
1 head cauliflower, salt, 2 cloves garlic (peeled), 2–3 tbsp butter plus for the baking dish, ¼–½ cup heavy cream, 1–1½ cups grated cheddar or other melting cheese, ½ cup grated Parmesan cheese, a few sprigs of thyme (optional), toasted bread crumbs (optional; see p. 176).

Including all but the rattiest leaves and the base of the stem, cut the cauliflower into small florets and thinly slice the core and leaves. Heat the oven to 400°F. In a large pot of boiling water salted to taste like pleasant seawater, boil the leaf and stem pieces and the garlic for 5 min, then add the cauliflower florets and boil until just cooked, another 5 min. Drain. Butter a baking dish that will fit the cauliflower piled up a bit. Add the cauliflower. In a bowl, chop or smash the boiled garlic, add the cream, cheddar, and Parmesan and stir together. Pour over the cauliflower. Nestle in thyme (if using). Dot with butter. Bake for 30 min, adding bread crumbs (if using) for the final 10 min. Cool for 5 min before eating.

CELERIAC, COOKED

Cooked celeriac can be used anywhere another cooked root vegetable can. Also try it in the Hot Toasty Broccoli (p. 20), Any Vegetable Mash (p. 8), Any Vegetable Minestra (p. 8), Any Vegetable Salad (p. 9), Any Vegetable Curry (p. 9), or Swiss Chard Stem Gratin (p. 89). Or add to Fried Rice (p. 205), Pan-Fried Farro (p. 224), or Minestrone (p. 210).

CELERIAC, HUGE

CÉLERI RÉMOULADE *(35 min)*
1 celery root, white wine vinegar, salt, 1 cup crème fraîche or mayonnaise,
2 tbsp capers (drained; roughly chopped if big), freshly ground black pepper,
lemon juice (optional).

Hack off the warty outside of the celeriac with a knife. Cut what's left
into matchsticks and place in a bowl. Douse them with vinegar and season
with salt. Let them sit for 20 min, mixing if you remember, then move to a
colander to drain, pressing down well to dry, saving the salty vinegar for Basic
Vinaigrette (p. 376). Transfer to a bowl. Stir in the crème fraîche or mayonnaise, taste and add more if you want it creamier. Add the capers and a lot of
black pepper. I like to add a squeeze of lemon juice, if I have a lemon. This is a
good accompaniment to fried food.

CELERY, WILTED

One of the first science experiments many children do is to put celery and
food dye in a cup of water and watch it ascend the stalk's arteries. Celery can
be revived by arranging bendy stalks in cold water, which will course up its
veins and give it new life. Or make:

BRAISED CELERY WITH HERBS *(20–25 min)*
1 bunch celery (cut into 2-inch pieces, leaves reserved), ¼ cup broth or water,
¼ cup olive oil, a bouquet garni (rosemary, thyme, and marjoram), ¼ tsp salt
plus to taste.

Put the celery in a pan that holds it in a single-ish layer. Add the broth or
water, olive oil, bouquet garni, and salt. Bring to a bubble, then cover, reduce
to a simmer, and cook until very tender, 15–20 min. This is a delicious side
dish, or very good on rice.

BRAISED CELERY WITH LEMON *(20–30 min)*
1 bunch celery (cut into 2-inch pieces, leaves reserved), 2 tbsp butter, ¼ tsp
salt plus to taste, ⅔–1 lemon (sliced into the thinnest possible rounds), ½ cup
toasted bread crumbs (see p. 176), chopped parsley or mint leaves.

Put the celery, butter, and just enough water to cover into a pan that holds the celery in a more or less single layer. Season with the salt, then layer the lemon rounds over the top. Bring to a bubble, then cover, reduce to a simmer, and cook until very tender, about 15–20 min. Check periodically, adding water if needed to keep it from sticking. When the celery is tender, uncover the pan, increase the heat to high and cook until it's not liquid-y, and there's just a tiny bit of thick sauce at the bottom. Taste for salt and adjust. Top with the toasted bread crumbs and herbs and eat.

Or use wilted celery to make a mirepoix (see p. 6) and freeze it. Or make chicken or tuna or tofu salad for tomorrow's lunch, where it won't matter if the celery isn't perfectly crisp, because the celery in those salads never is.

CELERY HEART

BRAISED CELERY HEART *(20 min)*
1–2 tbsp olive oil, 1 celery heart (halved lengthwise), ⅛ tsp salt plus to taste, ½ cup broth or water.

Heat a small pan over medium heat. Add the olive oil and then add the celery heart, cut-side down, and sear until browned and caramelized. Flip the heart, salt it, add broth or water, cover, and cook until very tender, 15–20 min. Taste for salt and adjust. Good with rice. (Adapted from Tom Hunt)

CELERY LEAVES

Celery leaves are especially good in four constellations: 1) With eggs: Whisk a few eggs and softly scramble them in butter, then stir in a handful of chopped celery leaves. If you're feeling omelet-y, mix chopped celery leaves into whatever cheese you want in your omelet. If you're boiling or poaching eggs, once they're cooked and salted, scatter celery leaves directly on top. Or, for the best use of both leftover celery leaves and leftover pasta, combine in a Pasta Frittata (p. 363). 2) In a nutty gremolata: Chop celery leaves and combine them with an equal quantity of chopped toasted walnuts and lemon zest, then add a clove of minced garlic and flaky salt. Sprinkle *this* over scrambled eggs or boiled vegetables or pasta or grilled meat and breathe deep the odd ingenuity of the combination. Add olive oil to the sprinkle and it becomes a spoonable sauce, good wherever the sprinkle would have been. 3) In a piquant rémoulade: Combine ½ cup mayonnaise, ⅓ cup chopped celery leaves, ½ tsp chopped capers, ½ tsp salt or to taste, 1 tsp rice vinegar or white wine vinegar. Stir together well and dollop at will. This is delicious on Yankee Fish Cakes (p. 273), or any battered and fried food, or *with* any battered and fried food mixed in. 4) In celery salt: In a 125°F oven, dehydrate the leaves on a baking sheet until they're papery and dry, 4–6 hr. Crumble by hand and combine with salt in a spice grinder and pulse.

CELERY BOTTOM

MORE CELERY (*a few weeks/months, but all waiting*)
Bottom of a celery stalk, 4 toothpicks, sunlight.

Fill a jar with enough water to cover the bottom of the celery with the bits of stalk still above water. If using toothpicks, insert them into the root end of celery about 1½ inches from the bottom (this is to suspend the celery). Or make sure there's an inch or so of space under the base of the celery. Place near a window with good natural light. Change the water every few days. Do not worry if the outer stalks brown. Leaves will sprout. They will continue to sprout, and then, eventually, roots will. When the roots are 1 inch long, transplant the celery into potting soil, in a partly sunny spot, covering the roots and leaving the new leaves and bits of stalk above the soil. Water as you would any plant, keeping it damp but not wet. Harvest by the stem or leaf, or pick the whole bunch. The celery plant will eventually tire, as we all do.

CHAYOTE, COOKED

Use cooked chayote in the Any Vegetable Minestra (p. 8). It is also good in Minestrone (p. 210), as everything is.

CHICORY, WILTED

Wilted chicory makes a wonderful soup addition. Chop whatever hasn't liquefied and use it as a spur to make Minestrone (p. 210). Or stir it into any leftover lentils or beans while they're warming. Or heat a pan, add olive oil, add a smashed clove of garlic, then chicory leaves, a sprinkle of salt, a shake of chile flakes, and a drizzle of water, and cook until melted and tender. Eat on a piece of garlic-rubbed toast, with an anchovy laid languidly on top.

See also Greens (p. 45).

CHILES, WILTED

Pare off any brown parts, then immediately chop and freeze whatever didn't brown, storing in plastic bags or in ice cube trays. These stay good, frozen, forever and can be chipped off in tsp- or tbsp-size pieces and used directly wherever needed.

CHILE SEEDS AND VEINS

PIZZA SPRINKLE *(6 hr, but all waiting)*
Any amount of seeds and veins (ribs) from trimmed chiles.

Heat the oven to 125°F. Place the seeds and veins on a sheet pan and dehydrate until completely dry. Crumble or grind, and sprinkle on pizza wherever you would chile flakes. Also good mixed with salt to rim cocktail glasses or to dip mango or jicama into.

CHIVES, WILTED

As soon as they threaten to wilt, chives must be gone through remorselessly. Whatever is liquefied should be composted, and whatever isn't should be chopped and mixed into room-temperature butter to make chive butter. Chive butter is delicious, and it's the only way—other, I suppose, than chive sour cream and chive yogurt and chive cream cheese and chive chèvre—to halt the inevitable and steep decline of chives.

See also Herbs (p. 52).

CILANTRO, STEMS

Cilantro stems can be used like cilantro leaves wherever the flavor of cilantro is needed and the herb will be finely chopped or pureed to obviate the stems' toughness. My favorite cilantro stem destination is Puerto Rican Sofrito (p. 7).

COLLARD GREENS, COOKED

Use in Greens Gratin (p. 46), Greens Frittata (p. 46), Greens Sandwich and Toast (p. 47), Greens Pesto (p. 47), Greener Greens and Beans (p. 47), Greens Risotto (p. 47), Italian Creamed Greens (p. 48), Greens Dip (p. 48), Greens Kuku (p. 48), Ribollita (p. 178), Fast Ribollita (p. 179), Bean and Salami Soup (p. 213), Farro Soup (p. 225), Pan-Fried Farro (p. 224), or Farro Soup (p. 225).

See also Greens (p. 45).

COLLARD GREEN STEMS

Use in the Garlicky Stem and Core Pesto (p. 21), or thinly slice and add to a soup like Ribollita (p. 178) or Minestrone (p. 210) very early, when you add the liquid, so they have a long time to cook.

CORN, COOKED

Leftover cooked corn is sweetness in kernel form. It can be added to good effect to just about anything. Try:

SWEET CORN SALAD *(5 min)*
2–3 cups cooked corn kernels, 2 tbsp olive oil, 1–2 cloves garlic (thinly sliced), ½ bulb spring onion or 3 scallions (thinly sliced), ¼ tsp salt plus to taste, 1 small handful halved cherry tomatoes or ½ cucumber (quartered lengthwise and thinly sliced crosswise), or both, a few drops red or white wine vinegar, 1 small handful torn fresh basil leaves, 1 tbsp fresh marjoram leaves (chopped).

Cut the kernels from the ears of corn if not already done: Hold the ear of corn vertically with one end set in a bowl and slice off the kernels directly into the bowl. Heat a heavy-bottomed pan over medium heat. Add the olive oil, garlic, and spring onion or scallions, and salt, and cook until beginning to soften, 3–5 min. Add the tomatoes or cucumbers (or a combination). Let sizzle for 2 min, then add the corn. Increase the heat, stir once or twice, taste for salt and adjust, then add the vinegar. Mix through. Remove from the heat, add the herbs, and eat.

This can be varied by changing the herbs, or made into a richer, glossier dish by the addition of 1 tbsp heavy cream or sour cream or crème fraîche at the end.

CORN PUDDING (1 hr)

3 tbsp butter plus for pan, 3 tbsp all-purpose flour, 2 cups whole milk, ½ cup freshly grated Parmesan cheese plus for pan, ½ tsp salt plus to taste, 3 eggs (separated), 2 cups cooked corn, ½ tsp freshly grated nutmeg, freshly ground black pepper.

Make béchamel: In a saucepan, melt the butter, add the flour, whisking it in very well, then gradually add the milk, whisking the whole time. Continue to whisk as it comes to a boil. At this point, the béchamel should be thickened. Reduce to the lowest possible heat and cook, stirring occasionally, until it no longer tastes floury, 20–30 min. Add the Parmesan and salt, then taste for salt and adjust. It should be highly seasoned. Position a rack in the center of the oven and heat the oven to 400°F. Whisk the egg yolks into the béchamel mixture one by one. Mix in the corn. Add the nutmeg and black pepper to taste. Taste for salt and adjust. In a stand mixer (or by hand), whip the egg whites until just past soft peaks. Lightly butter a 1½-quart shallow pie dish or round cake pan, then coat lightly with Parmesan. Gently fold the beaten whites into the béchamel-corn mixture, then add to prepared dish. Bake until puffed and just set, 25–30 min.

Or add leftover cooked corn to Any Vegetable Minestra (p. 8) or Minestrone (p. 210). Or add to Fried Rice (p. 205) or use in Best Grain or Bean Salad (p. 206), Tacos (p. 306), or Fancy Succotash (p. 214). Or add any amount of corn to congee, polenta, grits, or risotto, either fresh or while reheating. Leftover corn is also delicious mixed into corn bread and corn muffin batter before baking. Good, good, good.

CORN COBS

CORN STOCK *(2 hr)*
In a pot, cover the corn cobs with water by 2 inches. Add a sprig of parsley, an onion peel, a garlic clove or peel, a few peppercorns, and a bay leaf. Bring to a boil, reduce to a simmer, and cook until the liquid tastes faintly of corn, 1–2 hr. If you need to add more water, do. This is also delicious with a Parmesan rind or two added. Strain and use for vegetable soup, or for extra corny corn chowder, or corn and shrimp risotto. Corn husks and silk can be included!

CORN HUSKS

Corn husks are good wrappers. They can be used for tamales or steamed sticky rice or steamed fish, or anything else in need of steaming. Season whatever it is, wrap tightly in fresh husks, then place on a grill, or in a hot oven. Husks can also be used instead of parchment paper to cover food to be stored or to line a steamer basket to keep food from sticking, or added to Corn Stock (p. 38). Dried corn husks make excellent kindling.

CORN, OLD

Old corn lacks the swollen sweetness of fresh sweet corn, but can still be used. Shuck the ears and cut the kernels from the cobs with a sharp knife. Add these to a pan of cooking greens, toward the end, perhaps with a handful of cherry tomatoes. Or sizzle them in hot oil with a tiny sprinkle of sugar and eat as slightly crisp corn on hot rice. Or add to Fried Rice (p. 205) or serve on a bowl of noodles.

CREAMED SPINACH

SPINACH RICOTTA GRATIN *(20–30 min)*
1 cup or more creamed spinach, half as much ricotta cheese as spinach, salt.

Heat the oven to 400°F. In a bowl, combine the creamed spinach and ricotta, leaving some pockets of ricotta for deliciousness. Add salt to taste. Spoon into a baking dish that will hold the mixture 2 inches deep or so. Bake until hot and bubbling, broiling for an instant at the end if you like. Cool to just above room temperature before eating.

CUCUMBERS, OLD

SIMPLE TZATZIKI (*5 min*)
½ cucumber (peeled), 1 clove garlic, 5 tbsp whole-milk yogurt, salt.

Cut off any liquidy and mushy bits of the cucumber, and grate what remains. Add a few grates of a garlic clove directly to the grated cucumber. Mix with the yogurt and add salt to taste.

STIR-FRIED CUCUMBERS (*10 min*)
1–2 cucumbers, 1 tbsp olive oil, 2 cloves garlic (sliced), ¼ tsp salt plus to taste, 2 dried chiles (crumbled), ⅛ tsp sugar, 1 tsp chopped fresh herbs (mint, basil, cilantro, or scallion tops).

Partially peel the cucumbers and cut off any liquidy and mushy bits. Halve lengthwise and scoop out the seeds. Cut crosswise into thin half-moons. Heat a cast-iron skillet or wok. Add the olive oil, garlic, and salt, and cook until the garlic has just softened, about 30 sec. Add the chiles and spread it all out to sizzle. The instant the garlic has begun to turn golden, add the cucumbers in a single layer along with another sprinkle of salt and cook, stirring only occasionally, letting the garlic and chiles darken. When the cucumbers have begun to get nicely cooked, add the sugar and stir through. Cook until just tender, and becoming translucent, 5–6 min total. Mix in the herbs, and eat.

If you find yourself with cucumbers you cut yesterday, blend them with yogurt and ice for a refreshing drink. Or drain them, pressing out excess liquid, then mix with beaten eggs and a few drops of fish sauce, sliced scallion, and sesame seeds and cook into a novel omelet.

DAIKON RADISH, HUGE

Finely grate leftover daikon into oroshi, a bright, refreshing garnish for soba or meat or fish, or an addition to Tempura Dipping Sauce (p. 405).
See also Radishes, Old (p. 78).

DANDELION FLOWERS

FRIED DANDELIONS *(20 min)*
Any amount dandelions (from unsprayed grass), Tempura Batter (p. 139), peanut or grapeseed oil for deep-frying, lemon for serving (optional).

Clean the dandelions well, soaking them to remove insects, and cleaning off the dark green bracts. In a bowl, whisk the egg with water or milk. Make the tempura batter and keep on ice. In a deep, medium pot, heat 3 inches of oil to 350°–365°F. Drop batches of dandelion into the batter and let excess drip off. Fry in batches until crisp. These are a good addition to any fritto, which can be as plain as onion rings, or as dainty as fried leaves of shiso.

DANDELION GREENS

Dandelion greens can be treated like any other cooking green: cooked in olive oil with chopped garlic and a pinch of salt until sunken and delicious. I especially like cooked dandelion greens on ricotta- or fresh mozzarella–topped, garlic-rubbed toast.
See also Greens (p. 45).

DILL, WILTED

Remove any truly soggy bits, then make a dill dip by combining 1 tsp minced dill, sour cream or Greek yogurt or crème fraîche (or any combination), a squeeze of lemon (optional), a tiny bit of pounded or grated garlic, and salt to taste. Good with potato chips. A variation is to add chopped toasted walnuts or lemon zest, or both. Or combine rescued dill with room-temperature butter for dill butter to spread on hot cooked meat or potatoes or eggs.

EGGPLANT, COOKED

When I briefly lived in Bangkok, my favorite curries included Thai eggplants, for which any leftover cooked eggplant is an acceptable substitute. Chop what you have left into rough cubes. Add it to any Thai curry recipe you have (or find) or to the Any Vegetable Curry (p. 9) or Any Vegetable Thai-Style Curry

(p. 10). Or, heat a pan, add 2 tbsp oil, then add a combination of chopped garlic, chopped onion or scallion, chopped chile, and chopped cilantro stems; or a little spoonful of curry paste. Let it sizzle. Add the eggplant and ½–1 can coconut milk, and any other leftover cooked vegetable you have. Bring to a simmer, taste for salt, adjust, and eat on rice. Or if you find yourself reheating a leftover vegetable sabzi, add leftover cooked eggplant in any quantity, and warm it all together. Leftover cooked eggplant can also be simply warmed with a drizzle of water and smashed a bit, then eaten on rice, sprinkled with ponzu and sesame seeds, or steeped in dashi. Or make:

EGGPLANT PASTA (*30 min*)

2–3 tbsp olive oil, 2 cloves garlic (chopped or sliced), ½ tsp salt plus to taste, 2 cups chopped tomatoes (fresh or canned), 1–2 cups cubed cooked eggplant, ½–1 lb short pasta or spaghetti, ¼–½ cup ricotta salata or fresh ricotta or freshly grated Parmesan cheese, basil or parsley (if available, sliced or chopped).

Heat a heavy-bottomed pan. Add the oil, garlic, and salt and let it cook until just tender, 30 sec–1 min. Add the tomatoes, then cook over medium heat until the tomatoes are slightly broken down and saucy, 5–8 min. Add the eggplant, reducing the heat if needed. Cook until tender and combined, another 2–3 min. In a large pot of boiling water salted to taste like pleasant seawater, cook the pasta. Reserve ½ cup pasta water just before draining. Add the pasta to the sauce, drizzling in the pasta water as needed. Taste for salt and oil and adjust, then sprinkle in the cheese. Top with herbs and eat.

SABICH (*5–20 min*)

2 Boiled Eggs (p. 139), Techina (p. 393), 1 cup sliced or cubed cooked eggplant, salt, pita for serving, ½ cup chopped arugula or cilantro, amba for drizzling, s'chug or other hot sauce (optional).

If you need to boil the eggs and make the techina, do. Bring the eggplant to room temperature. Peel and slice the eggs and salt them. Warm pita and cut the top if there's a pocket. Dollop amba and techina amply, adding s'chug if you like. Add the eggplant, then egg. Add the arugula or cilantro.

SIMPLEST BABA GHANOUSH (*5 min*)

Cooked eggplant, ½ clove garlic (chopped), salt, whole-milk yogurt.

In a food processor, combine the eggplant, garlic, and a little pinch of salt. Pulse to smooth. Add about as much yogurt as eggplant, unless you only have a little leftover eggplant and need to add more yogurt to make it worth the time and food processor. Pulse. Taste for salt and adjust. Eat as a dip with chips or vegetables.

ENDIVE, WILTED

Endive is like other layered vegetables in that its outer layers may wilt while its inner ones stay fresh and crisp. Remove leaves until you're at a good part and begin an endive salad with those. Or pare off whatever looks discouraging and sauté what's left in butter.

ESCAROLE, WILTED

Trim off what's gone bad and immediately use the rest in a salad, with toasted walnuts added and a Blue Cheese Dressing (p. 143). Or sauté it, as you would *Wilted chicory (p. 35)*.

FENNEL, COOKED

FENNEL POTATO PUREE (*45 min*)
2 medium potatoes (peeled and cubed), salt, ½–1 cup sliced roasted fennel, 4 tbsp (½ stick) butter, ¼ tsp ground fennel seeds, 1 tsp white wine.

In a small pot, combine the potatoes with water to cover by 2 inches, salt liberally, and bring to a boil. Boil until completely tender, 10–15 min. Drain, reserving the water. In a saucepan, warm the fennel with 2 tbsp butter, fennel seeds, white wine, and a little of the potato cooking water and cook until completely tender, 10–15 min, depending how tender the fennel was to start with. In a food mill or blender, puree the fennel. Rice or mash the potatoes. Combine the two, add the remaining 2 tbsp butter, and a drizzle of the potato water if needed, and delicately stir until just combined.

FENNEL, OUTERS AND TOPS

Fennel outers and tops are among the most valuable scraps in the vegetable scrap kingdom. They should be quickly rinsed, then frozen. Even one or two make such a profound impression on Beans and Rice (p. 203) and Meat Stock (p. 246) and Fish Stock (p. 247) that I mete my frozen ones out parsimoniously, allowing only one or two scraps per pot of beans or stock.

FRENCH FRIES

Do not be discouraged by the refrigerator smell of leftover fries. Try:

MOST BUTTERY ROAST-Y SMASH (10–15 min)
3 cups French fries, 1 clove garlic (peeled), ⅓ cup heavy cream, salt.

In a small pot, combine the fries, 1 cup water, and the garlic, and cook over medium heat, at a simmer, until the water is evaporated and absorbed and the fries are very soft and smashable. Smash well, including the garlic if it's soft enough, then add the cream over low heat, continuing to smash. Smash and smash until the cream is absorbed and the potatoes are hot and beginning to balloon up. Taste for salt and eat, in astonishment.

This is very good with a tadka (see p. 208) spooned over the top, too.

CAL'S FRENCH FRY FRITTATA (15–20 min)
6 eggs, 1 tsp salt, 3 tbsp olive oil, 1–2 cups French fries, 4 scallions (thinly sliced).

Heat the oven to 375°F. In a bowl, whisk the eggs, salt, and 1 tbsp of the olive oil. Heat the remaining 2 tbsp olive oil in an ovenproof pan over medium, then add the fries to crisp slightly, then the scallions. Cook until it all starts to crisp and sizzle, 2–3 min. Add the eggs, moving and smoothing them a few times, then cook over medium-low heat until the bottom is set, another 1–2 min. Place the pan in the oven and cook until the eggs are just set, 8–12 min. Let cool and eat. (Adapted from *Burnt Toast and Other Disasters* by Cal Peternell)

Or, use leftover French fries for the Fish and Chips Hash (p. 278).

GARLIC PEELS

GARLIC PEEL STOCK *(1 hr, but all waiting)*
Garlic peels (collected until you have a handful, or about ¼ cup), 1 bay leaf, a few peppercorns, Parmesan rind (optional).

In a small pot, combine all the ingredients and add 4 cups water. Bring to a boil, reduce to a simmer, and cook for 1 hr. Strain and use as stock.

Or use garlic peels instead of garlic cloves in Savory Stock/Broth (p. 247).

GARLIC, CHOPPED

Place in a small shallow bowl and coat with olive oil to prevent oxidizing. It is bacterially inadvisable to keep this for long, so you must remember to use it very soon.

GARLIC, OLD

This can be used in Garlic Peel Stock (p. 44), Savory Stock/Broth (p. 247), Beans and Rice (p. 203), or Braised Meat (p. 298). Pare off anything terrible, and if the green germ has emerged, halve the garlic and remove it before proceeding.

GINGER, CHOPPED

Chopped ginger freezes well and, like chiles, can be used directly from the freezer. I peel and chop and freeze ginger whenever I buy any, so I only chop it at all every few months.

GINGER PEELS

GINGER HONEY TEA *(15 min)*
Ginger peels (rinsed), honey.

In a saucepan, combine the ginger peel with water to cover by 2 inches. Bring to a boil, reduce to a simmer, and cook for 10 min. Add copious amounts of honey while warm, then strain.

GREENS

The category of cooking greens is broad and deep, including any leaf that tastes good cooked—from collard greens and spinach and kale to greens that arrive attached to other vegetables, like beet greens and radish and turnip tops. To remember that the second category qualifies, it can be helpful to quickly snip them off their bottoms, soak them in water to get rid of any grit (this might take two soaks), then shake them dry and store them however you store collard greens and kale, etc.

If you don't already consider cooked greens one of the most versatile ingredients in the kitchen, this is all perhaps putting the cart before the horse. All the recipes that follow rely on them, and there are more throughout this book. With only cooked greens and stale bread or cornmeal or rice you have a meal—as you do with cooked greens and eggs, or cooked greens and beans. You often have greens' stems, too, for which I have suggestions (see Greens Stems, p. 49).

All recipes for cooking greens should begin by acknowledging that greens are interchangeable and that each can be turned from raw to cooked in the same way. Knowing this lets you develop a pattern for greens cookery. Then any time you spend stemming, chopping, washing, and cooking any is your time because your actions are habitual.

When I cook greens, I am resolute. I follow a fixed set of steps with only slight variations. For kale, collards, beet greens, and chard, I tear or cut the stems from the leaves, then tear or chop the leaves. Depending on the size of the stems, I finely chop and include them with the leaves, or set them aside for longer cooking in Minestrone (p. 210) or Garlicky Stem and Core Pesto (p. 21). For broccoli rabe and turnip greens, I cut the whole bunch into pieces of diminishing length—1 inch long at the leaf end and ⅛ inch at the stem—discarding the bottom bits of stem where the very center turns white, which indicates woodiness. I put the leaves directly into a sink or large bowl full of cold water. These soak while I chop or slice a clove of garlic per bunch—slicing is faster—and place my greens pan, which is big, on a burner over high heat. I add enough olive oil to cover the bottom of the pan, then the garlic and a pinch of salt. I reduce the heat immediately after adding the salt because garlic is quick to burn, then drop batches of wet greens directly into the pan, continuing until they're all hissing away. Then, it's a matter of high heat and trust: Trust that all the water will evaporate, and that the greens will go from unyielding to tender and nicely oiled and sizzly. When the greens look done, I remove a little pinch to a cutting board, let it briefly cool, then taste. If I instinctively reach for a second bite, they are done; if not, I let them cook longer, adding a touch more salt, another drizzle of olive oil, a little pour of water if things seem dry, and continue cooking until they are.

For what to do with them once cooked, and with any leftovers, try:

GREENS GRATIN *(1–1½ hr)*
1 tbsp butter plus butter for the gratin dish, 1 tbsp flour, 1 cup whole milk, 3 tbsp freshly grated Parmesan cheese, 2 cups cooked greens, salt.

Make the béchamel: In a saucepan, melt the butter, add the flour, whisking it very well, then gradually add the milk, whisking the whole time. Continue to whisk as it comes to a boil. Reduce to the lowest possible heat and cook, stirring occasionally, until it no longer tastes floury, 20–30 min. Add 2 tbsp of the Parmesan. Heat the oven to 400°F. Butter a gratin dish. Mix the greens and béchamel well. Add salt to taste. It should be highly seasoned and rich. Spoon into the prepared dish and top with the remaining 1 tbsp Parmesan. Bake until it's bubbling, rotating once during the cooking, about 35–45 min. Cool to just above room temperature before eating.

GREENS FRITTATA *(10–15 min)*
Up to 3 cups chopped cooked greens, 8 eggs, ⅛ tsp salt plus to taste, up to 1 cup chopped cilantro leaves (optional), a lot of olive oil, freshly grated Pecorino Romano or Parmesan cheese.

Heat the oven to 375°F. Beat the eggs with salt. Add greens, and cilantro if using. Heat an ovenproof skillet. Coat well with olive oil. Add the egg mixture and move the set part toward the middle a few times. As soon as the sides have cohered, transfer to the oven. Cook until the top is just set, checking after 8 min, then again until it's done. Cool briefly in the pan, invert it, drizzle with olive oil, and top with cheese.

GREENS SANDWICH AND TOAST *(10 min)*

2 thick slices of bread, 1 clove garlic (halved), olive oil for drizzling, thickly sliced fresh mozzarella or fresh ricotta, ¼–½ cup chopped cooked greens. *Optional additions:* a scattering of chile flakes, a few very thin slices of quickly pickled onion, a squeeze of lemon juice.

Toast the bread, then rub one side of each with the cut side of the garlic and drizzle with olive oil. Add the cheese, then the greens. Add the chile flakes, pickled onion, or lemon juice. Drizzle with more olive oil, top with the second piece of bread and eat. Turn this into a Greens Toast by using only one slice of bread.

A variation is to first warm the cooked greens in a pan.

GREENS PESTO *(10 min)*

1 clove garlic, ¼ tsp salt, 1½–2 cups cooked greens, ¼ cup toasted nuts (pine nuts, walnuts, almonds, or pistachios), ½ cup freshly grated Parmesan cheese, ½ cup olive oil.

Pound the garlic to a paste with the salt. In a blender, combine half the greens with the nuts, garlic paste, and Parmesan, then add the remaining greens and the olive oil. Pulse to blend, using a wooden spoon or blender insert to make sure everything gets chopped and mixed, aiming for a thick, uniform paste with as little blending as possible.

GREENER GREENS AND BEANS *(20 min)*

Any amount of cooked beans, 3 cloves garlic (peeled), ½ bunch of cilantro, ¼ tsp salt plus to taste, 2 tbsp olive oil, ¼ cup bean cooking liquid or water, ¼–½ cup cooked greens.

If the beans are canned, drain and rinse. If cooked, proceed. Pound the garlic and cilantro to a paste with the salt. Heat a medium pot. Add the oil and cook the garlic-cilantro paste over low heat until just softened, 1–2 min. Add the cooked beans and bean cooking liquid or water. Add the greens. Bring just to a simmer, taste for salt and adjust, and eat. Very good on rice or grits or with tortillas alongside.

GREENS RISOTTO *(25 min)*

Any amount of cooked greens make a vibrantly verdant risotto. Puree cooked greens with a bit of olive oil and a spoonful of water to a smooth paste. Follow the directions for Risotto (p. 206), adding the greens puree just as the risotto is about to be done cooking, then stirring until the paste is just integrated and the risotto is still "all'onda," rippling like an ocean wave. Add cheese and eat.

ITALIAN CREAMED GREENS *(10 min)*
2 cups cooked greens, 4–5 tbsp butter, salt, 1½ cups freshly grated Parmesan cheese.

In a food processor, pulse the greens until almost smooth. In a pan, melt the butter and add the greens and salt to taste. Fry until buttery, 2–4 min. Remove from the heat and add the Parmesan. Stir through and eat.

GREENS DIP *(15 min)*
2–3 cups cooked greens, 3 cloves garlic (unpeeled), salt, 3–4 tbsp olive oil, ½ tsp chile flakes, ¼ tsp ground cumin, ¼ cup pitted dry-cured black olives, lemon juice.

Chop the greens finely. In a small pot, boil the garlic in very salty water until cooked. Remove the skins. Heat a pan and add the olive oil, chile flakes, and cumin and cook until just aromatic, then remove from the heat and add the greens, garlic, and olives, smashing it all together. Taste for salt and adjust. Sprinkle with lemon juice to taste and eat on flatbread or crackers or rice. (Adapted from *This Is Camino* by Russell Moore and Allison Hopelain with Chris Colin)

GREENS KUKU *(20 min)*
5 tbsp olive oil, 1 onion (finely chopped), salt, 2–4 cups cooked greens, enough soft fresh herbs (cilantro, parsley, dill, arugula, lovage, fennel fronds, sorrel, celery leaves) to equal 5–6 cups including cooked greens, 5 eggs (beaten), 1 tsp baking powder, ½ tsp ground turmeric.

Heat a 9–10-inch ovenproof pan. Add 2 tbsp of the oil, the onion, and a pinch of salt and cook until tender, 5–10 min. Remove to a bowl. Heat the oven to 375°F. In a food processor, pulse the greens and herbs. Add the eggs, baking powder, turmeric, and 1¼ tsp salt to the onions. Whisk, then add the greens-herb mixture. Reheat the pan, add the remaining 3 tbsp oil, then add the eggs-greens mixture. Cook over medium heat until the bottom is nearly set, then reduce the heat to low, cover, and cook for 4–5 min, checking often. Uncover, place in the oven and cook until just set, another 8–10 min or so. Let cool to room temperature and eat.

LEMONY VEGETABLE SOUP *(40 min)*
4 tbsp (½ stick) butter, ½ onion (finely chopped), ½ tsp salt plus to taste, 1 clove garlic (chopped), 4 cups chicken stock, 1–2 potatoes (chopped), 1–2 cups leftover cooked vegetables (kohlrabi, broccoli, cauliflower, cabbage, squash, etc.), 2–4 cups chopped cooked greens, 1 tbsp lemon juice.

Heat a soup pot. Add 2 tbsp of the butter, the onion, garlic, and salt and cook, stirring occasionally, until tender, 5–10 min. Add 1 cup stock. Bring to a boil, then reduce to a simmer and cook for 5 min. Either puree to smooth, or leave as is. Add the remaining 2 tbsp butter and 3 cups stock, then the potatoes, cooked vegetables, and greens. Simmer until everything is cooked, 20–30 min. Add the lemon juice, taste for salt and adjust. Delicious drizzled with Parsley Oil (p. 68).

A variation is to make this with Garlic Peel Stock (p. 44) or another vegetable stock.

Or use leftover greens in Beans and Greens and Egg (p. 212), Ribollita (p. 178), Fast Ribollita (p. 179), Bean and Salami Soup (p. 213), Pan-Fried Farro (p. 224), Farro Soup (p. 225), Farro and Turnip and Turnip Green Salad (p. 224), or Teaism Soup (p. 275).

GREENS, OLD

First, sort through old greens with a bullish, unwavering practicality. If any are melted or a color opposite their original one, cut off the bad bits or cull the whole leaf. Rinse what's left and then stem and slice. Cook whatever the amount is and have leftover cooked greens. Or, set a bowl of the clean and cut and mostly green greens near the stove, and add them to whatever you cook.

GREENS STEMS

The stems of cooking greens are fibrous. They should be first sliced across. Then they can be cooked alongside their leaves, added to the pan first and cooked until tender before the leaves are added. Or, cook them on their own, as you would their leaves (*see Greens, p. 45*), with garlic and oil plus enough water or stock to cover them by half so that they cook through before they begin to fry. Cooked stems are delicious in a Greens Frittata (p. 46), Greens Sandwich and Toast (p. 47), or Greens Kuku (p. 48), or combined with any other cooked vegetable in the Best Grain or Bean Salad (p. 206). Greens stems can also be left long and reedlike, and then pickled. Clean and pack them in a jar and cover them in a boiling mixture of equal parts water and vinegar heavily seasoned with sugar and salt. If they are stems of Swiss chard, *see Swiss Chard Stems (p. 89)*.

Or use in the Garlicky Stem and Core Pesto (p. 21).

GREEN BEANS, COOKED

GREEN BEANS WITH AILLADE *(15 min)*
1 cup cooked green beans, Aillade (p. 395), olive oil for drizzling.

Bring the beans to room temperature. Mix in a spoonful of the aillade and drizzle with olive oil.

A variation is to add some lemon zest.

GREEN BEAN FRITTATA *(20 min)*
10 eggs, salt, ½–1 cup cooked green beans, 1 tbsp sauce (Basil Pesto, p. 394; Aillade, p. 395; Salsa Verde, p. 398; or Parsley Oil, p. 68), olive oil, 1 cup freshly grated Parmesan cheese.

Heat the oven to 375°F. In a large bowl, whisk the eggs with a small pinch of salt. Roughly chop the beans. Mix them with the sauce, then add to the eggs. Heat an ovenproof pan over medium-low heat and coat the bottom with olive oil. Add the mixture, and cook until the bottom is set, then put into the oven until cooked, 12–15 min. Top with Parmesan.

A variation is to add thinly sliced scallions to the egg mixture before cooking. For more detail on cooking frittatas, see Frittata (p. 140).

GREEN BEANS, OLD

Old green beans just need more care and more butter.

BUTTERY GREEN BEANS (*10 min*)
1 clove garlic, salt, ½–1 cup green beans, 1 tbsp butter.

Pound the garlic to a paste with a little salt. Slice the beans into thin ribbons, lengthwise, imagining you're going to be tying each slice into a knot. In a skillet, melt the butter. Add the beans and a sprinkle of salt, then about ¼ tsp of the garlic paste. Toss until sizzling and beginning to fry and eat.

A delicious variation is to add a handful of toasted bread crumbs (see p. 176) for the last 10 sec.

GREEN BEANS, CANNED

These are not leftover but they need as much attention as if they were.

SPICY GREEN BEANS (*10 min*)
1 clove garlic, ½ tsp salt, ½ cup almonds (toasted), 1 tbsp olive or vegetable oil, 1 can green beans (dained and rinsed), 2 tsp chile flakes, 2 tsp lemon juice or red wine vinegar.

In a mortar or food processor, pound the garlic to a paste with the salt, then pound in the almonds. In a skillet, heat the oil to almost smoking. Add the beans in a single layer, cook over high heat without moving until they're clearly browned on the bottom, 30–60 sec. Flip the beans as deftly as you can—canned beans are mushy, and you're trying to keep yours together. Add the chile flakes and let brown on the second side. Stir in the garlic-almond mixture, then stir in the lemon juice or vinegar, still being economical with your stirring. Taste for salt and adjust. Good over hot rice.

GRILLED VEGETABLES

The first thing is to ensure that leftover grilled vegetables weren't left under-seasoned, underoiled, undercooked, or any combination. When you remove them from the refrigerator, if it seems as if their oiling or cooking was rushed or unfinished, heat the oven to 400°F. Spread the vegetables on a sheet pan, gloss them nicely with oil, then roast them until they are sunken and browned in places. Taste for salt and adjust. Now substitute grilled vegetables for caponata or peperonata in any recipe, 1:1. Or, lay them on hot, toasted bread, drizzle with olive oil, and add fresh herbs like basil or parsley or arugula. Add mozzarella or ricotta or goat cheese, if you have it. Or chop and stir leftover grilled vegetables into cooked rice. Or, add them to Bread Salad (p. 181), or use them in Any Vegetable Salad (p. 9). Or warm them in a small pan with olive oil and add them, in a final flourish, to a burger or a sausage or a hot dog or a piece of grilled fish or tofu.

HERBS

There are certain storage methods that increase herbs' longevity. Basil does well on the stem, in a glass of water. Everything else seems happiest clean and dry, on the stem or plucked off, then laid between layers of paper or cloth towel in an airtight container in the refrigerator. No matter what you do, herbs eventually wilt and must be dealt with on new terms. If the entire bunch smells like old flower water, compost it. If *some* do, keep an open mind. Pick through them under lightly running water, deciding who can be salvaged. Set the survivors on a towel to dry. Compost what can't be saved.

When you neither see nor smell a rotting plant, preserve what's left in fat. Pesto is herbs preserved in fat (nuts, cheese, oil). So is salsa verde (oil) and herb butter (butter). Herb mayonnaise, tartar sauce, and tzatziki are all herbs in fat. (Salt plays a protective role, too.) Make Parsley Oil (p. 68), Salsa Verde (p. 398), or dill dip (p. 40), or simply chop whatever herb you've rescued, pound a clove of garlic with a sprinkle of salt, and cover it in oil. Use this for all-purpose drizzling at your next meal and the following, until it's gone, refrigerating between meals if that feels right to you, and giving it 20–30 min to come back to life at room temperature before eating. If you notice that your herbs *often* wilt before you use them, rather than giving up on herbs, employ this strategy earlier, using some of a bunch of herbs immediately and then making a pesto or herb oil or herb butter or mayonnaise or yogurt sauce out of the rest instead of putting it away to wither.

To decide which herbs can replace each other, note: 1) Where the herb grows and is used: Herbal affinities tend to be geographical; herbs that grow near each other cooperate, and can usually be substituted. 2) The texture of the herb: rosemary and thyme and sage are hardy leaves. They are generally cooked along with aromatics rather than eaten raw. Basil, cilantro, and chervil are tender herbs generally added at the end. Replace like with like and you will not go astray. To decide how much of an herb to use beyond the confines of a recipe: Taste the herb and then taste what you plan to add it to. Add the herb gradually as you figure out how it behaves. If the herb's flavor is subtle and the dish needs color, be promiscuous.

HIJIKI, COOKED

Leftover hijiki is good on hot rice. Make rice or warm any you have, place the leftover hikiji on top with a little bit of mirin or leftover tempura dipping sauce, or seasoned rice vinegar, and choose one or two other additions, like a halved boiled egg, or sliced avocado, or pickles, then scatter toasted sesame seeds over it all.

ICEBERG LETTUCE CORE

Iceberg core is bitter and hard, but not inedible. Taste it, and if you don't mind the bitterness, use it in Grace Young's Stir-Fried Iceberg (p. 54).

ICEBERG LETTUCE, OLD

SAUCY BLUE CHEESE SALAD (*15 min*)
1–2 slices bacon, ¼ cup crumbled blue cheese, ¼ cup mayonnaise, 3–4 tbsp whole-milk yogurt, 1–2 cups old shredded iceberg lettuce.

Cook the bacon to crisp, then slice or tear. In a bowl, smash the blue cheese and mayonnaise together. Add the yogurt and mix vigorously. If you like the taste and consistency, leave as is. If you want it more drizzleable, add up to 1 tbsp water. In a bowl, mix the lettuce and blue cheese dressing. Top with bacon and eat.

PIZZERIA SALAD *(15 min)*
¼ cup thinly sliced red onion, ¼ tsp salt plus to taste, red wine vinegar to just cover, 2 cups old shredded iceberg lettuce, ¼–⅓ cup thin ribbons of deli meat (bologna, mortadella, ham, or similar, or any combination), 1 cup small mozzarella balls (halved), 1 cup combined roughly chopped olives and other cured and pickled vegetables (giardiniera, cherry peppers, dilly beans, or any combination), ¼ cup thinly sliced celery, 2 tbsp olive oil or Pizzeria Salad Dressing (p. 432), ½ cup toasted croutons (optional; see p. 176).

In a small bowl, combine the red onion, salt, and vinegar to cover, and marinate for 10 min. In a large bowl, combine the lettuce, sliced meat, mozzarella, olives/pickled vegetable mixture, celery, olive oil or vinaigrette, and the onions and some of the vinegar they marinated in. Mix well, taste for salt, adjust, and eat, topped with croutons if desired.

GRACE YOUNG'S STIR-FRIED ICEBERG *(5 min)*
½ head old iceberg lettuce, 1 tsp soy sauce, 1 tsp sesame oil, 1 tsp rice wine or sherry, ½ tsp sugar, ½ tsp freshly ground white or black pepper, 1½ tbsp vegetable or peanut oil, 4 scallions or 1–2 shallots (sliced), 3 cloves garlic (sliced), salt.

If not already shredded, cut the iceberg into ribbons. In a small bowl, combine the soy sauce, sesame oil, rice wine or sherry, sugar, and pepper. Heat a heavy-bottomed skillet or wok over high heat. Add the oil, scallions, and garlic and cook until garlic is golden, 5 sec. Add the lettuce and stir-fry to wilt, about 1 min. Add the sauce, stir through another min, salt to taste, and eat on rice. (Adapted from Food 52 website)

Or use in Almost a Hot Sausage Po'boy (p. 342).

JERUSALEM ARTICHOKES, COOKED

Use in the Any Vegetable Salad (p. 9). Also delicious chopped and tossed with shaved Brussels sprouts, cooked or raw, along with a big handful of parsley and a squeeze of lemon.

KALE, COOKED

Leftover cooked kale is like any other leftover cooked green. Use it everywhere, including Greens Gratin (p. 46), Greens Frittata (p. 46), Greens Sandwich and Toast (p. 47), Greens Pesto (p. 47), Greener Greens and Beans (p. 47), Greens Risotto (p. 47), Italian Creamed Greens (p. 48), Greens Dip (p. 48), Greens Kuku (p. 48), Ribollita (p. 178), Fast Ribollita (p. 179), or Beans and Greens and Egg (p. 212). For its stems, *see Greens stems (p. 49)*.

KOMBU, USED

KOMBU TSUKUDANI *(30 min)*
2 oz used kombu (thinly sliced), 1 tbsp sake, 1 tbsp mirin, 1 tsp rice vinegar, 2 tbsp soy sauce, 1 tsp sugar, ½ tsp katsuobushi (optional), 1 dried red chile pepper (optional; thinly sliced or left whole), ½ tsp toasted sesame seeds.

In a small pot, combine the kombu, 1 cup water, sake, mirin, vinegar, soy sauce, sugar, katsuobushi (if using), and chile (if using). Bring to a boil, then reduce to a simmer. Simmer until the liquid is almost gone and the kombu is tender and delicious, 20–25 min. If it's not tender yet, add a bit of water and cook until it is. Sprinkle with sesame seeds and eat on rice! (From Just One Cookbook website)

Or use in Furikake (p. 434).

LEEKS, COOKED

Leftover cooked leeks are uniquely delicious with eggs, a coupling that can be achieved mostly by arranging: Thinly slice and drape them over soft-cooked eggs. Or chop leftover leeks and add them to beaten eggs to be scrambled, or to beaten eggs to be cooked into a Frittata (p. 140). Or make:

LEEK AND HERB PASTA *(20–30 min)*
1½ cups broth/cream in any ratio, 2 tbsp butter, ½–¾ cup cooked leeks, salt, ½ lb pasta (maltagliati, orecchiette, or mezze maniche), 1 cup combined herbs (rosemary, parsley, and celery leaves, or any combination of herbs that go together), Parmesan or Pecorino Romano cheese for grating (optional).

In a sauté pan, combine the broth and cream, butter, and leeks. Bring to a boil, then remove from heat. In a large pot of well-salted boiling water, cook the pasta until very al dente. Add the pasta to the pan and cook until the pasta is fully cooked and is coated with the buttery leeks, about 5 min. Remove from the heat and stir in the herbs. Eat topped with grated cheese if you like.

IMPROVED GREENS (*15 min*)
Olive oil, ¼–½ cup cooked leeks, a sprinkle of chile flakes (optional), stemmed and chopped greens, salt, lemon juice.

Heat a pan, add a few tablespoons of olive oil, then add the cooked leeks and chile flakes (if using). Stir, add the greens and a little salt—the amount can depend on how heavily salted your leeks are—and cook until perfectly tender and delicious. Taste for salt and adjust. Add a big squeeze of lemon juice and eat.

LEEK POTATO SMASH (*25 min*)
Any amount up to 1 cup cooked leeks, salt to taste, 4 large potatoes (peeled or unpeeled, cut into large chunks), 4 tbsp (½ stick) butter, a drizzle of cream.

Place the leeks in a large bowl and let come to room temperature. In a large pot of boiling salty water, cook the potatoes until tender. Drain. Add the potatoes to the bowl with the leeks, then add the butter to the hot potatoes. Smash to combine. Add cream, mix through. Taste for salt and adjust. Eat warm.

Any leftover leek-potato smash can be put through a food mill then thinned with milk into vicchyssoise. Or, use it in any recipe for leftover *Mashed potatoes* (*p. 59*). Cooked leeks can also be substituted for onions in any recipe.

LEEK TOPS

Leek tops are some of the best additions to any stock pot or any pot of beans, ranking just behind fennel scraps. Rinse leek tops, shake them dry, then store them in a section of your freezer devoted to scraps for stock and beans. Try to remember them when you next begin a pot of either. If you forget, write yourself a note and post it so you don't forget the following time.

LEEKS, OLD

Even when leeks look old and tired, they remain lively within. Cut off whatever has wilted, starting with the top and the outermost layers. When you reach the inner leek, use it as you had originally planned.

LEMON BALM, WILTED

Use in Herb Tea (p. 10).

LETTUCE, BOLTING

If your lettuce starts to flower or bolt, use it in Grace Young's Stir-Fried Iceberg (p. 54).

LETTUCE, WILTED

A 20-min bath in ice cold water is often all it takes to perk lettuce up. Pare off any browning leaves. With a sharp knife, cut the remaining leaves into salad-size pieces. Fill a bowl with very cold water, and add the lettuce. In 20 min, you may find it revived, in which case you should spin it dry in batches, letting it do the last bit of its drying laid in a single layer on kitchen towels. Now you have fresh, sprightly lettuce to dress as you like. *(See p. 376 for vinaigrette recipes.)*

Or make Cream of Lettuce Soup, which is better than it sounds.

CREAM OF LETTUCE SOUP *(15 min)*

4 tbsp (½ stick) butter, 1 onion or leek white (chopped or sliced), ½ tsp salt plus to taste, a handful of parsley or chervil or a few leaves tarragon, a few heads lettuce (chopped), 2 tbsp heavy cream, croutons (see p. 176) for garnish.

Heat a soup pot. Add 2 tbsp of the butter, the onion or leek white, and the salt, and cook over medium-low heat until completely tender, 5–10 min. Add the herbs and 3 cups water and bring to a boil. Add the lettuce, then remove from the heat. Let sit until the lettuce is totally wilted, 2 min. Puree in batches until completely smooth. Return to the heat and add the cream and remaining 2 tbsp butter. Taste for salt and adjust. Eat hot, topped with croutons.

Or make this soup, which is for when you really want a warming vegetable soup, but the only vegetable in sight is a head of old lettuce:

RICE AND LETTUCE SOUP *(40–50 min)*

2 tbsp butter, 1½ onions (medium diced) or 1 bunch scallions (sliced), ½ tsp salt plus to taste, ⅓ cup parsley or cilantro leaves (roughly chopped), ½ cup Arborio rice, 8½ cups chicken stock (or a combination of chicken stock and water), 1 star anise (optional), 1 head lettuce (cored and sliced into thin ribbons), olive oil or drizzling sauce (equal parts soy sauce and black vinegar, with slivered fresh ginger mixed in).

Heat a soup pot. Add the butter, onions or scallions, and salt, and cook until softened, 5–10 min. Add the parsley or cilantro. Add the rice, stock, and star anise (if using), and cook until the rice is beginning to break down, 40–50 min. Remove from the heat, taste for salt and adjust, add the lettuce and eat, topping either with the olive oil or with the drizzling sauce.

LO BAK GO, COOKED

Lo bak go can be refrigerated for days and then reheated by being brought to room temperature, then pan-fried till crisp. They also freeze well. Thaw then pan-fry.

LOVAGE, WILTED

Lovage tastes like celery leaves and has a similar affinity for eggs. Pick through carefully, compost anything liquid or yellow, and chop and mix what's left into mayonnaise, which makes the laziest possible tartar sauce. Or use it in Sauce Gribiche (p. 396), actual Tartar Sauce (p. 396), or Salsa Verde (p. 398).

MARJORAM, WILTED

MARJORAM PARSLEY OIL *(5 min)*
1 tbsp wilted marjoram, Parsley Oil (p. 68), olive oil, salt.

Pick through carefully, composting any leaves that have fully browned. Chop what remains. In a bowl, combine the marjoram and parsley oil, adding more olive oil as needed to make it a little swimmy. Taste for salt and adjust. Dollop at will. Especially good with meat.

MARJORAM STEMS

If you are about to make a pot of beans or a stock, the stems can be added, along with any other herbs or herb stems you plan to include. Otherwise, compost.

MASHED POTATOES

PIEROGIS *(45 min)*
Pierogi Dough (p. 350), 2 tbsp butter plus more (optional) for serving, ½ cup chopped onion, ½–1 tsp salt, 1 cup mashed potatoes, ½ cup grated cheese (cheddar or Gruyère), freshly ground black pepper (optional).

Make the pierogi dough. Heat a pot. Add the butter, onion, and salt and cook over medium heat until completely tender and beginning to brown, about 10 min. Set aside half for serving. Pour the remaining cooked onion into the mashed potatoes. Add the cheese and a few grinds of black pepper (if using). Mix, taste for salt and pepper, and adjust. Scantly fill pierogi dough rounds with 1½ tsp of the filling. In a large pot of boiling water, cook the pierogis until they float. Serve with melted butter and the reserved onion.

MASHED POTATO PANCAKES *(10 min)*
1½ cups mashed potatoes, 2 tbsp all-purpose flour, 1 egg (beaten), salt if needed. *Optional additions:* 1 tbsp chopped green chile, ¼ tsp finely minced fresh ginger, 1–2 tbsp chopped cilantro, ½ tsp chaat masala. Olive oil or neutral oil or ghee for pan-frying.

In a large bowl, combine the potatoes, flour, and egg, adding a tiny pinch of salt if the potatoes weren't highly seasoned. Add any add-ins you like. Shape into fat pancakes. In a medium skillet, heat the oil over medium heat. Fry the cakes in batches if needed, flipping when you can just see the golden brown moving up the bottom of each cake, 1–3 min per side. Fry until both sides are crisp and golden brown. Good with any sauces or condiments.

An Italian variation is to crush 1 cup uncooked vermicelli into pieces ⅛ inch long and combine them with a little flour, form the mixture into croquettes, roll them in the combination of crushed noodles and flour, and fry as above. These are crunchy and festive.

POTATO DUMPLINGS *(15 min)*
2 cups mashed potatoes, 1 egg (beaten), 1 tsp salt, 1½ cups all-purpose flour.

In a bowl, stir together the mashed potatoes, egg, and salt. Add 1 cup of the flour, mixing until just combined. Knead a few times, then spread the remaining ½ cup flour on a board and tip out the potato mixture. Knead to just combine. Cut into 6–8 portions. Working with one portion of dough at a time (and keeping the rest covered with a towel), roll into a long snake about ½ inch thick, and then cut with a sharp knife or pastry cutter into ½–1-inch pillows, moving finished ones to a floured sheet pan as you go. In a large pot of boiling water salted to taste like pleasant seawater, cook the dumplings until they float to the top. Sauce with Parsley Oil (p. 68), or butter and chives, or herb butter, or leftover meat ragu, or toss with warmed leftover cooked greens. These can also be refrigerated, covered, until ready to cook, or frozen.

Mashed potatoes are also wonderful in the unanticipatedly delicious Sardine Croquettes (p. 286).

MATAR PANEER

Substitute for aloo gobi in the Aloo Gobi Samosas (p. 12) or for saag paneer in Saag Paneer Shakshuka (p. 83). Or add broth or water to turn into a stew, or use it in an omelet.

MILKWEED PODS, TINY

FRIED MILKWEED (*1 hr 15 min*)
Salt, milkweed pods, buttermilk (or buttermilk substitute, see p. 138) for soaking, fine cornmeal for breading, neutral oil (peanut or grapeseed) for frying, optional dipping sauce (hot sauce or ranch or raita or rémoulade).

In a large pot of boiling water salted to taste like pleasant seawater, briefly boil the milkweed pods, then remove and drain. Soak in the buttermilk just to cover for 1 hr, then remove and lightly coat each with cornmeal. In a small pot, heat 4 inches of oil to 350°–375°F. Fry in batches until crisp, stirring occasionally for uniform frying. Let them drain on paper towels or a cooling rack, salting immediately after retrieving from the oil. Eat when just slightly cooled, with any dipping sauce you like.

MINT, WILTED

MINT PARSLEY OIL (*5 min*)
1 tbsp chopped mint, Parsley Oil (p. 68), olive oil, salt.

Pick through carefully, composting any leaves that have fully browned. Chop what remains. In a bowl, combine with the parsley oil, adding more olive oil as needed to make it a little swimmy. Taste for salt and adjust. Dollop at will. Especially good with summer vegetables.

Leftover chopped mint is also wonderful for mixing into yogurt for another general drizzler.

MINT STEMS

MINT VINEGAR *(a few weeks, but all waiting)*
Mint stems, white wine vinegar or red wine vinegar.

In a jar, cover the mint stems with wine vinegar. Let sit several weeks. When the vinegar is nicely minty, remove the stems and use the vinegar for a mignonette or vinaigrette.

Or use mint stems in Herb Tea (p. 10).

MIREPOIX, COOKED

Freeze it in an ice cube tray! Cubes can be popped into hot fat directly from the freezer. It is worth remembering that many leftovers can be stored as frozen cubes—even various ones in a single tray—then popped out as needed.

MIREPOIX, RAW

Mirepoix's ingredients—carrots, onion, and celery or fennel—are among the longest lasting in the kitchen. Store leftover uncooked mirepoix in a little container toward the front of your fridge and begin the next thing you make with it, whether or not the recipe suggests it. If you roast a chicken, scatter the mirepoix in the pan. If you make a soup, add it to the other vegetables, and so on. Another approach is to remember that mirepoix is made of the same vegetables used in stock, and add it to any pot of stock or beans. A third approach is to quickly cook it in olive oil with a little salt, then freeze it and have frozen cooked mirepoix.

MUSHROOM SOAKING LIQUID (FROM DRIED MUSHROOMS)

Strain well through a double layer of cheesecloth in a fine-mesh sieve. Now you have mushroom stock. This can be used to make mushroom soup or mushroom pasta sauce or for Risotto (p. 206) or Braised Meat (p. 298).

MUSHROOM STEMS

Mushroom stems improve any pot of water, broth, stock, or braise. Drop them directly into the liquid, then strain their fibrous cadavers out before serving, or collect them in a bundle of cheesecloth or muslin, tie it up, submerge, and then fish the bundle out when its work is done. To make a stock of mostly mushroom stems, combine a cup of mushroom stems with water to cover by 3–4 inches in a soup pot. Add 1–2 hard cheese rinds, 1 bay leaf, 1–3 garlic skins, and a few sprigs of thyme. Bring to a boil, then reduce to a simmer and cook until it tastes like broth. Strain and use for any soup, Risotto (p. 206), or Braised Meat (p. 298).

MUSHROOMS, OLD

CREAMY MUSHROOM TOAST *(10–15 min)*
½ lb old mushrooms, 1 slice good bread, 1 clove garlic (halved), 4 tbsp (½ stick) butter, 1 sprig thyme or rosemary, ½ cup finely chopped shallot (or scallion or onion), salt, 1 tbsp wine, 2 tbsp heavy cream.

Remove the stems and freeze for stock. Wash the mushrooms under water, cutting off any rotten bits. Dry on a kitchen towel, then chop medium-fine. Toast the bread, then rub with the cut side of the garlic. Heat a pan. Add 2 tbsp of the butter. Add the herb sprig, chopped shallot, garlic, and a little sprinkle of salt and cook until just softened, 3–5 min. Add the mushrooms and wine and increase the heat to medium-high. Cook, stirring occasionally, until the mushrooms are cooked, another 5 min or so, adding the remaining 2 tbsp butter when the pan dries. Add the cream, taste for salt and adjust, and remove from heat. Remove the garlic and herb stem, spoon the mushrooms over the toast, and eat. The creamy mushrooms can also be used as a pasta or polenta sauce, if you'd prefer.

If you've had to jettison most of a box of mushrooms and have only several that haven't rotted, freeze them along with your fennel scraps and leek tops and parsley stems to add to stock or beans.
See also Mushroom stems (above).

NASTURTIUM BUDS

These make a good stand-in for capers. Bring a jar of leftover caper brine to a boil, then add a dash of water, vinegar, and sugar to freshen it. Or make a brine from scratch: Combine water and white vinegar in a pot, add salt and sugar, in about equal parts, bring to a boil, taste, adjust. Fill a little jar with nasturtium buds. Pour in the hot brine, close the lid, then let sit for 3 days before eating. These will keep in the refrigerator for months.

NASTURTIUM LEAVES

Nasturtium leaves add a peppery bite to salads or rice dishes. Mix them in and warn the tender-tongued.

NETTLES

Nettles are another wild green that should be sautéed with garlic and salt in olive oil. For further details, *see Greens (p. 45)*.

NETTLE STEMS

NETTLE TEA *(15 min)*
Clip clean nettle stems into a teapot. Top with boiling water, steep 5 min, add honey if you want, and drink.

NORI

Leftover nori is lovely thinly julienned and sprinkled over hot cooked rice.

OKRA, COOKED

OKRA FRITTERS *(30 min)*
½ cup all-purpose flour, ½ cup cornmeal, ½ tsp baking powder, ¼ tsp salt plus to taste, freshly ground black pepper, 1 egg (beaten), 3 tbsp milk, 1 cup

chopped cooked okra, ¼–½ cup corn kernels (optional), peanut or grapeseed oil for frying.

In a bowl, combine the flour, cornmeal, baking powder, salt, and black pepper. Add the egg and milk and mix well. Taste the batter for salt and adjust, then add the okra and corn (if using). Heat oil in a cast-iron skillet. Fry the fritters, about 1 tbsp each, in batches, flipping when crisp and brown, 1–3 min. Flip and cook on the other side. Continue until all are done. Good with hot sauce.

ONIONS, CHOPPED

If you have chopped onions and 10 min, heat a pan, add oil to coat the bottom, then add the onions and a pinch of salt and cook until totally tender, about 10 min. These can be frozen in an ice cube tray, or stored in a clear jar and used tomorrow as the start of sautéed vegetables, or Any Vegetable Minestra (p. 8), Amy's Pilaf (p. 206), or dozens of other recipes. Or use chopped onion, more finely minced, in place of shallot in Basic Vinaigrette (p. 376).

ONIONS, BURNED

CHARRED ONION BURGER SAUCE *(5 min)*
1 cup chopped burned onion, ¾ cup mayonnaise, ¼ cup chopped cornichons, any herbs.

Combine well and use as a burger sauce.

ONIONS, OLD

Old onions are fine for many things, including caramelized onions. Remove any soft, browned layers and then slice and cook the rest with a lot of butter, a bit of water, and a sprinkle of sugar and salt until deep golden. Any acridness will fade in the long, buttery cook. Or, if you feel bold, remove the soft browned layers and then use the rest as an onion, ignoring the strong smell, in (momentarily) blind faith.

ONION FROM MARCELLA'S TOMATO SAUCE

My favorite tomato sauce is from a recipe by Marcella Hazan. It can be found on p. 394. The recipe leaves behind two hemispheres of a collapsed, salted, slightly tomato-y onion. And what an onion it is!

GREENS WITH BUTTERY ONIONS—AND MAYBE CHERRY TOMATOES *(10 min)*
1 Marcella Sauce onion (any excess sauce still clinging), olive oil, 1–2 cloves garlic (optional; sliced), salt, 1 bunch cooking greens (kale or collards; stemmed, roughly chopped, and washed), a handful of halved cherry tomatoes (optional).

Slice the onion halves lengthwise into thin half-moons. Heat a large pan. Add olive oil, then garlic (if using), along with a little pinch of salt. Sauté until it just begins to soften, 20–30 sec, then add the sliced onion and greens. Cook, stirring occasionally, until the greens are tender, adding a sprinkle of water if and as needed to keep them cooking without burning. When they're almost done—when you taste them, think they might be, then decide against it—add the cherry tomatoes (if using) and increase the heat to high. Cook, stirring occasionally, until the cherry tomatoes have broken down and burst a bit. Taste for salt and adjust.

Or use the Marcella Sauce onion in Fān Qié Chǎo Dàn/Tomato and Egg Stir-Fry (p. 91).

ONION PEELS

The flavors of onion and garlic (and other alliums) thrive in their vellum paper skins and puckered tops and bottoms. Store them together, as you peel, in a bag in the freezer. Then, to make any stock or broth or Beans and Rice (p. 203) or Braised Meat (p. 298) or a long-cooking grain like farro, retrieve the bag, break off a piece, and include the odiferous iceberg instead of fresh onion or garlic.

Another strategy is to leave an empty pot on a back burner and drop onion and garlic peels directly into it over several days, during which you can also locate other freezer-burned but useful aromatics like carrot peels and parsley stems and fennel fronds and perhaps a chicken carcass, dropping each into the pot as you encounter it. When there are at least 2 cups of homely but useful bits and bobs in the pot, add water to cover by an inch or two, bring it to a boil, reduce it to a simmer, and let it cook while you do something else, adding water if it boils off. After 1–2 hrs, turn the burner off and let the brew stay there until you have time to strain it into a jar—which I have learned to label "broth" if I want it to be used. Several of these jars often inhabit my refrigerator at once, but they take up less physical and mental space than untended peels and tops. A bit of lovely botanical and semantic trivia: The potency of alliums, which makes even their most attenuated parts good for cooking, is ephemeral. The "lachrymatory factor," of alliums (what makes you cry) is a result of highly reactive compounds that very quickly lose reactivity, proving that in onions, as in loss, the passage of time is the best medicine.

Onion peels also make:

CLOTH OR EASTER EGG DYE (1–2 days, but mostly waiting)
This makes a sand-brown dye. Combine peels with 4 cups of water in a pot. Bring to a boil, simmer for about 40 min, then turn off the heat to let it steep as it cools to room temperature. Remove peels and add wet clothing directly to it, or strain and use as you would any clothing or egg dye.

ONION RINGS

Use onion rings in place of tempura in Tempura Miso Soup (p. 91). Or, toast onion rings or just their coating in a toaster oven, 5 min or so. Mix into cooked rice for a wonderfully exciting crunch. Or chop crispy batter bits and add to a maki roll with canned tuna and sriracha mayonnaise, and scallions if you have them, or to any other filling, like sliced avocado, or crab.

OREGANO, WILTED

OREGANO PARSLEY OIL (10 min)
1 tbsp wilted oregano, Parsley Oil (p. 68).

Pick through and discard any completely brown leaves. Chop the rest. Combine with parsley oil and dollop and drizzle away.

PARSLEY

Leftover parsley can be quickly chopped and used for perking up anything that requires reviving. Scatter it with wabi-sabi artistry over the top, or mix into olive oil or butter for a sauce, or cunningly sprinkle it to cover up where you cut into the chicken three times to check for doneness.

Here is an incomplete list of other uses for parsley, from which you should summon inspiration where you like. 1) Scatter chopped parsley over chicken broth or clam cooking liquid or cold rice with dashi, and once it's warm, consider it soup. 2) Add it to pasta with butter. 3) Add it to pasta with red sauce. 4) Add it to pasta with cheese sauce. 5) Add it to pasta with seafood. 6) Add it to: rice, fried rice, congee, risotto. 7) Add it to chicken soup with rice or 8) chicken soup with noodles or 9) any soup of any ingredient, any texture, any temperature. 10) Add it to boiled potatoes, 11) fried potatoes, 12) roasted potatoes, 13) roasted vegetables, 14) sautéed vegetables, or 15) boiled vegetables. I also count on parsley to enhance the appearance and flavor of 16) roasted meat, 17) boiled meat, 18) fried meat, 19) fried anything, plus 20) scrambled, boiled, poached, or fried eggs, and 21) any salad of any vegetable, 22) any salad of any meat, 23) any salad of any egg or dairy product, and 24) toast topped with anything savory, whether cheese or vegetables or eggs . . . I'm sure there are more.

Or use chopped parsley to make Parsley Oil.

PARSLEY OIL
1 bunch parsley, ½–1 clove garlic, ¼ tsp salt plus to taste, ½ cup olive oil plus to taste.

Pick the parsley leaves from the stems, saving the stems to use in stock or beans. Finely chop the leaves. Pound the garlic to a paste with the salt and combine in a bowl with the parsley. Add enough olive oil to make a rich dollop-able oil—much swimmier than pesto. Taste for salt and adjust.

For parsley-lemon oil, add the zest of ½ lemon; for parsley-walnut oil, add chopped toasted walnuts; for a crunchy herby bread crumb sauce, add an equal amount of toasted bread crumbs or croutons crisped with olive oil and salt in a 400°F oven for 10 min; for parsley tapenade, add a handful of chopped olives, a few chopped capers, and a chopped anchovy. For parsley pesto, add freshly grated Parmesan until the sauce is creamy, then a spoonful of pounded toasted pine nuts or walnuts; for a brightening sauce to serve over boiled meat or eggs or vegetables, make Salsa Verde (p. 398).

PARSLEY BUTTER *(5 min)*
Up to ¼ cup parsley leaves, 1 shallot (finely chopped), 8 tbsp (1 stick) room-temperature butter, salt.

Chop parsley. In a bowl, mix the parsley, shallot, and butter, add a sprinkle of salt. Good on anything from meat to eggs to soup to toast.

PARSLEY YOGURT SAUCE *(5 min)*
Parsley, whole-milk yogurt, chaat masala (optional).

Chop the parsley finely and add to the yogurt. Add a little of the masala (if using). This is a good dolloping sauce.

PARSLEY MAYONNAISE *(5 min)*
Parsley, mayonnaise, a little lemon juice or lemon zest.

Chop the parsley finely and add to the mayonnaise, along with the lemon juice or zest. Very good on BLTs or ALTs!

PARSLEY STEMS

Parsley stems are like Parmesan rinds in their ability to add flavor to water or broth or oil, contributing a discernible greenness without which no soup or broth or pot of beans ever tastes quite like itself. Keep a bag in the freezer and add to and withdraw from it as needed.

PARSNIPS, COOKED

Anything that is true of a *Carrot, cooked (p. 27)* is true of a parsnip.

PARSNIPS, HUGE

PARSNIP RÉMOULADE (*35 min*)
Substitute parsnip for celeriac in the recipe for Céleri Rémoulade (p. 32).

PEAS, COOKED

RICE AND PEAS (*25 min*)
1 cup rice of your preference, water or broth at the right ratio for your rice,
½ tsp salt, 1 tbsp butter or ghee, ¼–½ cup cooked peas, chiffonade-cut parsley
or mint (optional), yogurt for serving (optional).

Soak the rice as needed. In a small pot, combine the rice, water or broth,
salt, and the butter or ghee and bring to a boil. Cover and reduce it to a bare
simmer and cook until done, probably 15–20 min. Open the pot just long
enough to tip in the peas, then close it again. Let sit another 10 min, then fluff
and eat, with herbs and a dollop of yogurt if you like.

PEA PUREE (*5 min*)
1 cup cooked peas, 2 tbsp chopped fresh herbs (cilantro, mint, dill, or a combination), 2–3 tbsp olive oil, salt to taste.

In a blender, puree everything together to whatever smoothness you like. This
is delicious at room temperature as a topping for rice or toast, or as a dip, and
it's especially delicious mixed through cooked green beans or cooked broccoli
for an extra green experience.
    If you're dipping, you might also add half an avocado and a little spoonful
of sour cream or whole-milk yogurt.

PEA PODS

PEA STOCK (*1 hr*)
Pea pods, tops or peels of 1–2 onions, a small handful of parsley stems, 2–3
peppercorns.

In a pot, combine everything and add water to cover by 2 inches. Bring to a
boil, then reduce to a simmer and cook until it tastes of pea. Strain and use

to begin any soup, especially a pea one. Also good in Risotto (p. 206) or Any Vegetable Minestra (p. 8).

PEAS, OLD

PISELLI BRASATI *(1 hr)*

2 tbsp olive oil, 2 tsp butter, ½ onion (finely chopped), ½ tsp salt plus to taste, 2–3 cups old peas, 1 sprig rosemary, sugar (optional).

Heat a small pot. Add the olive oil, butter, onion, and salt and cook until tender, about 10 min, stirring and adding a few drops of water if it browns. Add the old peas, 1 cup water, and rosemary. Reduce the heat and cover. Cook, stirring occasionally, until sweet and collapsed, 40 min–1 hr. If they are tender but lacking sweetness, add a little pinch of sugar and stir through. Taste for salt and adjust.

PEPERONATA

Peperonata improves with time and accommodates itself according to need. To use leftover peperonata as a pasta sauce, put it into a pan with its oil and set over low heat. Add a small handful of drained capers and/or chopped olives and/or chopped anchovies and/or a scattering of chile flakes if you like. In a large pot of boiling water salted to taste like pleasant seawater, cook the pasta. Reserve ¼ cup pasta water before draining. When the pasta is done, mix it well with the peperonata, then top it with Parmesan or Pecorino Romano and scatter chopped parsley or basil or both over the top.

Cook eggs in leftover peperonata by heating it in a wide skillet, adding a chopped tomato or a bit of tomato sauce or a drizzle of water to make it saucy. When the peperonata is hot and bubbling, make a few wells with a spoon, crack eggs into ramekins, and then tip the eggs into the wells, salting each egg. Reduce the heat to low, cover the pan, and cook until the eggs are as you like them. If your peperonata threatens to burn on the stovetop, the egg cookery can be done in a 375°F oven instead. This is especially good with garlic-rubbed toast or pita or tortillas.

Or include leftover peperonata in a sandwich of grilled sausage or mozzarella and cooked garlicky greens, or sliced sandwich meat and cheese. Or make a bowl of rice and spoon peperonata on top. Or add peperonata to fried rice of any kind. Or add it to gazpacho, or to a different soup . . .

PEPERONATA OIL

Peperonata oil is thick and rich and indispensable. It should always be saved. Use it to drizzle over rice or pasta, regardless of what else is in either. Or cook fried rice in it, or start a pasta sauce with it, or start a vinaigrette with it. Or whisk it into scrambling eggs, or whisk it into mayonnaise. Just do not, under any circumstance, discard it, because it is delicious.

PEPPER PEELS

If you peeled your peppers (because the peels were tough, or because a recipe told you to), the peels can be dehydrated in a 125°F oven until completely dry and papery, then blended to a powder in a spice or coffee grinder and mixed with salt to make a slightly sweet, slightly savory seasoned salt.

PEPPER TOPS

Pepper tops are a good addition to Braised Meat (p. 298). Put them into the pot when you add other vegetable scraps like onion tops or carrot peels. If you're not braising meat, freeze the tops in a bag labeled "for a braise." Alternatively or in addition: A neat trick is to cut around the circumference of the pepper, close to the stem, remove its top as a lid, then upturn the pepper and tap out the seeds, helping with your fingers as needed, then pop the stem through the pepper top, leaving a little pepper ring, which you can now just use as a slice of pepper.

PEPPERS, OLD

Cut out the bad bits and use in Peperonata (p. 73).

PEPPERS, TOO MANY

I have found myself with a glut of peppers, for which there is no remedy like making peperonata. This recipe is written per pepper, and should be scaled according to your glut.

PEPERONATA *(1 hr)*
1 pepper, ½ onion, 1 clove garlic, olive oil, salt.

Slice the pepper into lengthwise strips about ¾ inch wide. Slice the onion lengthwise into thin half-moons. Thinly slice the garlic. Heat a heavy-bottomed sauté pan or skillet. Add ¼ inch of olive oil. Cook the peppers and onions together, salting well, over medium-low heat, covering and uncovering as needed, until they are softened and a little sizzly. Add the garlic and more oil. Cover and uncover and worry occasionally, cooking until they are truly melted into the oil and tender but not mushy, 45 min–1 hr.

POKE BERRIES

These can be made into jelly, but I would feel safer using them for a clothing or Easter egg dye. Heat in a pot of water, without boiling, until it is deep magenta, about 2 hours. Add wet clothing or eggs, let them sit overnight, then remove. For clothing rinse well, then hang to dry.

POKEWEED SHOOTS

I've never cooked pokeweed. But I have read many recipes for it, because it is a food of necessity. I can say with authority that pokeweed should be boiled to be entirely cleansed of its toxins for 14–30 min, and that the number of times it needs to be boiled and then drained ranges from one to three. It is traditionally further cooked in bacon fat after having been expunged. Some people add onion, sautéed in the bacon fat at the same time (which I would) and others add molasses (which I would replace with wine vinegar).

It is so hard for potatoes to shake the taste of having been refrigerated that I often leave mine out, covered, on the counter overnight. If your kitchen is hot, or it is summer, this may encourage unwelcome pungency, or more quickly molding potatoes. But if your kitchen is cool, it is a useful if daring trick. The next day, spared any bad influence, my leftover potatoes are nearly as delicious as they were the day before. Wherever they are stored, leftover cooked potatoes are adaptable.

This recipe is written per baked potato and should be scaled accordingly. Though it is too late for this note now, in the future, it's best to scoop the baked insides from the potatoes before storing them—the insides will come out more cleanly when warm and the peel will better keep its integrity.

TWICE-BAKED POTATO (*25 min*)
1 baked potato, 1–2 tbsp butter, ¼ cup milk or cream, 1–2 tbsp grated cheddar or Gruyère cheese, ¼ tsp salt plus to taste.

Heat the oven to 400°F. Scoop the inside of the potato out into a small pot. Over low heat, warm it with the butter and milk or cream. Mash with a fork or a potato masher to rice-size pieces. Add the cheese and salt, and warm until the cheese is just melted. Taste for salt and adjust. Fill the potato skins with the potato mixture, using a fork to make crisscross lines on top if you feel nostalgic for that look. Bake until crisped and browned, and bubbling, about 15 min.

POTATO BIRYANI (*35–45 min*)
1 cup basmati rice, 1 bay leaf, 4 cardamom pods, ½ star anise, a few whole cloves, 1 tbsp coriander seeds, ½ tsp cumin seeds, ½ tsp fennel seeds, ½ tsp black peppercorns, a sprinkle of cinnamon, 1 tbsp neutral oil, 1 small onion (sliced into thin half-moons), 1 tsp salt plus to taste, 1¾ cups liquid (water, stock, a combination of water and coconut milk), ¼ tsp ground turmeric, ¼–2 cups cubed cooked potatoes, 1 cup chopped cilantro.

Soak the rice. Meanwhile, in a spice grinder, combine the bay leaf and all the whole seeds and spices and grind, then mix in the cinnamon. In a small-medium pot, heat the oil. Add the onion and salt and cook until just beginning to brown. Add the drained rice and liquid. Add 1 tsp of the spice mixture—the rest can be kept—and the turmeric. Bring to a boil. Reduce to a simmer and cook until the rice is almost cooked through, about 15 min. Add the potatoes and cilantro, quickly mixing through. Cover and continue cooking over the lowest heat another 5–7 min. Taste for salt. Very good drizzled with yogurt.

FRIED POTATOES *(15 min)*

Cooked potatoes, cornstarch or flour or a combination, ghee or olive oil, salt.

Spread the cooked potatoes onto a tray and lightly dust them with cornstarch or flour or both. Shake off the excess, flip them to the other side, and reflour, again shaking off the excess. Heat a heavy-bottomed pan. Add ⅛ inch of ghee or olive oil. Let it get quite hot and shimmery. Lay the potatoes in the fat in batches so they don't get crowded (there should be enough room around each piece to easily maneuver). Cook on their first side until the brown begins to creep up the side of the potato. Flip each piece. Once you have two crisp sides, don't worry about carefully turning to a third. Remove to a sheet pan, continue until done, salt well, and eat.

HERBY POTATO SALAD *(15 min)*

Cooked potatoes, lemon zest, ½ cup onions or shallots (cut into thin half moons) or chopped scallions, lemon juice, salt, olive oil, freshly ground black pepper, chopped fresh herbs (parsley, cilantro, celery leaves). *Optional additions: a scattering of well-drained capers, thinly sliced sorrel or purslane, a scattering of chopped olives.*

If you can, store the leftover potatoes with lemon zest to get lemony overnight. In a bowl, combine the onions, shallots, or scallions with enough lemon juice to cover, along with a little pinch of salt. Let sit for 10 min. In another bowl, combine the potatoes, lemon zest if the potatoes weren't stored with it, a squeeze of lemon juice, and ample amounts of olive oil and mix through. Taste for salt and adjust. Add black pepper and herbs. Drain the onion and add to the potatoes, along with any other optional additions.

POLPETTONE GENOVESE *(1 hr)*

1½ cups chopped cooked potatoes, salt, about 2 cups green beans, 2 cloves garlic (minced), 1¼ cups freshly grated Parmesan cheese, 2 eggs (whisked), 1 tbsp fresh marjoram leaves (chopped), ½ cup olive oil, ¾ cup fresh bread crumbs (p. 176).

Bring the potatoes to room temperature if they're not. In a large pot of water salted to taste like seawater, cook the green beans until just cooked, 3–5 min. Drain. Heat the oven to 350°F. Chop the green beans roughly, then mash with the potatoes or pass through a food mill. Add the Parmesan, eggs, marjoram, garlic, and ¼ cup of the olive oil. Taste for salt and adjust. Lightly brush a heavy-bottomed 10-inch cast-iron skillet or cake pan with olive oil. Add the vegetable mixture and top with the bread crumbs, then drizzle with the remaining ¼ cup olive oil. Bake until cooked through and golden brown, about 40 min.

Leftover cooked potatoes can also be chopped, skin on or off, and added to soup, whether Any Vegetable Minestra (p. 8), Lemony Vegetable Soup (p. 49), Minestrone (p. 210), or any other. Add with enough time for the potato to warm through.

POTATO COOKING WATER

On the spectrum of used cooking liquids, potato cooking water occupies a space at the useful end. It contains potato starch, which, like cornstarch, is good at thickening. Even at a hard, fast boil, potatoes cook long enough for their thickening starch to release into the pot. For a pureed vegetable soup, use potato water for some of the liquid. If you have meat drippings and want to make a quick gravy, heat the pan, add potato water while scraping, and you have gravy. Or use potato water to make a velouté sauce like the one for Oysters Rockefeller on p. 423. Use potato water instead of some of the cream in mashed potatoes and they will be airier but no less flavorful. Potato water can also be used for some of the liquid in a quick bread or a yeast-risen loaf. Make sure to taste any potato cooking water carefully for salt before using it. If the potatoes are properly seasoned, the water will be salty and need further watering down. Potato water can stay in the fridge for a few days or be frozen.

POTATOES, OLD AND TURNING GREEN

For legal reasons, I should say that green potatoes are poisonous. The following is a description of my own approach to them. It perhaps has some neutralizing effect on their toxins, since I have followed it for years and survived. I pare out the eyes, cut what remains into cubes, boil them in well salted water, and drain. I mash this with a potato masher, add lots of butter, and salt, and eat.

POTATO PEELS

CRISPY POTATO PEELS WITH SCALLIONS AND CHEESE *(25 min)*
Potato peels, olive oil, salt, a gratable cheese (Gouda or cheddar), as much thinly sliced scallions as you like (I like a lot).

Heat the oven to 400°F. In a bowl, toss the peels with a lot of olive oil and salt. Spread on a sheet pan. Bake until very crispy, 15–20 min, mixing at least once. Remove from the oven to a plate, blanket with grated cheese and scallions, and eat. These are best eaten immediately.

PUMPKIN, COOKED

Use in the Any Vegetable Mash (p. 8), Any Vegetable Minestra (p. 8), Any Vegetable Potage (p. 8), Any Vegetable Sabzi (p. 9), Any Vegetable Salad (p. 9), Any Vegetable Curry (p. 9), or Any Vegetable Thai-Style Curry (p. 10). Leftover cooked pumpkin can also be smashed with olive oil and eaten on garlic-rubbed toast with grated Parmesan or Pecorino Romano and black pepper over it all at the end, or added to warming bean or greens or rice or dal.

PUMPKIN SEEDS

TOASTED PUMPKIN SEEDS *(30 min)*
Pumpkin seeds, olive oil, salt.

Heat the oven to 400°F. Put all the stringy innards and seeds in a big bowl of water as you remove them and sift the seeds out, directly onto sheet pans. Drizzle heavily with olive oil and roast to browned and crisp, 10–20 min, depending on the seeds. Salt and eat. Let cool completely before storing.

PURSLANE

Purslane is a common edible garden weed. Dress it with lemon, olive oil, and salt, then add a roasted vegetable, like squash or carrots or beets, and bits of goat cheese. This is very early aughts, but also good.

RADICCHIO, WILTED

RADICCHIO WITH BEANS *(15 min)*
2 tbsp olive oil plus for serving, 1 clove garlic (sliced), ⅛ tsp salt plus to taste, up to ¼ cup radicchio (thinly sliced), cooked beans (see the recipe for Beans and Rice, p. 203), a small handful of roughly chopped parsley leaves (optional), freshly grated Parmesan cheese (optional).

Heat a small pot. Add 1 tbsp of the olive oil, garlic, and salt and cook over medium heat until just softened, 30 sec–1 min. Add the sliced radicchio and stir through, sautéing. Add the beans, along with some of their liquid, or a drizzle of broth or water if you don't have bean liquid, and warm over medium heat, stirring. Taste for salt and adjust. Add parsley if using. Drizzle with the remaining 1 tbsp olive oil and top with Parmesan if desired. Good with Parsley Oil (p. 68) or Marjoram Parsley Oil (p. 59) spooned on top.

RADICCHIO CORE

If you're making a salad, thinly slice the core, and include it with the leaves.

RADISHES, OLD

ROASTED RADISH FRITTATA *(30–45 min)*
2–3 cups chopped or quartered old radishes, rotten bits pared off, olive oil, ⅛ tsp salt plus to taste, 8 eggs, chopped thyme (optional), up to 2 cups greens (fresh spinach, cooked onions, thinly sliced scallions, or chopped soft herbs such as parsley, cilantro, or chervil).

Heat the oven to 400°F. In a bowl, toss the radishes with olive oil and salt and lay on a sheet pan. Roast to caramelized and golden brown, checking after

10 min. Let cool and reduce the oven temperature to 375°F. Beat the eggs with salt. Add the radishes and a pinch of chopped thyme (if using) and greens, onions, or herbs. Stir to combine. Heat an ovenproof skillet. Coat well with olive oil. Add the egg mixture and move the set part toward the middle a few times. As soon as the sides have cohered, transfer to the oven. Cook until the top is just set, checking after 8 min, then again until it's done. Cool briefly in the pan, then invert. Like most frittatas, this is better at room temperature than hot.

For this next you need a total of 1½–2 cups radishes and cucumber combined.

RADISH CUCUMBER IKURA SALAD *(20 min)*
¾ cup old radish matchsticks, 1 large cucumber (partially peeled, seeded, and julienned), a few leaves shiso (or mint or Thai basil), 3 tbsp ponzu, 2 tbsp sesame oil, 1 tbsp rice vinegar, ½ tbsp soy sauce, ⅛ tsp sugar, 2 tbsp ikura (salmon caviar).

Briefly soak the radish in cold water to crisp it. Pat dry and combine with the cucumber and shiso. In a small bowl, whisk together the ponzu, sesame oil, vinegar, soy sauce, and sugar to make a dressing. Pour the dressing over the salad, without mixing. Top with ikura. (Adapted from Just One Cookbook website)

RADISH GREENS

RADISH PESTO *(10–15 min)*
1 clove garlic, ¼ tsp salt plus to taste, 2 bunches radish greens (washed and dried), ¼ cup lightly toasted pistachios or pecans, ½ cup freshly grated Parmesan or Pecorino Romano cheese, ½ cup olive oil.

Pound the garlic into a paste with the salt. In a blender, combine the radish greens with the nuts, garlic, and cheese, then add the olive oil. Pulse to blend, using a wooden spoon or blender insert to make sure everything mixes, aiming for a thick, uniform paste. Taste for salt and adjust. This is good in all the usual constellations, and can be smoothed out with a bit of crème fraîche or extra cheese if it's too sharp.

If this pesto seems too radish greeny, next time use radish greens for up to half the basil in Basic Pesto (p. 394). Or try:

MULO SHAAK PITHALI (*1½ hr, but mostly waiting*)
3 tbsp masoor dal (red lentils), 2 tbsp mustard oil or a neutral oil like peanut, ½ tsp panch phoron (or any combination of ground fennel, ground fenugreek leaves, ground cumin, and ground onion seed or onion powder), 1 whole dried red chile (broken) or ½ tsp red chile flakes, ½ tsp ground turmeric, 1 bunch radish greens (finely chopped), scant ¼ tsp salt plus to taste.

Soak the dal in water to cover for 1 hr. In a mortar or spice grinder, grind the dal to a paste with a tiny bit of soaking water. Heat a pan, then add the oil. Add the panch phoron and chile and cook over medium heat until aromatic, 20–30 sec. Add the dal paste and cook, stirring, until roasted and cooked, 2–3 min. Add the turmeric, greens, and salt. Cook, stirring, until the greens are tender, 1–2 min. Taste for salt and adjust. Very good with yogurt and rice. (Adapted from Fork Tales website)

I'm leaving this in my friend Olivia Tincani's words, because while she excludes details normally included, she includes details normally omitted. For additional measurements, try 3 tbsp oil and 1 clove garlic.

OLIVIA'S RADISH GREEN PASTA (*25 min*)
"Wash radish greens, rough cut. Combine with whatever else you have that needs to go away from the fridge (turnip tops, erbette [chard], arugula, pea tips, or nothing.) Boil pasta. Save a little pasta water. Heat oil and sliced garlic in a pan with peperoncini [chile flakes] to your liking. Add radish greens. Toss cooked pasta in the pan with radish greens and add a little pasta water to bind, and a touch of butter if you like, on low flame. 2 bunches of radish greens gets you a serving size of pasta for 3 people, usually. Radish greens should be beetle bitten and ugly. They will still be scrumptious. Best is combined with tops of turnips."
See also Greens (p. 45).

RATATOUILLE

RATATOUILLE PASTA *(20 min)*
1–2 cups ratatouille, olive oil, salt, ½ lb short pasta, ½–1 cup chopped herbs like parsley and basil, 1–2 tbsp drained chopped capers, ½ cup chopped pitted Niçoise or other good olives (optional).

Bring the ratatouille to room temperature or heat in a small pot on the stove, adding a little olive oil and a sprinkle of water while it heats. In a large pot of boiling water salted to taste like pleasant seawater, cook the pasta. Reserve ¼ cup pasta water just before draining. In a big bowl, toss the pasta, ratatouille, herbs, capers, and olives (if using), drizzling in a little olive oil as you mix it all together. Add a little pasta water if it's a bit dry. Taste for salt and adjust. Eat at any temperature. This is good with freshly grated Parmesan or Pecorino Romano.

EGGS IN RATATOUILLE *(10 min)*
1–2 cups ratatouille, olive oil, 2 eggs, salt, chopped herbs if you have them.

In a small pot or pan, heat the ratatouille with a drizzle of water and olive oil until just bubbling. Crack the eggs into ramekins or teacups. Make small wells in the ratatouille, drop an egg in each, lightly salt them, especially the yolks, and cover the pan. Check after 2 min and then frequently until the eggs are cooked as you like them. Scoop into a bowl, drizzle with olive oil, scatter with herbs, and eat, ideally with garlic-rubbed toast.

Or just toast thickly cut bread, rub it with a garlic clove, then drizzle with olive oil. Add cold ratatouille cold, then chopped parsley or torn basil, a diamond on the toast's diadem.

ROMAINE, OLD

One of the best destinations for wilted romaine is rice. This can take the form of Rice and Lettuce Soup (p. 58), or it can be more informal: Add a handful of romaine to Fried Rice (p. 205) or stir it into heating congee, where it softens into the porridge but retains enough structure to keep bites interesting. Or make:

BRAISED LETTUCE ON TOAST *(10–15 min)*
1 head romaine lettuce, ½ clove garlic, salt, 6 anchovy fillets, 6 tbsp room-temperature butter, 6 slices rustic bread, ¼ cup chicken or vegetable stock, grated zest of ½ lemon.

Remove the outer leaves from the romaine, reserving them for soup (see Gazpacho-ish Verde, p. 82). Cut the rest into thin wedges. Pound the garlic with a tiny pinch of salt. Pound the anchovies to a paste with the garlic to a paste paste, then mash in 3 tbsp of the butter to make anchovy butter. Toast the bread. Meanwhile, in a pan, melt the remaining 3 tbsp butter. Once it's melted, add the stock and then the romaine. Cook over medium heat about 2 min, flip wedges, and scatter with lemon zest. Cook until the lettuce is totally tender and the liquid is absorbed. Taste for salt and adjust. Spread the toasts with anchovy butter. Remove the lettuce from the pan and chop roughly, then arrange over the anchovy-buttered toast. Weird but so good.

GAZPACHO-ISH VERDE *(5 min)*
2 cups chopped romaine lettuce, 1 cup chopped peeled cucumber, 1½–2 cloves garlic (sliced), 2 tbsp sherry vinegar, 1 cup packed chopped soft herbs (with stems; parsley, basil, sorrel, cilantro, arugula, chervil, tarragon, celery leaf, in any combination), 1 tsp salt plus to taste, ½ cup olive oil plus to taste.

In a blender, combine all the ingredients and blend until smooth and frothy. Taste for olive oil by noting whether the richness you taste at the end is enough, or you want a little more, and adjust. Taste for salt and adjust. Refrigerate until well chilled, then eat or drink, garnished any way you like.

ROSEMARY, OLD

Even rosemary that's been languishing on a countertop for weeks should be used. If you see your rosemary beginning to dry out, use it more energetically. Put a few sprigs into a roasting pan with your roasting squash or potatoes, or into the pan with the chicken, or into a pan in which you'll cook hamburgers or mushrooms, or drop it into your potato cooking water, or add it to beans. Before long you will be wishing for more rosemary.

ROSEMARY FROM A ROASTING PAN

HERBY BREAD CRUMBS *(10 min)*
Bread, olive oil, salt, roasty rosemary.

Heat the oven to 400°F. In a food processor, pulse stale bread into fairly coarse, irregular crumbs. In a bowl, toss the crumbs with enough olive oil to make everything slightly moist and ready to roast. Tip onto a sheet pan and toast in the oven, checking at 10 min, until the crumbs are crisp and golden. Salt to taste. Crumble in rosemary. Use this to top Bean Gratin (p. 212) or scatter over pasta or roasted meat or eggs or vegetables or tofu, as you would a sauce.

RÖSTI

Refry any leftover rösti in ghee, then top with sour cream or yogurt and caviar!

SAAG PANEER

SAAG PANEER SHAKSHUKA *(30 min)*
2–3 tbsp olive oil, ½ onion (thinly sliced lengthwise), ½ tsp salt plus to taste, 2 cloves garlic (sliced), 2–3 cups saag paneer, 4 eggs. *Optional for serving:* fresh or pickled chiles, roughly chopped cilantro, yogurt.

Heat a heavy-bottomed skillet or pot. Add the oil, onion, garlic, and the salt. Cook, stirring, until tender, 5–10 min. Add the saag paneer and ½ cup water, stir through, and bring to a simmer. If it seems dry, add a little more water. Taste for salt and adjust. Crack the eggs into ramekins or teacups. Make slight wells in the saag, then tip an egg into each. Salt each lightly. Cover and cook until the eggs are cooked as you like them. If desired, garnish with chiles and cilantro. Serve with yogurt on the side (if using). Very good with warm bread or rice. (Adapted from Genevieve Ko in the *Los Angeles Times*)

Leftover saag paneer also makes a great topping for pizza, especially white pizza. It is worth ordering a pizza just to experience the transcendent combination. Top pizza, briefly heat, dollop with cilantro chutney if you have, and transcend.

SAGE, WILTED

SAGE TEA WITH HONEY *(5–10 min)*
Wilted sage, honey.

Heat some water, pour it over the sage, let steep for 3–5 min. Remove the sage and add as much honey as you like, and be warmed and calmed.

SCALLIONS, WILTED

Scallions that have wilted beyond salvation are a chimera. The outermost layer of a scallion may wilt. The wilt may even penetrate a layer or two. But the most commonly used part of the scallion—the inner bottom several inches—will endure. If your scallion is browned and wilted, trim it down to where it's not, then proceed as you would with any scallion.

Scallions are alliums, like onions and shallots and leeks, and can replace other alliums until they're used up. When you notice yours beginning to wilt, substitute them in a soup or sauce or mirepoix or sofrito or vinaigrette or use in stock or beans or pots of grains.

SCALLION TOPS

SCALLION TOP SAUCE *(5 min)*
1 bunch scallion greens (chopped), 1 clove garlic (chopped), ½–1 tsp salt, olive oil, citrus juice (optional).

Pound the scallion tops and garlic to a paste with salt. To use this as a marinade, add oil and a squeeze of citrus juice if desired. To make a delicious dollop-y sauce for rice or eggs or noodles or soup, add oil gradually and stop when it seems saucy.

Or use scallion tops wherever you would use part of an onion, or an onion skin, or an onion top.

SCALLION ROOTS

MORE SCALLIONS *(a few weeks, but mostly waiting)*
Scallion roots (with ¼–½ inch scallion white attached), potting soil, sunshine.

Stand the bottoms in a little jar and add just enough water to cover the roots, leaving the whites above water. Place somewhere with good natural light, changing the water every few days, and ensuring there's always some water in the jar. When the new green shoots are 4–5 inches long and the roots have grown, put in potting soil or in the ground. Harvest by snipping, and they will continue growing, until, eventually, what emerges is too hollow and tough, usually when the plant flowers. Use the flower blossoms, and whenever you are ready, begin again. (From All Recipes website)

SHALLOTS, TOO MANY

VINEGAR-ROASTED SHALLOTS *(45 min)*
2 lb shallots, 1 tsp salt, 2 tbsp olive oil, 2 tbsp red wine vinegar, 1 tbsp white wine or sherry, a few sprigs of thyme (optional).

Heat the oven to 400°F. Trim the root ends from the shallots, trying to leave their layers connected at the roots. Halve or quarter lengthwise (through the root end) if they're bigger than a golf ball, leaving any small ones whole. Peel and lay them tightly in a single layer in a deep roasting pan. Sprinkle with the salt and drizzle with the oil, vinegar, white wine or sherry, and ¼ cup water. Scatter the thyme over (if using). Cover the pan tightly with foil and put it in the oven. Check for doneness after 30 min by undoing the foil carefully and piercing the shallots with a knife. A knife should slide through easily. If it doesn't, re-cover tightly, and continue cooking until it does. Check periodically, adding a drizzle of water if the pan gets dry. When completely tender, remove the foil and return the pan to the oven. Cook, uncovered, until any remaining liquid has evaporated and the shallots have browned. These are as good at room temperature as hot.

SOFRITO

Freeze leftover sofrito in an ice cube tray or plastic bag. Use it directly from the freezer.

SPINACH, WILTED

Wilted spinach should be mercilessly picked through for yellowed leaves—which should be composted. Whatever survives should be immediately wilted further with a sprinkle of water in a hot pan, and added to any pesto or soup or eggs or warming leftover beans.

STUFFED CABBAGE

STUFFED CABBAGE STEW *(30–40 min)*
3 tbsp olive oil, 1 cup finely chopped cilantro (stems are ideal for this), ½ cup finely chopped onion (or scallion or shallot or any combination), ¼ cup finely chopped garlic, 1 tsp chile flakes, 1 tsp salt plus to taste, 3 tbsp tomato paste, 1 bay leaf, 1–2 stuffed cabbages (chopped), yogurt to garnish.

Heat a medium-small pot. Add the oil, cilantro, onion, garlic, chile flakes, and salt. Cook over medium heat for about 10 min, until everything has softened. Reduce the heat or add a few drops of water if needed to keep things from browning or sticking. Add the tomato paste and stir for 1 min until darkened. Add the bay leaf and 6 cups water. Bring to a boil, then reduce to a simmer, add the chopped stuffed cabbage, with all its stuffing and any liquid. Cook at a simmer until the soup has thickened, 15–30 min. Top with yogurt and eat.

SWEET POTATO, BAKED

FRANNY'S SWEET POTATOES *(10 min)*
2 baked sweet potatoes, 1 cup Greek yogurt, 3 tbsp lemon juice, ¼ cup olive oil plus for drizzling, ¼ tsp salt, 2 tbsp toasted sesame seeds, ¼ cup medium-diced red onion or scallions, ¼ tsp finely minced garlic, 1½ tbsp Thai fish sauce, 1 tbsp finely chopped pickled chiles or 1 tsp chile flakes, ¼ cup coarsely chopped parsley, flaky sea salt.

Bring the sweet potatoes to room temperature. Slice them into rounds ½ inch thick, including skin. In a bowl, whisk together the yogurt, lemon juice, and 2 tbsp of the olive oil. Spoon it onto a big serving plate. In a bowl, stir together the remaining 2 tbsp olive oil, the salt, sesame seeds, onion or scallions, garlic, fish sauce, chiles, and parsley. Spoon over the sweet potatoes. Top with flaky salt and an extra drizzle of olive oil.

SLIGHTLY PERUVIAN SWEET POTATO SALAD (10 min)

1–4 baked sweet potatoes, 1 shallot (thinly sliced), juice of 2 limes, ¼ tsp salt plus to taste, 1 jalapeño (finely chopped), ½–1 cup chopped cilantro, ¼ cup roughly chopped roasted peanuts.

Bring the sweet potatoes to room temperature. Slice them into rounds ½ inch thick, including skin. In a bowl, soak the shallot in the lime juice with the salt for 10 min. Add the sweet potatoes, jalapeño, cilantro, and peanuts to the shallots and toss together. It's fine if the sweet potato breaks into pieces! Taste for salt and adjust.

Or use leftover baked sweet potatoes in the Any Vegetable Mash (p. 8), Any Vegetable Minestra (p. 8), Any Vegetable Potage (p. 8), Any Vegetable Sabzi (p. 9), Any Vegetable Salad (p. 9), Any Vegetable Curry (p. 9), or Any Vegetable Thai-Style Curry (p. 10).

SWEET POTATO FRIES

Use leftover sweet potato fries instead of French fries in the Most Buttery Roast-y Smash (p. 43).

SWEET POTATO PUREE

SWEET POTATO SCONES (25–30 min)

2¾ cups (320 g) all-purpose flour, ⅓–½ cup (65–100 g) sugar (depending how sweet you like scones), 1 tbsp baking powder, ¾ tsp salt, ½ tsp combined sweet spices like cinnamon and nutmeg, 8 tbsp (4 oz/113 g) cold butter (cut into small pieces), ½ cup sweet potato puree, ½ cup whole milk or cream, 2 tsp vanilla extract.

Heat the oven to 425°F. Place parchment paper on a baking sheet. In a bowl, whisk together the flour, sugar, baking powder, salt, and spices. Cut the butter into the flour mixture to coarse crumbs. In a second bowl, whisk together the sweet potato puree, milk, and vanilla. Add the sweet potato mixture to the flour mixture and mix until just combined. Briefly knead on a well-floured surface. Form into an 8 x 3-inch rectangle 2 inches thick. Cut with a bench scraper into 5 pieces, then cut each into a right triangle, place at least ½ inch apart on the baking sheet and bake until just firm, 15–18 min.

SWEET POTATO MUFFINS (*30–40 min*)
8 tbsp (4 oz/113 g) room-temperature unsalted butter plus for muffin tin, ¾ cup (150 g) granulated sugar, 2 eggs (whisked), 1¼ cups sweet potato puree, 5 tbsp whole milk, 1½ cups (180 g) all-purpose flour, 2 tsp baking powder, ¼ tsp salt, ½ tsp ground cinnamon, ½ cup chopped pecans or walnuts or raisins (optional). *Optional streusel topping:* 3 tbsp all-purpose flour, ½ cup chopped almonds, 3½ tbsp room-temperature butter, 3 tbsp brown sugar.

Heat the oven to 400°F. Grease a 12-cup muffin tin. In a stand mixer, beat the butter and sugar until very fluffy, about 5 min. Beat in the eggs. Add the sweet potato and milk to the mixer and beat until combined. In another bowl, combine the flour, baking powder, salt, and cinnamon. Add to the ingredients in the mixer and stir until just combined. Mix in the nuts or raisins (if using) by hand. Spoon the batter into the prepared muffin cups. Combine the streusel topping (if using). Sprinkle the topping over the muffins. Bake until a skewer emerges almost clean, 22–25 min. Let cool briefly in the tin, then finish cooling on a rack.

SWISS CHARD, COOKED

Leftover cooked Swiss chard is good anywhere another cooked green would be. Try it in Greens Gratin (p. 46), Greens Frittata (p. 46), Greens Sandwich and Toast (p. 47), Greens Pesto (p. 47), Greener Greens and Beans (p. 47), Greens Risotto (p. 47), Italian Creamed Greens (p. 48), Greens Dip (p. 48), or Greens Kuku (p. 48). Or in Ribollita (p. 178), Fast Ribollita (p. 179), Beans and Greens and Egg (p. 212), Bean and Salami Soup (p. 213), Pan-Fried Farro (p. 224), or Farro Soup (p. 225).

SWISS CHARD STEMS

SWISS CHARD STEM GRATIN *(1 hr)*

Stems from 1–2 bunches Swiss chard, salt, 1 cup Béchamel (p. 395), butter for greasing pan plus a little bit cubed, thinly sliced mozzarella cheese (optional), freshly ground black pepper, freshly grated Parmesan cheese, bread crumbs (optional).

Cut the chard stems into 2–3-inch lengths. In a pot of very salty boiling water, cook them in batches until tender, 3–4 min (depending on their size and age). Scoop them out. Make the béchamel. Heat the oven to 375°F. Butter a gratin dish large enough to hold the stems in two layers. Add a layer of stems, then a little béchamel, then mozzarella (if using). Add the remaining stems and top with béchamel. Top with black pepper and Parmesan, then bread crumbs (if using). If you like, put a few little cubes of butter on top of everything. Bake until bubbling and golden brown, 20–30 min.

AL DI LA CHARD STEMS *(25–30 min)*

Stems from 1–2 bunches Swiss chard, salt, ½ cup olive oil plus for drizzling, 4 anchovy fillets, 2 cloves garlic (finely chopped), 1 tbsp lemon juice or red wine vinegar.

Cut the chard stems into 5–6-inch lengths. In a pot of very salty boiling water, cook the stems in batches until just tender, 3–4 min (depending on their size and age). Drain the stems. Heat a grill or indoor griddle to medium heat. Drizzle the stems with olive oil and grill until nicely charred in places. Meanwhile, pound the anchovy and garlic together with a tiny pinch of salt, then add the lemon juice or vinegar. Stir in the ½ cup olive oil. In a bowl, toss the chard stems with some of the anchovy mixture, using only as much of it as you like. Taste, adjust the salt, add more lemon or olive oil if you want, then eat. Very good with garlic-rubbed grilled bread. (Adapted from Food 52 website)

Chard stems can also be pickled. *See Greens stems (p. 49).*

TARO, COOKED

Cooked taro is delicious cut into chunks and added to a beef or other meat or root vegetable stew. It is also good cut into steak fries and pan-fried, then topped with herbs and scallions, as in Yuca Fries with Herb and Scallions (p. 94).

TARRAGON, WILTED

If it tastes good, proceed. Otherwise, use only the stems to add light licorice-ness to boiling or poaching or confit liquid, then fish out and compost.

TATER TOTS

TATER WAFFLES (*20 min*)
1 tbsp butter, 1–3 cups Tater Tots.

Heat a waffle iron to medium-high and butter well. Line the iron tightly with Tater Tots, making sure they're as close as possible and only using as much of the iron as you can fill tightly. Cook over medium heat at least 10 min per side if frozen, less if thawed or cooked. Cook until perfectly golden and coherent and waffle-y. Good with sour cream, guacamole, hot sauce, cheese . . . even ketchup, if that's your style.

TEMPURA VEGETABLES

SCALLION OMELET CREPE (*5–10 min*)
1 tbsp Shao Xing wine or sherry, 1 tbsp cornstarch, 1 egg, 2 egg whites, ½ tsp salt, 2 scallions (whites and light-green parts, thinly sliced on a diagonal, green tops thinly sliced, all kept separate), 1 tsp sesame oil, 1 cup sliced or chopped tempura, 1–2 tbsp peanut or vegetable oil.

In a small bowl, stir together the wine or sherry and the cornstarch. In a medium bowl, whisk the whole egg and egg whites with the salt until well combined. Add the cornstarch mixture and scallion whites and light-green parts. Stir in the sesame oil and tempura. In a skillet, heat the peanut oil until shimmery. Add the batter and spread as thinly as you can, moving cooked parts away and tilting uncooked batter underneath. When it is set, flip, using all of your gumption. Cook until just set on the other side. Tip onto a plate. Garnish with scallion greens and eat. Good drizzled with soy sauce, or a combination of soy sauce and black vinegar. Also good made with seafood tempura. (Inspired by *China: the Cookbook* by Kei Lum Chan and Diora Fong Chan)

TEMPURA MISO SOUP *(20 min)*

2–4 pieces tempura (left whole or chopped into bite-size pieces), 2–3 cups miso soup (made with dashi and miso), cubed tofu (optional), noodles (optional), sliced scallions.

Toast the tempura in a toaster oven to just warm, 5 min or so. In a pot, heat the soup along with some tofu and/or noodles (if using). Top with scallions. Add the toasted tempura just before eating.

TOMATOES, CUT YESTERDAY

FĀN QIÉ CHǍO DÀN/TOMATO AND EGG STIR-FRY *(10–15 min)*

2 eggs, ½ tsp salt, 2 tbsp neutral oil (peanut or grapeseed), 1 scallion (sliced), ½–1 cup chopped tomatoes, ½ tsp sugar (optional), hot rice for eating.

In a bowl, beat together the eggs and ¼ tsp of the salt. Heat an omelet pan. Add 1 tbsp of the oil, then the eggs, and lightly scramble until just set, then pour onto a plate. Heat the pan again, add the remaining 1 tbsp oil, then add the scallion, tomatoes, sugar if using, and remaining ¼ tsp salt and stir-fry until the tomatoes have begun to break down and release juice, 1–2 min. Return the eggs to the pan and mix through briefly. Eat on rice.

If you have only a half a tomato, or a handful of chopped ones, heat a small skillet, add 1-2 tbsp olive oil, then add the tomatoes and a little salt and cook them until they've just broken down and become a spoonful of saucy tomatoes. This can be added to sautéeing greens (see Greens with Buttery Onions, p. 66) or be used to make bruschetta or included in scrambled eggs or used in the Pan con Tomate (p. 93).

TOMATO CORES

Tomato cores can be added to Braised Meat (p. 298) or to any meat, fish, or vegetable stock.

TOMATOES, GREEN

Fried green tomatoes transform unripe late summer tomatoes from a sadness into a stroke of luck. It's best to bread these just before frying.

FRIED GREEN TOMATOES (*45 min*)
Green tomatoes, 1 egg, milk or buttermilk, cornmeal, salt, neutral oil (grapeseed or peanut); Rémoulade Sauce (p. 396) or mayonnaise for serving.

Slice tomatoes into ½-inch-thick slices. In a wide shallow dish, whisk together the egg and a bit of water, milk, or buttermilk. In another dish, combine finely ground cornmeal—I like corn flour best, but any cornmeal works—with a big pinch of salt. Set out a large cooling rack, and then bread the green tomatoes by dipping them first in the egg mixture, then in the cornmeal. In a deep, heavy bottomed pan or large pot, heat 1–2 inches of grapeseed or peanut oil until it just sizzles when you drop in a speck of cornmeal. Fry tomatoes in batches, flipping when you see golden brown beginning to move up the sides. Drain on the cooling rack and salt lightly. Keep warm if needed in a low oven. Good on their own or with rémoulade sauce or with mayonnaise or just hot sauce.

Green tomatoes are also a perfect addition to any Thai-style curry. Chop or slice into wedges and add to any Thai curry you have leftover, or any recipe for one, or use in the Any Vegetable Thai-Style Curry (p. 10).

TOMATOES, JUICE FROM THE CAN

Juice from a can of tomatoes is the perfect liquid for Braised Meat (p. 298), Minestrone (p. 210), Bean and Salami Soup (p. 213), Ribollita (p. 178), or any other bean soup.

TOMATOES, MOLDY

PAN CON TOMATE/PAN AMB TOMAXET *(10–15 min)*
1 or more old tomatoes, 3–4 thick slices rustic bread (ideally slightly stale),
1 clove garlic (halved), best possible olive oil, flaky sea salt.

Cut the tomato(es) in half, ignoring the rotten bits unless they're much deeper
than the skin. Toast the bread. Immediately rub the toasts with the cut side
of the garlic, then with the cut side of the tomato, letting the seeds and juices
sauce the toast lightly. Drizzle with olive oil and sprinkle with flaky salt. Eat
soon after making. If you ever find yourself in possession of fresh sardines, a
hot grilled fresh sardine atop each toast is a deep delight.

Once any rotten bits have been pared out, rotting tomatoes can also be turned
into a sauce or puree. Cut out the core and stem end of the tomato. Cut out
any bits that are clearly rotten. Roughly chop the remainders into a pan. Add
butter or olive oil, a sprinkle of salt, and a sprig of basil, and simmer until the
tomatoes have broken down and taste sweet, 15–30 min. Remove the basil,
returning the leaves to the sauce if you like and composting the stem. Use as
you would any tomato sauce, or freeze.

TURNIPS, WILTED

TURNIP SOUP *(40 min–1 hr)*
2 tbsp butter, 2 tbsp olive oil, ½ onion (thinly sliced lengthwise into half-
moons), ½ tsp salt plus to taste, 1–2 cups turnip, 1 potato (peeled and chopped)
or 1½ cups any other root vegetable (chopped), a pinch of thyme leaves, flavorful stock (chicken, mushroom, Parmesan, dashi), a drizzle of cream (optional).

In a medium pot, add the butter and olive oil. Add the onion and salt and
cook over medium-low heat until tender, 5–10 min. Add remaining ingredients other than the cream, and cook at a simmer until completely tender,
15–20 min. Blend in batches for a smooth soup, or leave as is. Add the cream,
taste for salt and adjust, and eat. Also good topped with chopped parsley.

YAMS

A real yam is a tuber in the Dioscoreaceae family. There are more than eight hundred varieties and they form one of the pillars of West African cooking. In the United States, the word "yam" is generally used to refer to orange-fleshed sweet potatoes. If you are looking for leftover sweet potato recipes, turn to *Sweet potato (pp. 86–88).*

YUCA, COOKED

YUCA FRIES WITH HERB AND SCALLIONS *(15–20 min)*
Cooked yuca, peanut or grapeseed oil for frying, salt, 1–2 scallions (thinly sliced on the diagonal), a handful of chopped cilantro, grated lemon zest, a tiny bit of finely minced garlic.

Cut the yuca into steak fry–size pieces. It's fine if they're shaggy. In a small, deep pot, heat 3–4 inches of oil to 350°–375°F. Set a plate or tray lined with paper towels beside the stove. Fry the yuca pieces in batches until all the shaggy edges are golden, removing them to the plate to drain. Lightly salt each batch as it drains. When all are done, shake onto a platter. In a small bowl, combine the scallions and cilantro, then add lemon zest to taste and the minced garlic, and mix. Shower the fries with it.

CHEESY YUCA BALLS *(20–30 min)*
Cooked yuca (preferably still warm), salt, finely chopped cilantro or scallions or both (optional), grated or tiny-cubed melty cheese, fine bread crumbs, peanut or grapeseed oil for frying.

Smash the yuca, or puree in a food processor. Season with salt to taste. It should be fairly highly seasoned. Add cilantro and/or scallions (if using). Form into balls the size of golf balls, then flatten into pancakes and press a tiny bit of grated or cube of cheese into each, then form into a ball, surrounding the cheese. Roll in the bread crumbs. In a small, deep pot, heat 3–4 inches of oil to 350°–375°F. Fry the balls in batches until golden, 2–4 min. Remove to a paper towel to drain. Good with lemon or lime or hot sauce or salsa verde or as is.

ZUCCHINI, COOKED

LITTLE PUFFED PUDDINGS *(1½ hr)*

2 tbsp butter, 2 cups sliced leeks (in half-moons), ½ tsp salt plus to taste, 4 cups chopped or smashed cooked zucchini, a pinch of saffron, 1 tbsp chopped fresh dill or parsley, 2 eggs (separated), 4½ tbsp crème fraîche, 1 egg white, softened butter and freshly grated Parmesan cheese for the cups or ramekins.

Heat the oven to 275°F. Put a deep roasting pan large enough to hold six cups or ramekins and a few inches of hot water on the middle rack of the heating oven. In a large skillet, add the butter over medium heat. Add the leeks and salt and cook until tender, 2–3 min. Add the zucchini and saffron and stir through to warm. Stir in the herbs. Let cool slightly, then puree to smooth in a food processor. Cool for another 5 min, then add the egg yolks and crème fraîche. Taste for salt: It should be slightly overseasoned. Butter six 6–7 oz ovenproof cups or ramekins, then dust lightly with Parmesan. Whip the egg whites to just past soft peaks, stopping while they are still shiny. Whisk one-third of them into the vegetable-yolk mixture to lighten it. Fold the rest of the whites into the mixture. Divide among the cups or ramekins. Lower them into the hot water bath and cook until just firm, 45–55 min.

Cooked zucchini also makes some of the best Big Toasts (p. 175). These are especially delicious made with cold, olive oily, garlicky smashed cooked zucchini on hot, garlicky grilled bread. Smash 1–2 cups cooked zucchini in its own little bowl with a drizzle of wine vinegar, a handful of herbs, and a long pour of olive oil. Taste for salt and herb and oil, adding more of whatever you need. Spoon onto garlic-rubbed toast and eat. Cooked zucchini is also good added to fried rice, once the grains are crisp and fried.

ZUCCHINI BLOSSOMS, FRIED

Leftover fried zucchini blossoms can be added in any quantity to a frittata along with other things that taste good with squash blossoms, like herbs, cheese, onions, and squash.

BUTTERED ZUCCHINI *(45 min)*

1 huge zucchini or more smaller ones, 1 tbsp olive oil, 1 tbsp butter, 1 clove garlic, ½ cup chopped spring or regular onion, salt, 1 dried chile (optional), ¼ cup basil leaves, 1 tbsp heavy cream, ¼ cup chopped other herbs (dill, parsley, fennel frond, or chives), freshly ground black pepper.

Cut the zucchini into ½-inch cubes, removing any bruised or rotten bits. Heat a deep pot. Add the oil, butter, garlic, and a pinch of salt. Cook, stirring, over low heat, 1–2 min. Add the zucchini, chile (if using), and half the basil leaves. Cover and cook over low heat, letting the zucchini self-braise, for about 15 min, checking and stirring once or twice. Uncover and cook, adjusting the heat as you like, covering and uncovering, until it begins to sizzle and loses a bit of its liquid. Stir vigorously, so the zucchini fries a bit. Taste for salt and adjust. Over high heat, add the cream and stir until it's integrated. Add the rest of the herbs and a lot of black pepper. Eat hot or at room temperature, on its own, on toast, on pasta, on rice, etc.

CREAMY ZUCCHINI SOUP *(25 min)*

3 tbsp olive oil or butter, ½ cup chopped spring or regular onion, salt, 1 huge zucchini or more smaller ones, 1 potato (peeled and chopped), 4 cups vegetable stock (or Garlic Peel Stock, p. 44, or water), 2 tbsp finely chopped fresh dill, ½ cup heavy cream, little croutons (optional), yogurt or crème fraîche (optional).

Cut the zucchini into ½-inch cubes, removing any bruised or rotten bits. Heat a medium pot. Add the oil or butter, onion, and a pinch of salt and cook until onion is tender, stirring as needed, 5–10 min. Add the zucchini, potato, and stock and bring to a boil. Reduce to a simmer and cook until the zucchini and potato are tender, another 15 min or so. Let cool slightly. Add the dill. Blend in batches until quite smooth. Add the cream. Taste for salt and adjust. Eat as is, or heat further without boiling, or chill the soup and eat cold, garnished with croutons and/or yogurt or crème fraîche, if using.

ZUCCHINI, UNRIPE

Unripe zucchini is starchier and less flavorful than its ripe successor. A good strategy is to add it early to a flavorful soup or stew. Cut it small—more surface area means more places for flavor to occupy. Or, go in the opposite direction. Slice the squash very thinly, dip it in batter, like the Tempura Batter (p. 139), and fry it. You'll scarcely notice the zucchini through the crunch.

HOW TO FLOURISH
Fruit and nuts

The plum survives its poems.

—*Wallace Stevens, "The Comedian as the Letter C"*

W e would have more delicious things to eat if we saw in every overripe or
bruised fruit the latent potential of a brown banana—which we trust to be
baked into bread, or muffins, or cake. We should similarly trust browning apples and
overripe berries and soft peaches and plums and pineapples, giving all fruit the banana
benefit of the doubt.

Unripe fruit is less inviting; its latent sugars are chains of polysaccharides, only
capable of dimly foretelling fruit's future ripe sweetness. It can still be used but is best
treated as a texture—thinly sliced if it tastes good raw, or sliced more thickly if it doesn't.
In the first case, it can be dressed with sharp acid and fat to become a salad, and in the
second it can be fried. Add toasted nuts (for crunch and depth), hard cheese (for umami),
fresh herbs (for color and liveliness), and pickles (for salt and acid), and the fruits of your
labor will be cherished.

Buy fruits in their seasons when you can. Then, you can eat as many as you want when
they are neither overripe nor underripe. If the season begins to turn, and you haven't
eaten your fill, freeze some for winter. Or combine a few cups in a pot with sugar and
pectin for jam. Then spend the cold months in a state of ripening desire. This fosters a
healthy lust for each fruit in its turn and keeps you from wasting time resenting fruit.

Here are a few good approaches for making the most of fruit (and nuts):

BASIC GALETTE DOUGH

2 cups (240 g) all-purpose flour, 1 tbsp brown or white sugar, ½ tsp salt, 12 tbsp (6 oz/170 g) cold butter (salted or unsalted, cut into small pieces), ⅓–½ cup ice water.

In a stand mixer fitted with the paddle (or in a large bowl), mix the flour, sugar, and salt. Using the paddle (or a pastry cutter if by hand), cut in the butter until the dough looks like damp sand with a good number of pea-size chunks, and just holds together when you pinch it. Drizzle in the ice water by the spoonful and paddle until it just forms a ball. Shape into a disc, wrap in parchment or wax paper, and refrigerate 15 min before rolling out. (From *Vegetarian Cooking for Everyone* by Deborah Madison)

NO ONE'S THE WISER FRUIT GALETTE

Any sliced fruit or berries to make up 1½–2 cups for a thin layer of filling or 2½ cups for a thicker layer, Basic Galette Dough (recipe above) or any other galette dough you like (chilled for 15 min after making it), ⅓–½ cup crumbs (biscotti, bread crumbs, or other similar), 2 tbsp melted butter or heavy cream, 1 egg, 2 tbsp sugar (optional).

Go through the fruit, composting any that has rotted. Rinse whatever's left. If you're not sure if you can use it, taste it. Combine with any fresh fruit you have. Heat the oven to 425°F. Roll the dough out to 15–16 inches, not worrying about the shape. Place on the back side of a sheet pan or a rimless cookie sheet. Sprinkle all but a 2- to 3-inch border with bread or cookie crumbs, not worrying too much about evenness. Cover with fruit, leaving a 2–3-inch border all around. Fold the ends of the dough over roughly, to make a rustic crust. In a small bowl, whisk together the melted butter or cream and the egg. Brush the crust with the butter-egg mixture. If desired, sprinkle the crust and fruit with the sugar. Bake 15 min, then reduce the oven temperature to 375°F and bake until the crust is browned and fruit cooked, another 20–25 min. Good with ice cream or mascarpone or Greek yogurt or crème fraîche.

ANY FRUIT CRISP

Butter for the baking dish, 1 tbsp cornstarch, ½ cup granulated sugar, 6 cups sliced or chopped very or overripe fruit, 1 tbsp lemon or lime juice, 1½ cups oats, 1 cup all-purpose flour, ½ cup brown sugar, ½ tsp salt, 8 tbsp (1 stick) butter (melted).

Heat the oven to 350°F. Grease a medium baking dish with butter. In a large bowl, combine the cornstarch and granulated sugar, then add the fruit and the lemon or lime juice and mix. Add to the baking dish. In a small bowl, combine the oats, flour, brown sugar, salt, and melted butter. Crumble it over the fruit, unevenly is fine. Bake until juice bubbles out, 30–35 min. Cool slightly, then eat. (Adapted from Kitchn website)

BASIC SCONES

2¾ cups (326 g) all-purpose flour, ⅓ cup (65 g) sugar, ¾ tsp salt, 1 tbsp baking powder, 8 tbsp (4 oz/113 g) cold butter (cut up in small pieces), 2 eggs (beaten), 1 tsp vanilla extract, ½–⅔ cup cream or milk, chopped dried or fresh fruit or nuts (optional).

Heat the oven to 425°F. Line a baking sheet with parchment paper. In a large bowl, mix the flour, sugar, salt, and baking powder. Work the butter in by hand until the pieces are like large pebbles. In another bowl, whisk the eggs, vanilla, and cream or milk. Add the egg mixture to the flour-butter mixture and mix until just combined. Flour a work surface and tip the dough onto it. Form into an 8 × 3-inch rectangle 2 inches thick, then cut into 5 pieces. Cut each into 2 right triangles. Place the scones spaced apart on the baking sheet. Bake until golden brown, 18–20 min. (Adapted from King Arthur Baking website)

BASIC MUFFIN BATTER

8 tbsp (4 oz/113 g) room-temperature butter plus for tin, ½ cup (100 g) brown sugar, ¼ cup (50 g) granulated sugar, ½ cup (120 g) sour cream or Greek yogurt, 2 eggs, 1¼ cups (220 g) all-purpose flour, 1 tsp baking soda, 1 tsp baking powder, ½ tsp ground cinnamon, ¼ tsp salt, ¼ cup whole milk.

Heat the oven to 350°F. Grease a muffin tin. In a stand mixer, beat together the butter and both sugars. Beat in the sour cream or yogurt and eggs. In a second bowl, whisk together the flour, baking soda, baking powder, cinnamon, and salt. Add the flour mixture in several additions to the butter-egg mixture, alternating with the milk. Divide the batter into the prepared muffin cups. Bake until golden and crisp at the edges, 20–25 min. Any dried fruit or nuts or seeds, or any jam, or any chopped raw fruit, or, or, or . . . can be added to the batter.

SIMPLE SYRUP

Water and sugar in a 1:1 ratio; optional: any other flavors you want, e.g., mint stems for mint simple syrup, grapefruit peels for grapefuit simple syrup, pineapple cores for pineapple simple syrup.

In a pan, bring the sugar and water plus any additions to a boil, stirring to dissolve the sugar. Let cool, strain, and store in the refrigerator. Use in cocktails or combine with seltzer for homemade sodas.

JAM THUMBPRINT COOKIES

12 tbsp (6 oz/170 g) butter (at room temperature), ½ cup (100 g) sugar, 1 egg, 1 tsp vanilla extract, 1¾ cups (220 g) all-purpose flour, ½ tsp baking powder, ½ tsp salt, ½ cup any jam (at room temperature).

In a stand mixer, beat the butter and sugar. Add the egg and vanilla, continuing to beat. In another bowl, combine the flour, baking powder, and salt. Add the flour mixture to the mixer, beating until just combined. Refrigerate until the dough is easy to roll into balls, about 1 hr. Meanwhile, heat the oven to 350°F. Line two baking sheets with parchment paper. Roll dough into small balls, set on the parchment, and press a thumbprint in each. Add small dabs of jam to the well in the middle. Bake until just firm, 13–14 min. Cool and eat.

JAM SCONES

2 cups (240 g) all-purpose flour, ¼ cup (50 g) sugar, 2 tsp baking powder, ½ tsp baking soda, ½ tsp salt, 8 tbsp (4 oz/113 g) cold butter (cut into tiny cubes), 1 egg, ½ cup any jam, ½ tsp mixed spices (optional: ground cinnamon, mace, nutmeg).

Heat the oven to 375°F. Line a baking sheet with parchment paper. In a large bowl, mix the flour, sugar, baking powder, baking soda, and salt. Work the butter in until the pieces are like large pebbles. In another bowl, whisk the egg, jam, and any optional spices. Add the egg mixture to the flour-butter mixture and mix until just combined. Flour a work surface and tip the dough onto it. Form into an 8 × 3-inch rectangle 2 inches thick, then cut into 5 pieces. Cut each into 2 right triangles. Place on the lined baking sheet with space between them. Bake until golden brown, 15–20 min. (Adapted from King Arthur Baking website)

JAM YOGURT SMOOTHIE

1 tbsp–⅓ cup any jam, 1–2 cups yogurt, a drizzle maple syrup, an ice cube (optional).

Blend and drink! Leftover smoothies make good ice pops.

JAM PASTRY GLAZE

3–4 tbsp any jam.

In a small pot, combine jam and 1 tsp water and warm to combine and melt. Use a pastry brush to brush over any crust you're about to bake, for extra shine.

UNRIPE FRUIT SALAD

1–2 unripe fruit, ¼ tsp salt plus to taste, lemon juice, thinly sliced fennel (optional), Niçoise or other good olives (optional), olive oil, strong tasting grating cheese (Parmesan or Pecorino Romano), mint or parsley leaves (torn or chopped), freshly ground black pepper.

Thinly slice the fruit. In a bowl, mix the slices with the salt and a squeeze of lemon juice and let sit 5 min. Taste for salt and adjust. Lay out on a plate. If desired, scatter with fennel and olives. Drizzle it all heavily with olive oil. With a vegetable peeler, peel off long pieces of cheese and scatter them over the fruit. Top with herbs, then black pepper. Good at room temperature.

TO TOAST NUTS

Heat the oven to 400°F. Spread the nuts on a baking sheet just large enough to fit them in a single layer. Check after 5 min, then every 2–3 min until tanned, shaking onto a cool surface like a plate or tray immediately after retrieving.

ALMONDS, CHOPPED

Use instead of pine nuts in Basil Pesto (p. 394) or Carrot Top Pesto (p. 28); or instead of walnuts in Aillade (p. 395). Or use in the Any Vegetable Salad (p. 9) or Best Grain or Bean Salad (p. 206). Or scatter over lunchtime rice, or use to make almond parsley oil by mixing any amount of chopped almonds into Parsley Oil (p. 68).

See also Nuts (p. 125).

APPLES, OLD

APPLE CIDER VINEGAR *(months and months, but mostly waiting)*
Apples, raw apple cider vinegar.

Cut apples (cores included) into chunks and puree in a blender. Pour into a jar. Add a long pour of cider vinegar or a vinegar mother. Stir well and cover with a permeable layer like a cheesecloth or thin kitchen towel and secure with a rubber band. Stir daily for a week, then strain out the fruit. Leave undisturbed, smelling and tasting occasionally, until it tastes like vinegar. When you like it (a month or 2 later), move to a clean jar and refrigerate, since it will go on changing.

APPLESAUCE *(45 min–2 hr)*
Apples.

Peel and core apples and cut into pieces, reserving cores if you like, for vinegar. In a pot, combine apple pieces with 1 cup water. Simmer, stirring occasionally. Cook to very caramelized, soft, and delicious, adding water as needed to prevent burning. If you're nearby and can stir often, this can all be done in 45 min because the heat can be higher and you can stir all the time to keep it from sticking. If you have (or want) to be doing something else while the applesauce cooks, once the apples have come to a simmer, cook it over very low heat. It will take longer but requires little tending. This can be eaten as is or turned into Apple Leather (p. 108).

APPLE PEELS

APPLE SCRAP VINEGAR (*months and months, but mostly waiting*)
Apple peels and cores (moldy parts removed), ¼ cup sugar, raw apple cider vinegar or a vinegar mother.

Combine the sugar and 1 quart water in a 3-quart jar and stir or shake well. Add the peels and cores. Add a long pour of raw apple cider vinegar or a vinegar mother. Cover with something permeable like a cheesecloth or thin kitchen towel. Stir daily for a week, then strain out fruit. Leave undisturbed, smelling and tasting occasionally, until it tastes like vinegar. When you like it (a month or 2 later) move to a clean jar and refrigerate. (Adapted from *Dappled* by Nicole Rucker)

APPLE TWIGS (*4 hr or longer, but mostly waiting*)
Olive oil, 1 cup apple peels, a scrape of cinnamon, 1 tbsp sugar.

Drizzle a roasting pan with olive oil. In a bowl, toss the peels with the cinnamon and sugar, add to the pan, and dehydrate in an oven at 170°F or in a dehydrator until dried and crisp. A good children's snack. (Adapted from Martha Stewart website)

APPLESAUCE

This is the most common use of leftover applesauce in my house. It is simple and it is beloved.

APPLE LEATHER (*12–15 hr, but mostly waiting*)
Applesauce, honey or maple syrup (optional).

Taste the applesauce for sweetness and add honey or maple syrup if you like. Blend briefly if it's not smooth. Spread onto parchment-lined baking sheets ⅛–¼ inch thick. Dehydrate in a 170°F oven, or in a dehydrator, until none of the surface is tacky. Allow to cool slightly, cut into strips, roll, and store in an airtight container. If you want a different flavored leather, blend another kind of fruit, fresh or frozen, into the sauce. Adding blueberries will produce blueberry leather, strawberries strawberry leather, and so on.

APPLESAUCE BUNDT CAKE *(1 hr 15 min)*
Butter and flour for the pan, 2 cups (240 g) all-purpose flour, 1 tsp baking powder, ½ tsp baking soda, ½ tsp salt, 1 tsp ground cinnamon, ½ tsp ground cloves (or ground fennel or ground cardamom), 10 tbsp (1¼ sticks) room-temperature butter, 1 cup (100 g) sugar, 1 egg plus 1 egg yolk, 1½ cups applesauce, powdered sugar for dusting (optional).

Heat the oven to 350°F. Butter and flour a 10-inch Bundt pan, tapping out the excess flour. In a medium bowl, mix the flour, baking powder, baking soda, salt, cinnamon, and ground cloves. In a stand mixer, cream the butter and sugar until fluffy, about 3 min, scraping down the sides as needed. Add the whole egg and yolk. Add the flour mixture in several additions, alternating with the applesauce, mixing to combine after each addition. Pour the batter into the prepared Bundt pan. Bake until a skewer emerges clean, about 1 hr. Cool in the pan on a rack for 15 min, then invert and dust with powdered sugar if you want. (Adapted from *The Apple Lover's Cookbook* by Amy Traverso)

APPLESAUCE MUFFINS *(30 min)*
Butter for the muffin tin, 1¾ cups (220 g) all-purpose flour, 1½ tsp baking powder, 1 tsp baking soda, ½ tsp salt, 8 tbsp (4 oz/113 g) room-temperature butter, a quite scant ⅔ cup (135 g) sugar, 1 egg, ½ cup applesauce, ⅔ cup buttermilk (or buttermilk substitute, see p. 138).

Heat the oven to 350°F. Butter a 12-cup muffin tin. In a medium bowl, mix the flour, baking powder, baking soda, and salt. In a stand mixer, cream the butter and sugar. Add the egg and applesauce and mix. Add the flour mixture in several additions alternating with the buttermilk, beating after each addition. Divide the batter among the prpared muffins cups. Bake until a skewer emerges clean, 20–25 min. Cool briefly in the pan, then invert onto a rack.

Applesauce is not jam and jam is not applesauce, but the leftovers of each can be used similarly. Applesauce makes good Jam Scones (p. 104), which should then be considered applesauce scones.

APPLE BUTTER

Use interchangeably with *Applesauce (p. 108)* recipes.

APRICOTS, OLD

APRICOT LEATHER (*12 hr, but mostly waiting*)
Halve the apricots and remove the pits. Remove any moldy bits. Cook in a pot with a little water until the fruit is sweetened and caramelized, about 30 min. Transfer to a blender and blend to very smooth. Spread out on parchment to ⅛–¼ inch thick and dehydrate in an oven at 170°F or in a dehydrator for 8 to 12 hr.

Or use old apricots in a smoothie or an ice pop, or a smoothie and then an ice pop.

APRICOTS, UNRIPE

Use unripe apricots in the Unripe Fruit Salad (p. 105).

APRICOT PITS

NOYAUX EXTRACT (*3 months, but mostly waiting*)
25–30 apricot pits, 1¾ cups liquor (vodka, bourbon, or light rum).

Heat the oven to 300°F. Take a hammer to your front sidewalk, spread the pits out on newspaper or an old sheet, and one by one, tap them as hard as needed to crack them to extract the kernels inside. Remove the kernels. If they are wet, allow them to dry outside, then place on a baking sheet and toast for 10 min. Toasting is essential for safety and flavor. Remove from the oven and allow to cool. Put in a jar and cover with the liquor. Cover and let sit for 3 months or longer, shaking occasionally. Use as you do vanilla or almond extract. (Adapted from Samin Nosrat in *New York Times Cooking*)

APRICOT JAM

Use the last little amounts of apricot jam for the Jam Thumbprint Cookies (p. 104), Jam Scones (p. 104), Jam Yogurt Smoothie (p. 104), or Jam Pastry Glaze (p. 104).

You know what to do with overripe bananas. This is here in case you discover that you have misplaced the banana bread recipe you usually use.

BANANA BREAD OR MUFFINS *(1 hr 15 min)*
Butter and flour for the pan, 2 cups (240 g) all-purpose flour, 1 tsp baking soda, ½ tsp salt, ½ tsp ground cinnamon, 8 tbsp (4 oz/113 g) softened butter or vegetable oil, ¾ cup (150 g) sugar, 2 eggs, 1 tsp vanilla extract, 1¼–1⅓ cups mashed bananas (2 or 3 bananas).

Heat the oven to 350°F. Butter and flour a loaf pan or a muffin tin, tapping out the excess flour. In a medium bowl, whisk the flour, baking soda, salt, and cinnamon together. In a stand mixer, beat the butter or oil and the sugar until fluffy. Beat in the eggs one by one, then the vanilla and bananas. Add the flour mixture and mix until just combined. Pour into the prepared loaf pan or muffin tin and bake until a skewer emerges clean or with a couple of crumbs still clinging, 50–60 min for the loaf, 15–30 min for the muffins (depending on the size of your muffins). Cool in the pan for 5 min, then move to a rack to cool completely. (Adapted from Spend with Pennies website)

And for those who can't eat flour:

GLUTEN-FREE BANANA BREAD OR MUFFINS *(25–30 min)*
Butter and gluten-free flour for greasing the pan, 2 cups almond or another nut flour, ¾ tsp salt, 1 tsp baking soda, ¾ tsp ground cinnamon, ½ cup unsweetened shredded coconut, 3 eggs, ½ cup olive oil, ⅓ cup maple syrup or ½ cup brown sugar, 1 cup mashed bananas (about 2 bananas).

Heat the oven to 350°F. Butter and flour a loaf pan or muffin tin, tapping out the excess flour. In a bowl, combine the nut flour, salt, baking soda, cinnamon, and coconut. In a second bowl, whisk the eggs, oil, maple syrup or brown sugar, and banana. Stir the egg mixture into the nut mixture. Spoon the batter into the prepared loaf pan or muffin tins and bake until set and a skewer emerges clean, 40–50 min for the loaf or 20–22 min for the muffins. This freezes well.

Or peel and freeze overripe bananas, cut in halves or thirds. Combine in a blender with yogurt and honey or maple syrup. Add anything else you like. Leftover smoothies make good ice pops.

GREEN BANANA CURRY (*30 min*)

3 green bananas, 3–4 tbsp neutral oil, 1½ tsp black mustard seeds, 4–6 fresh curry leaves, heaping 1 tbsp grated fresh ginger, ½ onion (thinly sliced), 1–2 tsp chopped chiles, ½ tsp salt plus to taste, 2 tsp ground turmeric, pinch of hing (asafoetida), chopped cilantro leaves (optional), fresh lemon or lime wedges for squeezing over (optional), hot rice for serving.

Remove the tips and tails of the unpeeled bananas and cut crosswise in half. In a pot of simmering water, cook the banana halves until the peel is easily pricked with a sharp knife, 15–20 min. When cool enough to handle, peel and cut into cubes. Heat a heavy-bottomed pan. Add the oil and mustard seeds and let sizzle a moment. Then add the curry leaves and ginger and cook over medium heat for 20 sec until the ginger begins to cook. Add the onion, chiles, and salt and cook until the onion begins to soften and becomes translucent, 5–10 min. Add the turmeric and hing and stir through. Add the banana and cook for about 30 sec, stirring. Add a few tbsp of water, cover, and cook until the banana can be smashed with a spoon, 2–3 min. Garnish with cilantro and sprinkle with lemon or lime juice if you like. Eat on rice. (Adapted from Swasthi's Recipes website)

GREEN BANANA TOSTONES (*20 min*)

Green bananas, oil for frying, salt, chaat masala (or chile powder or any spices you like).

Peel the green bananas with a knife. Cut into rounds about ¾ inch thick. In a saucepan, heat 2–3 inches of oil to quite warm, about 325°F. Fry the rounds until they just begin to turn golden. Remove to paper towels or a rack, leaving the pot of oil on the stove. Smash each round once with a ramekin or bottom of a mug to make them into tostones. Turn the heat on under the oil again. Heat to about 360°F. Fry the tostones until just browned and crisp. Drain on a paper towel. Salt well and season with chaat masala. Delicious with raita or another yogurt dip.

BANANA PEELS

Though this dry-fried dish isn't the only way I've eaten banana peels, it is my favorite. If you peel bananas at breakfast time and plan to cook the peels later, soak them in water with lemon or vinegar or a piece of turmeric.

BANANA PEEL THORAN (DRY-FRY) *(30–40 min)*
Peels of 3–4 bananas, 2 cloves garlic (minced), 2 tsp minced peeled fresh
ginger, 1 tsp ground cumin, 1 tsp ground coriander, ¼ tsp ground turmeric,
1 tsp salt, 1 tbsp fat (peanut, canola, or coconut oil, or ghee), 1 tsp black
mustard seeds (or cumin seeds or a combination), 1 small onion (diced), 1 tsp
hing (asafoetida), 10 curry leaves, 1 hot chile (sliced) or a bunch of sliced
pickled chiles, ¼ cup unsweetened shredded coconut, cilantro (optional), lime
juice (optional).

Wash and dry the banana peels, removing the ends and any big brown spots,
and slice crosswise, thinly. Pound or pulse the garlic, ginger, cumin, coriander, turmeric, and salt into a paste. In a large pan, heat the fat. Add the
mustard seeds. When they start to pop, add the onion/garlic-spice paste, hing,
and curry leaves. Sauté until they just begin to soften, about 3 min. Add the
banana peel, chile, coconut, and 2–4 tbsp water, depending on whether you
want it saucy or dry. Cook until the peels are tender and delicious, 15–20 min.
If desired, garnish with cilantro and a squeeze of lime. This is delicious on hot
basmati rice.

BLACKBERRIES, OLD

Taste to make sure they don't taste of mold. Remove any that do. Use what's
left in the No One's the Wiser Fruit Galette (p. 102), which can host a whole
assortment of berries and stone fruits. Or make Any Fruit Crisp (p. 102). Or
blend into a smoothie, or make into an ice pop, or add to Basic Scones (p. 103
or Basic Muffin Batter (p. 103). If you are left with only a few berries, freeze
them. Continue to add to the bag in the freezer until you have enough to do
something with.

BLACKBERRY JAM

Use little bits of leftover blackberry jam in Jam Thumbprint Cookies (p. 104),
or in Jam Scones (p. 104) where they will make a loverly purplish black marble,
or in a Jam Yogurt Smoothie (p. 104).

BLUEBERRIES, OLD

As with blackberries, taste these to make sure they don't taste of mold, and remove any that do. Use those that are left in the No One's the Wiser Fruit Galette (p. 102), or blend them into a smoothie or make into an ice pop. Or make Any Fruit Crisp (p. 102). Or add them to Basic Scones (p. 103) or Basic Muffin Batter (p. 103). If you only have a few left after culling, as with other berries, freeze them, and continue to add to the bag in the freezer until you have enough to do something with.

BLUEBERRY JAM

Use small amounts of blueberry jam in Jam Thumbprint Cookies (p. 104), Jam Scones (p. 104), or Jam Yogurt Smoothie (p. 104).

CASHEWS, CHOPPED

As long as they aren't rancid, use leftover chopped cashews in the Any Vegetable Salad (p. 9) or Best Grain or Bean Salad (p. 206). Or scatter them over lunchtime rice. If they are rancid, compost.

See also Nuts (p. 125).

CHERRIES, OLD

Cherries are remarkably resistant to mold and stay good for longer than berries. Taste and discard any that are pockmarked or bruised. Add what's left to Basic Scones (p. 103) or Basic Muffin Batter (p. 103). Or dehydrate them in an oven at 170°F or at 125°F in a food dehydrator until raisin-like. Their volume will shrink but their flavor will endure!

CHERRY PITS

Substitute cherry pits for apricot pits in the Noyaux Extract (p. 110) for a delightful cherry version. Or turn them into cherry syrup, by drying them, boiling them in a syrup of 1:1 sugar to water, letting it sit for 2–3 hr, then straining. Refrigerate the syrup for making homemade sodas by combining with seltzer.

CHERRY STEMS

Cherry stems are a folk remedy of the highest order. They have been credited with the dissolution of kidney stones, the cleansing of the urinary tract, and the resolution of gout. The path to all of this wellness is to dry the stems in a low oven or dehydrator to prevent rot, then store them in an airtight container. From there you can steep them in boiling water for cherry stem tea, or grind them into a powder then fill tea bags with it, and proceed to heal.

CHERRY PIE FILLING

Use in Jam Thumbprint Cookies (p. 104).

CHESTNUTS, ROASTED

If you find yourself with leftover roasted chestnuts, make a salad of escarole or radicchio or chicory in as many colors as you can find. Make a Garlicky Vinaigrette (p. 400) and dress the greens to taste. If you have pears or persimmons, thinly slice 1–2 and toss them through. Top with chopped roasted chestnuts.

CHUTNEY

This is for the last little bits of fruit chutney that sometime take up long-term residence on refrigerator shelves.

BAKED BRIE WITH CHUTNEY (*10–15 min*)
1 wheel brie (in its rind), ¼ cup chutney.

Heat the oven to 350°F. Line a pan with foil or parchment paper. Place the brie on the lined pan and top with the chutney. Bake until melty, about 10 min, and eat with little baguette toasts or crackers.

CITRUS PEEL OR ZEST

Even a small bit of peel or zest is worth saving. It is often all it takes to smarten up any dish, leftover or newly made. One method for saving zest is to zest or peel citrus before cutting into it. I would not do this to oranges for children, who would be insulted by the practice. Otherwise, it can be done with a zester or a vegetable peeler or cheese grater, or knife. Then you have zest, ready to be deployed, and the fruit itself, still to be used. Another method is to zest peels you've peeled off. This is messy but sometimes worth it. Another is to save peels you've peeled off, then when they've dried, scrape off as much of their bitter white pith as you can and use what remains. Do not feel guilty if you forget to do any of this. Remembering when you remember will suffice.

Grated citrus zest keeps well in the refrigerator. Store it in a small glass jar or well-labeled opaque one and use it until it is gone. One of the simplest ways is to put a pinch of zest into a pot of reheating rice. This makes citrusy rice, which is simple but good. Or, add citrus zest to leftover potatoes. They become infinitely better than any stored without.

For more of a to-do, combine citrus zest with smashed up leftover boiled egg yolks. Add a little pounded-up garlic, a tiny smidge of Dijon mustard, and olive oil. Stir the mixture vigorously then dollop it over cooked vegetables like asparagus or broccoli or cauliflower or over rice, or over toast, or a salad, or over eggs. Or make:

GREMOLATA (*5 min*)
Zest or finely minced peel of 1 citrus fruit, ¼–½ cup finely chopped parsley leaves, ½ clove garlic (finely chopped), ¼–½ tbsp flaky salt like Maldon.

In a bowl, combine the citrus zest, parsley, garlic, and salt, breaking the salt up a bit. Taste for salt, adjusting as needed. This is the best finishing touch for any braised meat or other rich, stew-y thing, like beef stew, and also over boiled buttered new potatoes.

CITRUS SUGAR (*times vary*)
Citrus peel or zest (dried), sugar.

Once peel is dry enough to blend in a spice grinder, scrape off all the pith you can. If using zest, simply proceed. Grind the peel or zest with sugar. Use as a bittersweet topping for holiday cookies or sprinkling over muffins.

CITRUS KOSHO *(times vary)*
1 cup citrus zest, ¾ tsp salt, 1–2 Thai chiles (minced), 3–4 tbsp citrus juice,
2 tsp lime juice.

In a spice grinder, blend the zest and salt to a paste. Add the chile(s) and
blend further. Add citrus juice, place in a jar, and let sit somewhere cool for a
few days to a few weeks. Refrigerate once you like the taste.

Or, add any zest to Basic Vinaigrette (p. 376) to make a citrus vinaigrette,
which makes the world seem sunny.

Or mix ground dried zest with a combination of salt and dried chile flakes,
then cut up fruit and dip it into the citrus-chile salt. Or use on the rim of
a margarita glass. Or, dry peels in long strips. Dried orange or mandarin or
clementine peels are called chen pi, and with them, you can make Chen Pi
Beef (p. 125).

CLEMENTINES

If you have ever cursed the fact that clementines are sold in such big bags,
quickly rinse and zest several the next time you bring a bag home. Refrigerate
the zest in a jar. Serve the fruit in a Citrus Olive Onion Salad (p. 126). Use the
zest (*see Citrus peel or zest, p. 116*) over the next 2 weeks. If this still leaves you
with enough that some dry out or rot, next week, zest and peel and squeeze
half the bag and drink fresh orange juice. Use the rest as intended.

COCONUT MILK

Rice benefits enormously from having any amount of coconut milk added.
Pour the amount you have leftover into a measuring cup, make up the difference of required rice-cooking liquid in water or broth, and cook as planned.

COCONUT SHELLS

Coconut shells make good kindling. Let them dry, crack them, and store them by the wood stove or fireplace. Though the making is laborious, they also make good bowls. First, the coconut water and meat must be removed, then the shell sanded and waterproofed with a natural oil . . . then dried, and sipped from.

CRANBERRY SAUCE

Leftover cranberry sauce makes delicious Jam Thumbprint Cookies (p. 104). It also provides a reason to make a Thanksgiving-style turkey or chicken sandwich, which tastes as good in March as in November.

DATES

If you are cleaning out the pantry and need a destination for the last few dates, this is a wonderful one.

TAHINI DATE BALLS (*40 min*)
4 pitted dates, 3 tbsp tahini, 3 tbsp unsweetened cocoa powder, 1 tsp vanilla extract, tiny pinch of flaky sea salt, sesame seeds or unsweetened shredded coconut for coating.

In a food processor, puree the dates to a sticky paste, scraping down the sides as needed. Add the tahini, cocoa, vanilla, and salt and pulse until it's a uniform paste that sticks together when pinched. Spread sesame seeds or shredded coonut on a plate. Roll the date mixture into small balls and roll the balls in the seeds to coat. Place on a parchment-lined plate and refrigerate 30 min to set. Keep refrigerated. (From Talbott & Arding, Hudson, New York)

FIGS, OVERRIPE

FAST FIG JAM *(30–40 min)*
10 overripe figs, ½ cup sugar, grated zest of 1 lemon, juice of ½ lemon.

Remove the stems from the figs and cut the fruit into small pieces. In a jam pan or deep sauté pan, combine all the ingredients and cook to 220°F for jam that sets up, 30–40 min. Add water as needed to keep it from burning.

FIGS, UNRIPE

These are an acquired taste.

PRESERVED FIGS
1 lb unripe figs, 1¾ cups sugar, strips of zest from 1 lemon (removed with a vegetable peeler) and juice of 1 lemon, 3–4 whole cloves.

Wash the figs and trim their stems. In a pot, combine the figs with water to cover. Bring to a boil and boil for 10 min. Drain, rinse the pot, and repeat. After rinsing the pot again, combine the figs, 5 cups water, the sugar, lemon zest strips, and cloves. Bring to a boil, then add the lemon juice and cook until the figs glisten, the liquid has reduced by half and approaches 218°–220°F. If the figs are getting too soft, scoop them out and cook the liquid until it's the right consistency, planning to reunite everything later. Cool the figs in their liquid in jars with lids and let sit for a week before eating. These are good on top of labneh or ricotta or goat cheese on toasted bread.

FIG JAM

Use the last bit of fig jam in the Jam Thumbprint Cookies (p. 104) or in the best peanut butter and jelly (fig jam) sandwich ever.

FRUIT SALAD

FRUIT COMPOTE *(30 min)*
In a jam pan or deep sauté pan, add fruit salad with its liquid. Bring to a boil.
Add one-third to one-half as much sugar as there is fruit salad and a squeeze
of lemon juice and boil to thicken slightly. This will not set, but will taste good
on ice cream or yogurt or in the Any Fruit Crumble Coffee Cake (p. 477).

FRUIT SALAD SMOOTHIE *(5 min)*
2 cups fruit salad, 1 tbsp honey, 1 cup whole-milk yogurt, 1 tbsp grated lemon
or lime zest (optional).

Blend and drink.

GRAPEFRUITS

If you find yourself with a leftover half grapefruit, juice it before any guilt sets
in and add seltzer and, if it is after 5 p.m., gin. Zest the peel and you'll have
made the most of things.

KIWIS

Overripe kiwis make disconcerting jam and smoothies, and unripe kiwis are
tannic and unpleasant. I have little to offer but a word of caution. Only buy
kiwis if you're confident in their ripeness and the likelihood of their being
promptly eaten.

KUMQUATS, SOUR

COCKTAIL GARNISH *(1 min)*
Even if these are sour or overripe, thinly slice them and drop into any drink
with Campari or sweet vermouth as a cocktail garnish.

LEMON JUICE

CAPER BUTTER LEMON SAUCE *(5–10 min)*
2 tbsp butter, 2 tbsp lemon juice, 1 tsp drained capers (roughly chopped if large), 1 tsp grated lemon zest (optional), 1 tsp chopped parsley.

In a little saucepan, melt the butter. Add the lemon juice, capers, and zest (if using). Bring to a simmer, then cook over low heat for about 30 sec, moving the pan to emulsify. Add the parsley. Drizzle over cooked chicken or fish or vegetables or poached eggs or boiled potatoes.

Any small amount of lemon juice you worry will go bad can also be frozen. And lemon juice can be used interchangeably with vinegar in any vinaigrette.

LEMON ZEST

LEMONY AVOCADO TOAST *(5 min)*
½ clove garlic (peeled), salt, 1 avocado, ¼ tsp grated lemon zest, a slice of thickly cut good bread, olive oil.

Pound the garlic to a paste with a tiny pinch of salt. Add the avocado and lemon zest and mix well. Taste for salt and adjust. Toast bread, drizzle with olive oil, spread with lemony avocado smash. Also good with Guntur Sannam chile, Marash chile, or other flavorful chile flake or powder on top.

If you ever have leftover lemon zest and leftover cooked potatoes, store them together. This is akin to alchemy. The potatoes absorb all the sweet citrusiness of the zest and then when you fry them into a hash, or warm them, or even eat them as they are, the potatoes are somehow both brighter and more likably potato-y.

LIMES

What is true of the lemon is true of the lime. *See Citrus peel or zest (p. 116)* and *Lemon zest (above)*.

MACADAMIA NUTS, CHOPPED

See Pine nuts (p. 130). The two are obviously different, but similarly high in delicious fats, which is the thing to consider when dealing with leftovers of either.

MANGOES, OVERRIPE

Mangoes make the best smoothies and the best ice pops. Blend any with yogurt and a little honey and drink, then freeze what's left as ice pops, or blend the overripe mango all on its own, adding water if needed to get things moving, and freeze half in ice pop molds and combine the rest with yogurt to eat or drink.

MANGOES, UNRIPE

GREEN MANGO WITH CHILE SALT *(5 min)*
1–2 green mangoes, 2 tbsp ground chile powder, 2 tsp salt, lime wedges (optional).

Peel the mangoes and slice into wedges. Combine the chile powder and salt. If using lime, squeeze juice over the mango slices. Eat by dipping the slices into the chile salt.

GREEN MANGO SALAD *(20 min)*
1 tbsp sugar plus to taste, 3 tbsp lime juice, 2–3 tbsp fish sauce plus to taste, 1 green mango, 2–4 Thai chiles (sliced), 3 tbsp thinly sliced shallot (1–1½ large shallots), 2 tbsp toasted chopped peanuts, 1 tbsp roughly chopped cilantro, 2 tbsp julienned or torn mint.

In a small bowl, whisk together the sugar, lime juice, and fish sauce. Peel and julienne the mango. In a bowl, toss the mango with as much chile as you would like. Add the shallots, nuts, and herbs. Add the sugar-lime mixture. Mix through, taste for sugar and fish sauce, and eat. Good with sticky rice or other hot rice.

MARASCHINO CHERRY LIQUID

MARASCHINO CHERRY SODA *(5 min)*
Combine leftover maraschino cherry liquid with seltzer for cherry soda, or add it to lemonade to turn it pink.

MELON, OVERRIPE

Immediately blend any overripe melon and freeze it in ice pop molds. Or pour it into a baking dish and place in the freezer, then check it after 45 min and run a fork through it to start turning it into granita. Return the dish to the freezer to do it every 30 min thereafter, three or four times, then eat.

MELON, UNRIPE

TIANJIN SALAD *(10 min)*
2 cups strips of unripe melon, ½ tsp salt, 2 tbsp distilled white vinegar, 1 tsp sesame oil, 1 tbsp soy sauce, 1 tsp–1 tbsp sugar (optional), 2 tbsp vegetable oil, 1 tsp Sichuan peppercorns, 1 tsp minced fresh ginger, 1 tsp minced garlic, 1 tsp minced fresh chile.

Put the melon strips in a bowl. In a small bowl, mix the salt, vinegar, sesame oil, soy sauce, and sugar (if you like things sweet). Heat a skillet over medium-low heat. Add the vegetable oil, then the Sichuan peppercorns and cook until just fragrant, about 1 min. Add the ginger, garlic, and chile, stir, then add the vinegar/soy sauce mixture. Mix to combine, then pour over the melon. Stir. Eat warm or cold. (Adapted from *Land of Plenty* by Fuchsia Dunlop)

MELON RIND

This is for the green flesh, not the hard peel.

ROAST RIND AND PECORINO ROMANO SALAD *(15 min)*
1 cup or more cubed melon rind (hard skin pared off), olive oil, salt, shaved Pecorino Romano or Parmesan cheese, toasted seeds or nuts (optional), a handful of chopped parsley leaves (optional).

Heat the oven to 400°F. In a bowl, drizzle the rind with olive oil, then lightly salt. Move to a sheet pan and roast until caramelized and brown, 15–20 min. Remove from the oven to a plate. Let cool slightly, then cover amply with cheese. If desired, sprinkle with toasted seeds or nuts and parsley. Good warm or at room temperature.

A number of smooth melon rinds can also be pickled. Combine equal amounts water and apple cider vinegar in a pot. Add half as much sugar as water. Bring to a boil, add salt to taste, and when it is just savory, add any other warm spices (cloves, star anise, or cinnamon). Slice the rind and pack into a jar. Pour the brine over, cool at room temperature, then refrigerate. These are good for about a month.

MELON SEEDS

ROASTED MELON SEEDS (*20 min*)
Melon seeds, olive oil, salt.

Heat the oven to 400°F. In a bowl, toss the seeds with olive oil, not worrying if bits of melon are still clinging to them. Spread on a parchment-lined sheet pan and roast, stirring after 5 min, until caramelized and crisp, about 10 min. Salt amply, move to a plate to cool, and eat.

NECTARINES, OVERRIPE

Pare off any moldy or dark brown bits and then slice what's left onto a plate. Dollop with goat cheese, drizzle with olive oil, scatter with toasted nuts and perhaps a few leaves of parsley or mint, and eat. Or blend it into a smoothie, or freeze it for a future smoothie, or blend it with another fruit, or just some juice, and make ice pops. Or use it in the Any Fruit Crisp (p. 102).

NECTARINES, UNRIPE

Use unripe nectarines in the Unripe Fruit Salad (p. 105).

NUTS

Harold McGee says this: "The same high oil content that makes nuts nutritious and delicious also makes them much more fragile than grains and legumes." Nuts go bad—their oils are delicate and quickly spoil when exposed to oxygen or light or heat or moisture. If you don't keep bacon on the pantry shelf, you shouldn't keep nuts there. They last far longer in the refrigerator or freezer.

Which type of nut you have matters less than whether nuts taste good. Do not buy a type of nut simply because a recipe has suggested it. A cashew can act like a peanut, and a peanut like a pistachio. Worry less about the right kind of nut and more about right storage.

NUT DUST

The dust at the bottom of a bag of salted roasted nuts is a lovely, salty sprinkle—if it tastes good, which can be ascertained by dipping in your finger. If you like what you taste, substitute nut dust for salt in Parsley Oil (p. 68), or in Basil Pesto (p. 394), where it's an obvious improvement over salt, adding a desired nuttiness. Or sprinkle it over any lunchtime meal of beans and greens or Fried Rice (p. 205) or over any chocolate chip cookies, or brownies.

ORANGE PEEL

CHEN PI (*several months, but all waiting*)
Chen pi is traditionally made with tangerine peel. I peel whatever orange-type thing I have. If I've forgotten to remove it with a peeler, I scrape off what I can of the pith before drying, then lay the peel out in a single layer somewhere warm and dry until it's completely dry—usually 5 days to 1 week—store, then use it as long as it is fragrant. Especially for:

CHEN PI BEEF (*45 min*)
Dried peels of 3 oranges, ½ lb thinly sliced beef (skirt steak, flatiron, or other stir-fry cut), 2 tbsp soy sauce, 1 tbsp Shaoxing wine or dry sherry, 1 tbsp corn-starch, 1 tbsp baking soda, 2 tbsp neutral oil (peanut or grapeseed), 1 tbsp finely minced fresh ginger, 5–8 dried chiles (broken in half), 1 tsp Sichuan peppercorns, 2 tsp sugar, 1 tsp sesame oil, 3 scallions (thinly sliced), rice for eating.

Soak the chen pi (dried peels) in boiling water for 15 min to rehydrate. Drain and reserve the soaking liquid. Thinly slice the peels. In a bowl, toss the beef with 1 tbsp of the soy sauce and the wine or sherry. Add the cornstarch and baking soda and toss again. Cover and refrigerate 20–30 min. Heat a heavy-bottomed pan. Add the oil, then fry the beef in two batches, cooking until just crisp and browned, removing to a plate with a sieve. Cook the ginger, chiles, and peppercorns in the oil for 30 sec, then add the orange peel and cook until you can smell it, another 30 sec or so. Add the beef, remaining 1 tbsp soy sauce, the sugar, sesame oil, and scallions and toss to combine. Add a pour of the reserved soaking liquid to make it saucy. Eat on hot rice.

See also Citrus peel or zest (p. 116).

ORANGES, OLD

No matter what they look like, oranges can usually be juiced. The juice can be frozen into ice pops, or drunk, or used in a vinaigrette.

ORANGES, TOO MANY

CITRUS OLIVE ONION SALAD *(15 min)*
3 tbsp thinly sliced onion or shallot, ¼ tsp salt, wine vinegar, 1–2 oranges, flaky sea salt for serving, good olive oil, ¼ cup very thinly sliced fennel (optional), ¼ cup pitted good olives.

In a little bowl, combine the onion or shallot, salt, and enough vinegar to cover and let sit for 10 min. Meanwhile, peel the orange and cut across into slices ¼–½ inch thick, or peel and separate into wedges. Lay them out on a plate, lightly salt with flaky salt, then drizzle heavily with olive oil. If using fennel, add to the onion, mix through, and then scoop the onion and fennel out and drape over the oranges, reserving the vinegar for another vinaigrette. Scatter with the olives, drizzle again with olive oil, and eat.

ORANGE MARMALADE

Orange marmalade makes delectable Jam Thumbprint Cookies (p. 104), if you don't mind cookies with a slightly bitter filling. I don't.

PAPAYAS, OVERRIPE

BEST PAPAYA SMOOTHIE *(5 min)*
1 cup milk or coconut water or just ice, ⅓ cup sweetened condensed milk, 1–2 cups cubed/smashed papaya, a few ice cubes, 1 tsp lemon or lime juice (optional).

Blend all the ingredients and drink!

PAPAYA SEEDS

Seeds from a ripe papaya have a peppery flavor, and can be used instead of black pepper. Scoop the seeds out of the papaya and wash and dry well. Lay out on a kitchen towel and dry in front of a sunny window or dehydrate until completely dry and crackly. Use them all at once, so you're not forever deciding whether to use black pepper or papaya seeds you took the trouble of drying. A nice way to do this is to make a peppery dip.

PAPAYA SEED DIP *(10 min)*
1 tbsp cracked papaya seeds, ½ clove garlic, salt, ¼ cup mayonnaise, ¼ cup whole-milk yogurt or sour cream, lemon juice.

Lightly smash the seeds in a mortar and add to a bowl. Pound the garlic clove with a little salt. Add to the bowl along with the mayonnaise, yogurt or sour cream, and a squeeze of lemon juice. Taste for salt and adjust. Use for dipping chips or other dippable things.

PASSION FRUIT, OLD

Passion fruit is ripe when it's wrinkled and old. It may even end up with bits of mold here and there. Wipe them off and cut the fruit open. If the flesh is deep golden and it tastes good, eat it.

PEACHES, OVERRIPE

If you innately go outside and lean forward at the mention of the word "peach," it's likely this entry is irrelevant to you. But if you have a peach tree and limited appetite, it's good to remember that, like overripe mangoes, overripe peaches are wonderful blended into refreshing drinks or frozen into ice pops. Or use in the Any Fruit Crisp (p. 102).

PEACHES, UNRIPE

Unripe peaches make good Unripe Fruit Salad (p. 105). They can also just be sliced, dressed with vinaigrette, and eaten, dolloped with goat cheese or ricotta. If they are completely green, they can also be peeled and used instead of mango in the Green Mango Salad (p. 122).

PEANUTS, CHOPPED

As long as they aren't rancid, even a spoonful of chopped peanuts can transform a salad or rice from basic to exciting. They are also a good and transformative thickener for a stew or sabzi or curry, and I often find myself adding the odd leftover handful of chopped nuts to any while I'm simmering it.
See also Nuts (p. 125).

PEANUT SHELLS

Peanut shells make good kitty litter. Soak them in water, add biodegradable dish soap and mix through, let dry outside or in front of a window, then sprinkle with baking soda, and offer to your cat. Peanut shells can also be used as mulch or the packing material upon which the shape of the ubiquitous Styrofoam peanuts is based, assuming your recipient isn't allergic. They also make good kindling.

PEARS, OVERRIPE

There may be, as Emerson said, only ten minutes in its life for which a pear is perfect for eating, but overripe pears make good pear butter (or pear sauce). This is only a matter of peeling and cooking them with water until the mixture is caramelized and saucy. Eat however you eat applesauce or apple butter, or use in baked goods (see Applesauce, p. 107). Or dry it into fruit leather (see Apple Leather, p. 110). If pears are only barely overripe, they can be cored and poached in sweet wine and water with a piece of cinnamon and one of star anise, then cooled and eaten on ice cream. Or they can be sliced and used in the No One's the Wiser Fruit Galette (p. 102).

PECANS, CHOPPED

As long as they aren't rancid, pecans are wonderful in the Any Vegetable Salad (p. 9) or scattered over rice or salad. They are also good in Granola (p. 207) or in All-Day Muffins (p. 232).

See also Nuts (p. 125).

PINEAPPLE SKIN AND CORE

PINEAPPLE DRINK *(1 hr)*
Pineapple skin and core, 1 piece peeled fresh ginger (optional), a squeeze of lime juice (optional), sweetener (brown sugar, honey, or maple syrup).

Wash the skin well, then put in a pot with the core. Add ginger (if using). Add water to cover by 3–4 inches. Cover, bring to a boil, then reduce to a simmer and cook until very fragrant, about 1 hr. Remove large pieces with tongs, then strain the rest into a bowl or pot through a fine-mesh sieve. Taste. Add any lime juice (if using) and a sweetener to taste. Let cool, and drink. This also makes good ice pops.

PINE NUTS

Anything that is true of other nuts and the volatility of their oils is doubly true of pine nuts (and macadamia nuts) because they are higher in oil—delicious when they are stable and fresh, and bitter when rancid. Store them in the refrigerator or freezer, and then use even the last ½ tsp to make a tiny bit of pesto. Pound a little garlic with salt in a mortar, then toast your few pine nuts in a dry skillet until they just start to turn golden, then add them to the garlic. Chop a cup of a soft herb—like parsley, cilantro, basil, celery leaf—or a combination, mix it into the pine nut/garlic mixture, and add enough oil to make it a spoonable, barely swimmy paste. Mix in ¼–½ cup finely grated Parmesan or Pecorino Romano. Season with salt to taste. Now dollop this anywhere you like, from toast to eggs to soup to pasta. If you don't have time for any of that, simply toast the pine nuts until golden and sprinkle them over your next bowl of rice, or over Amy's Pilaf (p. 206).

PISTACHIO SHELLS

Pistachio shells make good mulch, or filler for the bottom of a potted plant pot, or kindling. Save them in a container by the fireplace and set a match to them when you feel chilly.

PLANTAINS, COOKED

PATACONES/TOSTONES CON PICO DE GALLO (30 min)
Cooked plantains, chopped tomato, chopped onion, minced fresh chile, salt, lime juice, leftover braised meat (optional), neutral oil for pan-frying, sliced avocado (optional), chopped cilantro (optional).

If these were fried but not smashed, take a flat-bottomed mug and lightly smash, so they burst a bit. If they were already smashed, proceed. In a bowl, make a pico de gallo by combining tomato, onion, chile, salt, and lime juice to taste. If you have any leftover braised meat, warm it in a small pot with a splash of water or hot sauce. Heat a heavy-bottomed pan and add ¼ inch neutral oil and heat to 350°–375°F. Working in batches if necessary, refry the plantains, letting them lightly brown on the first side, 1–2 min, then flip.

Remove to paper towels to drain. Remove them to plates, top with a little meat and/or avocado (if using), then with pico de gallo and cilantro (if using).

I also like leftover plantains as they are, without reheating, on hot rice at lunchtime, with a few slices of avocado, or just a scattering of cilantro and a few pickled chiles, or a drizzle of hot sauce.

For plantain peels, *see Banana peels (p. 112)*. Use interchangeably.

PLUMS, OVERRIPE

Overripe plums make a delicious Any Fruit Crisp (p. 102), once any mold and browned bits have been removed.

PLUMS, UNRIPE

Unripe plums make a good Unripe Fruit Salad (p. 105). They can also make a refreshing topping for a cold soup, where they can be surprisingly grape-like if they're carefully cut into very small cubes.

POACHING LIQUID FROM FRUIT

What is left after poaching fruit could rightly be referred to as liquid gold. Wonderful uses include: 1) Poach more fruit in it. 2) Put it in a glass, add ice, then add seltzer for a soda. 3) Boil it down to a syrup and drizzle it over ice cream or a pie or crumble or panna cotta. 4) Add to a juice or smoothie.

POMEGRANATE PITH AND SHELL

These are, apparently, a curative for everything from indigestion to acne. The formula is to dry them well in the sun—though I think a dehydrator set to 125°F would work, too. Then grind and store as a powder. For your complexion, add yogurt or water and spread the mixture on your skin. For digestion, make a tea. For everything else, do something in between.

RAISINS, OLD

Use very, very dry raisins for cooking, since they will rehydrate and no one will know the difference. In a little bowl, cover them with boiling water and let them sit 10–15 min until they're plumped. Drain, then add to Rice Pudding Muffins (p. 491), All-Day Muffins (p. 232), or cooked rice, along with a handful of toasted pine nuts or walnuts, a drizzle of olive oil, and a handful of chopped parsley or chives. Or add to stewing chicken or beef for a slightly medieval braise.

RASPBERRY JAM

Raspberry jam makes wonderful Jam Thumbprint Cookies (p. 104), and is also good spread on the bottom of galette dough, as a sort of shellac, before other fruit is added.

SEEDS

The best thing to do with small amounts of varied seeds is to add them to Granola (p. 207) or to the All-Day Muffins (p. 232). Neither requires a certain quantity of any nut or seed and often benefits from inconsistency. If the seeds are rancid, however, they must be composted.

SOUR CHERRY PIE FILLING

This also makes good Jam Thumbprint Cookies (p. 104), but is likely worth making a very simple Basic Galette Dough (p. 102) for and turning into a very small galette.

STRAWBERRY JAM, OLD

Strawberry jam is the best jam. When it acquires mold, I have a daring habit of removing any mold plus ⅓ inch or so below it, and tasting what's left. One is, however, supposed to dispose of the whole jar. Listen to your own inner voice, and follow its lead.

STRAWBERRY LEAVES

I recently learned from a friend named Wesley Brown that the little leafy crowns of strawberries are good in salads. They can also be steeped in boiled water and drunk as tea.

FRUIT AND NUTS

WALNUTS, CHOPPED

As long as they aren't rancid, use chopped walnuts in the Any Vegetable Salad (p. 9), Best Grain or Bean Salad (p. 206), Basil Pesto (p. 394), or Aillade (p. 395). Or sprinkle them over any salad, or any eggs or vegetables, or creamy pasta. They add fat and crunch, and a layer of experience. Or make walnut parsley oil by adding chopped walnuts to Parsley Oil (p. 68).

See also Nuts (p. 125).

WATERMELON, OVERRIPE

Remove the seeds. Blend it and drink it as juice or blend it and freeze it as ice pops!

HOW TO BE RENEWED

Dairy and eggs

Of a good beginning cometh a good end.

—*John Heywood*, The Proverbs of John Heywood

I t bears remembering that eggs and milk and yogurt and cheese demand much of the animals that produce them and the humans who tend the animals. They need sunlight and grass and hay and countless hours and immeasurable obsession on the part of their many makers. If they are good fresh eggs and milk, and carefully made cheese, they remain good for longer than conventional wisdom suggests. And when they teeter toward their ends they are, each and every, worthy of a dignified denouement.

Eggs and milk and yogurt and cheese should only be thrown away when their lives as usable ingredients have ended. You will know this because when you encounter any, your body will revolt at the brush with decay. Until then, they are changing, as we all are, all the time, and it shouldn't be held against them.

One good method for ensuring that small amounts of eggs and dairy get used up is to store the end of any with another ingredient. By storing ingredients together, you encourage the mingling that normally has to wait until a burner is lit. Think of this as "refrigerator cooking." A leftover boiled egg half can be stored in soup, where it will add umami and body. Or on leftover roasted broccoli or coleslaw or beans. Then, when you drizzle it with vinaigrette or warm it with rice tomorrow, the egg will add to the atmosphere. Leftover grated cheese can be carefully swept into the last of the pasta, or onto the leftover broccoli, or potatoes, or scrambled eggs, or onto the boiled egg, or into the salad dressing, or into the rice or squash or spinach. Or it can go into the soup, like the egg did. When you remove the container to transform its contents, a bit of your transformation will already have been done for you. A little bit of leftover cream can be whipped into more cream. Or the cream, or the bit of leftover yogurt, or both, can gloss the pasta sauce or roast chicken juices. Or either can be a pretty little dollop on the hot soup or beans. Or be added to any creamy vinaigrette.

Cheese rinds are treasuries of salt and umami and fat. As with leftover eggs or bits of leftover grated cheese, begin with storage. Keep a container labeled "cheese rinds" neatly inside your cheese drawer. When you cut a cheese down to the rind, store it in the container with its kin. Whenever you add herbs and vegetable scraps to a pot of cooking beans, dig out a rind and add it, too. When you season cooking water for farro, add a rind to the water. Or, if you have a little cache of rinds, make Parmesan Stock (p. 165). If you have a very, very little cache, make Savory Stock/Broth (p. 247). With an attitude of cautious optimism rather than zealous caution you can ensure the meals you make are better than ones involving fewer good ends.

Here are some foundational ways with dairy and eggs. The batters can be breakfast (other than the cornstarch one) or can turn vegetables or pickles or salad or rice into savory pancakes or waffles.

BUTTERMILK SUBSTITUTE

To make 1 cup of buttermilk-ish, in a measuring cup, combine 1 tbsp distilled white vinegar into a measuring cup and whole milk to come up to 1 cup. Let sit for 5 min before using.

PANCAKE BATTER

2 eggs (beaten), 1¼ cups milk, 3 tbsp melted butter or olive oil, 1½ cups (180 g) all-purpose flour, 2 tsp baking powder, ¾ tsp salt, 2 tbsp sugar.

In a bowl, mix the eggs and milk. Stir in the melted butter. In a second bowl, whisk together the flour, baking powder, salt, and sugar. Combine, mixing well. Cook as you would any pancake. (Adapted from the King Arthur Baking website)

CORNMEAL PANCAKE BATTER

2 eggs (beaten), 1 cup milk, ¼ cup olive oil, 1 cup (120 g) all-purpose flour, 1 cup (138 g) cornmeal, 2 tbsp sugar, 1 tsp salt, 4 tsp baking powder.

In a bowl, mix the eggs, milk, and olive oil. In a second bowl, mix the flour, cornmeal, sugar, salt, and baking powder. Combine, mixing well. Cook as you would any pancake.

CORNSTARCH BATTER FOR SAVORY PANCAKES

1 egg, 3 tbsp buttermilk (or buttermilk substitute, recipe above), 1½ tbsp cornstarch, ½ tbsp oil, 1 tsp salt.

In a bowl, whisk everything together well, then add whatever savory leftovers you like. Especially good with leftover noodles or kimchi or both. Cook as you would any pancake.

SOURDOUGH STARTER PANCAKE BATTER

2 cups sourdough starter discard, 1 egg, 1 tbsp sugar, ½ tsp salt, 4 tbsp olive oil, 1 tsp baking soda dissolved in 1 tbsp water, oil or butter for cooking.

In a bowl, whisk together the starter, egg, sugar, salt, and olive oil. When ready to cook the pancakes, whisk in the baking soda in water. Cook as you would any pancake. (From What's Cooking America website)

SOURDOUGH STARTER WAFFLE BATTER

1 cup sourdough starter discard, 2 eggs, 2 tbsp sugar, ¾ cup whole milk, 1 tsp salt, 1½ tsp baking powder, 1 cup (120 g) all-purpose flour, 3 tbsp melted butter.

In a bowl, mix together the starter, eggs, sugar, and milk. In a second bowl, mix the salt, baking powder, and flour. Combine, mixing well, then stir in the melted butter. Cook as you would any waffles. (Adapted from Serious Eats website)

CREPE BATTER

1½ cups beaten eggs, 2 cups all-purpose flour (240 g), 3½ cups whole milk, ½ cup melted butter, ¼ tsp salt.

In a bowl, combine everything, let sit up to an hour, then make crepes, using about ¼ cup batter per crepe, and buttering the pan as needed.

TEMPURA BATTER

2¾ (300 g) cake flour, ½ tsp salt, 2 cups cold seltzer, 2 egg yolks, peanut or grapeseed oil for frying.

In a bowl, combine the flour and salt and put it in the freezer. Keep the seltzer and egg yolks cold. Just before frying, add the cold seltzer and yolks to the flour and salt, mixing until just barely combined, with big lumps still throughout. Heat the oil to 365°–375°F to fry.

BOILED EGGS

Place eggs in a pot of cold water. Bring to a boil, partially covered or covered. Remove from the heat, cover, and let sit 5 min for yolks that just cohere, and 6 min and on for increasingly firmer yolks. If the eggs are fresh, they will be hard to peel. Forgive the fresh eggs and peel them under running water.

POACHED EGGS

Bring a pan with a least 4 inches of water to a boil. Reduce the water to a simmer and add an unmeasured tsp of distilled white vinegar, which will help the whites seize more quickly and collect around the yolks. If you're nervous, be more liberal with the vinegar. Decrease the amount as you feel more comfortable. Crack each egg into a ramekin or teacup or other sharp rimmed cup or bowl. (If an egg breaks, save it to scramble tomorrow.) Adding one egg at a time, slide the eggs into the barely simmering water. If loose strands of egg white drift away from the yolks, collect them back toward it with a spoon. After about 90 sec, or whenever the eggs look like poached eggs, lift them with a slotted spoon and prod lightly. When each is cooked, its white will be firm and its yolk will still have give. Let each drain briefly in its spoon, then remove it to its destination. If you want to poach a number ahead of time, leave them sitting in a bath of water in the refrigerator and rewarm in a pan of hot water to serve.

OMELET

2–3 eggs, salt, 1–2 tbsp olive oil or butter or ghee.

In a bowl, beat the eggs with a little pinch of salt. Heat a small cast-iron skillet or other well-cured pan. Add the oil, butter, or ghee over medium heat. Reduce the heat slightly before adding the eggs. Let them set for 3–4 sec. Then use a silicone spatula to move everything toward one side of the pan so you can tip the still unset eggs into the empty space. Reduce the heat further if things seem to be happening too quickly. Do the same—gathering and tilting and pouring—again at a measured pace in easy motions, pulling some egg that looks like it's getting firm toward one side of the pan or the middle and tilting and nudging more liquid into its place. Remove the pan from the heat the instant the bottom has cohered and before any of it is brown, smoothing any remaining wobbly bits to the pan's margins. Let the inside of the omelet still have some softness to it. Add any filling or fold as is. Slide onto a plate or into a shallow bowl if the filling is wobbly.

FRITTATA

3–8 eggs, ¼ tsp salt, up to 3 cups other ingredients (leftover cooked vegetables, leftover pasta, leftover chopped herbs, or really anything at all), 3 tbsp olive oil.

Heat the oven to 375°F. Decide how many eggs to use based on the quantity of other ingredients being used: 3 eggs for 3 cups other ingredients, 8 eggs for only a few spoonsful—and the logical range between. In a bowl, whisk the eggs and salt, stir in the other ingredients. Heat an 8–9-inch ovenproof skillet over medium heat. Coat well with olive oil. Add the egg mixture and move the set part toward the middle a few times. As soon as the sides have cohered, transfer to the oven. Cook until the top is just set, checking after 8 min, then again until it's done. Cool briefly in the pan, then invert. Frittatas are better room temperature than hot.

ASIAGO RINDS

Anything that remains of Asiago can be used interchangeably with the remains of Parmesan or any other hard cheese. Use it in Creamy Mac and Cheese (p. 144), Variable Cheese Sauce (p. 144), Fromage Fortissimo (p. 145), Cheese Soufflé (p. 145), Homemade Cheez-Its (p. 146), Cheese Scones (p. 146), or Gougères (p. 146). Asiago rinds, like all hard natural cheese rinds, are also good all-purpose improvers.

BLUE CHEESE, CRUMBLED

BLUE CHEESE MAYONNAISE *(5 min)*
Mix crumbled blue cheese and mayonnaise in a ratio of 1:1. Slather on a burger or dip chips into it.

BLUE CHEESE DRESSING *(5 min)*
¼ cup crumbled blue cheese, ¼ cup mayonnaise, 3 tbsp yogurt.

Mix well to combine.

BLUE CHEESE OATMEAL!
This is just blue cheese spooned on top of oatmeal with lots of olive oil drizzled on, and freshly ground black pepper. Don't knock it till you try it.

BRIE, MOLDY

Cut off any fluffy blooms of mold and taste what's left. If it tastes good, use it in the Creamy Mac and Cheese (p. 144) or Variable Cheese Sauce (p. 144)—which will be especially delicious with brie included—or in a Cheese Soufflé (p. 145) or in Cheesy Savory Bread Pudding (p. 368).

BRIE RIND

Use in Fromage Fortissimo (p. 145).

BRINE, MOZZARELLA OR FETA

The brine in which mozzarella or feta is sold is salt water—that primordial liquid from which so much good emerges. With additional water added, it's good for cooking rice or other grains or pasta or vegetables. It is also a good starting point for a meat or fish brine. Take a sip to see how salty it is, then add water and a bit of sugar if you like, until it tastes slightly salty, slightly sweet—like good strong brine—and soak a chicken, or chicken thighs, or pork chops, or a trout or piece of salmon in it, refrigerated, overnight. Cook it the next day.

BUTTERMILK, SPOILING

Oh stop. I waive legal responsibility, but I don't discard buttermilk unless it's growing vicious green or blue mold. If you share my sentiments, shake it and use it in your biscuits or chicken brine.

CHEESE, ODDS AND ENDS

CREAMY MAC AND CHEESE *(15 min)*
Up to 2 cups finely grated odds and ends of cheese, Parmesan as needed, salt, 1 lb short pasta, 1 cup heavy cream, 8 tbsp (1 stick) butter.

Put the grated odds and ends into a bowl. Add enough Parmesan to get a total of 2 cups grated cheese. In a large pot of boiling water salted to taste like pleasant seawater, cook the pasta. Drain well. If you like mac and cheese browned on top, heat the broiler or heat the oven to 425°F. In a small pot, combine the cream and butter, bring to a simmer, and cook 2–3 min. Remove from the heat and whisk in the cheese. Taste for salt and adjust. Toss the pasta and cheese sauce together. Serve as is or transfer to a baking dish and bake or broil until the top is browned.

VARIABLE CHEESE SAUCE *(25 min)*
1½–2 tbsp butter, 1 tbsp flour, 1 cup milk (or any combination of milk and pasta cooking liquid or potato cooking liquid), salt, 1 cup finely grated odds and ends of cheese.

In a saucepan, melt the butter, whisk in the flour, add the liquid, and whisk over medium-high heat until it boils and thickens. Reduce to the lowest possible heat and cook, stirring occasionally, until it no longer tastes floury, 20–30 min. Remove from the heat and stir in the cheese until melted. Taste for salt and adjust. This can be poured over boiled vegetables or over toasted bread or mixed with pasta or poured over nachos, or, or, or . . .

FROMAGE FORTISSIMO *(5 min)*

½ lb odds and ends of cheese plus any soft edible rind, 1 clove garlic, salt, ¼–⅓ cup white wine or sherry (depending how boozy you like things), 2 tbsp heavy cream or butter, a few leaves fresh thyme (optional).

Finely chop any leftover cheese and edible rinds and place in a food processor. Pound the garlic to a paste with salt and add to the processor, along with the wine or sherry, the cream or butter, and thyme (if using) and process to smooth. Good on little crostini or crackers, accompanied by more wine.

A variation I learned of in the book *Company* by Amy Thielen is to add 2 tbsp crushed pork rinds. Another is to substitute soft goat cheese for the heavy cream.

CHEESE SOUFFLÉ *(45 min–1 hr)*

Butter and grated Parmesan cheese for the baking dish, 3 tbsp butter, 3 tbsp flour, 1¼ cups milk, 4 eggs (separated), 1 cup finely grated odds and ends of cheese, salt.

Heat the oven to 400°F. Butter a 6-cup soufflé or 8-cup gratin dish, then dust with grated Parmesan. Make the béchamel: In a saucepan, melt the butter, add the flour, whisking it very well, then gradually add the milk, whisking the whole time. Continue to whisk as it comes to a boil. Reduce to the lowest possible heat and cook, stirring occasionally, until it no longer tastes floury, 20–30 min. Beat in the egg yolks one at a time, then the cheese. Season with salt to taste, then set aside. In a bowl, beat the egg whites with a tiny pinch of salt to just past soft peaks. Add in three additions to the soufflé base. Pour into the prepared soufflé dish and transfer to the oven, then reduce the oven temperature to 375°F. Cook until just golden and still slightly wobbly inside, about 30 min. Eat! (From *Vegetarian Cooking for Everyone* by Deborah Madison)

HOMEMADE CHEEZ-ITS *(1½ hr, but mostly waiting)*
1½ cups finely grated odds and ends of cheese, 1 cup (120 g) all-purpose flour, 1½ tsp cornstarch, a very heaping ¼ tsp salt, 6 tbsp cold butter (cut into small cubes), 2 tbsp ice water.

In a food processor, pulse the cheese, flour, cornstarch, and salt. Add the butter and pulse to a wet sand consistency. Add the ice water. Pulse until the dough forms a ball. Pat into two 6-inch squares, cover, and refrigerate for at least 45 min. Heat the oven to 350°F. Line a sheet pan with parchment paper. Roll each square of dough out to ⅛ inch thick. Cut each sheet into about 64 crackers and mark each with the tines of a fork. Bake on the lined pan, rotating front to back halfway through, until crisp and lightly golden on the edges, 16–20 min. (Adapted from Sally's Baking Addiction website)

CHEESE SCONES *(40–60 min)*
2 cups (240 g) all-purpose flour plus for dusting, ½ tsp salt, 1 tbsp baking powder, 1½ cups odds and ends of cheese (finely grated), 2 eggs (beaten), ⅓ cup whole milk (or cream, sour cream, or ricotta), 6 tbsp cold butter (cut into small cubes).

Heat the oven to 375°F. Line a baking sheet with parchment paper. In a bowl, whisk together the flour, salt, and baking powder. Mix the cheese through the flour mixture, using your hands. In a small bowl, whisk the eggs and milk. Mix the butter into the flour to pebble-size crumbs. This can be done by hand or in the food processor. Add the egg-milk mixture and mix until everything is just moistened. It will be very sticky. Heavily flour a cutting board and tip the dough onto it. Pat the dough into an 8 x 3-inch rectangle 2 inches thick, then cut into 5 pieces. Cut each into 2 right triangles. Place the scones spaced apart on the baking sheet. Bake until golden brown, 20–25 min. Eat warm.

GOUGÈRES *(45 min)*
3 tbsp butter (cubed), ¼ tsp salt, freshly ground black pepper, ½ cup (60 g) flour, 2 eggs, ¾ cup finely grated odds and ends of cheese.

Heat the oven to 425°F. Line a baking sheet with parchment paper. In a small saucepan, heat ½ cup water, the butter, salt, and a tiny bit of black pepper until the butter is melted. Add the flour and stir vigorously until the dough pulls easily away from the sides and forms a smooth ball. Remove from the heat and let cool for 2–3 min. Move to a stand mixer with the paddle attachment and add the eggs, one at a time, mixing well. It will be lumpy then smooth. Let cool to a comfortable touch. Reserving some of the cheese for sprinkling on the gougères, add the rest of the cheese to the dough, mixing through. Put the dough into a plastic storage bag or pastry bag, then snip the corner and pipe the dough into little mounds the size of cherry tomatoes onto the lined baking sheet. Sprinkle each with a tiny bit of the reserved cheese. Place in the oven and bake for 5 min. Reduce the oven temperature to 375°F and bake to golden brown, 20–25 min. These can be frozen before being baked and then baked from the freezer, or baked, then frozen, then warmed in a 350°F oven just before friends arrive for a drink. (Adapted from David Lebovitz)

CHEESE, MOLDY

I cut the moldy bits off cheese and taste what remains. If my visceral self revolts at what I've tasted, I sigh and discard. If it calmly bears up, I use what's left as planned. You must listen to your own viscera, with whom you are better acquainted than you are with mine.

CHEESE RINDS

Washed cheese rinds are edible. Some options are: 1) Eat the rind along with the inside as you go. 2) Make Fromage Fortissimo (p. 145). 3) Include them in beans or soups for richness, then scoop them out before eating.

See also Parmesan rinds (p. 165).

CONDENSED MILK

CONDENSED MILK BUTTER COOKIES *(45 min)*
2 cups (240 g) all-purpose flour, 1 tsp baking powder, ¼ tsp salt, 10 tbsp room-temperature butter, ½ cup condensed milk, 1 tsp vanilla extract.

In a small bowl, whisk together the flour, baking powder, and salt. In a stand mixer, whisk the butter and condensed milk. Whisk in the vanilla, then the flour mixture. Form into a ball, then refrigerate for 20 min. Heat the oven to

375°F. Line a baking sheet with parchment paper. Roll out the dough ⅛ inch thick, then cut with a cookie cutter (scraps can be rerolled and cut into more cookies). Arrange on the baking sheet and bake until just set, 6–8 min. (Adapted from Manu's Menu website)

COTTAGE CHEESE

VOGUE'S COTTAGE CHEESE SOUFFLÉ *(1 hr)*
3 tbsp butter plus more for the pan, ⅓ cup (40 g) all-purpose flour, ½ cup milk, ½ tsp salt, 1 cup cottage cheese, 2 eggs (separated).

Heat the oven to 300°F. Butter a loaf pan. In a small pot, melt the 3 tbsp butter, then add the flour and stir through. Slowly add the milk, whisking. Add the salt and cottage cheese and whisk over low heat until just a bit thicker, 5–10 min. Remove from the heat. Whisk the egg yolks, then add to the cottage cheese mixture. In a bowl, whisk the egg whites until just past soft peaks. Fold into the cottage cheese mixture. Pour into the prepared loaf pan and bake until just set and lightly browned on top, about 45 min.

CRÈME FRAÎCHE

Use any small amount of leftover crème fraîche interchangeably with sour cream or yogurt in any recipe, especially when there's just a little left. Or add it at the very end of cooking to beef stew or pesto or polenta or any other dish with a bit of swim to it. Any will remain itself but become glossier.

DEVILED EGGS

BETTER EGG SALAD *(15 min)*
Deviled eggs, garlic, salt, grated lemon zest, chopped chives (or chervil or celery leaves), freshly ground black pepper, chopped cornichons or chili sauce like sriracha but not both (optional), mayonnaise (store-bought or homemade, p. 395).

In a bowl, smash the leftover deviled eggs with a fork or potato masher. Pound a touch of garlic to a paste with a little salt and add a dab of it to the eggs along with the lemon zest and a big handful of chopped herbs. Add the black pepper, cornichons or chili sauce (if using), then add the mayonnaise judiciously, tasting almost maniacally to add just what tastes good. Enjoy! Especially good on dark bread or rye or crackers. Add any other herbs or pickles you think will go well.

EGGS, BOILED

Though this gastronomic fact is often snubbed, it is only at room temperature that leftover eggs regain their composure and elegant manufacture—half lean, half lush. (This is also true of cheese, which goes from chalky to smooth.) Bringing leftover eggs (and cheese) to room temperature before turning them into another dish is well worth the trouble. The least finicky way is to leave them either out of the refrigerator with enough time before the next meal.

I don't dispute that bacteria thrive at the range—between 45°F and 80°F—that I counsel. It is referred to in food safety courses as "the danger zone" because it is the ideal breeding temperature for bacteria. It is also true that more food-borne illnesses come from ingredients we don't rush to refrigerate—fruits, nuts, leafy vegetables—than from ones we do. There was a recent salad recall for listeria, a species of bacteria that thrives in cold rather than warm temperatures. If you are curious about what a big difference it makes for eggs (or cheese) to warm calmly on their own, try leaving leftovers of either out after breakfast. Taste them three hours later. If you find yourself happier than when you ate or cooked with them straight from the refrigerator, you can now at least accurately assess the risks and benefits yourself.

I boil extra eggs when I'm boiling any eggs. I also peel them so all the doing is done. Cut in half, lightly salted and drizzled with olive oil, with a parsley leaf or round of pickled chile or anchovy added, such an egg is a reminder that not all the best things are complicated. To make a leftover egg into a meal, add some garlic-rubbed toast and a tin of fish and some wedges of tomato, or leftover cooked vegetables drizzled with new oil and adorned with some chopped herbs, or, or, or . . . If you have more time, salt and wedge the egg, cut a tomato into wedges and salt them, too, then drape anchovies here and there, and eat it with garlic-rubbed toast.

Or make a composed salad. Make sure all the ingredients are close to room temperature.

VARIABLE COMPOSED SALAD *(10 min)*
Salt, a head of leaf lettuce or the equivalent (washed in cold water and dried), Basic Vinaigrette (p. 376), cooked vegetables (green beans, broccoli, cauliflower, squash, beets, potatoes), oil-packed tuna, 1–2 boiled eggs (quartered and salted), 3–4 anchovy fillets (optional), freshly ground black pepper.

In a medium bowl, lightly salt the lettuce and drizzle in the vinaigrette judiciously, mix, and taste. Tip the lettuce onto a plate, then quickly dress the leftover vegetables in the same bowl with whatever vinaigrette remains. Put that in a pile on the greens. Put the tuna in another pile, eggs on their own. Salt everything, drape here and there with anchovies if using. Top with black pepper.

Even though the soft eggs at ramen restaurants are cooked to remain perfectly soft throughout with a jelly center, eggs boiled a regular way provide nearly the same eating experience with less planning and technology.

BETTER RAMEN OR OTHER LUNCHTIME SOUP *(5 min)*
Cooked ramen or other soup (such as bean or lentil soup, Teaism Soup, p. 275, Savory Miso Rice Stew, p. 255, or Kimchi Jjigae, p. 435), 1 boiled egg, sliced scallions and/or sliced nori (optional).

In a pot, heat the soup to the temperature you like it, then place a halved boiled egg in the pot and let it warm for another 30 sec to heat the egg. Add the scallions and/or nori (if using) and eat.

EGG SALAD *(5 min)*
Boiled eggs, mayonnaise, garlic, salt, grated lemon zest, minced chives.

Smash the eggs with a fork and mix in mayonnaise sparingly. You can always add more. Pound the garlic to a paste with a little salt. Add ⅛–¼ tsp garlic paste per every 2 eggs, then a sprinkle of lemon zest and minced chives. Mix, taste, adjust, and eat.

PAN BAGNAT (*2 hr, but most of it is waiting*)
4–6-inch length baguette (halved horizontally as for a sandwich), 1 clove garlic, olive oil, oil-packed tuna, 1 boiled egg (thinly sliced), salt, 6–7 Niçoise or other dark olive (pitted and halved), 3–4 anchovy fillets, lemon juice or red wine vinegar, fresh basil or parsley leaves.

Toast the baguette until just warm and crisp. Rub the toasted side with the clove of garlic, then drizzle with olive oil. Lay on the tuna, then the egg, salting lightly. Dot with olives, drape with anchovy fillets, and then very lightly add a few drops lemon juice or vinegar. Scatter basil or parsley leaves, closely. Close and wrap tightly in foil. If you can, weight down with a pot or heavy pan for ultimate blending and melding of flavors. Let sit at least 2 hr, then eat.

Leftover boiled eggs can also be used in the Sauce Gribiche (p. 396) or Tartar Sauce (p. 396). Or they can be added to a taco or fried rice or sprinkled on top of a boiled vegetable . . .

EGGS BENEDICT

This recipe is somewhat optimistic. Do what you can.

EGGS BENEDICT SPAGHETTI (*30 min*)
Salt, 4 oz dried spaghetti per leftover egg, eggs Benedict, olive oil as needed, heavy cream, freshly grated Parmesan cheese.

Remove the eggs and sauce and Canadian bacon from their English muffins. Reserve the English muffins for retoasting tomorrow. Thinly slice the Canadian bacon to use now or store it away to crisp up for your English muffin. If using, in a small pan with a drizzle of olive oil, cook the slices to crisp, then set aside. In a wide, heavy saucepan over the lowest possible heat, warm any salvageable hollandaise sauce with a long pour of heavy cream and a good deal of Parmesan. Once it's bubbled, turn off the burner. In a large pot of boiling water salted to taste like pleasant seawater, cook the pasta. Reserve ¼ cup of pasta water. Scoop the pasta out of its cooking water with tongs directly into the hollandaise and stir well, adding additional water and the Canadian bacon (if using). Carefully lower the poached egg into the pasta water and leave to warm, 30 sec or so. Scoop the pasta into a bowl, gently retrieve the egg and place it atop the pasta, lightly salt the egg, drizzle it all with olive oil, and top with Parmesan. This can also be made without the poached egg.

EGGS, FRIED

COLD FRIED EGGS AND HERBS (*10 min*)
1–2 fried eggs, 1½–2 tbsp chopped cilantro (or mint, or basil, or a combination), 1 tsp sesame seeds, 2 tsp crunchy thing (fried shallots, fried onions, crushed sesame sticks, crushed Funyuns, crushed pretzels, or crushed potato chips), 2–3 splashes fish sauce, a squeeze of lime juice, a few slices pickled chiles. *Optional add-in:* ¼ cup leftover cooked vegetables (broccoli, cauliflower, or kale, etc., thinly sliced). *For serving:* a bowl of hot rice, or soba noodles; or a lettuce salad; or the Dumpling Rice Salad (p. 354).

Slice the egg(s) into long ribbons so they look as close to noodles as cold fried eggs ever can. In a shallow bowl, combine the eggs with the remaining ingredients. Mix it all together, taste for salt, and eat.

Leftover fried eggs make good classic egg salad, too.

FRIED EGG EGG SALAD (*10 min*)
1 fried egg (cut into rough pieces), 1–2 tsp mayonnaise, a few drops lemon juice or rice vinegar, 2 drops of sriracha or other chili sauce, chopped celery leaves (or cilantro or parsley). *Optional additions:* 1–2 tsp finely chopped shallots or scallions (soaked in ice water or lemon juice for 5 min), finely chopped radishes, or finely chopped cornichons. *For serving:* crackers (saltines, Ritz, or other) or 1 thin slice sandwich bread (toasted).

Place the fried egg pieces in a bowl and smash with a fork or potato masher. Add 1 tsp mayonnaise, lemon juice or vinegar, and sriracha and mix well, adding more mayonnaise if it seems dry. Add the herbs and continue smashing. Add any of the optional additions. Taste for salt, adjust. Serve on crackers or toast.

TAHINI EGG SALAD (*10 min*)

1–2 fried eggs, 1 tbsp chopped parsley or cilantro, 2 tbsp Techina (p. 393) or 1 tsp tahini well mixed with 2 tbsp water, salt, pounded garlic, lemon juice, freshly ground black pepper.

In a bowl, smash the fried egg pieces with a fork or potato masher. Add the parsley or cilantro, techina or tahini, a sprinkle of salt, a tiny bit of garlic, a squeeze of lemon juice, and mix well. Adjust the lemon and salt until you like it. Add black pepper to taste. This makes a great dip, like hummus or guacamole, or a delicious sandwich.

FRIED EGG SALAMI SANDWICH (*10 min*)

4–6-inch length baguette (halved horizontally as for a sandwich), olive oil or butter or mayonnaise, thinly sliced salami, arugula or other peppery green like cress, 1 fried egg, salt.

Toast the baguette until just warm and crisp. Drizzle with olive oil, or spread with butter or mayonnaise on both sides. Meanwhile, in a small skillet, fry the salami until just warmed and sizzled. Add the greens to the salami, then put on the bread. Slide the cold fried egg into the hot pan for 20–30 sec, salt, then add to the sandwich, close, and eat.

EGGS, POACHED

I once cooked in a restaurant in which eggs were poached ahead of time, then rewarmed in hot water when orders came in. I subsequently ran a restaurant where I copied the practice because the idea of each poached egg order hinging on the equanimity of the egg cook was harrowing. If you end up with leftover poached eggs at home, think of yourself as a highly organized cook, ready for service. Store the poached eggs in cold water in the refrigerator. Warm a shallow pan of water and gently reheat them when you have a piquant vinaigrette and crisp bacon and frisée ready for salade lyonnaise, or a soup, rice, cooked beans, or buttered toast prepared to receive them.

Leftover scambled eggs are not only bearable but adaptable and, moreover, delicious. They can always simply be briefly warmed in a pan or microwave and eaten in a bagel or sandwich, or on lunchtime rice, with a spoonful of pickled chilies added. Plus, half the fried rice recipes in the world insist that you separately scramble an egg before proceeding. With one leftover and a bit of old rice, you already have:

EGG FRIED RICE *(5–10 min)*
1–2 tbsp neutral oil, 1 cup cooked rice, salt, leftover scrambled egg. *Optional add-ins:* sliced scallions, pickled chilies, fresh cilantro or Thai basil, chopped crisp vegetables.

In a wide skillet or wok, heat the oil until it shimmers. Add the rice and spread it over the surface of the pan and salt to taste. When it seems like every grain has had a moment to fry, scoop the rice all together, and tip the leftover scrambled egg into the pan. Mix well and then garnish with any optional additions.

This next sounds very strange until you ponder the other egg sauces of the world, which include hollandaise, mayonnaise, gribiche, carbonara, and a dozen more, and are all various constellations of elbow grease and egg. This one is very simple.

GARLICKY EGG SAUCE *(5 min)*
1 clove garlic, salt, leftover scrambled egg.

In a mortar, pound the garlic to a paste with a little salt. Add the leftover scrambled egg to the garlic paste and pound it all into an even smoother, yellower paste. This sauce is for dolloping over hot vegetables or for spreading on sandwiches or eating over hot rice.

If you're dolloping over cooked vegetables, a scattering of quickly pickled onions can be a nice complement. Turn this into a gribiche sauce by adding a scant tsp chopped cornichons, a scant tsp drained capers, up to ¼ cup chopped mixed soft herbs, and a drizzle of olive oil.

EGG YOLKS, COOKED

ANOTHER GARLICKY EGG SAUCE *(5 min)*

1 clove garlic, salt, 2 cooked egg yolks, a very scant ⅛ tsp Dijon mustard, ¼ cup olive oil.

In a mortar, pound the garlic to a paste with a little salt. Add the egg yolks and mustard, and then add the olive oil gradually, while pounding. This is delicious over asparagus, or on fish, or on grilled or fried chicken, or over cooked broccoli or cauliflower, or used to dress a salad.

FAST PSEUDO CAESAR *(5 min)*

1 clove garlic, ⅛ tsp salt plus to taste, 2 anchovy fillets, 1 cooked egg yolk, juice of ½ lemon, ⅓ cup grated Parmesan cheese, ¼–⅓ cup olive oil.

In a mortar, pound the garlic to a paste with the salt. Add the anchovies and egg yolk and pound or whisk. Add the lemon juice, then the Parmesan, and then add the olive oil gradually, while pounding or whisking. Taste. It should be very potent! Dress bitter greens or chicories like radicchio and escarole.

A variation is to add ¼ cup mayonnaise and a bit more Parmesan (up to ¾ cup total) for a thicker dressing.

I happened to be contemplating leftover egg yolks from my son's fried eggs one day as I warmed a pot of dashi to make miso soup. As the dashi came to a simmer, I almost unconsciously ladled some from the pot into the rejected yolks, and then a bit more and, using a mortar, blended in the dashi. The combination went from chalky to creamy and, after I added a third spoonful, airy. The yolks absorbed the liquid thirstily, and when it was smooth and light, I spooned the result onto a sesame seeded cracker, and ate it, stunned by the simple richness of the combination.

EGG YOLKS, RAW

Raw egg yolks add shine and lushness. If you can get over the initial queasiness at the idea of eating a raw egg yolk, experiment by tipping one over roasted mushrooms, à la Cafe Mutton in Hudson, New York, or into a bowl of pasta with butter and cheese, or into hot rice, and watch it become its own sauce. Or, if you are eating chicken soup, whisk an egg yolk with a pour of soup in a separate bowl, then add more soup by the slow drizzle until the mixture is thick, and then whisk this back into the soup, for a soup with added body and luster. Or do the same with the liquid from a braising meat, or from any stew. This is especially lovely with seafood soups.

Or make Mayonnaise (p. 395).

EGG WHITES, RAW

There was a decade, spanning my adolescence, when people ate egg white omelets. The practice has mostly died out, but I ate enough in those ten years to know that while they are not equal to whole-egg omelets, egg white omelets, cooked in butter, with chopped fresh herbs, are entirely reasonable to eat, especially with thick, well-buttered toast.

Or make meringues.

MERINGUES *(2–4 hr, but only 5 min of work)*
3 egg whites, ¼ tsp cream of tartar, ¾ cup superfine sugar, ½ tsp flavoring (optional; orange blossom water or rosewater or vanilla).

Heat the oven to 200°F. Line a baking sheet with parchment paper. In a bowl, whisk the egg whites and cream of tartar to soft peaks, then add the sugar, by spoonfuls, continuing to whisk, until you have stiff peaks. Add any flavoring near the end. Pipe the meringue mixture onto the baking sheet or spoon into mounds. Bake until just crisp, 1–2 hr. Turn off the oven and leave another 1–2 hr to cool and firm. These can be topped with chopped nuts or bits of chocolate before baking.

EGG WASH

The egg wash left after brushing a crust is perfect for whisking into a creamy sauce, like Rémoulade Sauce (p. 396), Tartar Sauce (p. 396), or Mayonnaise (p. 395) to make it extra airy and lush.

FETA, CRUMBLED

A neat trick is to pour 1 tbsp of boiling water over a small amount of crumbled feta, whisk it well, then add to cooking polenta or grits. Or use the softened feta to make a frittata with thinly sliced onion, celery, and chives, as they do in Trieste. Or don't dilute or warm the feta at all and just crumble it, as is, over thickly sliced cucumber, whole olives, and slices of sweet onion, dressed with salt, wine vinegar, crumbled oregano, and olive oil.

DAIRY AND EGGS

FONDUE

You do not need a full pound of fondue to do this. Melt whatever fondue you have with more cheese and cream and it will be great.

FONDUE MAC AND CHEESE (*1 hr*)
Salt, 1 lb short pasta, 1 lb fondue, ¾–1 lb grated cheese (cheddar or anything that didn't get added to yesterday's fondue), ½ cup heavy cream.

In a large pot of boiling water salted to taste like pleasant seawater, cook the pasta until just shy of al dente. Reserve 2 cups pasta water just before draining. Heat the oven to 400°F. In the now empty pasta pot, heat the leftover fondue along with the grated cheese, 1¼–2 cups pasta water, and the cream until all hot and melted, then add the pasta and mix to combine. Scrape into a medium-size baking or gratin dish. Bake until the pasta is fully cooked, the liquid is absorbed, and the top has begun to brown in places, 20–25 min.

FONTINA

Use in Creamy Mac and Cheese (p. 144), Variable Cheese Sauce (p. 144), Cheese Soufflé (p. 145), or Cheesy Savory Bread Pudding (p. 368).

FRENCH TOAST BATTER

Store leftover French toast batter in the refrigerator and use for more French toast, or use it to make Bread Pudding (p. 182), counting it as replacement for the eggs by volume.

FRITTATA

This is one of the world's great sandwiches.

PANINO CON LA FRITTATA (*10 min if you are in a hurry–2 hr*)
4–6-inch length baguette (halved horizontally as for a sandwich) or 2 slices other hard crusted bread, olive oil, 1–2 pieces frittata.

Toast the bread until just warm and crisp. Drizzle the cut sides lightly with olive oil. Add the frittata and wrap tightly in foil. Ideally let sit 2 hr. Eat.

A variation (I highly recommend) is to add a drizzle of chili oil. Leftover cooked greens are good here, too.

My next suggestion hinges on your sharing my textural preference for the spongy: Cut leftover frittata into thin slices and add to soup. The cold frittata plumps gratifyingly in warm broth.

GHEE, USED

Ghee—which is clarified butter—can be reused. Line a fine-mesh sieve with a double layer of cheesecloth and strain used ghee. Compost what's in the strainer, wash and dry the cheesecloth, and store the ghee in a jar with a lid.

GOAT CHEESE, OLD

Cut leftover goat cheese into rounds and store it, coated with olive oil, with several sprigs of hardy herbs (thyme, marjoram, or rosemary), salt, and fennel seeds in a mason jar. Let the goat cheese sit at least 3 days. Now you have herby, seasoned, preserved goat cheese, which needs only a small piece of toast or cracker or a plain green salad to become a distinguished snack.

If you didn't marinate it as above and yours has mold on it, follow your own instinct. I scoop or slice off mold, then taste what's left and use it if it tastes good.

GRUYÈRE

Use in the Creamy Mac and Cheese (p. 144), Variable Cheese Sauce (p. 144), Cheese Soufflé (p. 145), Gougères (p. 146), or Cheesy Savory Bread Pudding (p. 368).

HALLOUMI, COOKED

REFRIED HALLOUMI WITH OLIVES AND HERBS *(10 min)*
Halloumi, olive oil, a handful of oil-cured black olives, chile flakes, a handful of chopped parsley (or mint or a combination).

Cut the leftover Halloumi into cubes. Heat a heavy-bottomed skillet. Add oil to just coat the bottom of the pan. Add the Halloumi cubes and cook to retoast on each side, flipping them as needed. Remove to a plate and drizzle with olive oil. Sprinkle the olives over, then sprinkle with chile flakes, then with herbs. Eat with hot bread.

HEAVY CREAM

Be free of hand, heart, and mind when adding the last spoonful of heavy cream to a creamy dressing or anything you're baking, or any eggs you're scrambling. It will contribute much.

If heavy cream has begun to smell bad, make the recipe below. It is for cooking, not spreading on toast.

COOKING BUTTER *(variable but not long)*
Put any amount of cream in a stand mixer and whisk on medium-high until very thick, scraping it down as needed. Continue to whip until the liquid and the fat separate. This will take as long as it takes, and will happen eventually. If you find yourself worried yours is the only cream in the world that will not eventually coagulate into butter, distract yourself by reading an article far from the mixer until you hear the sound change from a whip into a thump. Separate the butter from the liquid. Taste the liquid. If it's just sour, use it as buttermilk. If it's bitter, discard. Squeeze the butter well, store it, and cook with it before you cook with any of your less artisanal butter. (Adapted from *Prune* by Gabrielle Hamilton)

HUEVOS RANCHEROS FRIED RICE *(15 min)*

2 tbsp olive or other cooking oil, ⅓–½ cup finely chopped onion, 1 clove garlic (finely chopped), 2 tsp chopped pickled or fresh chiles, ¼ tsp salt plus to taste, 1–2 cups cooked rice, ½ cup diced crunchy vegetable (cucumber, tomato, green tomato, or jicama), ¼–1 cup huevos rancheros (combined), 1–2 tsp distilled white vinegar or lime juice, ½–1 cup chopped cilantro (stems included). *For serving:* crumbled tortilla chips (or Fritos or other corn chip), lime wedges.

Heat a medium-large skillet over medium-high heat. Add the oil, onion, garlic, chiles, and salt and cook until beginning to brown, 1–2 min. Add the rice and spread out across the pan to fry the grains. Cook, moving it occasionally, until the rice seems hot and a bit fried. Add the crunchy vegetable and leftover huevos rancheros and stir through. Add the vinegar or lime juice and stir through. Taste for salt and adjust. Remove from the heat and add the cilantro. Serve topped with the chips, with lime wedges for squeezing, and eat.

Or substitute huevos rancheros for the enchiladas in Enchilada Stew (p. 355).

KUKU

Like frittata, kuku makes a good sandwich. Persian friends recommend making kuku sandwiches with barbari bread or lavash or pita, topped with torshi (Persian pickles) yogurt, olive oil, fresh sliced radishes, and lots of fresh herbs. That is the best version. It is also acceptable to use another bread, without too much crumb, and any fresh vegetables and pickles you have.

KULFI

KULFI MILKSHAKE *(5 min)*

Up to 2 cups kulfi, vanilla ice cream (if you only have a few spoonfuls of kulfi and want more milkshake), ¼ tsp ground cardamom, a few strands of saffron, milk.

Blend and eat with a spoon or sip with a straw. A drop of rose water is a nice addition.

LABNEH

Add small amounts of leftover labneh to guacamole for a creamier, tangier guacamole. Or combine it with mayonnaise in a ranch or blue cheese dressing. Or add it to the other ingredients in Caesar dressing. Or whisk it into eggs to be scrambled. Or dollop it onto scrambled eggs, or use it in the Tzatziki Omelet (p. 422), or add a little bit of pounded garlic to make an extra-rich toum and fill an omelet with that. Labneh is also thick enough to spread on a sandwich, which makes it an especially good accompaniment to leftover grilled or roasted vegetables or cooking greens. Add sambal or sriracha to labneh for a spicy yogurt sauce. Or do what is simplest: toast thick slices of crusty bread, rub it with the cut side of garlic, then spread as heavily as you like with labneh, drizzle it with olive oil, then, if you have energy, sprinkle with Greek oregano or za'atar and eat.

See also Yogurt (p. 170).

MANCHEGO, OLD

Old Manchego that is both too oily and too dry makes good grating cheese. It is a reasonable replacement for Parmesan or Pecorino Romano on pasta, in soup, in pesto, and so on. A trick that I play on myself is to put Manchego destined for grating in a container labeled "pasta cheese." This prevents my simple mind from rejecting it in favor of Parmesan. Another trick that works just as well is to grate Manchego as soon as you deem it unworthy for a cheese platter. Label this "grated cheese" and keep it in the refrigerator in plain sight.

MASCARPONE

Use small amounts of mascarpone interchangeably with crème fraîche, Greek yogurt, or heavy cream. Or use in The Best Coleslaw (p. 23), or instead of some of the sour cream in Any Pastry Sour Cream Coffee Cake (p. 478).

It is hard to tell when a good thing is about to end. The only real way to prepare for milk going bad is to note if you've had a carton for particularly long. If you have, first smell and taste it. If it smells and tastes fine but you're worried it won't be by tomorrow morning, extend its life by turning it into a substitute for buttermilk (see p. 138). This can be used to make buttermilk brine for fried chicken or buttermilk biscuits or scones or pancakes or, or, or . . .

It is extremely unlikely that sour pasteurized milk will hurt you. I use any that tastes sour, but not bitter, in pancake or waffle batter, or in scones or biscuits, or in muffins. Many of the baked goods my family has eaten have included milk I wouldn't drink in coffee. So far, so good.

This next is a good use for very sour milk, because the molasses balances it out nicely.

SOUR MILK SPICE CAKE *(1 hr)*

Butter and flour for the pan, 1 cup sour milk, 1 cup molasses, ½ cup (100 g) sugar, 2⅓ cups (280 g) all-purpose flour, 1½ tsp baking soda, ½ tsp salt, grated zest of ½ orange, ground nutmeg or mace, ground ginger, ground cinnamon, 4 tbsp (½ stick) melted butter.

Heat the oven to 350°F. Butter and flour a shallow 8–10-inch cake pan. In a large bowl, combine the sour milk, molasses, and sugar. In a small bowl, combine the flour, baking soda, salt, orange zest, and a pinch each of the spices. Add the flour mixture to the milk and molasses, then whisk in the melted butter. Pour into the prepared pan and bake until a skewer emerges nearly clean, 25–40 min, depending on your pan. Let cool in the pan for 10 min, then invert onto a plate. Good for breakfast or an afternoon snack. (Adapted from the *Boston Cooking-School Cookbook* by Fannie Farmer)

MOZZARELLA

What makes mozzarella so appealing is its sweet richness and meltiness. Use any small amount you have left for a single grilled cheese instead of your regular cheddar, or scramble it into eggs, or add it to a mixture of cheeses for Creamy Mac and Cheese (p. 144) or a Cheese Soufflé (p. 145).

If you inadvertently left fresh mozzarella on the counter overnight, and your kitchen is in a temperate clime, it may be fine. If the very outer layers seem sour and sticky, rinse and pare them off. Use the rest of it today. One simple option is to make Basic Galette Dough (p. 102), brush it with olive oil, fill it with leftover cooked greens, or scatter it with halved cherry tomatoes, and then add torn or sliced mozzarella, and bake. This is plain but makes the most of mozzarella, and is unobjectionable to most eaters.

MOZZARELLA STICKS

MOZZARELLA STICK FRITTATA (20 min)
3 eggs, ¼ tsp salt, about 2 cups fried mozzarella sticks (chopped), ½ cup chopped parsley or celery leaves (optional), 3 tbsp olive oil, freshly grated Parmesan cheese.

Heat the oven to 375°F. In a bowl, whisk the eggs with the salt. Stir in the chopped mozzarella sticks, adding the herbs (if using). Heat an 8–9-inch oven-proof skillet over medium heat. Add the olive oil, then the egg mixture. Cook, moving raw egg toward the empty pan space, until the bottom is just set and the border is just firm. Transfer to the oven and cook until just set, 10–15 min. Blanket with Parmesan, and eat at room temperature, along with any marinara sauce that came with the mozzarella sticks, if you like.

MUFFIN BATTER

If you ever find yourself with prepared muffin batter, not wanting to bake any more muffins, pour the leftover batter into muffin liners—silicone or paper—and freeze. When you find yourself re-energized, place the liners in muffin tins and bake directly from the freezer, adding a few min to the original cooking time to compensate for the freezing.

OMELETS

Like leftover scrambled eggs, leftover omelets have an almost inevitable destination in fried rice. Slice or chop into ribbons and add to the pan once the rice is nicely fried. Or turn to YouTube and watch any of a hundred instructional videos on making fried rice that instruct you to cook an omelet or eggs separately, then remove it from the pan to a plate, then reheat the pan, make the fried rice, and add the omelet back in at the end—but only watch the part after the egg has been cooked, since yours is.

A flat, unfilled omelet also makes a delicious stand-in for wheat or rice or buckwheat noodles in a lunchtime soup. Thinly slice the omelet into ribbons and then warm them in soup for the last min or so of its simmering.

Or make a Panino with Omelet. Follow the recipe for Panino con la Frittata (p. 158) but, because American omelets tend to skimp on olive oil, drizzle everything liberally with olive oil before putting the top piece of bread on your panino.

PANCAKE BATTER

If eaters will accept less lofty ones—which these will be, due to the diminished activity of their rising agent—you can refrigerate and use pancake batter to make more breakfast pancakes tomorrow. If flatter pancakes won't be eaten for breakfast, make them as crepes for lunch, rolling up kimchi and cheese, or scrambled egg and anchovy, or roasted mushrooms and greens. Or slice and eat the pancakes as noodles, as in Frittaten Suppe (p. 190). Or use the batter for savory leftovers pancakes, using a grain, or another leftover vegetable, like corn, or leftover cooked greens, or just kimchi, with some of its juice added to the batter.

PANEER

A small amount of paneer that didn't make it into a recipe is wonderful added to any other sabzi or masala sauce. Warm either with a little liquid added to keep things from burning, and add paneer. Eat as a warming if nameless accompaniment to rice. Paneer also makes good grilled cheese, especially with a little achar and cilantro chutney. Or make:

PANEER CHAAT (*5 min*)
¼ cup thinly sliced red onion, ¼ tsp salt plus to taste, lemon or lime juice, 1½ tbsp peanut or vegetable oil, 2 cloves garlic (minced), 2 small green chiles

(chopped), ¼ tsp ground turmeric, ¼ tsp ground cumin, ½ block paneer (cubed), ½ bunch cilantro (leaves and stems, chopped). *For serving*: a flatbread or paratha or a bowl of potato chips, yogurt.

In a bowl, combine the red onion, salt, and lemon or lime juice to cover. Let sit 10 min, then drain. Meanwhile, in a skillet, heat the oil. Add the garlic, chiles, and a sprinkle of salt. Cook until beginning to sizzle, then stir in the turmeric and cumin. Add the paneer and cook to warm. Stir in the cilantro, taste for salt and adjust. To serve: place flatbread or paratha or chips on a plate, top with the paneer chaat, drizzle with yogurt, and eat. (Adapted from Simon Majumdar)

PARMESAN, OLD

Parmesan is definitionally old. I scrape off any bits of mold that develop proceed. You must decide your own limits. Consider retaining the rind, regardless.

PARMESAN RINDS

The rind of Parmesan, or any hard grating cheese, makes an exemplary addition to beans, and minestrone, and ribollita, and pappa al pomodoro, and meat or vegetable stock. It adds indispensible umami. Fish the rind out before eating, and if there's anything left, rinse and reuse it once more before composting. Or make:

PARMESAN STOCK (*2–3 hr, but all waiting*)
5–6 Parmesan rinds, ¼ onion (or the peels of 1–3 onions), a little carrot peel, a few celery leaves or a piece of fennel frond, 1 bay leaf, 3–4 cloves garlic, a few parsley stems, a few sprigs of hardy herbs (optional; thyme and rosemary), ½ cup white wine.

In a stockpot, combine ingredients with 8–10 cups water. Bring to a boil, then reduce to a simmer and cook until it's flavorful and delicious, 2–3 hr. Strain well. This is a delicious base for bean soup, or vegetable soup, or Marcella Hazan's Passatelli in Brodo (p. 183), or risotto. This is unsalted, leaving room for salt whenever the next ingredients are added. You can reuse the rinds for another batch of stock if there's still cheese left on them.

If you have only 1–2 rinds, use them in the Savory Stock/Broth (p. 247), which is similar to the Parmesan Stock but needs fewer Parmesan rinds and can be made even more quickly.

PASTRY DOUGH

Leftover pastry dough is most charitably handed to the youngest person in the household, who can choose whether to twist or braid it, then brush it with melted butter, sprinkle with sugar, bake until golden, and eat.

PECORINO ROMANO

As with a number of other foods I've crudely lumped together, while Parmesan and Pecorino Romano are different, their leftovers function interchangeably. So, for the sake of relative brevity, I continue to lump.

See Parmesan, old (p. 165).

QUESO FRESCO

CORN AND QUESO (*10 min*)
1 tbsp neutral oil (peanut or grapeseed), 4 ears corn (shucked and kernels cut from cobs), 2 tbsp butter, ½ tsp ground chile powder (or ¼ tsp each cayenne and chipotle powder), 1 lime, ¼–½ cup crumbled queso fresco, chopped cilantro, salt.

Heat a cast-iron skillet. Add the oil and cook the corn until blackened in places. Remove from the heat, stir in the butter and chile powder, squeeze the lime over, then crumble queso over it all, and scatter with cilantro. Sprinkle with salt to taste.

SAVORY QUESO WAFFLES *(40 min)*
2 cups (240 g) all-purpose flour, 4 tsp baking powder, 1 tsp salt, 1¾ cups
milk, 2 large eggs, ½ cup melted butter or olive oil, 1 cup corn kernels, ½ cup
crumbled queso fresco, 1 chopped jalapeño (optional), olive oil or ghee for the
waffle iron. *Optional for serving:* fried eggs, sliced avocado, chopped cilantro,
hot sauce of choice.

In a bowl, whisk together the flour, baking powder, salt, milk, eggs, and
melted butter or olive oil. Stir in the corn, queso, and jalapeño (if using). Heat
the oven to the lowest setting. Heat a waffle iron and coat with olive oil or
ghee. Cook the batter in a waffle maker until crisp, about 3 min. Keep warm in
the oven as you make more waffles. Serve with any of the optional accompaniments. (Adapted from My Kitchen Love website)

RACLETTE

Use any leftovers in Creamy Mac and Cheese (p. 144), Variable Cheese Sauce
(p. 144), Fromage Fortissimo (p. 145), or Gougères (p. 146). For ideas on what
to do with raclette garnishes, see *crudités* (p. 463).

RICOTTA

Ricotta is its own self-contained transformation. If you have leftover ricotta
and cooked greens, you have an ideal sandwich. A dollop of ricotta makes
leftover pasta and leftover pizza infinitely more appealing. Or toss the last of
the ricotta with just-cooked pasta, where it will become a sauce. If you have
the will and the leftovers, leftover ricotta is miraculous mixed into leftover
creamed spinach, or leek and potato mash, or just mashed potatoes, and the
whole thing baked to bubbling and hot in a 400°F oven. This makes of two
rich things an even richer one. It is a filling delight.

Or if you have a good deal you're worried will go bad, make:

SAVORY BAKED RICOTTA *(45 min)*
2 cups leftover ricotta, 2 tbsp olive oil, 1 egg yolk, 2 tbsp chopped fresh thyme
or parsley leaves (or a combination), salt, freshly ground black pepper.

Heat the oven to 425°F. In a bowl, mix the ingredients well, then add salt and black pepper to taste, underseasoning slightly because water will evaporate during baking. Spread the mixture into a small gratin dish. Bake for 30–35 min, until toasted and brown on top. It will inflate, and then deflate, and be delicious throughout.

SHAKSHUKA

SHAKSHUKA SANDWICH (*10–15 min*)
4–6-inch length baguette (halved horizontally as for a sandwich), ½ clove garlic, 1–2 tbsp olive oil, ½ cup shakshuka, salt, 4–5 leaves fresh basil or a handful of cilantro leaves.

Toast the baguette until just warm and crisp, then immediately rub both with the cut side of the garlic. In a little pan, heat the oil and add the leftover shakshuka, not worrying what amount of tomato and pepper and egg you're warming but smashing it all up with a wooden spoon. Taste for salt and adjust. Smoosh the warm shakshuka onto the bottom piece of the baguette, including all the olive oil from the pan. Top with the herbs, then second baguette half, and eat.

SOUFFLÉ

Soufflés can be eaten cold or reheated in a 375°F oven for 5–10 min. I eat leftover soufflé on toast, because I like everything on toast. In a note to me on the subject, the author Deborah Madison recommended frying leftover soufflé in a bit of butter, pointing out that nothing has ever suffered from the treatment.

SOUFFLÉ BASE, RAW

Soufflé base that hasn't been souffléed can be refrigerated for 3 days without any change to the quality of the eventual soufflé. This is worth keeping in mind. If you want to make a soufflé but are anxious about it, make the base ahead, store it, covered, then bring it to room temperature before adding the egg whites and baking.

SOUR CREAM

A leftover sour cream problem is likely a real estate shortage—a spoonful left in a large container and shelf space needed for a fuller one. In that case, consolidate: Add the leftover sour cream to a newer container of sour cream. Or add it to a container of Greek yogurt, or crème fraîche, or ricotta, or mascarpone, which only differ by degrees.

STRING CHEESE

This is a reminder that string cheese is low-fat mozzarella. It's good on pizza, or on meatball or greens sandwiches, or anywhere else you use mozzarella. It also makes excellent fried mozzarella sticks. To make string cheese mozzarella sticks, roll string cheese in beaten egg, then in bread crumbs, and fry until hot and golden.

TEMPURA BATTER

As long as it has been refrigerated and smells fine, leftover tempura batter makes great, crisp onion rings.

ONION RINGS (*10 min*)
Peanut or grapeseed oil for deep frying, onion (cut into thin rings), ½–1 cup tempura batter, salt.

In a deep pot, heat 2–3 inches of oil to about 365°F. Dip the onion in the tempura batter, separating the rings. Fry in batches, until golden and crisp. Drain on paper towels, salt, and eat.

WAFFLE BATTER

Waffle batter can be refrigerated and used the following day to make waffles, or pancakes, or muffins. For waffles or pancakes, proceed, anticipating diminished rise. For muffins, whisk in an extra egg and any additions (grated carrot, chopped nuts, seeds, grated coconut, dried fruit, etc.) and bake at 350°F until a skewer emerges mostly clean, about 18 min.

WELSH RAREBIT

WELSH RAREBIT POUTINE (*5–30 min*)
French fries (homemade or frozen), Welsh rarebit, salt, snipped chives.

Cook the French fries. Meanwhile, in a small saucepan, reheat the rarebit over very low heat, stirring constantly, taking your time, to avoid breaking. Salt the fries, tip the rarebit over, garnish with chives, open a beer (or pour a glass of Gamay), and eat.

WHIPPED CREAM

BETTER COFFEE OR TEA
Leftover whipped cream, morning beverage.

Scoop as much whipped cream as you want onto your morning drink and enjoy.

YOGURT

Yogurt is soup if you need soup. It is dressing if you need dressing. It is spread, salad, sauce, smoothie—as the occasion demands. Yogurt is already fermented and takes ages to go bad. If it tastes acrid, dispose of it. Otherwise, even small amounts of yogurt can do everything and anything. Add finely chopped herbs, like dill or parsley or mint, to make a yogurt sauce for drizzling, adding olive oil or heavy or sour cream if the resulting sauce tastes lean. Or pound some garlic and add it to yogurt and drizzle it uninhibitedly, especially over rice. Or drizzle or dollop the yogurt, as is, on anything, from soup to salad to sandwich. A spoonful of yogurt works wonders in a vinaigrette in place of mustard, or whisked into mayonnaise, like lemon juice, for acid. Yogurt can be substituted for any amount of milk or buttermilk or sour cream in a cake or muffin recipe, and it's fine if just 1 tbsp of the overall amount is yogurt and the rest is milk or buttermilk, etc. Or make the simplest dip by combining a cup of well-roasted eggplant or zucchini or peppers, ½ cup yogurt, and ½ clove garlic (minced), plus a little pinch of salt in a blender and blend to semismooth, then eat with flatbread or vegetables or in a sandwich. Or make:

COLESLAW DRESSING (*5 min*)

Not just for coleslaw; use it for other things, too.

⅓ cup plain yogurt, 1 tbsp cider vinegar or rice vinegar, ½ tsp Dijon mustard, ¼–½ tsp salt, ½–1 tsp sugar.

In a bowl, whisk everything together. For coleslaw, mix into 2 cups thinly sliced cabbage. Top with freshly ground black pepper. To use this in a rémoulade, mix with julienned celeriac or beet or carrot. Add a dab more mustard and a handful of drained capers.

HERBY DRESSING (*5–10 min*)

½ clove garlic, salt, ½ cup mayonnaise, ⅓–½ cup plain yogurt, 2–3 tbsp olive oil, 2–3 tbsp chopped herbs (parsley, chives, dill), freshly ground black pepper, a few drops vinegar or lemon juice (optional).

Mash the garlic to a paste with a pinch of salt. In a bowl, combine the garlic, mayonnaise, yogurt, oil, herbs, 1–1½ tsp salt, and black pepper to taste. Taste for acid and add a few drops of vinegar or lemon juice if needed. Use to dress lettuce salads.

YOGURT PARFAIT

PARFAIT SMOOTHIE BOWL (*10–15 min*)

1 cup milk, 1 cup yogurt parfait, 1 cup frozen fruit (blueberries or strawberries, etc.), maple syrup.

In a blender, combine the milk, yogurt parfait, frozen fruit, and as much maple syrup as you want and blend until you like the consistency. If there was granola in the parfait, it will always be slightly textured. Chill for 10–15 min in the freezer and eat out of a bowl with a spoon with more fruit on top if you like. You can add whatever other nut, fruit, or dairy you have, as you are moved to.

HOW TO GROW OLD

Bread

> Grow old along with me! The best is yet to be!
>
> —*Robert Browning, "Rabbi Ben Ezra"*

S tale bread can't be asked to act like fresh bread. It will abstain. But if you regard it as it is—its dark brittle crust, its dry, absorbent crumb—and set your mind to work upon its new qualities, making plans to crisp it further into croutons, or grind it into bread crumbs, or poach it into panade, stale bread is dazzling in its flexibility and willingness.

I try to slice and freeze bread when it is long of fresh and short of stale. Then, any time I want, I can make a meal of it, and feel justified in having bought and eaten only half a loaf of good bread. I think of a meal thus made as Big Toasts, and I eat and serve it often, because it puts good bread and vegetables or cheese or fruit or eggs at the center of the plate, giving more proteinaceous matter the night off.

The procedure for making Big Toasts is variable, but the bones are the same. Remove as many slices of bread from the freezer as there are mouths (or two per mouth, depending). Place them in the oven or toaster oven at 400°F. While the toast is toasting, warm any leftover roasted or sautéed vegetables in a small pot with a sprinkle of water. Rub the toast with the cut side of a garlic clove, then drizzle it with olive oil and top it with the warmed vegetables. Drizzle this with *more* olive oil, if you like, and consider anything else you might like to add, like grated Parmesan or Pecorino Romano, or a drizzle of yogurt, or ricotta, or chili sauce, or salsa. Or, if it's summer, thickly slice a tomato or an avocado (or both), add salt and pepper abundantly, top with herbs, and eat. Or remove the cold delicious leftover baba ghanoush or tzatziki or hummus from the refrigerator. Treat any as you would vegetables, salting and oiling and accessorizing your toast attentively and slathering the leftover dip wall-to-wall, so that each bite offers some of the best of everything. That is a Big Toast, and though it is not a Big Meal, two of them make a medium-size one. Plus, once Big Toasts are part of your own pattern, you can elaborate. Put your garlic-rubbed toast in the bottom of a bowl, and scoop hot beans on top. Or make a little herb salad and put that on your toast and squeeze it with lemon. Or top garlicky toast with leftover fish mixed with olives and capers and pickled onion. The Toast will be the meal, and it is ever available as long as you have sliced and frozen bread.

When facing bread that is harder and dryer, and not easily sliced, remember that over the course of human history, there have been many instances of bread just that hard and dry. There exist delicious solutions for every circumstance. Somewhere in the world, someone has used bread so coarse and dry it would serve as a doorstop to make a salad, a sauce, a soup, and a supper. I've included all the stale bread recipes I know here. But the world is big. There are more, and there is wisdom in each.

Here are some pillars of stale bread cooking.

TO MAKE FRESH BREAD CRUMBS

Saw off the crusts if you can; if not, leave them. Cut what remains into cubes or chunks. If the bread isn't totally dry, set an oven to 200°F, spread in a single layer on a sheet pan, and leave in the oven until hard and dry, then remove and let cool to room temperature. Grind in a food processor to fine or semifine crumbs. If there are any crumbs too large to easily use, set a medium-mesh sieve over a bowl and pour the crumbs through. Store breadcrumbs a bag or jar in the freezer.

TO MAKE TOASTED BREAD CRUMBS

Heat the oven to 400°F. Saw off the crusts if you can; if not, leave them. Grind the bread in a food processor into rough crumbs. Toss with a good deal of olive oil, spread on a baking sheet in a single layer, and cook until golden brown and crisp, 5–12 min, checking on them and mixing throughout. Remove to another surface immediately to stop their cooking. Cool, then store breadcrumbs in a bag or jar in the freezer.

TO MAKE CROUTONS

Heat the oven to 400°F. Saw off the crusts if you can; if not, leave them. Tear the rest into pieces of similar size. Toss with a good deal of olive oil and salt, spread on a baking sheet, and bake until golden brown and crisp, 10–15 min, checking on them and mixing them midway. Remove to another surface immediately to stop their cooking.

BAGEL WITH CREAM CHEESE

BAGEL FRITTATA *(30 min)*

2 tbsp butter, ½ onion (chopped), salt, 1 tbsp chopped parsley (or sage or rosemary), 1½ cups cubed bagel, 1½ cups grated mozzarella cheese (or a combination of mozzarella and Parmesan or Pecorino Romano), 6 eggs, 2 tbsp olive oil.

Heat the oven to 375°F. Heat an ovenproof skillet. Add the butter, onion, and ½ tsp salt and cook over medium heat until the onion is tender, 5–10 min. Stir in the herbs. Add the cubed bagel and stir to coat. Remove to a bowl to cool for a few min. Add the grated cheese. Beat the eggs with a little pinch of salt. Add to the bowl with the bagel. Wipe out the skillet and heat over medium-high heat. Coat well with olive oil. Add the egg mixture and move the set part toward the middle a few times. As soon as the sides have cohered, transfer to the oven. Cook until the top is just set, checking after 8 min, then again until it's done. Cool briefly in the pan. This is better room temperature than hot and is good made with any bagel and any combination of bagel other than cinnamon raisin.

Use leftover cinnamon raisin bagels in Bread Pudding (p. 182).

BISCUITS, OLD

Staling biscuits can be sliced, toasted and spread with butter or jam or whipped cream and eaten. If they are more than a few days old, they can be placed in a plastic bag or kitchen towel and pummeled into crumbs. Freeze and use as extra-buttery bread crumbs. Or use 2 cups crumbled or chopped stale biscuits in Stuffing (p. 181) or Bread Pudding (p. 182), or substitute for corn bread in Corn Bread Dressing (p. 186). Or use instead of cookies in the Summer Trifle (p. 477).

BISCUIT DOUGH SCRAPS

BISCUIT BITES *(10 min)*

Dough scraps, 4 tbsp (½ stick) melted butter, za'atar or dukkah or a masala (or for a sweet version, cinnamon sugar).

Heat the oven to 350°F. Line a baking sheet with parchment paper. Cut the dough scraps into 1-inch pieces and bake until golden, 7–10 min. Brush with the melted butter and top with chosen spices.

BREAD, OLD

If stale bread can still be sliced, it should be. Then it can be frozen and toasted as needed for Big Toasts (p. 175), or turned into croutons (p. 176), or bread crumbs (fresh, see p. 176, or toasted, see p. 176), or used to make ribollita.

Ribollita is the best soup in the world, and ironically the one that comes to mind when I hear the word "soup." It is ironic because ribollita is thick enough to stand a spoon in. It is mostly brown and singularly delicious.

RIBOLLITA *(1–2 hr)*
Olive oil, 1 medium onion (diced), 2 cloves garlic (sliced), 2 stalks celery (diced), ½ tsp salt plus to taste, ½ cup combined parsley and rosemary (chopped), ½ tsp chile flakes, 3 whole peeled tomatoes (fresh or canned; chopped), 1 bunch leafy cooking greens (kale, collards, or chard, stemmed and chopped; or 1 cup leftover cooked greens), 2 cups cooked beans, 2 cups broth (bean cooking liquid or any combination of chicken stock, liquid from cans of tomatoes, or water), 1 piece Parmesan rind, 2 cups cubed stale bread, freshly grated Parmesan cheese, freshly ground black pepper.

Heat a large pot. Add ¼ inch of olive oil, onion, garlic, celery, and salt. Cook until they begin to soften, about 5 min, then add the herbs and chile flakes. Add the tomatoes and cook over medium heat for a few min so everything can get acquainted. Add the chopped greens and ¼ cup water, cover the pot, and cook over medium-low heat until the greens are just wilted, 3–5 min. Add the beans, broth, and Parmesan rind and bring to a boil. Reduce to a simmer and add the bread cubes, along with ½ cup olive oil. Cover the pot and cook over the lowest possible heat for at least 45 min, stirring occasionally and adding water if needed to keep things from sticking. It's done when the bread is completely melted into the soup. At which point . . . stir in another ¼ cup olive oil, taste for salt, remove the cheese rind, and serve warm, topped with Parmesan and black pepper. Ricotta, Parsley Oil (p. 68), or pesto are all good dollops and drizzles for the top.

If you find yourself with only stale bread and no beans or greens to make ribollita, follow the directions for Ribollita, minus the beans and greens, using any combination of vegetable cooking liquids—bean broth, meat broth, or tomato liquid for the broth. Make sure to season it well, drizzle it heavily with olive oil, shower with freshly grated Parmesan and top it copiously with any roughly chopped fresh herbs like parsley, basil, or celery leaves. This is a simpler bread soup but it is nearly as good. If you have ribollita ingredients but not ribollita time, here is a quick version:

BREAD

FAST RIBOLLITA *(30 min)*

Olive oil, 1–2 tbsp chopped onion, 1 clove garlic (sliced), ½ tsp salt plus to taste, a few leaves rosemary (roughly chopped), 4 leaves cooking greens (kale, collards, or chard, stemmed and chopped; or ¼ cup leftover cooked greens), 2 cups broth (bean cooking liquid, or any combination of chicken stock, liquid from cans of tomatoes, water), 1 piece Parmesan rind, 1 cup cubed stale bread, ⅓–½ cup cooked beans, freshly grated Parmesan cheese, freshly ground black pepper.

Heat a large pot. Add ¼ inch of olive oil, the onion, garlic, and salt, and cook until they begin to soften, about 5 min. Add the rosemary and greens, stir through. Add the beans, broth, Parmesan rind, and bread. Partially cover, opening to stir occasionally, breaking up the bread with a spoon when you do. Add water if needed to keep things from sticking. Simmer on medium-low heat for about 20 min. Serve topped with Parmesan and black pepper.

All of the following old bread recipes occupy places in my personal culinary Pantheon.

SQUASH PANADE *(3 hr)*

¼ cup olive oil, 4 onions (sliced lengthwise into thin half-moons), salt, 6 cloves garlic (sliced), 1 tsp thyme leaves, ½ cup white wine, 2–3 quarts combined stock and water, 1 autumn squash (Honeynut or butternut), 10–12 thin slices stale bread, butter for greasing foil.

Heat a large heavy-bottomed pot. Add the olive oil, onions, garlic, and salt, and cook until they're completely soft, about 15 min, adding the garlic halfway through. Add the thyme, and wine and cook for 5 min. Heat the oven to 375°F. Add the stock to the pot and simmer for about 20 min. Taste. It should be delicious and highly seasoned. Peel and slice the squash into thin, bread-like slices. Toast the bread in the oven until it just begins to crisp. Build the panade in a medium roasting or gratin pan by setting down a layer of toast, then topping it with brothy onions, then squash, then more onions and broth, and finally the remaining toast. Make sure the top layer of bread is well soaked. Cover tightly with buttered foil and bake until a sharp knife easily pierces the squash, about 45 min. Uncover and bake until the liquid is absorbed and the top is glossy and browned, pressing down occasionally with a flat spatula to check, 10–15 min. Delicious warm or at room temperature.

PAPPA AL POMODORO *(1½ hr)*

½ cup olive oil plus to taste, ½ onion (sliced), 3 cloves smashed garlic, ½ tsp salt plus to taste, 6 whole peeled tomatoes (fresh or canned; roughly chopped), 1–2 pieces Parmesan rind, a handful of fresh basil leaves (stems reserved), 4 cups cubed stale bread, freshly grated Parmesan cheese.

Heat a medium pot. Add ¼ cup of the olive oil, the onion, garlic, and salt. Cook until softened, 5–10 min. Add the tomatoes and their juice, another sprinkle of salt, the Parmesan rind(s) and basil stems (you can wrap the stems and rind(s) in cheesecloth for ease of retrieval, or just let them bob around). Cook over low heat, stirring often, 20–30 min. Add the remaining ¼ cup olive oil and the bread, cover, and cook for another 20–30 min. Remove from the heat, add the basil leaves and let sit for 30 min. Taste for salt and adjust. Serve just warm, drizzled with more olive oil and topped with Parmesan. (Adapted from the now-closed Franny's Restaurant, Brooklyn, NY)

SALMOREJO *(30 min)*

About 2 lb fresh or canned tomatoes, 2 cloves garlic (roughly chopped), ¼ cup good sherry vinegar or red wine vinegar, 5 cups cubed stale bread, ½ tsp salt plus to taste, 1 cup very good olive oil plus to taste. *Optional garnishes:* chopped boiled eggs, shreds of Spanish ham, croutons.

Core the tomatoes, saving any juice. In a blender, in two batches if needed, blend the garlic, vinegar, some of the stale bread, and a small pinch of salt. Add some of the tomatoes and blend further. Then add more bread and tomatoes and any saved juices. In a slow, steady stream, add the olive oil, dividing in half if you are doing two batches due to blender size. Decide whether to add more olive oil by tasting. It should be quite thick and rich, but not sticky, and to your liking. Add up to another 1 cup if needed, slowly, stopping when your instincts say to. When all the ingredients are blended, taste for salt and vinegar and adjust. Serve this chilled, topped with any or all of the optional garnishes, or just an additional drizzle of olive oil.

STUFFING *(1½–2 hr)*
Butter for the baking dish, 8 tbsp (1 stick) butter, 2 cups thinly sliced leeks (well washed), 2 cups thinly sliced celery, 1 tsp salt, 3–4 cloves garlic (minced), 8 cups cubed stale bread, ¾ cup combined chopped hardy herbs (rosemary, sage, thyme, and parsley leaves), 2 cups chicken broth, 2 eggs (beaten).

Heat the oven to 350°F. Butter a medium baking dish. Heat a heavy-bottomed sauce pan. Add the butter, leeks, celery, garlic, and salt, and cook until softened, 5–10 min. In a large bowl, mix the bread with the sautéed vegetable mixture and the herbs. Add the broth and the beaten eggs and toss to moisten. Transfer to the prepared baking dish and press down. Cover with foil and bake until bubbling and set, 30–45 min. Uncover and cook until the top is crisp, another 30 min.

BREAD SALAD *(25–30 min)*
½ onion (cut lengthwise into thin half-moons), ½ tsp salt plus to taste, ¼ cup red wine vinegar, 2 cups cubed stale bread, olive oil, 2 cups cooked vegetables at room temperature (or chopped tomatoes or cucumbers), 1 cup fresh herbs (roughly chopped; basil, parsley, chervil, celery leaves).

Heat the oven to 400°F. In a small bowl, combine the onion, salt, and vinegar. Let sit for 10 min. Meanwhile, in a bowl, toss the bread cubes with a lot of olive oil and a sprinkle of salt. Spread on a sheet pan and toast until just crisp, checking after 10 min. Let cool. Reserving the vinegar, drain the onion and place in a large bowl. Add the toasted bread, vegetables, and herbs. Judiciously add some of the reserved vinegar, drizzle copiously with olive oil, and toss. Let sit 10–15 min, and taste for vinegar, salt, and oil. Adjust and eat.

FRENCH TOAST *(20 min)*
½ cup milk, 1 egg, ¼ tsp salt, 1 tbsp maple syrup, a few slices stale bread, ghee or butter for the pan.

In a shallow dish, whisk together the milk, egg, salt, and maple syrup. Soak the bread slices in the custard until they're suffused, 2–3 min a slice. Pan-fry in ghee or butter and serve with more syrup. If you run out of the milk-egg mixture, make more.

BREAD PUDDING (*4–5 hr, but almost all waiting*)
1 egg, 1 cup heavy cream, ⅓ cup sugar, 1 tbsp melted butter, ⅛ tsp ground cinnamon, a grate of nutmeg, softened butter for the baking dish, 2 cups cubed stale bread.

In a bowl, combine the egg, cream, sugar, melted butter, cinnamon, and nutmeg. Butter a smallish baking dish. Place the cubed bread into the dish. Pour the egg mixture over the bread and let sit 3–4 hr or until fully swollen with custard. Heat the oven to 350°F. Bake until slightly risen and browned on top, 35–40 min. Enjoy!

A variation is to use cinnamon bread. Another is to add raisins.

BREAD CRUSTS

Save crusts in a paper bag until you have enough. They'll get stale and dry, which is what you want. Traditionally, upma is made as a savory pudding, à la cream of wheat, or with leftover chapati. In both cases it's a soft, highly spiced, almost porridge–style dish. This sort-of version is quite crunchy. The rest of the flavors are assertive enough you won't notice if these crusts have jam, or cheese, or butter, or peanut butter left on them.

A SORT OF UPMA (*30 min*)
3–4 cups bread crusts, 3 tbsp cooking oil (peanut or vegetable), 2 tsp cumin seeds, 6–7 fresh curry leaves, ¼ tsp hing (asafoetida), ¼ tsp ground turmeric, 1 tsp finely chopped fresh ginger, 2 chopped green chiles, ½ onion (very finely minced), ½ tsp salt plus to taste, 1 cup chopped tomatoes, ½ tsp ground chile powder, ½ cup roasted peanuts, lemon or lime juice. *Optional garnishes:* cilantro leaves, a sprinkle of something crisp like bel phuri or fried shallots.

In a food processor, pulse the crusts to large crumbs. In a large pan, heat the oil. Add the cumin seeds and curry leaves. When they are sizzling, add the hing, turmeric, ginger, chiles, onion, and salt. Add the tomatoes and chile powder and cook until the tomatoes have cooked down, 10–15 min. Add the ground crusts and peanuts. Mix well. Taste for salt and adjust. Add a squeeze of lemon or lime juice just before eating. Top with any optional garnishes.

BREAD CRUMBS

Bread crumbs are themselves the product of a leftover, which makes it even more remarkable that they can transform even the simplest food. Toast bread crumbs (see p. 176) and then scatter them onto cooked pasta, or any vegetable or bean gratin, or over salads or cooked vegetables. They act like Parmesan or herbs, providing the contrast and crunch that makes a meal feel considered.

Bread crumbs can also become a pasta called passatelli—because the noodles are formed by being passed through a food mill or potato ricer.

MARCELLA HAZAN'S PASSATELLI IN BRODO *(30 min)*
7 cups chicken or beef stock, salt, ¾ cup freshly grated Parmesan cheese plus for serving, ⅓ cup fine dried bread crumbs, scant ¼ tsp grated nutmeg, 2 eggs.

In a large pot, bring the stock to a simmer, adding a little pinch of salt if it was unseasoned, tasting it for salt, and adjusting once it's warm. Meanwhile, on a work surface or in a big bowl, combine the Parmesan, bread crumbs, and nutmeg and form into a mound. Make a well in the center and crack in the eggs. Using your hands, knead it all into a dough, until it's mushy and combined. If it's too wet, add more bread crumbs and Parmesan. Put the dough in a food mill with the biggest disk in it over the pot of boiling broth. Press it through the mill directly into the simmering broth. Cook 1–2 min, remove from the heat, let sit 4–5 min, then serve with more grated Parmesan for eating.

Bread crumbs also make good dumplings, a variation on the theme.

HERBY BREAD DUMPLINGS *(35–45 min)*
½ cup fresh or dried bread crumbs, ½ cup milk, 1–2 tbsp butter, ½ cup very finely chopped onion, 1 tsp salt, 1 egg (beaten), ¼ cup chopped fresh dill, 3 oz cream cheese or Boursin, ¼ cup finely chopped parsley (optional), freshly grated Parmesan or cheddar cheese for eating.

In a medium bowl, soak the bread crumbs in the milk. Meanwhile, in a saucepan, melt the butter. Add the onion and salt and sauté until tender, 10–15 min, then remove from the heat. Add the egg to the bowl of bread crumbs and mix well, then add the onion, dill, and the cream cheese or Boursin. Form into dumplings of a size and shape you like. Bring a deep sauté pan of lightly salted water to a very low simmer. Add the dumplings and cook until slightly swollen and tender and cooked through, about 20 min. Remove to a plate and blanket with chopped parsley and grated Parmesan or cheddar. Eat hot.

Also very good in broth.

BRIOCHE, OLD

Stale brioche makes some of the best Bread Pudding (p. 182).

BRUSCHETTA

Tomato bruschetta, with or without its toppings, can be included in Ribollita (p. 178). Cube, dump in, and proceed. For any other leftover bruschetta, scrape off the toppings and use the underlying toast in any recipe for *Bread, old (p. 178)*.

BUNS, BURGER OR HOT DOG

The preservatives that keep burger and hot dog buns soft and fluffy encourage them to become luxurious Bread Pudding (p. 182). Both types of bun subside into creaminess with a brief soak in eggs and cream, and can be baked immediately, considerably shortening one's pudding time. Burger and hot dog buns are also a shortcut to Ribollita (p. 178), which normally requires some patience as dry, brittle bread absorbs broth and flavor and fat. Buns are quick, and a long simmering soup becomes a fast one.

CHAPATI, OLD

Chapati (and roti) have dozens of next-stage dishes that Indian and Pakistani and North African cooks know more about than I do. The following ideas are those I've practiced. It is worth following your interest and finding more recipes by cooks who are more expert.

Fit fit is usually made with injera.

KIND OF FIT FIT WITH CHICKPEAS *(30 min)*
1 stale chapati, 3 tbsp olive oil, 1 cup finely diced onions, 1 tsp salt plus to taste, ½ tsp spice mixture of choice (one you like, like berbere, or a masala), 2 cloves garlic (minced), 1 tbsp tomato paste, 1 cup drained cooked chickpeas. *For serving:* fried eggs, or yogurt (or both).

Cut the chapati into ½–1-inch-wide strips and set aside. Heat a pan over medium-high heat. Add the oil, onions, and salt and cook until the onion has begun to soften, 4–5 min. Stir in spice mixture and cook, stirring, another 30 sec or so. Add the garlic and cook over medium heat another 1–2 min. Add the tomato paste and cook until it starts to darken, about 30 sec. Add ½–¾ cup water and the chickpeas and bring to a simmer, then cook until it's integrated, about 10 min. Taste for salt and adjust. Turn down the heat, add the chapati, stir through, until wilted, and eat topped with whatever you like.

Leftover chapati can also be used in A Sort of Upma (p. 182), Naanchos (p. 190), Dip Chips (p. 192), Fattoush (p. 192), Makhlouta (p. 193), Kottu Roti (p. 194), Seyal Phulka (p. 194), or Chilaquiles (p. 197).

CORN BREAD, OLD

Stale corn bread, like stale biscuits, can be retoasted to nearly newness in a hot oven, then amply spread with butter, and taste especially good with a cup of strong tea.

Corn bread is also an aging bread of the highest order. Once it is stale, it can be crisped in hot fat and eaten with bacon and cooked greens. Or broken into pieces and dropped in a bowl of hot beans to be doused with chili vinegar, or turned into a Southern-style stuffing that is filling enough to be a meal.

CORN BREAD DRESSING *(1 hr)*
3 tbsp butter plus for the baking dish, ½–1 cup flavorful cooked pork (cooked and crumbled Italian sausage meat, or cooked bacon lardons), 1 cup combined chopped onion and celery, 1 tsp salt, 1 tbsp chopped sage or a combination of rosemary and thyme, 2 cups crumbled corn bread, 1 egg (beaten), ½ cup chicken stock. *Optional for serving:* a salad of sharp herbs like parsley and celery leaves tossed with Basic Vinaigrette (p. 376).

Heat the oven to 350°F. Butter a baking dish large enough to fit the corn bread. In a skillet, melt the butter, then add the cooked pork to warm through. Once it's sizzled, add the onion-celery mixture and salt and cook over medium heat until the vegetables can be broken with a wooden spoon, about 10 min. Add the herbs and mix through. Remove from the heat. Add the corn bread and mix well. Add the egg and pour into the baking dish. Add the chicken stock. Bake until slightly risen and browned on top, about 35 min. Top with herb salad (if using) and eat.

CRACKERS, OLD

Old crackers, whether or not they are already crumbs, can become them via food processor or rolling pin. They can then be used as bread crumbs. Or they can be rejuvenated as crackers.

RECRISPED CRACKERS *(15–25 min)*
Crackers.

Heat the oven to 225°F. Spread the crackers in a single layer on a baking sheet and put it in the oven until the crackers are crisp again.

CROISSANTS, OLD

Stale croissants should be reheated briefly in an oven. Slice in half horizontally and use to make a sandwich, especially of soft cheese, like brie or Robiola, or goat cheese or squares of dark chocolate or Nutella! Or, if croissants are so stale they shatter when you try to cut them, turn them into bread crumbs or use in Bread Pudding (p. 182).

ENGLISH MUFFINS

English muffins are packaged in a number that often exceeds a household's interest in them. Store English muffins in the freezer so that they survive until affection for their nooks and crannies is rekindled. English muffins that are thawed and toasted but not eaten can be turned into my version of my father-in-law's favorite childhood meal: raw spicy sausage or 'nduja spread thinly over and the combination broiled until cooked. His was ground beef. It was the 1960s.

FOCACCIA, OLD

Stale focaccia can still be used for sandwiches. This is especially true if it's scooped like a scooped bagel: its shiny crust left intact and its inner crumb removed. The removed crumb can be staled in a 200°F oven and then ground into crumbs and frozen until bread crumbs are needed. The shiny golden crust can be briefly crisped in a 400°F oven and layered with prosciutto and thinly sliced mozzarella and leftover cooked greens. Or with gruyère and butter and ham, or with roasted eggplant and olive paste, and so on. Stale focaccia also makes good Stuffing (p. 181).

FRENCH TOAST

If leftover French toast is in good shape, freeze it. Now you have instant French toast for the morning that demands it. Reheat it in a covered pan in the oven, top with syrup, and eat. Or cube leftovers and freeze them. When you make your next Bread Pudding (p. 182), include the French toast cut in cubes. If the French toast wasn't too sweet, you might also include the cubes in Ribollita (p. 178).

GARLIC BREAD

GARLICKY CROUTONS (20 min)
Garlic bread (torn into 1–2-inch pieces or cubed), olive oil, salt.

Heat the oven to 400°F. In a bowl, toss the bread pieces with a good deal of olive oil, even if it's already quite buttery. Taste for salt and add if needed. Spread in a single layer on a baking sheet and bake until crispy, 15–20 min, stirring after 10 min. So good on a Caesar or bitter greens salad, or any pureed soup, like the creamy version of Any Vegetable Minestra (p. 8).

SAVORY FRENCH TOAST WITH AN EGG ON TOP (10 min)
2 eggs, ¼ cup milk, olive oil or butter, 1–2 pieces garlic bread, salt, a handful of fresh arugula (or parsley and basil or celery leaves), freshly grated Parmesan cheese, freshly ground black pepper, hot sauce or chili oil.

In a shallow bowl, whisk together 1 egg and the milk. In a skillet, heat the olive oil or butter. Batter the garlic bread and cook into French toast. Remove to a plate. Add more olive oil or butter to the same pan and fry the second egg. Cook until the white is set and the yolk is as you like it, remembering to lightly salt the egg. Meanwhile, pile arugula (or herbs) atop the French toast. When the egg is done, nestle it over the greens and top with Parmesan and black pepper. Drizzle with olive oil and hot sauce or chili oil and eat!

GARLIC BREAD CRUMBS (20–30 min)
Further stale leftover garlic bread in a 250°F oven. Cool, then grind in a food processor to fine crumbs. Store in the freezer and use to coat chicken cutlets, or mozzarella sticks, or for scattering over pasta.

If you have cycled through all those and yearn for something new, garlic bread also makes good, garlicky Pappa al Pomodoro (p. 180).

INJERA, OLD

Injera makes especially good Kind of Fit Fit with Chickpeas (p. 185). It also makes great Dip Chips (p. 192).

KULCHA

Leftover kulcha makes good Naan Pizza (recipe below), Avocado and S'chug Naan (p. 190), Naanchos (p. 190), Dip Chips (p. 192), Fattoush (p. 192), Makhlouta with Pita (p. 193), or Quesadillas (p. 196).

LAVASH, OLD

I grew up with a Middle Eastern father, so pita was the stalwart at our table. It remains my lodestar. Lavash may be your lodestar, and I apologize for my bias. In these recipes, lavash can be used interchangeably with *Pita, old (p. 192)*.

MATZO, OLD

If you like matzo brie, it is a solution tailor-made for old matzo. I grind leftover matzo into crumbs, freeze, and use as bread crumbs.

MTABAQ, OLD

Leftover mtabaq makes good Kind of Fit Fit with Chickpeas (p. 185). It can also be substituted for naan in Naan Pizza (recipe below), or Avocado and S'chug Naan (p. 190). It makes good Dip Chips (p. 192), as well as excellent Fattoush (p. 192) and Makhlouta with Pita (p. 193).

NAAN, OLD

Stale naan can be made soft and pliable again by being sprinkled lightly with water, wrapped in a kitchen towel and warmed briefly, still wrapped, in the toaster oven. Now it will make a wonderful sandwich, like Sabich (p. 41), or a simpler one of sliced boiled egg, labneh, olive oil, herbs, and pickled chiles. Or use it for:

NAAN PIZZA (*10–15 min*)
Naan, olive oil, salt, tomato sauce, fresh mozzarella cheese, any other pizza toppings, fresh basil or other herbs.

Heat the oven to 450°F. Place the naan on a baking sheet. Drizzle with olive oil, then salt to taste. Spoon on tomato sauce, dot with cheese and any pizza toppings. Bake until bubbling, 5–7 min. Remove from the oven, top with basil or other herbs, and eat.

AVOCADO AND S'CHUG NAAN *(5–10 min)*
Naan, olive oil, ½ avocado, flaky salt, S'chug (p. 398).

Heat the naan in a toaster oven, drizzle with olive oil, smash big chunks of ripe avocado over, top with flaky salt, drizzle heavily with s'chug, and enjoy!

NAANCHOS *(25 min)*
2 or more pieces naan, ½ cup warm refried or freshly cooked beans, ½–1 cup grated cheese, ½ cup finely chopped onion, 2 tablespoons pickled chiles, sour cream, guacamole, cilantro.

Heat the oven to 400°F. Cut the naan into bite-size triangles. Lay on a baking sheet and toast until crisp, 8–10 min. Remove from the oven, cover with the beans, cheese, and onion and return to the oven until the cheese is melted, another 5–10 min. Top with the chiles, sour cream, guacamole, and cilantro, and eat.

PANCAKES

These ideas for leftover pancakes apply best to plain pancakes. But if yours contain fruit (or chocolate!) and you yearn to venture into the occasionally rewarding frontier of sweet-and-savory, proceed at your own risk.

FRITTATEN SUPPE *(10 min)*
2–4 cups good strong broth, a few cloves garlic, salt, parsley stems, lemon juice, 1–4 plain pancakes, a few tsp chopped fresh parsley or dill (or a combination).

In a small pot, heat the broth with the garlic, a pinch of salt, a bunch of parsley stems, and a little water. Simmer until it tastes good and flavorful, about 10 min. Add a little lemon juice. Taste for salt and acid and adjust.

Strain the broth. Slice the pancakes into thin strips. Place a handful in each bowl, ladle soup on top, and garnish with herbs.

CHOPPED EGG AND HERB SANDWICH (*10 min*)
1 Boiled Egg (p. 139, boiled until just set), 1 tbsp chopped fresh dill, 1 chopped scallion, 1 tsp mayonnaise, a squeeze of lemon juice or drop of vinegar, salt, 2 or more plain pancakes.

Chop the egg. In a bowl, combine the egg with the dill, scallion, mayonnaise, and lemon juice or vinegar. Season with salt to taste. Use to fill pancake sandwiches!

An alternative is to make sandwiches with very thin sausage patties and thinly sliced cheddar cheese and/or a fried egg.

PAPAD/PAPPADAM

PAPAD KI SUBZI/SABZI (*5 min*)
1 cup whole-milk yogurt, 2 tbsp chickpea flour, ¼ tsp salt plus to taste, 1 tsp ground coriander, ¼ tsp ground turmeric, 1 tsp ground Kashmiri chile or cayenne, 1 tbsp finely chopped fresh ginger, 1–2 chopped green chiles, 2 tbsp peanut or vegetable oil or ghee, 1 tsp cumin seeds, 1 bay leaf, 3–4 whole cloves, pinch of hing (asafoetida), 1–2 cups crushed cooked papads, chopped cilantro (optional).

In a bowl, combine the yogurt, chickpea flour, salt, coriander, turmeric, Kashmiri chile or cayenne, and 1 cup water and mix well. Pound the ginger and green chiles to a paste with salt. Heat a heavy-bottomed skillet. Add the oil or ghee. Add the cumin seeds, bay leaf, cloves, and hing. Once they stop sputtering, add the ginger-chile paste and stir-fry for a few sec. Add the yogurt mixture, bring it to a boil, simmer for a couple of min, then stir in the crushed papads. Remove from the heat and top with cilantro (if using). Good with hot rice!

PARATHA, OLD

Use parathas to make Kind of Fit Fit with Chickpeas (p. 185) or as a substitute for tortillas in Quesadillas (p. 196), or reheat in a hot cast-iron skillet, spread with ghee, and eat, hot and toasty and buttery straight from the pan.

PITA, OLD

I grew up on these, always spiced with za'atar.

DIP CHIPS (*15 min*)
Pita, olive oil, salt, any spices you like.

Heat the oven to 400°F. Cut the pita into wedges. Drizzle or brush with olive oil and bake until crisp, 10–12 min. Add salt and spices you like to taste. Good for dipping.

FATTOUSH (*15 min*)
Pita, grapeseed or peanut oil for frying, ¼ tsp salt plus to taste, 1 tbsp sumac, 1 clove garlic, juice of 1 lemon, 1 tsp pomegranate molasses, ¼ cup olive oil, 3 cups medium chopped cucumber, 1 cup medium chopped tomatoes, ½ cup thinly sliced radishes, 3 tbsp very thinly sliced scallion, 4–6 cups thickly sliced romaine lettuce (optional), ½ cup chopped parsley and mint.

If the pita is the two layered, pocket kind, separate the sides of the pocket. Chop into 2-inch pieces. In a small pot, heat 2–3 inches of oil to about 350°F. Working in batches, fry the pita to golden brown, removing them to paper towels as done. Lightly salt, then scatter with sumac. Pound the garlic to a paste with salt, adding any sumac you didn't sprinkle. In a small bowl, combine the pounded garlic and lemon juice and let sit for 5 min. Add the molasses and olive oil. Taste for salt and adjust. In a large bowl, combine the cucumbers, tomatoes, radishes, and scallion. Drizzle with dressing and toss gently to mix, only adding as much dressing as you like. Add the lettuce (if using) and the herbs. Mix through well. Add the fried pita and mix through just before eating.

Here is another version of beans and stale bread, of which I could eat a variation every day. I've been served makhlouta only once, at a Lebanese restaurant in Brooklyn, and I've never forgotten its unapologetic simplicity. I love it.

MAKHLOUTA WITH PITA (*overnight, but mostly waiting*)
1 cup each of 4 types of dried beans, 1 cup cracked wheat or freekeh, 1 cup olive oil plus to taste, 2 cups finely chopped onion, 2 tsp salt plus to taste, a scrape of baking soda, 3–5 pieces pita, grapeseed or peanut oil for frying.

BREAD

Soak the beans and wheat or freekeh together overnight in water to cover by a few inches. The following day, heat a pot big enough to hold all the beans and grains. Add the olive oil, the onions, and salt, and cook until tender and lightly golden, about 10 min. Add the beans and grains and add water to cover by 2 inches. Bring to a boil, reduce to a simmer, and skim any scum. Taste the water for salt and adjust, it should be well seasoned, like soup. Add the baking soda and cook until all the beans are tender and some have begun to break down, 2–3 hr. Add water as needed. If the pita is the two layered, pocket kind, separate the sides of the pocket. Chop into 2-inch pieces. In a small pot, heat 2–3 inches of oil to about 350°F. Working in batches, fry the pita to golden brown, removing them to paper towels as done. Lightly salt. To eat, top each serving of makhlouta with a big handful of fried pita and stir through. Drizzle with more olive oil if you like.

Stale pita also makes good A Sort of Upma (p. 182), Kind of Fit Fit with Chickpeas (p. 185), or Chilaquiles (p. 197) if it is very, very stale.

POORI/PURI

Substitute poori for papads in Papad ki Subzi/Sabzi (p. 191).

POPOVERS

Leftover popovers can be reheated in a 350°F oven until they're warm and slightly browned. Then cold butter and flaky salt should complete the amelioration. Or cube, freeze, and include in Stuffing (p. 181) or Bread Pudding (p. 182).

ROLL, DINNER

When faced with a leftover dinner roll, I am afflicted by a festive desire to make a picnic sandwich of butter and salted cucumber or herby Egg Salad (p. 150). Slice rolls, warm them in a 375°F oven, then sandwich either filling or whatever else needs sandwiching. Leftover rolls can also be used for Ribollita (p. 178), Pappa al Pomodoro (p. 180), Stuffing (p. 181), or Bread Pudding (p. 182).

ROTI, OLD

These are all good enough to warrant making extra roti.

KOTTU ROTI (30 min)

½ cup warm water, 2 tsp any masala spice mixture, ¼ tsp freshly ground black pepper, ½ tsp cayenne pepper, ½ tsp ground cinnamon, 3 tbsp neutral oil (peanut), ½ cup minced onion, 1 tsp salt plus to taste, 3 cloves garlic, 1 tbsp minced fresh ginger, ¼ cup chopped green chiles, ¼ cup thinly sliced cabbage, ¼ cup thinly sliced carrot, 2 eggs (beaten), 2–3 cups sliced or chopped roti.

In a bowl, whisk together the warm water, masala, black pepper, cayenne, and cinnamon. Heat a large pan. Add the oil, onion, and a pinch of salt. Cook until just softened, about 5 min. Meanwhile, pound the garlic and ginger into a paste with the remaining salt. Add to the onion and cook for a few sec. Add the chiles and mix through. Add the cabbage and carrot and stir-fry for 1 min or so. Add the masala mixture and cook until the vegetables are just tender, 3–4 min. Stir the eggs into the vegetables. Add the roti, mix well, and cook until the roti are coated and softened, 3–4 min. Taste for salt and adjust. (Adapted from The Flavor Bender website)

SEYAL PHULKA (25 min)

1 tbsp neutral oil, ½ tsp mustard seeds, 4 cloves garlic (chopped), 1–2 green chiles (chopped), ½ tsp salt plus to taste, 7–8 curry leaves, 1½ cups finely chopped fresh or canned tomatoes, ½ tsp ground turmeric, ½ tsp ground coriander, ¼ tsp ground chile powder, 3–4 roti (sliced or chopped), chopped cilantro, lemon or lime juice (optional).

Heat a large pan. Add the oil, then the mustard seeds and cook until the mustard seeds begin to sputter. Add the garlic and chiles and a tiny pinch of salt and cook until beginning to soften, about 1 min. Add the curry leaves, then the tomatoes, remaining salt, turmeric, coriander, and chile powder and cook over medium heat until the tomatoes have begun to melt and break down, about 5 min. Add 1½ cups water, bring to a boil, then add the roti and cook at a simmer. Add the cilantro and continue cooking until the mixture is fairly dry and the roti has softened. Taste for salt and adjust. Remove from the heat. Add a squeeze of lemon or lime if desired, and eat. (Adapted from Sindhi Rasoi website.)

VAGHARELI ROTLI (*20 min*)
2 tbsp neutral oil, ½ tsp black mustard seeds, ¼ tsp cumin seeds, 1 tsp finely chopped fresh ginger, 1 green chile (chopped), ¼ tsp salt plus to taste, 7–8 curry leaves, ¼ tsp hing (asafoetida), ¼ tsp ground turmeric, 3–5 roti (chopped or torn), ⅔ cup yogurt, salt, chopped cilantro.

Heat a large pan. Add the oil, then the mustard and cumin seeds and cook until they begin to sputter. Add the ginger, chile, salt, and curry leaves and stir to combine. Add the hing, turmeric, and 1 cup water. Bring to a boil, then add the roti. Reduce the heat and cook until the water has evaporated and the roti is soft, about 10 min. Stir in the yogurt and simmer until combined, about 2 min. Season with salt to taste. Add the cilantro and eat. (Adapted from Vegetarian Medley website)

SCONES

Leftover scones can be run quickly under a dripping tap and then toasted back into warm crispness. They can also be used instead of cake in the Cake Crumb Muffins (p. 476).

STUFFING

I love Thanksgiving dinner in sandwich form and find my annual one a depen-dable delight. I mention it to remind you that you can make one any time of year, as long as you have stuffing. Chicken works as well as turkey, and marma-lade or jam as well as cranberry sauce.

Or use your stuffing for morning-after waffles. These are satisfying and simple.

SOURDOUGH STUFFING WAFFLES (*10 min*)
Sourdough starter discard, stuffing, butter.

In a bowl, add as much sourdough starter discard to leftover stuffing as needed to make it into a very thick batter. Butter a waffle iron and cook as waffles. Eat with chili crisp.

Leftover stuffing can also be substituted for bread in Ribollita (p. 178), Fast Ribollita (p. 179), or Crouton Soup (p. 380). Any will be fine with a mixture of some stuffing and some stale bread.

TOAST, BURNT

Burnt toast is delicious, and can be scraped and buttered and eaten as is for an inimitable campfire experience that is so distinct, the toast both too carbonized and too cold to absorb the butter. It can also be used in the Squash Panade (p. 179) or in a version of the panade by Cal Peternell in his book, *Burnt Toast and Other Disasters*, which replaces the squash with 3 large, thinly sliced onions, sautéed in olive oil, and added, along with ½ cup grated cheese, to the burnt toast, and baked.

TORTILLAS, OLD

QUESADILLA (*5–10 min*)
2 stale tortillas, ½–1 cup grated cheese or enough to cover the surface of one piece well. *Optional additions:* leftover beans, pickled chiles, cilantro or arugula.

Place a tortilla in a hot cast-iron skillet and scatter the cheese thickly over it. Add any other ingredients. Top with the second tortilla. Reduce the heat slightly, cover, and cook until the bottom is toasted and the cheese has begun to melt, 1–2 min. Uncover and flip. Cook until you can smell the melted cheese and both sides are lightly toasted. Remove and eat, with more herbs and anything else you like.

TORTILLA CHIPS *(5–10 min)*
Oil for frying (peanut, grapeseed, or vegetable), tortillas cut into sixths, salt.

In a heavy pot, heat ½ inch of oil to 360°–370°F. Fry the chips in batches until golden and crisp, 1–2 min per batch, removing them to a rack or paper towels to cool, salting as soon as they're on the rack or towel. These should stay crisp for nearly a week.

TOSTADAS *(20 min plus more, depending on your toppings)*
Oil for frying (peanut, grapeseed, or vegetable), any number of tortillas, salt, anything you want to top your tostadas (cooked beans, refried beans, braised meat, shredded cheese, sliced avocado, radishes, cilantro, chopped chiles, or all of the above).

In a heavy pot, heat 1 inch of oil to 360°–370°F. Fry the whole tortillas in 2–3 batches, until golden and crisp, 1–2 min per batch, removing them to a rack or paper towels to cool, and salting as soon as they're on the rack or towel. Top with any toppings, and eat.

CHILAQUILES *(30–40 min)*
2–3 tbsp bacon fat or vegetable oil, 4–6 stale tortillas (quartered), 3 cloves garlic (smashed and chopped), ½ medium red onion (diced), ½ red or yellow bell pepper (diced), 1 tsp salt plus to taste, 1 cup chopped canned or fresh tomatoes (drained if canned), ½ tbsp pickled chiles (or a few dashes Tabasco or other hot sauce), 4 eggs, 1 cup cilantro or mint leaves, lime wedges, and grated or crumbled cheddar or queso blanco (optional).

Heat the oven to 400°F. In an ovenproof sauté pan, heat the fat over medium-high heat until hot enough to make the edge of a tortilla piece sizzle when it touches the fat. Working in 2 batches, fry the tortilla pieces until just golden, removing to a plate. Reduce the heat to low and add the garlic, onion, bell pepper, and salt. Cook until the onion has begun to soften, about 5 min.

Add the tomatoes. Cook until they have become a little stewy, 5–8 min. Add the pickled chiles. Add the fried tortillas and stir through, then partially cover the pot, and cook until the tortillas are completely tender, opening to stir every few min and adding drizzles of water as needed to keep it from sticking, 15–20 min. Make 4 little wells in the tomato-chip mixture. Crack the eggs into ramekins or teacups, then tip each into a well. Salt the eggs lightly. Transfer the pan to the oven, uncovered, and roast until the whites are set and the yolks are as you like them, 5–10 min. Remove, top with herbs, and serve with wedges of lime and cheese, if you want.

WAFFLES

Leftover waffles should be frozen. Now you have instant waffles. Reheat in the toaster oven.

HOW TO SPEAK PLAINLY
Beans and rice

If one uses soft words, even plain rice tastes good.

—*Kashmiri proverb*

I f you have cooked beans or rice, you are a short step away from a meal. You are, moreover, a short step away from beans and rice, of which there are, conservatively, a million wondrous variations, all good.

Recipes for beans and rice tend to specify a type of bean, a type of rice, a flavor base, condiments, accompaniments, and so on—all vital to a recipe's mission to guide you to gallo pinto, or arroz con frijoles, or jeera rice and dal, or rice and peas . . . and so on. It is reassuring to know that thousands of eaters have settled on those details over millennia, and that those combinations reliably taste good. But they are not the only defensible details and combinations. Beans and rice meals don't have to be specific, if striving for specificity complicates making beans and rice. Other than beans, rice, salt, liquid, and fat, no ingredient is essential. (I'm not arguing that you don't need what you *know* you need to make your mother's beans and rice. I'm saying that if you are tired and hungry you can vary the formula to make yours.) The principle of the pairing is seasoned cooked beans that are warm and flavorful, hot rice, and, if you are in the mood, a contrast—like herbs, or hot sauce, or citrus, or yogurt, or, or, or . . .

With a pot of cooked rice, you are also only one short step away from fried rice, and rice salads, and rice soups, and more. They all store perfectly, cooked, and can be heated using basically any warming implement in the kitchen, from hot plate to microwave.

I've had to practice rice cookery for years to gain confidence. The best approach I've found to both rice cooking anxiety *and* rice cooking errors is to cook only one type for a duration—long enough to get good at it. I have been cooking Koshihikari rice for several years now. I stray. When I make sambar, I cook basmati rice, and when I make larb, I cook sticky rice, and when it is summer and there are tomatoes and basil, I cook farro. But I have the hang of Koshihikari, and I start many meals by rinsing two cups of it, bringing it to a boil with a pinch of salt, and letting it simmer for 20 min. By dinnertime I find several things to go on top.

For cooking grains other than rice, like spelt or farro, I have a slightly different method. I place a pot of water on the stove. Once it boils, I season it to taste like soup, rather than the pleasant seawater of a pasta- or vegetable-boiling pot. I then add garlic or garlic peels, and a bay leaf and a cheese rind if one's around. I add the grain and cook it at a low burble until it is completely tender and delicious—ascertained by tasting rather than obedience to a timer. I strain and keep the liquid, which is indispensable. *(See Farro Cooking Liquid, p. 225.)*

Grains thus cooked have wide-open futures. They can be eaten with beans or vegetables or tofu or meat or fried or turned into soups or stews or salads or porridges. As with any project you begin bravely, what to do next will reveal itself to you when it's time. Once you top farro with leftover cooked greens, you'll think of adding a fried egg, and a scattering of chaat masala or za'atar or another spice mixture over it all. Or after you've arranged a few lunar pieces of ripe avocado, adding a dollop of leftover techina and a shake of hot sauce will seem inevitable. Or something else will, that hasn't yet occurred to me.

When you find yourself with multiple bags each containing a small amount of different sorts of rice and grain, cook each on its own and them combine them afterward, with a handful of fried onions or shallots for crunch. Or, make congee or jook or a similar porridge, where all the grains are meant to burst anyway. For those, the contents of all the bags can be combined in a big pot with a lot of flavorful liquid and cooked until soft and uniformly porridge-y.

Other than lentils, which I cook as I do grains, I cook all beans according to one method. After a night-long soak in water (with or without salt; both are fine), beans are either drained and covered with ¼–½ inch new water, then put on the stove, or put directly on as is. There are those who claim that fresh water is the path to less windy digestion. I have a friend who was taught that pounding a bag of beans on the table before soaking and cooking is a more reliable path. Others say that beans make gas in our bodies regardless of what we do. I soak and drain and refill unless I don't.

Being judicious with the amount of cooking water is key. As Harold McGee wrote, "These seeds are best cooked in just enough water for them to soak up *and* to cook in." Too much water dilutes the beans, leaving them tasting watery; too little and they parch and crack. To a judiciously watered pot, I add a handful of salt, fennel stalks, a bit of carrot, a bay leaf, parsley stems, a garlic clove or peel, a cheese rind, and a tiny scrape of baking soda. Once the pot has boiled, I skim off the scum that rises, add a copious amount of olive oil, and lower the heat until the pot emits nothing but an occasional hiccup. I wait. The beans bathe, as they must. Harold McGee, on the temperature of a bean pot: "Though boiling temperatures speed cooking, the turbulence of boiling water can damage the seed coats and cause the beans to disintegrate; lower temperatures are slower but gentler." For silky beans whose skins are (mostly) unbroken and whose cotyledon (the meaty part) is tender and velvety, cook them at the merest bubble or just below it and continue until the beans are almost pudding-like inside yet structurally sound without. Add water as needed to keep the beans just submerged, as you would like to be in a bath. How long this bath takes varies with the bean and its age. But it produces the most delicious beans. Beans are done cooking when five are perfectly tender. If five do not meet that description, they are not done. After all the resources you've dedicated, it would be a shame for the effort to fall short. Cook beans until they are done, and you will be rewarded.

Beans store perfectly in both the refrigerator and freezer, and like any slow-murmuring food, are better after a day of post-cooking rumination. Beans make broth—much as the herbs and vegetable scraps in your bean pot make beans. The symbiotic development of the two ingredients is inviolable. Neglect the broth, and the beans will not be good; neglect the beans, and the broth will be lifeless. Attend to both and you will have made beans and soup, which you can use to their very lasts. I served a warm mug of bean broth with not a bean in sight to a friend too jittery to eat on the day of her wedding, and she credits it with her steadiness the rest of the day.

Here are some beans and rice things that matter:

RATIOS OF RICE TO LIQUID
Basmati: 1:1¾
Jasmine: 1:1¼
Short-grain Japanese white, like Koshihikari: about 1:1 or per package directions
Short-grain Japanese brown: 1:2
Medium-grain brown rice: 1:1½

FRIED RICE
1–2 tbsp peanut or vegetable oil, 2 shallots (thinly sliced), 1 chile (thinly sliced) or 1 tsp sliced pickled chiles, 2 cloves garlic (finely chopped), 1 cup leftover rice, ¼ tsp salt plus to taste, ½ cup chopped crisp vegetable (cucumber or radish), 2 cups chopped herbs (cilantro, basil, mint, or a combination), a squeeze of lime juice or a drizzle of wine vinegar, ½ tsp sugar, 2 tsp fish sauce. *Optional for serving:* 1 fried egg per person.

Heat a wide pan or wok. Add the oil. Once it's just begun to smoke, add the shallots, chile, and garlic. Fry for 5 sec, then add the rice. Spread the rice over the surface of the pan and add the salt. When it seems like every grain has had a moment to fry, scoop the rice all together, add the crisp vegetable, herbs, and lime juice or vinegar, sugar, and fish sauce, and toss and stir well. Taste for salt and adjust. Very good with a fried egg per bowl.

AMY'S PILAF

2 tbsp butter, ½ cup chopped white onion, 2 cups long-grain white rice, 3 cups meat or vegetable broth, 1 bouquet garni (1 sprig thyme, parsley stems, a bay leaf).

Heat the oven to 400°F. Heat an ovenproof pan. Add the butter, onion, and salt, and sauté until tender, 5–10 min. Add the rice and cook until just opaque. Add the broth and bring to a boil. Place the bouquet garni on top. Cover, transfer to the oven, and bake until the liquid is absorbed and the rice is completely cooked, about 17 min. My mother (Amy) always left the bouquet garni in the rice for serving, and I find its bedraggled aspect charming.

RISOTTO

3 tbsp butter, ½ onion (chopped medium-fine), ½ tsp salt plus to taste, 1 cup risotto rice (Arborio, Carnaroli, or Vialone Nano), ¼ cup white wine, 5–6 cups stock (meat, fish, vegetable or other), freshly grated Parmesan cheese, lemon juice, freshly ground black pepper.

Heat a medium pot. Add the butter over medium-low heat. Add the onion and salt and cook, stirring occasionally, until tender, 5–10 min. Add the rice, stir to coat with the butter and cook until opaque. Add the wine and cook until you can no longer smell it. Add the stock by the ladleful, stirring occasionally, adding more stock as soon as an empty spot appears on the pot bottom. Continue until the rice has absorbed the stock and is tender but not mushy and still has a slight soupiness to it. Taste for salt and adjust. Add Parmesan and a squeeze of lemon, then serve, topping with black pepper and more Parmesan if you want.

BEST GRAIN OR BEAN SALAD

Basic Vinaigrette (p. 376), 2 cups cooked grain or beans, 2 tbsp chopped fresh oregano, 2 tbsp drained capers, big pinch of chopped fresh chives, ½ cup roughly chopped almonds.

Make the vinaigrette. In a bowl, mix the grain or beans with everything but the vinaigrette. Drizzle in the dressing, tasting as you go, until it tastes wonderful. Good at room temperature.

FALAFEL

1 cup dried chickpeas, 1 cup chopped onion, ¼ cup combined chopped parsley and cilantro, 1 tsp salt, ½ tsp ground chile powder, 4 cloves garlic, 1 tsp ground cumin, 1 tsp baking powder, 4–6 tbsp chickpea flour, oil for frying.

Soak the chickpeas in water overnight. Drain and add to a food processor. Add the onion, herbs, salt, chile powder, garlic, and cumin and pulse until blended but not smooth. Add the baking powder and 4 tbsp of the chickpea flour. Pulse to smooth, then try to form into a ball. If it's still too wet, add the remaining flour. Remove to a bowl and refrigerate at least 1 hr. Form into walnut-size balls. In a deep pot, heat 3–4 inches of oil to 350°–375°F. Working in batches, fry the falafel. Drain on paper towels or a cooling rack. (Adapted from the Epicurious website)

FARINATA

1½ cups chickpea flour, ¼ cup olive oil, ½ tsp salt, 2 cups water.

In a blender, combine the chickpea flour, olive oil, salt, and water and blend on high. Let sit for 1 hr. Heat the oven to 450°–500°F. As the oven heats, preheat a pan at least 14 inches wide. Heavily oil the pan, add the batter, cook until set, then broil until lightly browned in places.

TORTA DI RISO

1 cup Arborio rice, 1 cup whole milk, salt, olive oil, 1 egg (beaten), 1 heaping tsp freshly grated Parmesan cheese, about 4 oz ricotta cheese.

Rinse and drain the rice. In a small pot, combine the milk and 1 cup water and bring to a boil. Once it's boiling, add a pinch of salt. Add the rice and cook over low heat until cooked through, 15–20 min. Remove from the heat, then leave to cool. Heat the oven to 350°F. When the rice is no longer warm to the touch, stir in 1 tbsp olive oil. When the rice is thoroughly cooled, add the egg, Parmesan, and half the ricotta. Heat a medium-size, heavy, ovenproof skillet over medium-high heat until warm, then coat the bottom with some olive oil. Press the rice mixture into it in a layer 1–2 inches thick. Remove from the heat, add the remaining ricotta in spoonfuls over the rice, pressing it in. Transfer to the oven and bake until set, about 10 min. Broil quickly to brown the top. Eat hot or at room temperature, cut into slices.

GRANOLA

5 cups rolled oats, 1¼ cups unsweetened shredded coconut, 1 cup sesame seeds, ¾ cup maple syrup, ½ cup olive oil, a scant ½ cup brown sugar, 1 tsp salt plus to taste.

Heat the oven to 300°F. In a large bowl, combine all the ingredients. Spread onto two sheet pans and bake for 15 min. Remove and stir and return to the oven, stirring and rotating every 10 min, until the granola is dry and toasted, about another 30 min.

ROASTED RICE POWDER (KHAO KHUA)

In a heavy-bottomed skillet, roast glutinous rice or jasmine rice in a single layer over medium-low heat until golden, 10–15 min. Remove from the heat, let cool, and grind in a mortar and pestle or in a spice grinder to a medium-fine, pebble texture.

A TADKA

In a heavy-bottomed saucepan or skillet, heat a few tbsp of a fat (ghee, coconut oil, or a neutral oil). Drop in any whole spice seeds (black mustard, cumin, fenugreek, coriander, cumin, nigella) as soon as the oil is hot enough to sizzle a seed. Let them sizzle until fragrant, a few sec. Add any larger spices and/or any dal (whole peppercorns, cracked cardamom, bay leaves, curry leaves, urad dal, chana dal) and sizzle until fragrant. Add any fresh aromatics that you want browned (ginger and onion), otherwise wait until the end. Add any ground spices (turmeric or hing/asafoetida, etc.). Add any dried chiles, then any fresh chiles, along with ginger and onion you don't want to brown. Add garlic, then remove from heat, add any chile powder you plan to add, and you are done! Be careful not to burn, and most vitally, take note of what you like and tailor your next tadka to your preferences.

ARANCINI

Arancini Poppers are a third generation leftovers dish, as the arancini themselves were likely made from leftover risotto. And they can continue to metamorphose.

ARANCINI POPPERS *(15 min)*
4 Arancini (p. 240, halved), 8 tiny cubes and 16 strips (2 inches wide) very thinly sliced cheddar cheese, 1 scallion (thinly sliced), a few slices pickled chile (finely chopped), 2 slices ham (cut into 8 pieces), freshly ground black pepper.

Heat the broiler. Arrange arancini halves cut side up on a baking sheet. On each half, place 1 cheese cube, a few slivers of scallion, some pickled chile and gently press. Drape each half with 1 piece of ham and 2 strips of cheese. Broil until golden, 6–8 min. Let cool on the pan, top with black pepper, then pop 'em. (From Danny Amend)

ARROZ CON GANDULES

Leftover arroz con gandules makes great Arancini (p. 240).

ARROZ CON POLLO

FRIED ARROZ CON POLLO *(10 min)*
2 cups arroz con pollo, 1–2 tbsp oil, 4–5 cloves garlic (finely chopped), salt, 2–3 thinly sliced scallions.

Shred or cut the meat from the arroz con pollo, then mix back in with the rice. Heat the oil in a wok or a large pan. Add the garlic and cook until it just begins to turn golden, salting lightly. Add the rice and meat. Stir-fry, trying to heat and fry the grains. Taste for salt and adjust. Add the chopped scallions. Eat. Also good with other herbs or pickled chiles added.

BARLEY, COOKED

BARLEY SALAD *(15–30 min)*

1–2 cups cooked barley, Basic Vinaigrette (p. 376), salt, 1 cup chopped (½-inch pieces) cooked or fresh vegetables (roast squash, turnips, parsnips, or carrots in fall and winter; fresh snap peas or radishes or cucumbers in spring; tomatoes in summer, etc.), 1 cup whole herb leaves (parsley, mint, celery leaves, cilantro, basil), ¼ cup toasted nuts (optional; pine nuts or chopped walnuts or almonds).

Bring the barley to room temperature. Make the vinaigrette. Lightly salt the vegetables. In a large bowl, mix 2–4 tsp vinaigrette with the barley. Add the vegetables, taste, and adjust salt. Add the herbs and nuts (if using).

A variation is to add a handful of thinly sliced scallions.

Cooked barley is also delicious in the Best Grain or Bean Salad (p. 206), or in place of rice in Savory Grain Pancakes (p. 238), A Version of Yam Kai (p. 239), or A Congee-esque Soup (p. 239). Like all other grains it can also be fried. Or substitute it for some or all of the beans or pasta in Minestrone (recipe below).

BEANS, COOKED

MINESTRONE *(1 hr–1 hr 20 min)*

½ cup olive oil, 1 cup mirepoix vegetables (any combination of onion, carrot, celery, leek, or fennel), 3 cloves garlic (sliced), ¼ tsp salt plus to taste, small pinch of chile flakes, the end of a piece of cured meat or hard salami (sliced), 1 cup herbs (any combination of parsley, thyme, marjoram, or basil leaves), 2–3 cups roughly chopped cooked or raw greens (any combination of kale, collard greens, Swiss chard, spinach, mustard greens, dandelion greens, broccoli rabe, escarole, cabbage—and their attendant stems, ribs, and cores), ½ cup chopped fresh tomatoes or drained and crushed canned whole peeled tomatoes, ½–1 cup chopped root vegetables (optional; if they are there and need to be cooked, or cooked and need to be eaten), 6 cups cooked beans, a Parmesan rind, 8 cups liquid (any combination of bean broth, stock, and liquid from cans of tomatoes), 1 cup small pasta (optional; orecchiette, tubini, small penne). *Optional garnishes:* Basil Pesto (p. 394), Olive Tapenade (p. 393), ricotta cheese, or parsley.

Heat a large pot. Add the olive oil, mirepoix vegetables, garlic, and salt and cook until tender, about 10 min. Add the chile flakes and any cured meat and stir to combine. Add the herbs, greens, tomatoes, root vegetables (if using), beans, and Parmesan rind, crushing the tomatoes against the side of the pot. Add the liquid to cover. Simmer until everything has agreed to become minestrone, 45 min–1 hr. Just before you eat the soup, cook pasta in a pot of boiling salty water, but only enough for the soup you're planning to eat that week. Stir the cooked pasta into the amount of soup you are serving. If you freeze minestrone, cook new pasta whenever you eat the minestrone you've frozen. Add any garnishes and eat!

For Pasta e Fagioli it is essential to use well-seasoned bean or farro broth. It is also best to refrain from making this with black beans or kidney beans, which will find happier homes elsewhere, like in Greener Greens and Beans (p. 47), Beans and Egg on Garlicky Toast (recipe below), or Beans and Greens and Egg (p. 212).

PASTA E FAGIOLI (15–20 min)

1–2 cups cooked beans, 2–3 cups well-seasoned bean or farro cooking liquid, 1 Parmesan rind, 1 sprig rosemary, salt, 1 lb short pasta (ditalini, orecchiette, lumache), 3–4 tbsp best-possible olive oil plus more to taste, freshly ground black pepper, freshly grated Parmesan cheese, lemon juice (optional).

In a large pot, combine the beans, cooking liquid, Parmesan rind, and rosemary and bring to a simmer. In a separate pot of boiling water salted to taste like pleasant seawater, cook the pasta. Or cook the pasta directly in the bean or farro broth, which means adding a good deal of extra water so that the pasta has somewhere to move around. Do this unreservedly, adding 1–2 more cups. If cooking in water, reserve ¼ cup of the pasta water just before draining. Remove the Parmesan rind from the beans. Tip the pasta into the bean pot (if it isn't already there) and stir well, adding the olive oil as you stir. Add a pour of reserved pasta water if needed. Add black pepper and top with Parmesan. I like the cozy richness of this, but if you are happier with a little contrast, a squeeze of lemon juice just before eating provides it.

BEANS AND EGG ON GARLICKY TOAST (5 min)

Optional cilantro-garlic paste (½ bunch cilantro, including stems, 2 cloves garlic, 2 tbsp olive oil, salt), ½ cup cooked beans, hard-crusted bread, 1 clove garlic, halved, 1–2 eggs, butter (or ghee or olive oil), Sichuan chili crisp or other beloved chili oil.

If your beans are canned, make the cilantro-garlic paste: Chop the cilantro and garlic, then pound to a paste with salt. Heat a small pot, add the oil, and cook the cilantro-garlic mixture over medium heat until it just begins to soften, about 2 min. In a small pot (the one with the cilantro-garlic paste if using), sprinkle the beans with a little water and warm them through. Toast the bread and rub with the cut side of the clove of garlic. In a small pan, fry the egg(s) in butter. When the beans are warm and the eggs cooked, spoon the beans over the toast, top with the egg, and dollop with chili crisp.

This is also good with sliced scallions on top. It is perhaps worth adding that beans are good in, on, or under any bread-like substance. Follow the procedure above, but spoon the beans over a tortilla, or in injera, or chapati or a dosa or a pita, and so on.

BEANS AND GREENS AND EGG *(10 min)*
¼–½ cup cooked beans, 1–2 cups leftover cooked greens (kale or collards or chard), 1–2 eggs, salt, olive oil, pickled chiles or a beloved chili oil (optional).

In a small pan, warm the beans and greens together with a sprinkle of water. When just bubbling, crack the egg(s) into the pan, salt each egg, then cover the pan and cook over low heat until the whites are set and the yolks as you like them, 3–5 min. Drizzle it all copiously with olive oil and eat topped with pickled chiles or chili oil (if using). Also good alongside or over toast.

BEAN GRATIN *(30–40 min)*
Olive oil, ¼ cup mirepoix (see p. 6) or 2–4 tbsp each chopped mirepoix vegetables (onion, carrot, celery or fennel), salt, 2–4 cups cooked beans, bean broth (or stock or water), 1–2 cups toasted bread crumbs (see p. 176), 1–2 tbsp chopped fresh herbs (parsley, rosemary, sage, or any combination).

Heat the oven to 375°F. Heat a small pot. Add a few tbsp of olive oil and warm the mirepoix (or cook the onion, carrot, and celery) with a pinch of salt until tender, about 10 min. Add the beans and mix lightly, then spoon into a small gratin or baking dish that will fit the beans in a 2-inch layer. Pour in enough bean broth to just begin to seep up around the edges of the beans. Bake until the beans are hot and the liquid is mostly evaporated and bubbling, about 10–12 min. Meanwhile, in a small bowl, combine the bread crumbs and herbs. Pull the baking dish out of the oven and layer the bread crumbs over the beans. Increase the oven temperature to 400°F and cook until the top is quite browned, 7–10 min.

BEANS AND SAUSAGE *(45 min–1 hr)*

Olive oil, several slices to 1 sausage per person (anything from a sweet or spicy Italian sausage to a hot dog to a German wurst to chorizo), ¼ cup mirepoix (see p. 6) or 2–4 tbsp each chopped mirepoix vegetables (onion, carrot, celery or fennel), salt, 2–4 cups cooked beans, bean cooking liquid (or stock or water), a few wedges of cabbage (optional; boiled in very salty water), 1–2 cups toasted bread crumbs (see p. 176).

Heat the oven to 325°F. Heat a medium pot. Add a drizzle of olive oil. Brown whatever sausage you're using, just to caramelize the outside. Remove to a plate. In the same pot, warm the mirepoix or cook the onion, carrot, and celery or fennel with a pinch of salt until tender, about 10 min. Add the beans, browned sausage, and bean cooking liquid to cover everything only by half. Transfer to the oven uncovered. After about 30 min, nestle in the cabbage (if using) amid the rest of it, and increase the oven temperature to 400°F. Cook until much of the liquid is gone and things look hot and a bit browned, 10–15 min. Scatter the top heavily with toasted bread crumbs, drizzle with olive oil, and broil until the top is browned and crisp.

If you don't have sausage, leftover braised meat works well here, too.

BEAN AND SALAMI SOUP *(20–30 min)*

1 cup olive oil plus to taste, ¼ cup chopped fennel or celery, ½ cup chopped onion, 1 tbsp chopped or sliced garlic, ½ tsp salt plus to taste, 2 tbsp chopped herbs (rosemary, parsley, cilantro, or savory), 2 tbsp tomato paste, ¼–½ cup chopped spicy or mild salami, ½–1 cup cooked beans, ½–3 cups bean liquid (depending on the quantity of beans), 1 big bunch cooking greens (kale, turnip, collard, broccoli rabe; stemmed and roughly chopped), ½ tsp ground cinnamon, ½ tsp Spanish smoked paprika. *Optional for serving:* toasted bread, Pecorino Romano or Parmesan cheese for grating.

Heat a medium pot. Add ½ cup of the olive oil, then the fennel or celery, onion, garlic, and salt. Cook until beginning to soften, about 5 min. Add the herbs and stir through. Add the tomato paste and salami and cook until the tomato paste begins to caramelize, another 5–10 min. Add the beans, bean liquid, and 3–5 cups water and bring to a boil. Reduce to a simmer and add the greens, cinnamon, paprika, and remaining ½ cup olive oil and simmer until the greens are tender, another 5 min or so. Taste for salt and adjust. If desired, serve over a thick piece of toast, drizzled with olive oil, and showered with cheese.

A variation is to put a fried egg on the toast and then ladle the soup on top.

FANCY SUCCOTASH (5 min)

1 tbsp butter or olive oil, ⅓ cup finely chopped fennel or celery, ¼ cup finely chopped onion, ½ tsp salt plus to taste, 1 cup cooked beans, 1 cup corn, 2 tbsp crème fraîche or sour cream, a few drops red wine vinegar.

Heat a sauté pan. Add the butter or olive oil, then fennel or celery, onion, and salt. Cook until beginning to soften, about 5 min. Add the cooked beans, corn, and crème fraîche or sour cream and stir through until all is warm and glossy. Add the red wine vinegar just before eating.

Also good with cooked bacon or a handful of fresh herbs sprinkled over the top, or topped with a fried egg.

Or use leftover beans in the Greener Greens and Beans (p. 47), Ribollita (p. 178), Fast Ribollita (p. 179), Best Grain or Bean Salad (p. 206), or Green Farro Soup (p. 225)!

BEANS AND RICE

FRIED BEANS AND RICE (25 min)

½ cup chopped peeled cucumber, salt, sugar, ¼ cup thinly sliced onion (or shallots or scallions), 1 tbsp plus 1 tsp rice vinegar, 1 tbsp olive or vegetable oil, 1–1¼ cups beans and rice, soy sauce, Spicy Mayonnaise (p. 396), a big handful of chopped herbs (cilantro, mint, basil, or any combination).

In a bowl, combine the cucumber with 1 tsp salt and 1 tsp sugar. Mix well, place in a sieve set over a bowl, then let sit for 10 min. (Use the cucumber liquid for a slightly salty soda, or drink as is, or add to a beer or gin.) Meanwhile, quickly pickle the onions by combining them in a bowl with

1 tbsp of the rice vinegar and a tiny pinch each of sugar and salt. Let sit for 10 min. Heat the oil in a pan, drain the pickled onion, and add to the pan, spreading it around. Cook for 10–15 sec, then add the beans and rice. Spread well, moving occasionally so it fries, but letting it stay and get browned and crisp in places. Add a sprinkle of soy sauce and the remaining 1 tsp vinegar and mix. When all the liquid has evaporated, scoop the rice and beans into a bowl, then top with spicy mayonnaise, cucumber, and herbs. (Adapted from *Superiority Burger Cookbook* by Brooks Headley)

BEANS, OVERCOOKED

If by the time your beans are tender, their skins have burst and they've turned to mush, blend them—leaving behind some of their cooking liquid—with a clove of pounded garlic and a long drizzle of olive oil. Now you have bean puree, which can top little crisp crostini or be spread on crackers or eaten like mashed potatoes with a hearty chop. A little pour of cream or a spoonful of ghee are good additions. Or, turn overcooked beans into soup by pureeing them with their liquid, adding a bit of stock or water if needed and a few drops of red wine vinegar. Or turn them into a version of hummus by blending them with a clove of pounded garlic, a squeeze of lemon juice, and a spoonful of tahini paste.

BEANS, UNDERCOOKED

Undercooked beans can be salvaged by being further simmered in flavorful fatty liquid. They will eventually surrender but may burst by the time they do. In that case, follow the instructions for *Beans, Overcooked (above).*

BEAN BROTH

Bean broth is already soup, albeit a subtle one. I am torn between rhapsodizing about the uses of bean broth, and leaving you the satisfaction of discovering them and finding your own evangelical language. In the meantime, use bean broth in Ribollita (p. 178), Fast Ribollita (p. 179), Minestrone (p. 210), Pasta e Fagioli (p. 211), Beans and Egg on Garlicky Toast (p. 211), Bean Gratin (p. 212) or Bean and Salami Soup (p. 213), and so many more . . .

BEANS, LEFT OUT OVERNIGHT AND FERMENTY

As with any food created by bacterial fermentation, fermented beans should be eaten at one's discretion. I have eaten these at my own and, discreetly, survived.

VERY SPICY BEANS *(20 min)*
Olive oil, at least 1 onion (chopped), a heck of a lot of garlic (sliced), a lot of spicy pickled chiles, a bunch of cilantro stems (finely chopped), salt, beans.

Heat a pot large enough to fit all your beans. Add a staggering amount of olive oil. Cook the onion, garlic, pickled chiles, cilantro stems, and a small pinch of salt over medium heat until the onion has softened, 5–10 min. Add the beans, leaving some of the liquid behind if you like. Stir and smash, simmer for 10 min, and then taste. They should be spicy and fatty and salty, with not a hint of fizz in sight. Very good with tortillas or any flatbread.

BIBIMBAP

BIBIMBAP FRIED RICE *(25 min)*
1 tbsp neutral oil (peanut or vegetable), 1 slice bacon (sliced), ½ tsp minced garlic, ½–1 cup sliced kimchi (drained), 1 cup bibimbap, 2 tbsp kimchi juice or 1 tbsp gochujang, 1 scallion (thinly sliced), ½–1 tsp sesame oil, 1 tbsp toasted sesame seeds, 1–2 fried eggs (according to your taste).

Heat a large pan over medium heat. Add the bacon and cook until it's beginning to crisp, about 5 min. Add the garlic and stir through. Add the kimchi and spread out. Add the bibimbap and cook, frying, until the grains have all had some time with the pan and are sizzling. Add the kimchi juice or gochujang and scallion, stir through. When the juice is absorbed, drizzle with the sesame oil to taste and remove from the heat. Serve topped with sesame seeds and fried eggs.

BIBIMBAP STEW *(5–20 min)*
1 cup bibimbap, 1 cup dashi (or miso or other strong savory broth), ¼–½ cup cooked and seasoned cooking greens, a sprinkle of gochugaru or other chile flakes, ½ block tofu (cubed), ½ tsp toasted sesame seeds.

In a pot, combine the bibimbap, dashi, greens, gochugaru, and tofu and bring to a simmer. Cook until just combined, then remove from the heat, garnish with the sesame seeds, and eat. Also very good with a halved, soft-cooked egg on top.

BIRYANI

BIRYANI PAKORA (*20–30 min*)

1 cup biryani, ½ cup finely chopped onion, 1 small green chile (finely chopped), ¼ cup chickpea flour, ¼ tsp salt, peanut or vegetable oil for frying, chaat masala (optional).

In a bowl, smash the biryani with a potato masher to a rough mash. Add the onion, chile, chickpea flour, and salt and smash well until the mixture can form a large ball. Lightly oil your hands and form the pakora into balls the size of golf balls. In a heavy-bottomed sauté pan, heat 3–4 inches of oil to 350°–375°F. Working in batches, fry the pakora until crisp and golden brown, 5–8 min. Sprinkle with chaat masala if you like. Very good with raita.

CASSOULET

BEANS AND EGGS WITH PARSLEY OIL (*10 min*)

1–2 cups cassoulet, 1 egg per person, salt, Parsley Oil (p. 68).

Remove any sausages from the cassoulet and slice into thick slices. In a small pot, brown the slices, then add the beans and bread crumbs, along with a few spoonfuls of water. Heat until warm. Crack eggs into individual ramekins. Make wells in the cassoulet and drop an egg in each, lightly salting each egg once it's in. Reduce the heat to very low, cover with a lid, and cook until the whites are just set and the yolks are as you like them. Remove from the heat, spoon into dishes, and drizzle copiously with parsley oil. Salsa verde is good here, too.

CHICKPEA PASTA *(30–45 min)*
1½–1¾ cups cooked chickpeas, 3 tbsp olive oil, 1 clove garlic (sliced), salt, freshly ground black pepper, ½ lb short pasta (orecchiette or fusilli or elbow macaroni).

In a small, deep pot, heat the oil over medium-low heat until the oil begins to shimmer. Stir in the garlic, reduce the heat to low, and cook until the garlic has softened, about 5 min. Add the chickpeas, a pinch of salt, and enough water to barely cover the chickpeas. Increase the heat to medium, so the liquid is bubbling around the edges. Let bubble softly for 30–45 min, adding small amounts of water as needed to keep the beans barely moistened. Continue simmering until the beans are very velvety and tender and some are beginning to fall apart. Reduce heat to lowest possible setting. Season to taste with black pepper. Meanwhile, in a large pot of boiling water salted to taste like pleasant seawater, cook the pasta. Reserve ¼ cup pasta water just before draining. In a large bowl, combine the pasta, chickpeas, and a few spoonfuls of water, stirring to help the beans' starch emulsify. Add more water if needed to keep things creamy and saucy. Taste and adjust as needed.

This next is very good baby food, as well as good adult food.

CHICKPEA PUREE OR SOUP *(25 min)*
½ cup olive oil, 1 onion (chopped), salt, ¼ tsp combined ground cinnamon and any garam masala (or either), ½–1 bunch beet (or other) greens (washed and chopped), 1-2 cloves garlic (sliced), 2–3 cups cooked chickpeas.

Heat a medium small pot. Add ¼ cup of the oil, onion, and a pinch of salt. Cook over medium-low heat, adding the spices and garlic when the onion has softened, 5–10 min. Add the beet greens and cook, stirring, until the greens are wilted, 1–2 min. Add the chickpeas and 1 cup water. Stir and simmer over low heat until the chickpeas have softened a bit, 10–15 min. Taste for salt, adjusting to make it well seasoned. When it tastes good, add the remaining ¼ cup olive oil, or more if you want, and puree to a texture you like.

SIMPLEST HUMMUS *(10 min)*

¼ cup tahini, 2 tbsp lemon juice, 1 cup cooked chickpeas, 1 small clove garlic (minced), 2 tbsp olive oil plus for serving, ¼ tsp ground cumin, ½ tsp salt plus to taste, 1–3 tsp cold water.

In a food processor, combine the tahini and lemon juice and blend to smooth. Add the chickpeas, garlic, olive oil, cumin and salt and blend. Add 1 tbsp water and blend to very fluffy, adding more if needed. Taste for salt, adjust, drizzle with olive oil, and eat.

CHICKPEA NUTS *(45 min)*

½ cup cooked chickpeas (patted dry), olive oil, salt, any dried spices you like (cumin, za'atar, sumac, chile powder, etc.).

Heat the oven to 400°F. In a bowl, drizzle the chickpeas with olive oil, then lightly salt. Mix with a shake of whatever spices you're using. Place on a sheet pan and roast until crisp, checking on them and stirring halfway, about 20–25 min. When golden brown and crisp, turn off the oven and let sit in the oven for 15 min to dry. Remove and eat.

Or use leftover cooked chickpeas in Best Grain or Bean Salad (p. 206), or Minestrone (p. 210), or Farro Soup (p. 225).
  See also Beans, cooked (p. 210).

BEANS AND RICE

CHICKPEA CAN LIQUID

The liquid from a can of chickpeas (called aquafaba) is a reasonable vegan substitute for eggs in baking or making mayonnaise. The ratio is 3 tbsp aquafaba for every 1 egg.

CHOLE OR CHANA MASALA

COCONUT STEW *(5–10 min)*

Chole or chana masala, canned coconut milk (well shaken), salt, lime juice (optional), achar.

In a pot, combine chole or chana and coconut milk. Bring to a boil, then reduce to a simmer and heat to bubbling. Taste for salt and adjust, add lime juice (if using). Drizzle with achar to eat.

A variation is to add any leftover rice when heating.

Chole or chana masala is also a perfect bed for cooking eggs, as in Shakshuka (p. 421) or Saag Paneer Shakshuka (p. 83). Warm leftovers in a pan, adding a little liquid if you need to keep it from burning, crack eggs into ramekins then tip in, cover and simmer on the stovetop or bake (in a 375°F oven) until the whites are set and the yolks are as you like them. Or substitute leftovers for aloo gobi in Aloo Gobi Samosas (p. 12). Or use in Samosa Chaat (p. 367).

CONGEE

MORE CONGEE *(5–10 min)*
1 cup congee, 1 cup strong broth or water.

Combine leftover congee with more broth or water. Cook at a boil or simmer. Voilà! More congee.

COUSCOUS

Add leftover couscous to any pancake batter (pp. 138–39) to make savory couscous pancakes, adding parsley or other herbs and vegetables, plus 1 tbsp sliced scallions if you have them. Or use to make a couscous rendition of Fried Rice (p. 205) or in the Best Grain or Bean Salad (p. 206).

DAL

STRETCHED DAL *(25–30 min)*
1 tbsp neutral oil, ½ tsp ground coriander, ½ tsp ground fennel, ½ tsp freshly ground black pepper, ½ cup cooked dal, ⅛ tsp hing (asafoetida), ⅛ tsp ground turmeric, ¼ tsp red chile powder, ¼ tsp amchur powder, salt.

Heat a small pot. Add the oil. Add the coriander, fennel, and black pepper. Add the dal and 1 cup water. Stir through, then simmer until warm and combined, about 10 min, adding more water if you want wetter dal. Add the hing, turmeric, chile powder, and amchur. Taste for salt and adjust.

KHICHDI *(30 min)*

½ cup uncooked rice, ½ tsp salt, 1 cup cooked dal, ⅛ tsp hing (asafoetida), 1 tomato (optional; chopped). *For the tadka:* 2 tsp ghee, ½ tsp cumin seeds, ½ tsp mustard seeds, 1 tsp finely chopped fresh ginger, 1 green chile (finely chopped). *For serving:* yogurt and achar.

Rinse and soak the rice for 30 min. Place the rice in a pot with 2 cups water and the salt. Bring to a boil, cover, then simmer over lowest possible heat for 20 min. Add the dal, hing, and tomato (if using). Make the tadka (see p. 208 for details) and pour over before eating. Eat with yogurt and achar. (Adapted from Cook with Manali website)

Leftover dal also makes good Coconut Stew (p. 219).

EDAMAME, COOKED

Once cooked, edamame should be eaten within 4 days; they freeze well, though, so try to freeze them as soon as they become leftovers. Or shell them and make one of the recipes below.

CRISPY EDAMAME *(20 min)*

1 cup cooked shelled edamame, ½ tbsp olive oil, 2 tbsp freshly grated Parmesan cheese (or a little more), ¼ tsp salt plus to taste.

Heat the oven to 400°F. Line a small baking sheet with parchment paper. In a bowl, mix the edamame with the olive oil, then with the Parmesan and salt. Spread onto the baking sheet. Bake until the cheese is lightly browned and adherent to the edamame, 12–15 min. Taste for salt, adjust, and eat. (Adapted from Homemade Hooplah website)

EDAMAME PESTO (*10 min*)

Salt, 1 clove garlic finely minced, 1 cup cooked shelled edamame, a squeeze of lemon or the grated zest of 1 lemon, 1½ tbsp olive oil, a small handful of cilantro or basil leaves (optional).

In a blender, combine the edamame and garlic, add lemon juice or zest, and puree to combine. Add the olive oil, herbs if using, and a drizzle of water, and puree to smooth. Taste for salt and adjust. Delicious with pasta or as a dip.

FALAFEL

This next is only a larb in using a lot of herbs and acid to nudge stodgier protein into a salad.

FALAFEL LARB (*15 min*)

¼ cup chopped cucumber, salt, ½ cup chopped falafel, ¼ cup chopped dill pickles (string bean or cucumber or other), 1 tsp sesame seeds or roasted rice powder (see p. 208), ½–¾ tsp lime juice, ¼ cup slivered basil (or a combination of basil and cilantro). *Optional for serving:* leftover sauces (hummus, techina, s'chug).

In a bowl, combine the cucumber with a pinch of salt and mix. Leave for 10 min, then drain. In a large bowl, combine the falafel, salted cucumber, pickles, sesame seeds or rice powder, and lime juice and mix well. Add the herbs. Dollop with any of the optional sauces as desired.

A variation is to add ¼ cup chopped jalapeño or a chopped Thai bird's eye chile. Good with rice or on lettuce leaves.

FALAFEL TOAST (*10 min*)

1–2 falafel balls, 1 slice multigrain bread, butter or olive oil plus for frying, avocado (or labneh or techina, or even goat cheese), 1 egg, salt, hot sauce (s'chug, etc.).

Slightly flatten the falafel balls. Toast the bread, and at the same time warm the smashed falafel on a bit of foil on the toaster tray. Butter or oil the toast. Press avocado on top (or dollop on labneh or techina or goat cheese). Place the flattened falafel on top. Fry the egg in olive oil or butter, salting as soon as you crack it into the pan. Lay the fried egg atop the falafel and top with hot sauce. (Adapted from Food52 website)

A variation is to add a tuft of salad greens or herbs under the falafel.

FALAFEL, RAW, MIX

Prepared falafel mix can be frozen as is, either as mix, or formed into falafel balls. It should be thawed before being fried.

FARINA, COOKED

FRIED MUSH (*10 min*)
Cooked farina, olive oil or butter. *For a sweet version:* honey or maple syrup. *For a savory version:* flaky salt, grated cheese, lemon juice.

Cut leftover farina into 1-inch slices or wedges, directly out of the container in which you stored it. Heat a heavy-bottomed pan like a cast-iron skillet and add olive oil or butter to coat the bottom. Fry the slices over medium heat, browning each side. Eat them hot, drizzled with honey or maple syrup if you want them sweet, or salted with flaky salt, grated with cheese, and squeezed with lemon if you want them savory. Experiment with additions of nuts and spices, or, or, or . . .

FARINATA

Farinata is supposed to be eaten only hot and only immediately. But, especially if you mutinously store it at room temperature overnight, it is delicious fried quickly in a hot pan and eaten as a snack, or used to make little sandwiches of cheese or soft-cooked egg or vegetable or thinly sliced salumi.

FARRO, COOKED

PAN-FRIED FARRO *(15 min)*

2 tbsp olive oil, ½ cup thinly sliced onion (leek, scallion, or shallot), salt, 1–2 cloves garlic (chopped), 1 cup cooked farro, a handful of herbs (fennel fronds, parsley, mint, cilantro, celery leaves; chopped), a squeeze of lemon juice or a drop of red wine vinegar (optional).

Heat a pan over medium heat. Add the olive oil, onion, and a pinch of salt and cook until tender, 5–10 min. Add the garlic and mix through until it just begins to sizzle. Add the farro and stir. Fry over medium-high heat, stirring, until crisp, 3–4 min. Add the herbs and toss through. Keep stirring and scraping for another min, then taste for salt and serve, adding lemon juice or vinegar if you like.

This is endlessly variable. Add cooked greens, bringing them to room temperature first. Or boiled eggs, wedged and salted, and fried onions or shallots and a sprinkle of za'atar or sumac or chaat masala. Any version is delicious with yogurt or raita drizzled on top. (Adapted from *This Is Camino: A Cookbook*, by Allison Hopelain, Chris Colin, and Russell Moore)

FARRO AND TURNIP AND TURNIP GREEN SALAD *(25 min)*

2 cups cooked farro, ½–1 bunch little turnips with their greens (separated and cleaned), 4 tbsp olive oil, ½ tsp salt plus to taste, ½ tsp thyme leaves, 2 tsp red wine vinegar, ¼ cup chopped parsley or celery leaves.

Bring the farro to room temperature and place in a bowl. Slice the turnips into thin wedges. Heat a skillet. Add 2 tbsp of the olive oil. Add the turnips and salt. Let them brown, add 3–4 tbsp water, just enough to let them steam, and cook until tender, about 10 min, covering if needed. Meanwhile, chop the turnip greens. Uncover the pan, add the thyme and turnip greens and remaining 2 tbsp olive oil, and fry until the greens are well fried and cooked. Tip the vegetables into the bowl of farro and add the vinegar. Taste for salt and adjust. Add the parsley or celery leaves and eat.

Another salad with leftover farro is the Best Grain or Bean Salad (p. 206). Or make this soup:

FARRO SOUP *(30 min)*

¼ cup olive oil, ¼ cup chopped onion or leek, ¼ cup chopped carrots, ¼ cup chopped celery or fennel, a sprinkle of chile flakes, salt, 2 cloves garlic (sliced or chopped), 2 tsp rosemary (chopped), 2 cups stemmed and chopped cooking greens (plus stems finely chopped), 4 cups farro cooking liquid (or a combination of farro liquid, bean liquid, water, or just water), 1 cup cooked chickpeas or borlotti beans, ½–2 cups cooked farro, 1 cup leftover roasted root vegetable (optional; squash, turnip, sweet potato), chili oil or olive oil for serving.

Heat a medium large pot. Add the olive oil, onion or leek, carrots, celery or fennel, chile flakes, and a little pinch of salt, and cook until tender, 5–10 min. Stir in the garlic and rosemary and cook until the garlic has softened, another 2–3 min. Stir in the greens, then add the farro liquid and chickpeas or beans and simmer 5–10 min. Stir in the farro and any root vegetables (if using), adding water if needed for a consistency you like. Cook until just warmed through, then taste for salt and adjust. Drizzle heavily with chili oil or olive oil and eat.

GREEN FARRO SOUP *(25 min)*

¼ cup olive oil, 1 bunch scallions (chopped, whites and green tops kept separate), 3 stalks celery (chopped or finely sliced), ¼–½ cup finely chopped carrots, 2 cloves garlic (chopped), salt, 1 bunch carrot tops (chopped), 1–1½ cups cooked beans (drained and rinsed if canned), 4 cups farro cooking liquid (or a combination of farro liquid, bean liquid, water, or just water), 1–2 cups cooked farro, 2–4 cups chopped cooking greens or finely sliced stems of cooking greens, olive oil for serving.

Heat a medium pot. Add the olive oil, scallion whites, celery, carrots, garlic, and a pinch of salt. Cook over medium heat until softened, 5–10 min. Stir in the carrot tops, scallion tops, and beans. Add the farro liquid and farro. Bring to a simmer, add the greens, and simmer until the greens are perfectly tender, 5–10 min. Taste for salt and adjust. Drizzle heavily with olive oil and eat.

FARRO COOKING LIQUID

When you cook farro, add a bay leaf, a bunch of herb stems, a clove of garlic, olive oil, and a cheese rind to the water. This makes delicious farro and delicious farro broth. If you follow these recommendations, the liquid drained from your finished farro is nearly ready to be served. I serve it, watered down, to my son as soup because he likes clear broth and few other soups. To use yours, ideally in more elaborate dishes, dilute it with water or broth. Now treat it as vegetable or other stock, labeling it accordingly to increase its chances of deployment.

FAVA BEANS, COOKED

Is this a dilemma anyone has ever faced? Well, just in case . . .

FAVA PASTE *(15 min)*
2 tbsp olive oil plus for drizzling, 1 clove garlic (sliced), ¼ tsp salt plus to taste, 1 sprig savory or rosemary (chopped), 1 cup cooked fava beans.

Heat a small pot. Add the olive oil, garlic, salt, and savory or rosemary, and cook until just softened, 30 sec–1 min. Add the fava beans and enough water to just be able to stir. Cook, stirring and smashing, 5–10 min, adding water as needed to make a rough paste. Taste for salt and doneness, and stop once the beans have broken down. Adjust salt. Drizzle with more olive oil just before serving. Best on rustic toast rubbed with garlic.

Or use leftover favas in the Farro Soup (p. 225) or Green Farro Soup (p. 225), garnishing it at the end with copious quantities of fresh herbs (fennel fronds, carrot tops, or celery leaves). Or add a small amount of pureed leftover fava beans to the mixture for Falafel (p. 206) before shaping into balls and frying.

FEIJOADA

SORT OF GALLO PINTO *(15 min)*
2 tbsp oil, ½ cup finely chopped onion, salt, 2 cloves garlic (finely chopped), 3–4 cups cooked long-grain rice, 1–2 cups feijoada, 2–3 tbsp liquid aminos or Maggi Seasoning, chopped cilantro, any salsa for eating (optional).

Heat a medium saucepan. Add the oil, onion, and a pinch of salt, and cook until slightly softened, 5–10 min. Add the garlic and cook until it can be broken with a spoon, another min or so. Add the rice, feijoada, and liquid aminos or Maggi Seasoning. Stir to combine, reduce the heat to medium-low, and cook until just warm, another 2–3 min, uncovering once it starts steaming. Increase the heat and let it get slightly fried and browned, another min. Remove from the heat, add the cilantro, and eat, topped with any salsa you like (if using).

A variation is to use raw rice and add the right ratio of liquid (see ratios on p. 205) using feijoada broth as part of the total amount and water or broth for the rest.

FONIO, COOKED

Use leftover fonio in the Best Grain or Bean Salad (p. 206), Barley Salad (p. 210), Pan-Fried Farro (p. 224), Farro Soup (p. 225), Savory Grain Pancakes (p. 238), A Version of Yam Kai (p. 239), or A Congee-esque Soup (p. 239). Or just heat with coconut milk and add a swirl of honey or maple syrup for a sweet porridge, or a swirl of chili paste or other spicy sauce for a savory one.

FREEKEH, COOKED

Freekeh and fonio are different grains, but their leftovers can be used inter-changeably. Use freekah in the Best Grain or Bean Salad (p. 206), Barley Salad (p. 210), Pan-Fried Farro (p. 224), Farro Soup (p. 225), Savory Grain Pancakes (p. 238), A Version of Yam Kai (p. 239), or A Congee-esque Soup (p. 239). Or heat into a porridge.

FRIED RICE

Rice can be fried twice. The rhythm and rhyme of that fact please me whenever I act on it. Twice-fried rice is really thrice *cooked* rice, which offers another brief mental tickle. In any case, if you make a pot of rice on Monday, you can fry it on Tuesday, fry it *again* on Wednesday, then add the twice-fried rice to a savory stew on Thursday. If this plan sounds repetitive, think of how different the direction of each can be. If Monday's rice was plain brown, eaten with tofu and mushrooms, on Tuesday it can be fried with lots of garlic and chiles. On Wednesday, you can tack, frying it Italian, in lots of olive oil, with

cooked greens and topped with frying peppers, or toasted nuts. Or you make
it all taste Thai, with lots of cilantro and mint and basil, and fish sauce, sugar,
lime, and why not chopped cucumber? By the time it's ready to be Thursday-
stewed, it will be a deeply flavorful and deeply loved green-y brown. Add just
enough broth or water to cover, heat, and eat. Or make any of the other lovely
things that can only be made once you have fried rice.

FRIED RICE OMELET/OMURICE—WITHOUT KETCHUP *(5 min)*
2–3 eggs, ¼ tsp salt, ½–¾ cup fried rice, 1–2 tbsp butter.

In a small bowl, beat the eggs with the salt. In a small pot, warm the rice with
a few drops of water. Warm a nonstick or well-seasoned pan to medium-low.
Add the butter and when it stops foaming, add the eggs, agitating any parts
that aren't in contact with the pan and pouring uncooked egg into the spots
formerly occupied by cooked egg. When it's just barely set, tip the rice into the
middle. Fold one side in, clumsily is fine, then tip the pan so it's easy to begin
to fold the other side over and flip onto a plate so the egg side is facing you.
Do your best with a kitchen towel to shape the egg like a football. Omurice
would now be topped with a mixture of about equal parts ketchup and tomato
puree with a little water added. I don't like ketchup, so I'm not recommending
that, but most people do, and they would.

CRISP RICE BALLS *(20 min)*
**2–2½ cups fried rice, 3 eggs, 6 tbsp all-purpose flour plus for dredging, panko
or other bread crumbs, peanut or vegetable oil for frying.** *For serving:* **lemon
wedges or yogurt, or another sauce into which you feel like dipping.**

In a bowl, bring the rice to room temperature. In another bowl, beat 2 of
the eggs and add to the rice along with 6 tbsp flour and mix well. Form into
balls. Set up three shallow dishes. Put flour for dredging in one, the remaining
egg, beaten, in the second, and the panko in the third. Dip the the rice balls
into the flour, then the egg, then the panko. In a deep pot, heat a few inches
of oil to 350°–375°F. Add the rice balls and fry until browned and crisp. Eat
squeezed with lemon or with yogurt or with any dipping sauce.

A variation is to add tiny cubes of cheese to each: To do that, flatten the
rice into a little patty, add the cheese, and then form the rice around the
cheese into a ball.

FUL, COOKED

HUMMUS WITH FUL *(30 min)*
½ cup ful, Simplest Hummus (p. 219), olive oil, wedges of hard-boiled eggs (optional), pita.

In a small pot, warm the ful. In a shallow bowl, spread the hummus, making a well in the middle. Add the warm ful, drizzle heavily with as much olive oil as will fit on the plate. If desired, tuck wedged eggs around the perimeter of the ful. Eat in blissful silence, scooping it up with pita until it's gone. You can sprinkle this all with sumac and/or parsley if that heightens your bliss.
See also Beans, cooked (p. 210).

GRITS, COOKED

Grits can be rewarmed with water or water and cream, and I've never done it so many times it was too many. If it seems boring to serve grits again, they can also be poured out on a cutting board like the Italian dish, Polenta Sulla Spianatoia, where everyone goes at the collective board with spoons. Or leftover grits can be poured into a baking sheet, refrigerated overnight, then cut into long batons or wedges and fried in olive oil until their cut sides are hot and crisp. These make a fine meal with a salad and some grated or sliced cheese alongside. Or make:

FRIED GRITS *(10–15 min)*
1 cup cooked grits, ¾ cup grated cheddar cheese. *Optional additions:* ½ cup chopped cooked bacon, ¾ cup chopped garlic chives, ¼ cup corn, chopped parsley or cilantro, ¼ cup thinly sliced ham. *For frying:* all-purpose flour, 1 egg (beaten with a spoonful water), bread crumbs, peanut or vegetable oil.

In a bowl, combine the grits with cheddar and any optional additions. Form into balls the size of walnuts in their shells. Set up three bowls for dredging: flour in one, beaten egg in another, and bread crumbs in the third. In a deep pot, heat 3–4 inches of oil to 350°–375°F. Roll the balls in the flour, then the egg, then the bread crumbs. Add to the hot oil and fry until browned and crisp. Drain on paper towels.

HUSH PUPPIES

Leftover hush puppies can stand in for arancini in Arancini Poppers (p. 209).

JAMBALAYA

JAMBALAYA SOUP (*20–25 min*)
2–4 cups jambalaya, 2–4 cups stock (chicken, pork, or ham stock, or another broth), 2–3 cups stemmed chopped cooking greens or 1 cup leftover cooked greens, 1 cup cooked black-eyed peas (optional), olive oil or Parsley Oil (p. 68).

In a medium pot, heat the leftover jambalaya with stock, bringing the mixture to a simmer. Add the cooking greens and black-eyed peas (if using). Simmer for 10–15 min to combine and lightly reduce the broth. Eat hot, drizzled with olive oil or parsley oil.

Use this general technique for any leftover rice stew you have stored away.

KASHA, COOKED

KASHA KIBBE (*10–15 min*)
¼ cup chopped allium (garlic and any combination of onion, shallot, scallion, or chives), 1 tsp salt, ½ cup chopped parsley, ⅓–½ cup cooked kasha, a tiny scrape each of cinnamon and cardamom, 1 egg, 1 lb beef or lamb.

In a blender, pulse the allium combination and the salt. Add the parsley and pulse again. Add the kasha and spices and pulse, then add the egg. Add the meat and pulse until a paste has formed. Form into batons, either on soaked skewers or off. Cook on a grill or in a cast-iron skillet about 3 min per side, or more if needed. Serve with rice or in sandwiches. Good with techina and s'chug.

KHICHDI

FRIED KHICHDI (10 min)

1–2 tbsp neutral oil or ghee, ¼–½ cup finely chopped onion or scallions, 1 clove garlic (chopped or sliced), ¼ tsp salt plus to taste, 1 tbsp chopped pickled or fresh chile (optional), 1–2 cups khichdi, lemon or lime juice.

Heat a pan. Add the oil or ghee. Cook the onion or scallions, garlic, and salt, and cook until tender, 5–10 min. Add the chile (if using). Add the khichdi, fry to warm, top with lemon or lime juice, and eat. Fresh herbs, like cilantro, are good, too.

LENTILS, COOKED

INAUTHENTIC TOMATO DAL (40 min)

2 tbsp ghee or butter, 2 chopped tomatoes (fresh or canned), ½ tsp salt plus to taste, ¾–1 cup cooked lentils, ¼ tsp black mustard seeds, ½ tsp cumin seeds, 2 cloves garlic (chopped), pinch of hing (asafoetida), ¼ tsp ground red chile powder, ¼ tsp ground turmeric, ¼ tsp kasuri methi (fenugreek leaves), a small handful of chopped cilantro (optional).

Heat a saucepan. Add 1 tbsp ghee or butter. Add the tomatoes and salt and cook until broken down, 5–10 min. Add the lentils and a little water to cover, simmering until the lentils are very soft and the tomato has melted into them, about 20 min. Smash with a spoon to a rough mash. In a small pan, heat the remaining 1 tbsp ghee or butter and add the mustard seeds, cumin seeds, and garlic. Cook until the garlic is just tender, 30 sec–1 min. Remove from the heat and add the hing, chile powder, turmeric, and methi. Pour into the dal, adding the cilantro directly to the pot (if using). Serve on hot rice! (Adapted from Swasthi's Recipes website)

SORT OF MUJADARA (45 min)

1 cup long-grain rice, ½ cup cooked lentils, 2 tbsp olive oil, 1 large onion (sliced lengthwise into thin half-moons), ½ tsp salt, 1 bay leaf, ½ tsp ground cumin, 2–3 tbsp toasted pine nuts, yogurt (optional).

Soak the rice in water for 20 min, then drain. Meanwhile, bring the lentils to room temperature and drain if in liquid (reserving the liquid for soup). Heat a small pot. Add the olive oil, onion, and ¼ tsp of the salt. Cook, stirring occasionally and reducing the heat as needed, until golden brown, about 20 min. Remove half the onion from the pot and set aside for garnish. Add the bay leaf, cumin, rice and the ratio of water appropriate to your rice (see p. 205), along with the remaining ¼ tsp salt. Bring to a boil, cover, then reduce to a simmer, and cook 20 min. Uncover, add the lentils, fluff through, cover and let sit off the heat for 10 min. Serve topped with the reserved onion and the pine nuts, with yogurt for garnishing if desired.

See also Dal (p. 220).

NASI GORENG

SAVORY NASI GORENG STEW *(5–10 min)*
1 cup nasi goreng, 1–2 cups miso broth, 1 soft-boiled egg (optional; p. 139), 1 scallion (white and light green parts only; thinly sliced on a diagonal).

In a pot, warm the nasi goreng and broth, adding the egg (if using) for the last min just to warm through. Top with scallions, and eat.

OATMEAL, COOKED

ALL-DAY MUFFINS *(25 min)*
Butter for the muffin tin, 1 cup (120 g) all-purpose flour, ½ cup (100 g) granulated or brown sugar, 1 tsp baking powder, 1 tsp baking soda, ¼ tsp salt, 8 tbsp (1 stick) melted butter, 2 eggs, 1 cup cooked oatmeal, 1 tsp vanilla extract, 1½ cups chopped combined dried fruit/nuts/seeds (raisins, thinly sliced dried apricots, sliced dried mango, sliced dates, cranberries, pumpkin or sunflower seeds, walnuts, pistachios), scant ¼ tsp ground cinnamon (optional), scant ¼ tsp ground cardamom (optional).

Heat the oven to 350°F. Butter a 12-cup muffin tin. In a large bowl, mix together the flour, sugar, baking powder, baking soda, and salt. In another bowl, mix the melted butter, eggs, cooked oatmeal, vanilla, and fruit/nut/seed mixture. Add the butter mixture to the flour and mix to combine. Spoon into the prepared muffin tin. Bake until a skewer emerges mostly clean, about 18 min.

PAELLA

PAELLA ARANCINI *(30–40 min)*
1 cup paella rice, 3 eggs (beaten), bread crumbs, 2 tbsp chopped paella seafood, meat, or vegetables, salt, ½ cup all-purpose flour, grapeseed or peanut oil for frying.

Remove any seafood, meat, or vegetables from the paella. Chop and set aside. In a bowl, combine the rice with 2 tbsp of the beaten egg and 2–3 tbsp of bread crumbs. Dampen your hands and flatten 1–2 tbsp of the mixture into a small pancake in the palm of your hand. Put a little bit of the chopped paella in the middle of each and close it into a ball. Keep going until all of the rice mixture is used. Set up three shallow dishes. Put flour in one, the remaining egg, beaten, in the second, and more bread crumbs in the third. Dip the rice balls into the flour, then egg, then bread crumbs. In a deep pot, heat a few inches of oil to 350°–375°F. Add the rice balls and fry in batches until browned and crisp, 5–8 min. Drain on a paper towel and eat warm.

PAELLA STEW WITH AIOLI *(25 min)*
1–2 cups paella, 3 tbsp olive oil, ½ cup chopped carrots, ½ cup chopped celery, 1 cup chopped leek or onion, ½ tsp salt plus to taste, 1 clove garlic (minced), 4 cups chicken or other stock, 2 cups chopped cooking greens (raw or cooked), Aioli (p. 395).

Remove any seafood, meat, or vegetables from the paella. Chop and set aside. Heat a medium pot. Add the oil, carrots, celery, and leek or onion, and salt. Cook until beginning to soften, about 5 min. Add the garlic and cook for an additional min. Add the stock, bring to a boil, and simmer for 5 min until slightly reduced. Add the paella rice and the cooking greens. Cook until the greens are tender, 3–5 min. Add any chopped seafood or meat and remove from the heat. Let sit for at least 10 min. While it's sitting, make the aioli. Eat heavily dolloped with aioli.

PIGEON PEAS, COOKED

PIGEON PEA STEW *(45 min)*
2 tbsp olive oil, 2 cloves garlic (finely minced), 1 onion (finely diced), 1 kabocha
or Honeynut squash (peeled and cubed), ¼ cup finely minced red or green
bell pepper or 1 finely minced chile, 1 bunch cilantro (leaves and stems, finely
chopped), ½ tsp salt plus to taste, 1½ cups cooked pigeon peas, 4 cups chicken
stock or a combination of chicken stock and water.

Heat a pot. Add the olive oil, garlic, onion, squash, bell pepper or chile, half
the cilantro, and the salt and cook until the onion is just tender, 5–10 min.
Add the pigeon peas and stock, bring to a boil, reduce to a simmer, and cook
until the peas have begun to break down and the squash is totally tender,
another 25–30 min. Add the remaining cilantro. Taste for salt and adjust.
(Adapted from Selha Graham)

POLENTA

One of polenta's most admirable qualities is its willingness to go from hot to
cold and hot to cold until it's gone. If you liked polenta the first time, reheat
it again with water and more butter and eat it anew, perhaps with a different
sauce. Or serve it, rewarmed, Sulla Spianatoia, on a cutting board with sauce
or other adornments. Or make it into something entirely new.

POLENTA PASTICCIATA FROM OLIVIA *(45 min–1 hr)*
Béchamel (p. 395), butter and bread crumbs for the baking dish, cooked
polenta, leftover hard cheese.

Heat the oven to 375°F. Make the béchamel and remove from the heat. Butter
a baking dish and then scatter the bottom with bread crumbs. Cut leftover
polenta into slices ¼–½ inch thick, not worrying about the shape. Lay the
polenta over the bread crumbs. Top with a layer of béchamel, then grate on a
layer of leftover cheese. Repeat with polenta, then béchamel, then cheese, continuing with as many layers as you have ingredients for and adjusting to the
size of your pan, ending with a final layer of béchamel, then cheese on the very
top. You will likely have béchamel left over. Bake until browned and crisped on
top, about 25 min.

POLENTA GNOCCHI *(50 min)*

1½ cups cooked polenta, scant 2 cups (190 g) all-purpose flour plus as needed for rolling out, 1 egg yolk, 5 tbsp freshly grated Parmesan or Pecorino Romano cheese, salt to taste, semolina (optional).

In a bowl, combine all the ingredients and knead into a dough. Line a baking sheet with parchment (or sprinkle with semolina). On a lightly floured surface, roll the dough into snakes as thick as you'd like your gnocchi. Cut crosswise into pieces ¾–1 inch long, placing on the lined baking sheet as you go. Cover and refrigerate until ready to eat. In a pot of boiling water salted to taste like pleasant seawater, cook the gnocchi in batches. Toss with tomato sauce or pesto or other sauce or just melted butter, and grate heavily with cheese.

POLENTA, RAW

POLENTINA *(1½ hr)*

2 tbsp olive oil, 6 cloves garlic (sliced), salt, 8 cups chicken stock, 1 small bouquet garni (parsley stems, thyme, sage), ½ cup uncooked polenta.

Heat a large pot. Add the oil, garlic, and a small pinch of salt. Add the chicken stock and bouquet garni and bring to a boil. Reduce to a simmer. Add the polenta slowly, whisking it in. Cook for 1 hr or a bit longer, until it no longer tastes like soap. Remove the bouquet garni. Eat as is or topped with a poached egg. More olive oil drizzled over is welcome.

PORRIDGE, COOKED

Leftover porridge of any kind can be rewarmed with water, stock, or cream, and made into a savory lunch. I depend heavily on various Sichuan and Hong Kongese chili oils to make my rewarmed porridges into appetizing meals, but grated cheese, drizzles of olive oil or herb oil, piles of fresh herbs, pickled chiles, fried eggs, and fried shallots all labor to the same end.

SAVORY TART WITH A QUINOA CRUST *(1 hr)*

For the crust: 1½ cups cooked quinoa, ¾ cup grated Parmesan cheese, 1 egg (beaten), salt, butter for the pie plate or tart pan. *For the filling:* 6 eggs (beaten), ½ cup half-and-half, 1 tsp salt, 4 cups any cooked or raw vegetables (greens, or a combination of greens and tomatoes, herbs, roasted vegetable, or other).

Heat the oven to 375°F. *Make the crust:* In a bowl, combine the quinoa and Parmesan and mix well. Add the egg and mix. Taste for salt and adjust. Butter a medium pie plate or tart pan. Press the quinoa mixture in evenly, leveling with a measuring cup or ramekin. Bake until the crust is just set, 10–12 min. Remove and cool completely. Leave the oven on. *Make the filling:* In a bowl, whisk together the eggs, half-and-half, and salt to make custard. Add the vegetables to the pie shell and slowly pour the custard over—you may not use it all. Transfer to the oven and bake until the custard is set everywhere but the very center, 30–40 min. Cool and eat. (Adapted from Erin McDowell)

CRUNCHY QUINOA SALAD *(15 min)*

1 tbsp onion (chopped), lemon juice, ¼ tsp salt plus to taste, 1–2 tbsp sauerkraut (or curtido or sliced kimchi), 2 tsp rice wine or other light vinegar, 2 tbsp olive oil, ½ cup cooked quinoa, ½ cup chopped toasted nuts, ½ cup large, craggy toasted croutons (see p. 176), ¼ cup roughly cubed feta cheese (or mozzarella or goat cheese), ¼ cup chopped pitted olives, ¼ cup roughly chopped hard-boiled egg, ¼ cup roughly chopped strong acerbic green herb (parsley or parsley and mint or carrot tops), salt, a handful of cleaned and dried lettuces, freshly ground black pepper.

In a bowl, soak the onions in lemon juice to cover, along with the salt. Let sit 10 min. Add the sauerkraut and vinegar and mix well. Add the olive oil, quinoa, nuts, croutons, cheese, olives, egg, and herbs and mix well. Season with salt to taste. Add the lettuces and black pepper and eat.

REFRIED BEANS

REFRIED BEAN HUMMUS *(5–7 min)*

½ cup refried beans, 1 clove garlic (finely minced), 1½ tbsp lemon or lime juice, 3 tbsp tahini, ⅛ tsp ground cumin, ½ tsp salt plus to taste. *Optional garnish:* olive oil, sumac or za'atar.

In a blender or food processor, blend all the ingredients well, adding 1 tbsp water. Taste for salt and adjust. If desired, garnish with a drizzle of olive oil and sprinkling of sumac or za'atar. Delicious where chickpea hummus is.

REFRIED BEAN RIBOLLITA *(25–40 min)*

¼ cup olive oil, 1 clove garlic (sliced or minced), ½ tsp salt plus to taste, 2 tbsp chopped fresh sage and rosemary (or sub parsley for one of the two), a sprinkle chile flakes (optional), 3–4 leaves cooking greens (optional; stemmed and sliced into ribbons), 1–2 whole peeled tomatoes (fresh or canned; chopped), 1 cup refried beans, 2 cups ½–1-inch pieces good stale bread (without fruit or nuts or seeds, crusts removed), piece of Parmesan rind (optional).

Heat a medium pot. Add 2 tbsp of the oil, garlic, and salt. After about 1 min, add the herbs and chile flakes (if using). Stir in the kale (if using), then add the tomatoes, refried beans, 3 cups water, the bread, and the Parmesan rind if using. Partially cover, opening to stir occasionally, breaking up the bread with a spoon when you do. Add water if needed to keep things from sticking. Simmer until the bread is completely melted into the soup, about 25 min. Garnish as in Ribollita (p. 178).

RICE, COOKED

Fried rice is the best use of leftover rice. Here is what matters in rice-frying: 1) It's no use frying fresh rice. It gets mushy and leads to fried rice insecurity. Fried rice is a next-day affair, and needs dried-out rice. 2) The pan in which you fry rice can't be medium hot, or a temperature from which you can walk away. It must be cranked up, high-flame, dauntingly hot. 3) There must be enough fat in the pan to let each grain of rice fry. They don't need to deep-fry, but grains must encounter shimmering oil, not dry pan. 4) Frying rice is not constant motion. It is start and stop. Press grains into a hot sizzling layer (at which point you may need to reduce the heat slightly to keep them from burning), wait to see browned crust moving up the sides of the rice grains, gather and mound the rice up, and then spread, press, wait, gather again, so that each grain has time in the hot fat. 5) A good order to keep in mind is: hot pan, fat, any aromatics (garlic, onion, ginger, chile), a quick stir, then rice, then once it has really crisped, other dry ingredients (leftover meat, egg, cooked vegetables), then finally any liquids or sauces, or watery vegetables (cucumber and tomato), which must be added last. Herbs can enter off the heat.

Here is a list of some of the fried rice recipes in this book: Adobo Fried Rice (p. 303), Fried Rice (p. 205), Bibimbap Fried Rice (p. 216), Egg Fried Rice (p. 154), Egg Salad Fried Rice (p. 381), Fried Beans and Rice (p. 214), Fried Rice Cheeto Salad (p. 465), Fried Rice Omelet (p. 228), Huevos Rancheros Fried Rice (p. 160), Kimchi Fried Rice (p. 435), Mapo Fried Rice (p. 332), Morimoto Fried Rice (p. 304), Shrimp Fried Rice (p. 290), and Sort of Naam Khao/Larb Fried Rice (p. 331).

To turn leftover rice into beans and rice, instead of into fried rice, consider the flavor of your rice. If you cooked it in coconut milk, consider making a tadka (see p. 208) and then warm up some beans with onion and ginger and garlic. If you cooked rice in chicken stock, warm your beans with a sprig of thyme. If it's rice stained golden with annatto, warm a can of pigeon peas. And so on. As you match beans with your rice, look for meat or vegetables to add to your warming beans. Add any directly to the beans along with a little liquid if needed to avoid sticking. With all this underway, find condiments or sauces or herbs or grated cheese or yogurt or scallions to scatter on top of the beans and combine it all with optimism. If you are determined to turn leftover cooked rice into a salad, let the rice come to room temperature before dressing it or it will taste disconcertingly sandy.

SAVORY GRAIN PANCAKES (10 min)
Cornstarch Batter for Savory Pancakes (p. 138), 1¼ cups finely julienned kimchi (or scallions or chives, or a combination), a drizzle of kimchi juice, ½ cup cooked rice or other grain, olive oil.

Make the pancake batter. Whisk in the kimchi and kimchi juice. Mix in the cooked rice. Heat a heavy-bottomed pan to medium-high and add olive oil to just coat the bottom of the pan. Drop about 1 tbsp pancake mixture at a time into the pan as little pancakes. Don't worry about how liquid-y the batter seems; cornstarch firms up as soon as it hits the pan. These cook quickly. Flip and eat topped with more kimchi, or scallions, or dip in a combination of black vinegar and soy, or eat plain.

A VERSION OF YAM KAI (*5 min*)
4 eggs, salt, about 1½ tbsp lime juice or rice vinegar, 1½ tbsp fish sauce, 1 tsp sambal oelek or other chili-garlic paste, 1 cup cooked rice, 1 large onion or 5 shallots (thinly sliced), 3 tbsp vegetable oil, 1–2 cups fresh herb leaves (cilantro, basil, mint, or a combination), 1 chile (optional; chopped).

In a small bowl, whisk the eggs with a small pinch of salt. In a medium bowl, mix the lime juice or vinegar, fish sauce, sambal. Add the rice and onion or shalllots. Heat a heavy-bottomed pan. Add the oil, pour in the eggs and cook over medium-high heat into a flat omelet with very crispy edges. Remove from the pan to a plate, leaving oil in the pan. Add the rice mixture to the pan and cook over very high heat to become just crisp, too. Remove from the heat, layer over the omelet, shower with the herbs, the chile if using, and eat. (Adapted from the Epicurious website)

A CONGEE-ESQUE SOUP (*25 min*)
½ cup leftover cooked pork shoulder or other slow-cooked meat, ½ cup cooked rice, 2½–3 cups strong broth, 1 star anise, 2 tbsp peanut or vegetable oil, 2 cloves garlic (sliced), soy sauce, fried shallots (see p. 7) or chopped roasted peanuts. *Optional garnishes:* a soft-boiled egg, sliced scallions.

In a saucepan, heat the meat until any fat has melted. Add the rice, broth, and star anise and simmer for 20 min. Meanwhile, heat a small pot. Add the oil and garlic and fry to just golden, then remove from the heat. Add the garlic to the soup. Taste the soup and adjust with soy sauce. Add fried garlic. Garnish with fried shallots or chopped roasted peanuts. If desired, add a soft-boiled egg and sliced scallions.

Or use small amounts of leftover rice in a Savory Miso Rice Stew (p. 255) along with any leftover cooked greens and fish.

RICE, BURNT

If you burn rice to the bottom of the pot, scoop what you can out of the pot without agitating the burnt layer. Give what you scooped out time to settle, then taste it with an open mind. If it tastes slightly smoky or scorched, turn it into the Best Grain or Bean Salad (p. 206). The added flavors and textures will balance out the smoke. If it doesn't taste smokey, simply proceed. Add a drizzle of water and butter or oil to what's stuck to the bottom of the pan and heat it up, covered, so it steams a bit. Open and check on it, scraping with a metal spoon or sharp-edged wooden spatula. Store what comes up separately and make it into a Savory Miso Rice Stew (p. 255), where the miso's flavor will complement the burnt rice.

RICE, RAW

This is for the various bags in your pantry each containing a little bit of different kinds of rice.

CHICKEN SOUP WITH RICE (*20 min*)
Any amount of chicken broth, rice.

In a pot, bring the chicken broth to a boil. Add the rice. Cook at a low boil until the rice is well cooked, 20–25 min. Let cool slightly and eat drizzled or dolloped with your favorite condiments.

RISOTTO

ARANCINI (*30–40 min*)
½ cup all-purpose flour, salt, 2 eggs (beaten), bread crumbs plus for coating, 1 cup risotto, 2 tbsp finely chopped fontina or mozzarella cheese, grapeseed or peanut oil for deep-frying, lemon wedges.

Set up three shallow dishes. Put the flour in one, beaten eggs in the second, and bread crumbs in the third. Dampen your hands, take 1–2 tbsp of the risotto and flatten into a small pancake in the palm of your hand. Put a dab of cheese in the middle of each and close it into a ball. Continue until all of the arancini are formed. Roll each in flour, then egg, then bread crumbs, and place on a rack. In a deep pot, heat a few inches of oil to 350°–375°F. Add the arancini and fry in batches until browned and crisp, 5–8 min. Drain on paper towel and eat warm with lemon wedges for squeezing.

A variation is to add a dab of braised meat or meat sauce along with the cheese, then proceed.

TORTA DI RISO

Any leftover torta di riso is good at room temperature and can be gotten that way by being left out on the counter for 1 hr. Alternatively, heat a pan, add a little olive oil, add leftover torta, reduce the heat, cover, crisp, and eat.

HOW TO NOT STEW
Soup

All things make broth.

—*A Neopolitan proverb*

I f you have soup left from yesterday, it has begun to transform. Its starches have seeped into its broth; some of its liquid has evaporated heavenward; all of its flavors have mingled. Your soup can today be reheated as soup, with a little pour of water added to compensate for what the angels took. Or it can be reheated with heartifying additions like leftover cooked greens, roasted vegetables, cooked chickpeas, cold rice—at which point it will have become stew. Or it can be warmed and then poured over cooked grains as a wonderful fragrant sauce. Or the soup, if it is just a little, can spur you toward more soup, with what's left of this one used to fortify the next. Or, a little bit of soup can be a lovely replacement for a drizzle of cream or cooking liquid, added when you mash potatoes, or cauliflower, or turnips. If it is a chicken or beef or mushroom soup, its noodles, etc., can be strained out and its broth used to braise meat. Or your little bit of soup can add to a savory bread pudding or mixed with another leftover soup—have you ever had miso clam chowder? Why not?

Most of the leftover soup ideas in this chapter call for broth *or* water. To decide which you will use, taste whatever broth you have on hand. One might assume that chicken stock tastes like chicken stock and the liquid reserved from rehydrating dried mushrooms like deep and earthy mushrooms. But some purchased chicken stock tastes like cardboard, and mushroom liquid tastes like dust if the mushrooms were old. And, sometimes liquid that tasted good yesterday spent the night going sour. Taste what you have and if it tastes bad, you can always use trusty water, whose taste you know and like. If broth is cold, and you can't bear a sip, warm a few spoonfuls, then taste it.

If you are set on broth and have none, you will have to make some. There are a number of ways to do this. The first is to approach the problem head on and add the bones of meat or fish or mushroom stems, a few branches of herb or herb stems, a bit of carrot, an onion peel, perhaps a bay leaf to a pot of water. Putting this brew on a burner is making stock. This can cook for as little as 20 min and still accomplish something or up to several hours for a full-throated broth.

Another approach is to make a bay leaf-garlic stock. You can use whole garlic cloves or only garlic peels, saved in a pot near the stove as they're produced. Put a handful into a pot, cover them with water by several inches, add a little bunch of herbs or herb stems, a bay leaf and a pour of leftover white wine if you want. Bring it to a boil, then reduce it to simmer and let it cook for 30 min. Strain and you have a delightful slightly earthy broth. (The word "barley" comes to mind when I sip mine, even though there's no barley in sight.)

A third strategy is to save and freeze the liquid from boiling or braising anything, whether pasta or potatoes or broccoli or farro or beans—separately or together, in jars or ice cube trays or some other receptacle—and treat the salty and strongly flavored liquid as bouillon, to which you can add water to make broth. Another strategy yet is to keep the shelf-stable ingredients for dashi (kombu and bonito, which last forever) or instant dashi powder on hand. Then, you can have that versatile, subtle broth ready within 15 min. A fifth option is to add boiling water to one of the flavoring packets from instant ramen noodles that abscond to the backs of kitchen cupboards or drawers. These are full of all sorts of -dextrins and -ichlorides and so on, but the broth they make is universally delicious, and to harness the flavor and textural benefits of a -dextrin is no crime. A sixth path illustrates the depth of my own frugality (which is indemnified by extravagance elsewhere). I can't discard an empty bottle of soy or fish sauce or chili sauce or a jar of miso without splashing boiling water or another liquid around inside it (see p. 501). What I pour out after shaking is faintly savory, and it suits as broth. And there are yet other liquids that can be combined to make something more flavorful than water, like the liquid in a can of tomatoes, kimchi juice, chicken drippings, and, and, and . . . The vital thing is that what you use tastes good, not bad, because flavors can be added to good plain water, but they cannot be removed from bad-tasting broth.

Here are some stock/broth specifics:

MEAT STOCK

Enough bones to half fill a stockpot, 1 cup total aromatic vegetable scraps (carrot ends, onion skins or tops, fennel fronds, celery outers, parsley stems, mushroom feet, a few black peppercorns). *Optional additions:* 1 star anise, cilantro stems.

In a pot, combine the bones and vegetable scraps and any other additions. Add water to cover by 2 inches. Bring to a boil, skim off the scum that rises with a spoon or skimmer, reduce to a simmer, and cook until it tastes like broth, 2–4 hr, skimming periodically as the scum rises. Taste it after about 2 hr by scooping some into a spoon, lightly salting it, and deciding if it tastes like light broth. If it does, it's done. If not let it cook until it matches that description. Strain, cool, and freeze or use.

Fish bones freeze perfectly. Freeze until you have the full amount. Heads count.

FISH STOCK
2–3 lb fish bones (thwacked into pieces), ½–1 cup chopped onion (or leek or shallot), ½ cup chopped fennel scrap, 2 tbsp butter, 2 whole tomatoes (fresh or canned), ¼ cup white wine, bouquet garni (parsley stems and a bay leaf), ½ tsp black peppercorns, ¼ tsp fennel seeds, ¼ tsp coriander seeds.

In a pot, combine all the ingredients. Bring to a boil, then reduce to a simmer. Cook until it tastes delicious, 30 min–1 hr. Strain through a fine-mesh sieve and use to make soup or risotto or chowder!

DASHI
½ ounce (a few pieces) kombu (dried kelp), 3 cups lightly packed bonito flakes.

Wipe the kombu with a wet cloth. In a soup pot, combine 8 cups water and kombu and bring to a simmer, then turn off. Remove and reserve the kombu for Kombu Tsukudani (p. 55). Add the bonito flakes to the pot and stir. Let sit 3–4 minutes. Strain through a fine-mesh sieve, reserving the bonito for Furikake (p. 434), and use for anything and everything. This freezes well.

SAVORY STOCK/BROTH
1 piece cheese rind, 2–4 cloves garlic or 8 garlic peels, any piece of onion top or peel (or scallions tops or leek tops), a few sprigs of hardy herbs (thyme, rosemary, sage, parsley stems), 1 bay leaf, ¼ cup white wine.

In a pot, combine all the ingredients along with 6 cups water. Bring to a boil, reduce to a hard simmer. Cook for 1 hr. Taste. If it tastes like stock, strain and store it. If not, cook for up to another hr, then taste it again. In either case, strain, then freeze or use!

BEAN SOUP

FASTEST BEANS AND RICE *(15 min)*
1–2 tbsp neutral oil, 1 tbsp Puerto Rican Sofrito (p. 7), 1 cup bean soup, 1–2 cups cooked rice, salt, 1 tbsp chopped fresh herbs (optional; cilantro, parsley, mint).

Heat a small pot. Add the oil, and sofrito and cook until softened, 2–3 min. Add the bean soup and stir through, adding a drizzle of water if needed to make it stirable. Add the rice, stir through, then reduce the heat to low, cover, and cook until it's all warm and combined, another 4–5 min. Uncover, stir, taste for salt and adjust. Add herbs (if using) and eat.

SO MUCH BETTER BEAN SOUP *(5 min)*
2 cups bean soup, 4 kale leaves (stemmed and sliced into thin ribbons), ½–1 tsp Bengali hot sauce (Mr Naga), 1–2 tsp ghee, plain yogurt or raita (optional).

In a small pot, combine the bean soup, ¼ cup water, the kale, hot sauce, and ghee and heat to a simmer. Stir well, top with yogurt or raita (if using), and eat.

BEEF STEW

Macaronade is so good that it's worth making beef stew for.

MACARONADE *(30–40 min)*
Butter for the baking dish, salt, 1 lb rigatoni, 2 tbsp butter, 2 cups beef stew (mostly liquid), ½ cup grated Parmesan cheese, ½ cup fresh ricotta cheese.

Butter a large gratin or roasting dish. In a large pot of boiling water salted to taste like pleasant seawater, cook the pasta until al dente. Drain and transfer to a bowl. Add the butter and stew, mix, and let sit for 15 min. Add half the pasta to the prepared baking dish. Top with half the Parmesan, then the remaining pasta, and remaining Parmesan. Top with dollops of ricotta. Let sit another 10–15 min. Turn the broiler on low. Bake the macaronade under the broiler until the top is slightly crisped and the ricotta has begun to brown, 5–10 min.

BOUILLON CUBES

Bouillon cubes are good for seasoning rice. If you find yourself with a single straggling bouillon cube, make a batch of bouillon and use it to cook rice, or Amy's Pilaf (p. 206).

BROTH OR STOCK

Their swimminess implies a truth: Broth and stock are indifferent to boundaries. You never need the precise amount called for in a recipe. Any dish that asks for 4 cups of chicken stock can be cooked with 3 cups of water and 1 cup of broth, or 1 cup of cooking liquid, 1 cup of feta brine, 1 cup of water, and 1 cup of whatever liquid remained when you last cooked spinach. The total amount should be upheld and the details disregarded.

CHICKEN SOUP

Obviously, you can just reheat leftover chicken soup, adding more chicken broth if you have it, or water if you don't, plus fresh herbs, soy, etc. if you like them. Or, put the leftover soup in a pot, add cold cooked rice, allowing the pleasant and unusual comingling of starches, and a drizzle of water as needed to keep the warming soup from sticking. If you only have a small amoung of soup left, add broth or water, or water and cream and make it into more soup. Chopped parsley will reliably freshen this up.

CHOWDER

POT PIE (*2 hr, though much is resting the dough*)
Pie dough (Basic Cream Cheese Dough, p. 350, Basic Galette Dough, p. 102, or store-bought), 1 potato, 1 cup chowder, salt, ½ cup frozen peas (or corn or both), 1 tsp cornstarch, chopped fresh herbs (parsley, celery leaf, fennel frond, tarragon), melted butter or heavy cream.

If making homemade dough, make it and let it rest. Wash and peel the potato and cut into ½-inch cubes. In a pot, combine the chowder and potato and simmer until tender, about 10 min, adding water if needed. Taste for salt and adjust. Add the peas. Remove 2 tbsp warm chowder to a small bowl, whisk in the cornstarch, then add it to the chowder and stir over low heat. Add the herbs. Heat the oven to 375°F. Roll out enough dough to top a small, deep gratin or soufflé dish. Freeze the remaining dough for another time. Add the chowder to the gratin or soufflé dish. Top it with dough, sealing around the sides by pressing down, and make vents with a sharp knife. Brush with melted butter or heavy cream and bake until the top is browned and the chowder is hot, about 45 min.

CONSOMMÉ

I don't know if anyone has ever wondered what to do with leftover consommé, but there are so many pleasing and divergent words for clear broth—consommé, broth, bouillon, and stock—that it bears remembering that all can be used interchangeably. If you have a little consommé left, think of it as whichever—broth, stock, bouillon, or consommé—you use most often.

DASHI

Dashi can be used for reheating any soup or stew. Most vitally, it does not need restricting to Japanese cuisine. Cook beans in dashi, or use dashi to cook vegetables or as some of the liquid in Braised Meat (p. 298).

EGG DROP SOUP

EGG DROP CORN RAMEN *(5 min)*
1 package ramen, ¼ cup frozen or leftover cooked corn, ½ cup egg drop soup.

Cook the ramen according to package directions, adding the corn when you add the noodles. Add the leftover soup, stir through, and eat!

FISH SOUP

Reheat what's left and serve over little garlic-rubbed toasts. Leftover fish soup also makes excellent pasta sauce. Heat a small amount in a large pan. Cook pasta in well-seasoned boiling water until al dente, meanwhile heating the soup and letting some of the liquid boil off. Add the drained pasta, some pasta water, and a little butter, and let it finish cooking all together. Drizzle with olive oil and top with chopped parsley.

FRENCH ONION SOUP

FRENCH ONION SOUP PANADE *(1½ hr)*
Butter for the baking dish, 2 cups French onion soup, 2 cups broth or water, salt, 4–6 slices staling rustic bread (or more if it's a skinnier loaf like a baguette), 1 cup grated Gruyère or other good melting cheese.

Heat the oven to 375°F. Butter a small baking dish. In a small pot, combine the leftover onion soup (with or without its bread and cheese) and the broth or water and bring to a simmer. Taste for salt and adjust. It should be highly seasoned. Spoon half the hot soup mixture into the prepared baking dish, top with half of the sliced bread, fitting it tightly, then top with half the cheese, then with more soup mixture and the rest of the bread. Press down the top layer. It should be submerged in liquid when you press. If it's not, add a bit more broth or water. Cover and bake until it is all easily pierced with a sharp knife and seems like a soggy, but coherent mess, 30–45 min. Uncover and cook until the liquid is absorbed, another 20–30 min, adding the remaining cheese for the last 10–15 min.

GAZPACHO

Leftover gazpacho can be dealt with in three ways: 1) Pour what's left into a glass with ice, and drink it. 2) Make a savory ice pop by pouring gazpacho into an ice pop mold (or several) and cool down the next hot day without a sugar rush. 3) Make more gazpacho, and include what you have left in the blender instead of some of the olive oil and vinegar. Face the quandary anew tomorrow.

GUMBO

Leftover gumbo can be stretched by adding enough broth or water to turn it into stew. Heat until very hot, adding any leftover cooked meat or sausage or greens or all of the above as it warms. Or make Arancini (p. 240).

LENTIL SOUP

Leftover lentil soup makes a So Much Better Bean Soup (p. 249) nonpareil. *See also Bean soup (p. 249).*

LOBSTER STOCK

Lobster stock is more important to lobster stew than is lobster, and a perfectly satisfactory one can be made without any lobster meat.

LOBSTER STEW *(30 min)*
Ghee or olive oil, ½ cup finely chopped onion, 1 cup chopped raw or cooked potatoes, ½ cup finely chopped carrots, any other vegetables you want in your stew, 4 cups lobster stock, salt, heavy cream, croutons or oyster crackers (optional), a few strands of saffron (optional).

Heat a pot. Add the ghee or olive oil and onion and sauté until tender, about 10 min. Stir in the potatoes, carrots, and any other long-cooking vegetable you want. Add the stock and bring to a boil, then reduce to a simmer and cook until the potatoes, carrots, or longest-cooking vegetable are tender. Season with salt to taste, then add any quick-cooking vegetables (corn and peas), then as much cream as you like. Eat hot as is or with toasted croutons or oyster crackers. If the lobster stock didn't contain saffron, a few strands can be added at the start of the stew-making.

Or use lobster stock in Onion Soup (p. 27). I prefer the lobster broth version to the beef broth version.

MENUDO

Menudo improves on its own, and it's hard to come up with a needful intervention. I add a bit of water or stock, reheat it, top it heavily with chopped onion, cilantro, and lime juice, and eat it until it's gone.

MINESTRONE

Minestrone can be reheated with added broth, especially bean broth, or chicken or vegetable broth or water, and eaten again as minestrone! Or it can evolve into:

MARCELLA HAZAN'S MINESTRONE FREDDO ALLA MILANESE
(3–4 hr, but mostly waiting)
2 cups minestrone, ½ cup Arborio or other short-grain rice, 1 tsp salt plus to taste, 8–10 basil leaves (julienned), ¼ cup freshly grated Parmesan cheese, good olive oil for drizzling.

In a pot, combine the minestrone and 2 cups water and bring to a boil. Stir in the rice and salt, reduce the heat to medium-low, cover, and cook until the rice is just cooked through, 12–15 min. Taste for salt and adjust, then remove from the heat. Add the basil and Parmesan, mix well, and let cool to room temperature. Serve at room temperature, with a drizzle of olive oil. This is a summer soup.

MINESTRONE RIBOLLITA *(40 min)*
1 cup minestrone, ½ cup cubed stale crustless bread, salt. *For serving:* freshly grated Parmesan cheese, olive oil for drizzling.

In a small pot, combine the minestrone, bread, and enough water to make things lightly soupy, starting with ½ cup. Bring to a boil then reduce to a simmer and cook, stirring occasionally, until the bread has completely broken down and becomes creamy, 30–40 min, adding sprinkles of water throughout if needed to keep things from burning and sticking. Taste for salt and adjust. Eat topped with Parmesan and a drizzle of olive oil.

MISO SOUP

I love miso soup. I always make more than I need and use what's left as a general reheating liquid, adding a few spoonfuls to anything and taking advantage of its salt and umami. I find that any bits of tofu or scallion left floating around in the result contribute to rather than detract from the overall next-day experience. I also often make:

SAVORY MISO RICE STEW *(5 min)*
½ cup miso soup, any amount of leftover cooked rice. *Optional add-ons:* a halved boiled egg or oil-packed canned or leftover cooked fish, furikake or julienned nori.

In a small pot, combine the miso soup and rice and bring to a simmer. Cook until the rice is warm. If desired, add the halved egg and/or fish and cook until just warm. Remove from the heat and eat, garnished with furikake or nori if desired.

MUSHROOM SOUP

MUSHROOM PASTA SAUCE *(25 min)*
3 tbsp olive oil, 2 tbsp finely chopped shallot or onion, 2 cups mushroom soup, ¼–½ cup heavy cream, ½ cup grated Parmesan cheese plus to taste, salt, 1 lb short pasta (rigatoni or mezze maniche), 2 tbsp butter, ½ cup chopped parsley, freshly ground black pepper.

Heat a pan large enough to hold the pasta. Add the olive oil, shallot or onion, and ½ tsp salt and cook until the shallot is totally tender and transparent, about 3 min. Stir in the mushroom soup, bring to a boil, and cook to reduce by half. Add the cream. Remove from the heat, add the Parmesan, taste for salt and adjust. In a large pot of boiling water salted to taste like pleasant seawater, cook the pasta. Reserve ¼ cup pasta water before draining. When the pasta is done, remove it directly into the pan, and return to the heat and add the butter, tossing well to coat and adding pasta water if needed. Add the parsley, black pepper, and any more cheese you like to the sauce and eat.
   The sauce can also be used as a sauce for polenta.

POZOLE

Like menudo, pozole improves with age and should just be warmed and eaten, with new julienned cabbage, new cilantro, new lime, and old salsa, until gone.

RAMEN, LEFTOVER

Leftover ramen can have broth or water added to turn it into a respectable quantity for lunch. Bring it to a boil with added liquid, taste for salt and adjust, then crack in an egg. Stir through and eat.

RAMEN FLAVORING PACKETS

I love these adamantly and use them if I find them, which I do about once a season, tucked away between the pencils stubs and spare keys. I add the one I find to boiled water, taste the result, sing the praises of modern food engineering, then add some cooked rice and tofu and eat lunch.

RASAM

FAST RASAM RICE *(25 min)*
1 cup cooked basmati rice, 1 cup rasam, 2 tbsp ghee, 6 curry leaves, ¼ tsp mustard seeds, ¼ tsp cumin seeds, a tiny pinch of hing (asafoetida), chopped cilantro (optional).

Cook rice if needed, using the ratios on p. 205. In a pot, bring rasam to a simmer. Add the cooked rice and stir through. Remove from the heat and let sit for 5 min. Meanwhile, in a small pot, melt the ghee, then add the curry leaves, mustard seeds, and cumin seeds. When the seeds sizzle and pop, add the hing and remove from the heat. Pour over the rasam rice. Top with cilantro (if using).

RIBOLLITA

Bread soups, of which Ribollita is in my mind the queen, possess the magical properties of a bottomless cauldron. So much broth is absorbed overnight that warming the soup back up demands at least a ladleful or two of liquid before you can even get a spoon in to stir. This is as true on day 4 as on day 2, which makes the actual finishing of the soup a point that recedes . . . for longer than you'd think. If you actually want to finish your ribollita, make it into pancakes.

LILY MEYER'S RIBOLLITA SOURDOUGH PANCAKES (10 min)
1–2 cups ribollita, ½ cup leftover cooked broccoli (or cauliflower or other cooked greens), salt, ½ cup sourdough starter, olive oil.

Mix the ribollita with the broccoli until combined. Taste for salt and adjust. Whisk in the sourdough starter. Heat a pan. Add enough olive oil to just coat. Ladle out batter in the size pancakes you want, flipping when the top side of each pancake is well populated by little bubbles. Cook until just crisped on the second side. Good with a lettuce salad.

SAMBAR

FISH SAMBAR (15–20 min)
2–3 cups sambar, 1–2 cups bite-size pieces raw skinless white fish fillet, cooked rice for eating.

In a medium saucepan, bring the sambar to a simmer, stirring. Reduce the heat to the lowest possible simmer, then add the fish. Cook for 1 min on the lowest heat, then remove from the heat, cover, and let steam until the fish just flakes, another 3–4 min. Eat over hot rice.

SAMBAR BISI BELE BATH-ISH (20 min)
2 tbsp neutral oil (peanut or grapeseed oil), 1–2 cups chopped raw or cooked vegetables (optional; leftover zucchini, squash, carrots, peppers, etc.), salt, 1 cup cooked rice, 1 cup sambar, yogurt or raita (optional), cilantro (optional).

Heat a medium pot. Add the oil, the vegetables (if using), and a small pinch of salt. Cook over medium heat, stirring often, until tender, about 10 min. If you're not using vegetables, add the rice and sambar and cook, stirring occasionally, over medium heat, until hot, mushy, and combined. Good with yogurt or raita and chopped cilantro if desired.

SWEET AND SOUR SOUP

Treat leftover sweet and sour soup as a sauce. Add 1–3 tbsp toward the end of stir-frying noodles, or once fried rice has gotten a bit crisp, or use 1–3 tbsp of it in Empty Chili Sauce Noodles (p. 501).

TOM KA GAI

Add more coconut milk and liquid and you have more soup! Or add leftover roasted eggplant, squash, or zucchini and eat on rice.

VEGETABLE SOUP, BROTHY

As with most other soups, brothy vegetable soups—which are called minestras in Italy—can be extended by the judicious addition of more flavorful liquid, like dashi or bean broth or farro water or potato water, and made more substantial with rice or toasted croutons or bread.

VEGETABLE SOUP, PUREED

Adding liquid will turn a mashed vegetable into a vegetable soup, and removing liquid (which evaporation does on its own) will do the reverse. What you have left of a puréed vegetable soup (aka potage) can therefore be reimagined as a side dish: Heat with a bit of butter, with an additional cooked potato added if needed, then eat it as you would mashed potatoes, perhaps with gremolata or Parsley Oil (p. 68) or chopped nuts on top.

To turn leftover puréed vegetable soup into a new soup, put it in a pot and whisk it, as it heats, with additional liquid of any kind, along with whatever herbs or spices you're in the mood for. If it is squash soup, add a bit of red curry paste and coconut milk as it warms. If it appeals, poach some chopped shrimp in the redolent stew. If it's creamy bean soup, add broth and some sausage or tofu, heating it as you add so they have a chance to combine.

VICHYSSOISE

As a cold soup Vicchyssoise has the benefit of never having to be heated. I usually drink any leftovers. But if you don't want to drink yours, boil potatoes in water seasoned to taste like pleasant seawater, then drain. Rice or put through a food mill. Add a good deal of butter, then the leftover vichyssoise, then a drizzle of cream. Mix it all well, taste, adjust butter, salt, and cream, and eat.

soup

HOW TO FRY THE LITTLEST FISH

Seafood

A cook is quite as useful as a poet, And quite as wise, and these anchovies show it.

—*Athenaeus*, Deipnosophistae

I n cultures where fish is a mainstay, two truths inform its treatment. First, there are better and worse ways of slaughtering fish, and the prevailing way in the West, now, is a worse way. If, as in the Japanese method called ikejime, fish is immobilized and killed and cleansed of its blood immediately after being caught, then chilled to relax its muscles, it can last without measurable change for a week. Second is that not only can leftover fish find a home in countless sought-after dishes, like laap pla duk (Thai fried fish salad) and fish cakes and chowder and salads and croquettes and more, but so can their heads and fins and maws and frames.

If you can't find fish that have been killed using ikejime—and I can't—cook fish before it begins to smell strong. It lasts longer cooked than raw, and can always be drizzled with olive oil, left to chill, then brought back to room temperature before being flaked into pasta, or included in a composed salad, or eaten with hot rice, or turned into a curry or a soup or a chowder or a pot pie.

If you know you want to cook it for dinner tomorrow, there is some logic to seasoning fish lightly today. This will draw out water, whose oxygen hosts the sorts of bacteria that cause decay, and give it an extra longevity boost. Once fish has been served and its leftovers are ready to be stored away, use one of the world's genius strategies for cocooning a perishable in fat. It can be crème fraîche or butter or olive oil or duck fat or sour cream or mayonnaise. Versions of this approach comprise rich pâtés and dips and bagel toppings and salad ingredients and snacks. Or, liberally apply an acid to cooked fish, which can vary from lime juice (ceviche) to red wine vinegar and olive oil (in saor) to bottled Italian dressing (Raymond's Pickled Clams, p. 266). Another approach is to marshal the healing and charitable properties of starch. All of the fish cakes and fish balls and croquettes of the world take advantage of this principle, and, whatever this says of my discernment, I like almost all I encounter.

It is fortunate and unfortunate that in my custody most leftover fish is interchangeable. Anything I do tends to rely on the flakiness and general lightness of fish, and I can't pretend I distinguish carefully among species. I've listed everything under Fish (pp. 273–78), unless there is something else worth saying.

Temperature is paramount. Cold fish can be unnerving—as can cold eggs. Allow enough time for any fishy leftover to come back to room temperature before proceeding with a plan, because a fast heat-up will cause rubberiness—no improvement on the strange jellyness of cold fish. As with other leftovers that don't improve with further stewing or simmering, be bold and quick with leftover fish. Let crispness and chew and brightness and spice and sweetness work where the addition of fat and time won't, and add them with tenacity. Do not forget that the liquid left after cooking any fish or shellfish is more valuable than any other, carrying within it some of the salt and secret of the sea.

I've included a number of recipes here for canned fish. I don't live near a port and most of the fish we eat is canned. It's easy to keep canned seafood around, so on the occasion that you have no leftovers, several cans of fish and this chapter should help keep your frying pan full.

BLUEFISH

Bluefish is taut and clean tasting just after being caught, then quickly begins to act like a big sardine. Best is to turn any leftovers you have into Fish Curry with Rice Noodles (p. 276) or use it, with a good deal of salt added, instead of salt cod in Brandade Croquettes (recipe below).

BRANDADE

BRANDADE CROQUETTES *(30 min–1 hr)*
2 cups brandade, all-purpose flour, salt, 1–2 eggs (beaten), dried bread crumbs, neutral oil (peanut or grapeseed), flaky salt, wedges of lemon.

Form leftover brandade into little balls the size of falafel or into small cylindrical shapes. Set up three shallow dishes. Put the flour in one, the beaten egg in the second, and the bread crumbs in the third. Roll the balls lightly in the flour, tap off excess, then roll in the beaten egg, then the bread crumbs. Place on a cooling rack or plate or tray and refrigerate for 10 min. In a heavy-bottomed saucepan, heat ½ inch of oil to 365°F or so. Fry in batches, turning as needed, 3–5 min per batch. Drain on paper towels. Eat warm, sprinkled with flaky salt, with lemon wedges alongside.

CATFISH

Like bluefish, catfish has an urgency to it. For a leftover catfish sandwich, make Rémoulade Sauce (p. 396) or just mix mayonnaise with drained chopped capers and celery leaves, toast 2 slices of good white sandwich bread, butter well, put the catfish on one, add some hot sauce, then rémoulade, and imagine you were on a flat-bottom boat in calm water.

CAVIAR

Caviar is salt-cured and lasts longer than you'd think. If you somehow find a half jar, immediately make little pancakes. Locate sour cream or Greek yogurt or even a bit of cream- or cottage cheese. Dollop the pancakes with the sour cream, then spoon caviar over the top, with a tiny scrape of the most finely chopped onion or scallion or chive if you have.

CEVICHE

Drain leftover ceviche, saving the marinade (leche de tigre) to use in place of the sauerkraut juice in Sauerkraut Michelada (p. 441)—fishelada?—then use the ceviche itself in Fish Curry with Rice Noodles (p. 276) or Thai Fish Cakes (p. 273).

CLAMS, COOKED

PICKLED CLAMS (*30 min*)
1 clove garlic (sliced), ½ onion or 2 scallions (thinly sliced), ¼ tsp coriander seeds, ¼ tsp fennel seeds, chile flakes, ½ tsp salt plus to taste, 1 tbsp fresh lemon juice, 1½ tbsp white wine vinegar, ½ lemon (thinly sliced), 2 cups cooked clam meats, ½ tbsp chopped mixed herbs (celery leaves or fennel fronds), 3 tbsp olive oil plus to taste, ½ cup whole parsley leaves, freshly ground black pepper.

In a large bowl, combine the garlic, onion or scallions, coriander, fennel, chile flakes to taste, salt, lemon juice, vinegar, and sliced lemon. Let sit for 10 min. Add the clams and chopped mixed herbs and enough olive oil to make it all very juicy. Taste for salt and adjust. Let sit at least another 10 min or up to overnight. Just before serving, add parsley and black pepper to taste. Good on saltines.

RAYMOND'S PICKLED CLAMS (*5 min*)
2 cups cooked clam meat, store-bought Italian dressing.

A lobsterman named Raymond gave me this recipe: "Cook clams, remove the shells. Combine clams with Italian dressing in a Mason jar." A handful of chopped parsley is good, too, if you aren't on a lobster boat. These are also good on saltines.

HOI TOD *(5–10 min)*

1 clove garlic, ¼ tsp salt plus to taste, ½-1 cup bean sprouts, ½ cup tapioca flour or cornstarch, ½ cup seltzer or 7 Up, 1 egg, peanut oil (or grapeseed, or vegetable) for cooking, ½–1 cup cooked clam meat, 1–2 tsp fish sauce, 2–3 scallions (finely chopped).

Pound the garlic to a paste with salt, add the bean sprouts, and gently mix through. In a bowl, stir together the tapioca flour or cornstarch and seltzer or 7 Up. Whisk in the egg. Heat a large skillet. Add enough oil to coat the bottom. Add the batter, spreading thin, then sprinkle the clams over, and sprinkle with fish sauce. Scatter with the scallions. Reduce the heat slightly, and continue to spread. Let it get very crispy, then flip. Move it to the side of the pan. Add the bean sprouts and garlic and quickly cook. Spread the omelet, push the bean sprout mixture into it, fold loosely, and tip onto a plate. This does not have to stay together, or be neat at all. In Thailand, it's usually served cut in pieces.

COCONUT CLAM STEW *(15 min)*

2 cups total liquid (any combination of coconut milk, clam juice, and leftover clam liquid), ½ tsp some kind of curry paste, 2 cups thinly sliced stemmed cooking greens (kale, collards, or cabbage), 1 cup leftover cooked squash or potato, salt or fish sauce, ½–1 cup cooked clam meats, cilantro (or basil or Thai basil).

In a small pot, combine the liquid and curry paste and cook, whisking, until the curry paste is dissolved. Add the greens, squash or potato, and salt or fish sauce to taste and bring to a boil. Simmer until the greens are cooked, about 10 min. Add the clams and stir through to just warm. Eat topped with herbs. Good on rice or noodles, too, if you have any. This can be varied with whatever vegetables you have.

CLAM CHOWDER *(45 min)*

1 slice bacon (chopped), 2 tbsp butter plus to taste, ½ stalk celery (chopped), ½ onion (chopped), ¼ tsp salt plus to taste, ½ cup white wine, any liquid from cooking the clams, 2 bottles store-bought clam juice, pinch of chile flakes (optional), 2–3 smallish potatoes (chopped), a little frozen or fresh corn (optional), a few clam meats (whole or chopped), 1 cup heavy cream, any available chopped parsley.

In a pot, cook the bacon in the butter until just crisp. Add the celery, onion, and salt, and cook until tender, 5–10 min. Add the wine and cook until you can't smell it. Add the clam liquid, bottled clam juice, chile flakes if using, and 1 cup water, then add the potatoes. Bring to a boil, then reduce to a simmer and cook until the potatoes are tender, about 20 min. Add the corn (if using) and cook for 1 min. Add the clams and cream. Mix through, add the parsley, and eat.

CLAM COOKING LIQUID

I begin this recipe with the line of preface with which it was sent to me: "Defrost clam cooking water when you're feeling homesick for the sea."

OLIVIA'S CLAMLESS PASTA *(25 min)*
2 tbsp olive oil, 2 cloves garlic (smashed), 4 anchovy fillets, 1 slice dried pepperoncini or ⅛ tsp chile flakes, 8 cherry tomatoes (halved), 1 cup clam cooking liquid, 4 oz spaghetti or linguine, ¼ cup roughly chopped parsley.

Heat a pot. Add the oil, garlic, and anchovies and cook until the anchovies begin to melt, 20–30 sec. Add the pepperoncini or chile flakes, then the cherry tomatoes and clam liquid. Cook until reduced by half. Meanwhile, cook the pasta in unsalted water until very al dente. Add to the pot with the tomatoes and cook, over medium heat, until it's as cooked as you like it, adding the parsley toward the end.

MRS. GUEST'S CLAM BOUILLON *(10 min)*
A Mrs. Guest I do not know wrote this recipe a long time ago. Its sounds strange, but it is delicious: Bring cooking liquid to a boil, skim any scum that rises, taste, add a single grating of nutmeg if you know you really like nutmeg, then eat topped with whipped cream!

Or add cubed tofu and cooked rice to leftover clam cooking liquid. Heat to a bubble, taste, and eat. Add sliced scallions if you can bear to interrupt the serenity. Or freeze it and use where fish stock is called for.

If you're worried you won't remember the clam cooking liquid, intervene now on behalf of your future self and label it "seafood stock" before putting it away.

CLAMS, FRIED

Use any leftover fried clams in the Scallion Omelet Crepe (p. 90).

CLAMS, STUFFED

STUFFED CLAM PASTA *(25 min)*
12 stuffed clams, salt, as much pasta as you want, olive oil, 1–3 cloves garlic (chopped), a shake of dried chile flakes, 2–3 tbsp white wine (or clam juice or neither), 1 cup finely chopped parsley, 1–2 tbsp butter, grated lemon zest and/or a squeeze of lemon juice (optional), ½–1 cup toasted bread crumbs (see p. 176) for serving (optional).

Remove the clams from the shells, scraping all the stuffing with them, and set aside. Heat a wide pan. Add enough olive oil to well cover the bottom. Add the garlic, chile flakes, and a pinch of salt and cook over low heat until just tender, 1–2 min. Add the clams and let just warm. Add the wine and bring to a simmer, then add the parsley and remove from the heat. In a large pot of boiling water salted to taste like pleasant seawater, cook the pasta, reserving ¼ cup cooking water before draining. Add the cooked pasta to the pan, mixing well, adding a bit of pasta water if needed. Add the butter and, if desired, lemon zest and/or a squeeze of lemon juice. Scatter each serving heavily with bread crumbs (if using), before eating.

CLAMS, CANNED

These can, of course, be used to make a definitive linguine with clam sauce. But if you need something to take to a pot luck, try:

CLAM DIP *(overnight, but all waiting)*
One 6.5 oz can minced clams, 4 oz cream cheese, ¼ cup sour cream, 2–3 scallions (thinly sliced), juice of ½ lemon, ¼ tsp salt plus to taste, a few shakes of Tabasco.

Reserving the juice, drain the clams. In a bowl, combine the clams with the remaining ingredients plus a few spoonfuls of reserved clam juice. Mix well. Refrigerate covered overnight. Good on any cracker or any raw crisp vegetable. The same can be done with canned mussels or oysters.

CLAM SHELLS

These make beautiful soap holders. If the clams were small, so must be the soap. Thankfully, a number of clam species grow to the size of the average soap bar.

CRAB, COOKED

HAEMUL PAJEON *(20–30 min)*
1½ cups cooked crabmeat, 1 tbsp sesame oil, ¾ cup all-purpose flour, ¼ cup cornstarch, ¾ cup ice water plus a little more, ½ tsp gochugaru or chile flakes (or 1 tsp finely chopped fresh chile), 2 bunches scallions (very thinly sliced), vegetable or peanut oil for frying. *For dipping:* 1 tbsp soy sauce, 1 tbsp wine vinegar, 1 tbsp water, ¼ tsp sugar.

In a small bowl, combine the crab and sesame oil. In a large bowl, whisk together the flour and cornstarch, then whisk in ¾ cup ice water. The batter should be the consistency of heavy cream. Add 1–2 tbsp more ice water as needed for that consistency. Add the crab, gochugaru or chile flakes, and scallions. Heat a skillet. Add 3–4 tbsp oil. Ladle in half the batter and cook over medium heat until just golden brown, 3–4 min. Flip, add a bit more oil, cook another 3–4 min, then remove to a plate. Repeat with the rest of the batter and eat with the dipping sauce. (Adapted from Korean Bapsang website)

CRAB TOASTS *(20–25 min)*
Aioli (p. 395), 2–3 thick slices rustic bread or 4–5 baguette slices, ½–1 cup cooked crabmeat, 2 tbsp chopped celery leaves or fennel fronds, 1 small chile (finely chopped), 2 tbsp olive oil plus more for drizzling, ¼ tsp salt plus to taste, 1 drop Tabasco per toast (optional), lemon wedges (optional).

Make the aioli. Toast the bread. Meanwhile, in a bowl, combine the crabmeat, celery leaves or fennel fronds, chile, olive oil, and salt. Taste for salt and adjust. Drizzle the toast with some olive oil, then slather with aioli. Top with the crab mixture, then dab a little bit more aioli on each toast. Add a drop of Tabasco (if using). Can be good with a lemon wedge, too. (Adapted from the Epicurious website)

CRAB RICE BOWL *(30 min)*

1 cup short-grain rice, ½ cucumber (thinly sliced), 3 tbsp mirin, ½–1 cup cooked crabmeat, 2–3 shiso leaves (thinly sliced), 1 sheet nori (thinly sliced), 2 tbsp salmon roe or other caviar, 1 tbsp toasted sesame seeds, Kewpie mayonnaise (optional).

Cook the rice. While it's cooking, in a bowl, combine the cucumber and mirin and set aside. When the rice is done, divide between two bowls. On each bowl, arrange the ingredients in individual piles: crabmeat, drained cucumbers, shiso leaves, and nori. Place the salmon roe or other caviar in the middle and cover everything with the sesame seeds. If desired drizzle with Kewpie mayonnaise.

Or, add leftover crab to Fried Rice (p. 205) or use it to fill an omelet.

CRAB CAKES

CRAB CAKE LARB *(15 min)*

¼ cup thinly sliced shallot, 1 tbsp roasted rice powder (see p. 208) or sesame seeds, 2 tsp fish sauce, juice of 1 lime, ¼ tsp ground chile powder, scant 1 tsp sugar, 2–3 cooked crab cakes (crumbled or chopped), 1 cup chopped cilantro (or any combination of cilantro, mint, and basil).

In a large bowl, stir together the shallot, rice powder or sesame seeds, fish sauce, lime juice, chile powder, and sugar until well combined. Add the crab cakes, mix through, then add the herbs. Taste for a balance of hot, sour, salty, sweet. Adjust if you want. Eat as is or in cabbage or lettuce cups or on rice or with sticky rice. This same idea can be applied to any leftover chicken or fish or tofu.

CRAB, SOFT-SHELL, COOKED

The following ingredients are the amounts for 1 sandwich with 1 cooked soft-shell crab. Scale up as needed.

SOFT-SHELL CRAB SANDWICHES *(15 min)*
1 hamburger bun or potato roll or 2 slices sandwich bread, butter, 2 tbsp purchased or homemade mayonnaise (p. 395), ½ tsp capers (drained and chopped), 1 tbsp olive oil, 1 cooked soft-shell crab.

Toast the bun or potato roll or sandwich bread and butter both sides. In a small bowl, combine the mayonnaise and capers. Heat a skillet. Add the oil and crab and re-sauté until just warm and the bottom is beginning to crisp, about 2 min. Flip and cook to just crisp the top. Lay the crab on the bottom bread, heavily slather the top with caper mayonnaise, close the sandwich, and eat.

CRAB SHELLS

Use in place of the fish bones in Fish Stock (p. 247).

ESCARGOT

SCRAMBLED EGGS WITH SNAILS *(30 min)*
5 snails (out of their shells), 1 small clove garlic, ¼ tsp salt plus to taste, 6 tbsp room-temperature butter, 3–4 eggs, 1 tbsp finely chopped parsley.

Bring the snails to room temperature. Pound the garlic to a paste with salt. Add 3 tbsp butter to make garlic butter. In a bowl, whisk the eggs well, until very frothy, then add a tiny pinch of salt. In a small pan over the lowest possible heat, warm the snails in the garlic butter, adding parsley. Remove from heat. Heat a nonstick or cast-iron skillet. Melt the remaining 3 tbsp butter. When it stops foaming, turn it to the lowest heat, add the eggs, and scramble very, very softly, stirring patiently and consistently to get a tiny curd. When they are just set, tip them into a bowl, top with the snails, and serve or eat. (Inspired by Frenchette, New York City)

This is, in all seriousness, what every bagel needs.

WHAT EVERY BAGEL NEEDS *(5 min)*
⅔–1 cup flaked cooked fish (skin removed), 2 tbsp cream cheese (cut into pieces), 2 tbsp minced fresh chives, ½ tsp salt, ⅛ tsp ground coriander, scant ⅛ tsp ground cumin, a little freshly ground black pepper.

In a bowl, combine everything and smash well. You could add a tiny scrape of preserved lemon, as well.

If the leftover fish for the following fish cakes has skin, remove, reserve, finely chop, and include it. Its collagen is useful in binding. (So are eggs and bread crumbs, so it's not essential.)

YANKEE FISH CAKES *(30 min)*
For the fish cakes: 1½–2 cups flaked cooked fish (skin removed and reserved), 3 tbsp bread crumbs, 1 egg (beaten), scant ½ cup finely chopped onion, ½–1 clove garlic (chopped), 1½ tsp salt, a little freshly ground black pepper, a little finely chopped fish skin (optional), 1–2 tbsp finely chopped parsley or chives (optional). *For cooking:* bread crumbs (optional) for coating, peanut or grapeseed oil for frying. *For serving:* lemon wedges or Sauce Gribiche (p. 396) or Tartar Sauce (p. 396).

To make smoother fish cakes: In a food processor, combine all the ingredients and blend well until quite smooth and almost tacky, up to a few min. To make more textured fish cakes: Flake the fish by hand, then, in a bowl, whisk the egg, and combine all the remaining ingredients by hand. To cook: If desired, coat the fish cakes in bread crumbs. In a pot, heat 2–3 inches of oil until 350°–365°F. Add the fish cakes and fry 2–3 min on the first side and 2 min on the second. Drain on paper towels. Serve with lemon wedges or gribiche or tartar sauce.

A variation is to substitute leftover mashed potato for some or all of the fish.

THAI FISH CAKES *(10 min)*
1 cup flaked cooked fish (skin removed and reserved), a little finely chopped fish skin (optional), 1½ tsp Thai red curry paste, 1 egg yolk, 1 tsp fish sauce,

½ tsp sugar, 2 tsp cornstarch, 2 makrut lime leaves (slivered). *For cooking:* peanut or grapeseed oil for frying. *For serving:* lime or lemon wedges or any chili sauce you like.

In a blender, combine the cooked fish and a little of its skin, finely chopped, if you have it. Add the curry paste, egg yolk, fish sauce, and sugar and pulse to blend to a paste. Add the cornstarch and pulse. Test the mixture with your hand to make sure it stays together. Add the lime leaves and pulse once or twice more. Form into thick pancakes, 2–3 inches around. In a pot, heat 2–3 inches of oil to 350°–365°F. Add the fish cakes and fry 2–3 min on the first side and 2 min on the second. Drain on paper towels. Serve with lime or lemon wedges or a chili sauce for dipping. These are good on rice.

PORTUGUESE EGGS *(5–10 min)*
3–4 tbsp good olive oil plus to taste, 1 tbsp thinly sliced or chopped onion, ¼ tsp salt plus to taste, 1 small clove garlic (chopped), 2 eggs, ½ cup flaked cooked fish (skin removed), chopped parsley or sliced olives (optional).

Heat a pan. Add about 1½ tbsp olive oil. Add the onion and a little of the salt and cook over medium heat until just tender, 2–3 min. Meanwhile, pound the garlic to a paste with the remaining salt, then, in a bowl, whisk in the eggs and about 2 tbsp olive oil. Add the fish to the onion and mix through lightly. Add a final sprinkle of olive oil, then the garlic-egg mixture, and scramble over low heat, stopping just before the eggs are as you like them. Add some chopped parsley or a few sliced olives or both if desired.

FISH RILLETTES *(5 min)*
½ clove garlic, salt, 4 oz cooked fish, 1 tbsp room-temperature butter or crème fraîche, 2–3 tbsp finely chopped herbs (parsley, dill, or tarragon), ½ tsp Dijon mustard, a big squeeze of lemon, 1 tbsp thinly sliced scallions.

Smash the garlic to a paste with a little salt. In a bowl, combine the garlic, fish, butter or crème fraîche, herbs, mustard, and lemon and smash to fairly smooth. Mix in the scallion. Taste for salt and adjust. Good on crackers or on bagels or in lettuce cups.

YAM PLA DOOK FU *(25 min)*

1 cup neutral oil (peanut or grapeseed), 2 cups flaked cooked fish, ½ cup finely sliced green mango (or green papaya or carrot), 3 tbsp finely sliced shallots, 1–3 tbsp very hot chile like Thai bird's eye, 1 tbsp fish sauce or to taste, 1 tbsp sugar or to taste, lettuce leaves or rice for serving, 2 tbsp chopped toasted peanuts or fried shallots.

Heat a pan. Add the oil, then fry the fish, breaking it up lightly as you do, until golden. Remove with a hand-held sieve to paper towels. In a bowl, combine the mango, shallots, chile, fish sauce, and sugar. Mix well, combine with the crisp fish. Eat on lettuce leaves or rice and garnish with peanuts or fried shallots.

TEAISM SOUP *(3–5 min)*

2 cups miso soup, ½–1 cup cooked green vegetable (bok choy, broccoli, broccoli rabe, kale, or collards), ½ cup cooked rice or udon noodles (optional), 2 tbsp–¼ cup flaked cooked fish. *Optional garnishes:* chili paste, black vinegar, crisp fried shallots, toasted chopped peanuts, Crispy Fish Skin (p. 278).

In a saucepan, heat the miso soup and vegetables together until warm, along with the rice or noodles (if using). Remove from the heat and add the fish. Let warm off the heat. Garnish as desired and eat.

FISH, OVERCOOKED

A LITTLE FISH PASTA *(overnight, but all waiting)*

1 overcooked fish fillet, 1 tbsp finely sliced preserved lemon, salt, ½ tsp cracked coriander seeds, ½ tsp cracked fennel seeds, ¼ cup good olive oil, 1 tsp drained capers, ½ lb pasta, 2 tbsp butter, a handful of chopped parsley.

Flake the fish fillet and put in a small storage container, add the preserved lemon, ¼ tsp salt, the spices, and olive oil. Let sit in the refrigerator overnight. Bring to room temperature, then scoop out the fish, leaving a little oil behind, and mix in a bowl with capers. In a large pot of boiling water salted to taste like pleasant seawater, cook the pasta. Drain the pasta and toss with the fish mixture, 2 tbsp butter, and parsley. Use the oil for another batch of fish or for another seafood pasta sauce.

FISH CONFIT *(variable, 2 hr to overnight, but mostly waiting)*
3 tbsp salt, ½–1 lb raw fish, 2 cups olive oil, 2–3 cloves garlic (smashed), a few slices lemon or strips of lemon zest, a few sprigs of thyme, a few parsley stems, a bay leaf, 1 dried chile.

Salt the fish, cover, and refrigerate overnight. When you're ready to cook, remove the fish from the refrigerator, rinse off the salt, and pat dry. Cut any large pieces into 2-inch chunks. In a small, deep pot, heat the oil. Add the garlic, lemon, thyme, parsley, bay leaf, and chile. Once the oil is just warm, add the fish to the pot. Check it for doneness after a few min by retrieving a piece with a slotted spoon. The fish will be done when it just flakes. Let it cool in the oil off the heat, then store it in its oil in the refrigerator, where it will stay good for at least a week. The oil should be strained well, then refrigerated and used for cooking fish or for making more fish confit.

FISH CURRY WITH RICE NOODLES *(15 min)*
1 tbsp peanut or vegetable oil, 1 tbsp finely minced fresh ginger, 1 tbsp chopped or pounded garlic, 1–2 chopped chiles (optional), 2 tbsp yellow or green Thai curry paste, 1 can coconut milk (well shaken), 1 cup fish stock or clam juice, 1 tbsp fish sauce plus to taste, 2–3 makrut lime leaves (torn), 1 package rice noodles, 1–2 cups chopped raw fish, cilantro or Thai basil (optional).

Heat a medium pot. Add the oil, ginger, garlic, and chile (if using) and cook over medium heat until beginning to soften, 1–2 min. Add the curry paste and stir and smash. Stir in about ¼ cup of the coconut milk, breaking up any clumps in the curry paste. Add the remainder of the coconut milk, the fish stock or clam juice, fish sauce, and lime leaves. Bring to a boil, then reduce to a simmer. Taste and adjust with fish sauce, then remove from the heat. Cook the rice noodles according to the package directions and place into two bowls. Add the fish to the curry and briefly warm through. Pour over the noodles and serve, garnishing with cilantro or Thai basil if desired. Also good with udon or egg noodles.

FISH IN SAOR (*3 hr, but mostly waiting*)

¼ cup olive oil, 1 medium onion (sliced lengthwise into thin half-moons), 2 tsp salt, 1–2 fried fish fillets, 2 bay leaves, 1 tsp sugar, ¼ cup red or white wine, ¼ cup red or white wine vinegar.

Heat a heavy-bottomed pot or pan. Add the oil, onion, and salt and cook over low heat until the onion is quite soft but still holding shape, about 20 min. Meanwhile, put the fish into a shallow dish. The fish can be left whole or broken into a few large chunks. To the onion, add the bay leaves, sugar, wine, and vinegar and stir to combine. Remove from the heat and pour the mixture, including the bay leaves, over the fish. Let cool. Marinate at least 4 hr at room temperature and up to overnight in the refrigerator. If you refrigerate, bring it back to room temperature before eating.

The following is the amount for about 6 tacos, so scale depending on how much fish you have.

FRIED FISH TACOS (*20 min*)

2–3 tbsp finely sliced cabbage, salt, ½ red onion (sliced lengthwise into thin half-moons), lime juice or distilled white vinegar or rice vinegar, tortillas or large lettuce leaves, 1–2 pieces fried fish, ½ avocado (sliced), thinly sliced fresh or pickled jalapeño, wedges of lime, ¼ cup chopped cilantro, mayonnaise (optional; or Spicy Mayonnaise, p. 396).

Heat the oven to 400°F. In a small bowl, combine the cabbage with a pinch of salt. In another bowl, combine the onion and a pinch of salt, and add lime juice or vinegar to just cover. Let sit 10 min then strain, reserving the lime juice or vinegar for a vinaigrette. Press and drain any liquid from the cabbage. Warm the tortillas or set out lettuce leaves. Heat the fish in the oven until just warm, 5–10 min. Make tacos or lettuce tacos by placing a couple of pieces of fried fish per tortilla or lettuce leaf, top with avocado and salt the avocado. Top with cabbage and onion, jalapeño, then a squeeze of lime juice and cilantro. Drizzle with mayonnaise (if using).

FISH CAKES

Substitute any leftover fish cakes for crab cakes in Crab Cake Larb (p. 271).

FISH AND CHIPS

FISH AND CHIPS HASH (*25 min*)
3 tbsp butter, 1 cup diced carrot, 1 cup diced onion, ½ tsp salt plus to taste, 3 cups diced fish and chips, ½ cup frozen peas, 1 tsp finely chopped fresh dill or parsley, 1 tbsp malt vinegar or to taste, freshly ground black pepper. *For serving:* poached or fried eggs or whole-milk yogurt.

Heat the oven to 400°F. Heat a medium sauté pan. Add the butter. As soon as it begins to brown, add the carrots, onions, and salt and cook until lightly golden, about 3 min. Remove from the heat. In a medium bowl, combine the fish and chips, peas, and herbs. Add the cooked carrots and onions and mix well. Taste for salt and adjust. Transfer to a cast-iron skillet and roast in the oven until the hash has begun to brown, about 20 min. Sprinkle with the malt vinegar and black pepper. Serve with eggs or yogurt. (Adapted from Danny Amend)

FISH SKIN

CRISPY FISH SKIN (*5–7 min*)
Skin, in largeish pieces, olive oil.

Heat a cast-iron skillet. Add a drizzle of olive oil. Fry the fish skin shiny-side down, until it crisps, flipping as needed. Remove to a cutting board. Let cool 10 sec or so, slice, and eat on rice or in soup.

FISH HEADS

Fish heads are vital for the richness they contribute to fish broth. Any you have should be frozen until you have a good quantity of bones, then simmered with the bones, water, and aromatics into fish stock.

FRITTO MISTO

FRITTO MISTO HOAGIE *(15 min)*

¼ clove garlic, salt, 2 tbsp room-temperature butter, ½ cup fritto misto,
1 hoagie roll or similar (or a 4–6-inch-length baguette, halved horizontally
as for a sandwich), mayonnaise, a few slices pickled pepperoncini or chile,
2–3 tbsp shredded iceberg lettuce or The Best Coleslaw (p. 23), a squeeze of
lemon (optional).

Pound the garlic to a paste with a little salt. Add the butter to make garlic
butter. Heat the oven or toaster oven to 400°F. Lay the fritto misto on a tray
and warm, 5–7 min. Toast the roll. Spread the garlic butter on the bottom side
of the roll and the mayonnaise on the top. Lay the fritto misto over the butter.
Top with pepperoncini or chile, then the lettuce or coleslaw. Add a squeeze of
lemon (if using). Close and eat.

GEFILTE FISH

Leftover gefilte fish can be rolled into little balls, dipped in matzo crumbs
or bread crumbs, and deep-fried in peanut or grapeseed oil to crisp, 2–4 min
each. Finely minced fresh ginger, scallion, and cilantro can be added to the
mixture before it's rolled into balls and fried. If gefilte fish was not delicious to
start with though, it won't be improved by this treatment.

GRAVLAX

Gravlax is cured salmon, which can be finely chopped and mixed with spicy
mayonnaise and put into maki rolls, or Onigiri (p. 387), or eaten on a Rice
Bowl (p. 281). Or it can be eaten as is, on toasted thin brown bread covered in
butter, with 1–2 capers per triangle, and the finest paper-thin wisp of onion.

HERRING, JARRED

Herring are strongly flavored fish, which I like. Here is a common way of
eating herring and an easy one. Toast the darkest, sourest, brownest bread you
have, or find Wasa crispbreads in rye or another punchy flavor. Thickly spread

whatever bread or cracker you've chosen with butter, as thickly as you would cream cheese. Drain and lay herring over this in a single layer. Top with thinly sliced fresh or quickled onion (see p. 438). Chop a lot of fresh dill or parsley and scatter copiously over the toast or cracker.

HERRING BRINE

Herring brine can be used to pickle mackerel, herring, or sardines. Bring the brine to a boil. Taste. Add sugar, salt, white wine, and a little white wine vinegar, tasting as you do. It should be strongly flavored, slightly salty and sweet, and appealing. Lay fish in a single layer and pour boiling brine over. Let sit at room temperature to cool. Eat as described under *Herring, jarred (p. 279)* or laid on a warm potato salad.

LOBSTER, COOKED

Once lobster is cooked, heating it further leaves it rubbery. The two exceptions are in lobster risotto (which is just risotto made using lobster stock with any little bits of meat stirred in at the end) and Lobster Stew (p. 253).

Leftover lobster is best in a lobster roll. A straightforward version is: lobster (chopped), finely chopped celery (optional), mayonnaise, split-top hot dog bun, melted butter. Combine the lobster with celery (if using). Add just enough mayonnaise to hold it together. Heat a hot dog bun, brush heavily with melted butter, then fill with lobster salad, and drizzle on more melted butter if you like. The same lobster salad can be dolloped on potato chips or dolloped on endive and served as a very fine and fancy hors d'oeuvres. Or, if you are not feeling fancy, lobster salad is also good on plain hot white rice, adorned with a sprinkle of toasted sesame seeds.

LOBSTERS SHELLS

LOBSTER STOCK *(1 hr)*

In a stockpot, combine the lobster shells (from 4–8 lobsters, thwacked a little), any coral and legs, ¼ cup white wine, any herbs, a few threads of saffron, herbs, and water to cover by 1 inch. Bring to a boil, skim, reduce to a simmer. Cook until it tastes losbter-y and delicious, about 1 hr. Strain and use or freeze.

LOX

RICE BOWL *(20 min)*
1 cup freshly cooked short-grain Japanese rice, 1 tbsp seasoned rice vinegar (or regular rice vinegar with a little sugar and pinch of salt mixed in) plus to taste, toasted sesame seeds, 1 tbsp–¼ cup chopped or julienned lox, 1 tbsp seaweed salad (or julienned cucumber, basil, or shiso), 1 tbsp julienned pickled ginger, cubed avocado (optional), julienned toasted nori (optional).

In a bowl, combine the rice with the vinegar. Shake heavily with sesame seeds, then arrange the lox, seaweed salad, pickled ginger, avocado (if using), and nori (if using), each in its own little pile, and eat.

MACKEREL, COOKED

MACKEREL SALAD WITH SALSA VERDE *(variable, up to 45 min)*
Salsa Verde (p. 398), 1 fillet cooked mackerel, 1–2 small potatoes (optional), olive oil (optional).

If you have salsa verde on hand, tear the mackerel into a few large pieces and store it with the salsa verde, mixing it through lightly so the fish is coated in oil and herb. If you do not have salsa verde, make some. This is the work of 10 min and worth it. Spoon the sauce over the mackerel and lightly combine. Leave at room temperature 30–45 min to warm and accommodate. If using potatoes, place them whole in a pot of very salty boiling water and cook until tender, about 25 min. When cool enough to handle, slice the potatoes into rounds ½ inch thick, drizzle well with olive oil, and lay on a plate. Spoon the mackerel-salsa verde salad on top, adding extra salsa verde if you like things saucy. If you are omitting the potatoes, grill or toast a thick slice of bread and rub with a clove of garlic. Spoon the mackerel onto the garlic-rubbed toast.

MONKFISH LIVER, CANNED

Toast slices of bread (rustic rounds, baguette, or pain de mie) until just crisp. Butter well. Spread monkfish liver over and top with flaky salt.

MUSSELS, COOKED

Leftover cooked mussels are a delight. If they were hastily stored still in their shells, remove the meat today and make an especially wondrous version of Pickled Clams (p. 266), or Hoi Tod (p. 267), or Coconut Clam Stew (p. 267).

MUSSELS, RAW

Do the tap test to see if your mussels are alive, regardless of how long they've been haunting a refrigerator drawer. Take each one and tap its shell firmly against the edge of the sink. If it closes to protect itself, it is alive, and can be steamed in butter and wine. If it doesn't close, it has passed on, and must be discarded.

OCTOPUS, CANNED

OCTOPUS SALAD WITH POTATOES *(30–35 min)*
2–4 cups roughly cut or wedged waxy potatoes (fingerling, Yukon Gold, Magic Molly, etc.), salt, 1 bay leaf, 1 clove garlic, olive oil, 1 can octopus (at room temperature), Salsa Verde (p. 398), a 4-inch piece cured Spanish chorizo (optional; sliced on the diagonal), lemon juice.

In a pot, combine the potatoes, cold water, enough salt to taste like lightly salted seawater, the bay leaf, and garlic. Bring to a boil, then reduce to a simmer and cook until tender, 15–20 min. Drain the potatoes, reserving the potato water *(see Potato cooking water, p. 76)*. Drizzle lightly with olive oil. Drain the octopus, reserving the oil *(see Anchovy oil, p. 430)*. Make the salsa verde using octopus oil for some of the olive oil if you like. In a large bowl, combine the octopus, potatoes, and salsa verde. Mix lightly, taste for salt, acid, and olive oil, and adjust. If using the chorizo, heat a small pan. Warm the chorizo, letting it get crisped before flipping. Lay the octopus and potatoes on a plate, scatter the chorizo over the top, and squeeze lemon juice on top, then add a final drizzle of olive oil for good measure.

VERY PINTXO OCTOPUS ON BAGUETTE *(20 min)*
½ baguette (halved horizontally as for a sandwich), Aioli (p. 395), 1 can octopus, smoked sweet paprika, ¼ cup chopped parsley leaves.

Toast baguette until just warm and lightly crusty. Make aioli. Drain the octopus, reserving the oil *(see Anchovy oil, p. 430)*. Place a substantial blob of aioli on each slice of baguette. Top with a slice of octopus, dust with smoked paprika, then scatter with the parsley. Eat at room temperature.

OYSTERS, FRIED OR ROASTED

OYSTER OMELET *(10 min)*
Salt, 2–3 eggs (beaten), 3 tbsp Tabasco sauce, 1 tsp powdered sugar, 3–4 fried oysters, ghee or butter, Rémoulade Sauce (p. 396).

Heat the oven to 400°F. Lightly salt the eggs. In a little bowl, mix the Tabasco and sugar and set aside. Warm the oysters in the oven for 1 min. Heat a small skillet over medium heat. Add some butter or ghee. When it stops foaming, reduce the heat slightly and add the eggs, let spread and give them about 3 sec to set, then push what's cooked to the middle of the pan and let the unset eggs into the empty space. Reduce the heat where needed and continue nudging and filling empty spaces. When the bottom is just set, dollop the middle with rémoulade sauce and add the oysters. Tipping the pan toward you, fold over the half that's away, scoop onto a plate, and eat with more rémoulade sauce and the tabasco-sugar sauce in what I hope is happiness! If you don't eat fried oysters, try another fried filling, like fried fish or fried eggplant or fried tofu! (Inspired by Prune, New York City)

Leftover fried or roasted oysters also make good Hoi Tod (p. 267).

OYSTERS, RAW

Oysters in their shell keep, if refrigerated, for weeks. Shuck oysters when you're ready. You will be alerted by the telltale stench and putrefied appearance if they have gone bad. In the absence of those bad signs, make a mignonette sauce of chopped shallot, white wine vinegar, and white wine or champagne, and enjoy.

If you find yourself with a few leftover shucked oysters, make oyster stew.

OYSTER STEW (*10 min*)
4 shucked oysters (in their liquor), 1 tbsp butter, ½ shallot (minced), 1 cup whole milk, ½ cup cream, 1 bay leaf, salt. *Optional additions:* chopped parsley or chopped celery leaves, paprika or freshly ground black pepper, soda crackers or buttered toast for serving.

In a bowl, strain any liquor left in and around the oysters through a fine sieve. Heat a small pot. Add ½ tbsp of the butter and the shallot and cook until tender, about 5 min. Add the milk, cream, bay leaf, and the strained oyster liquid. Bring to just below a simmer and cook 2–3 min. Season with salt to taste. Add the oysters and cook until they just plump, 30 sec–1 min. Immediately add the remaining ½ tbsp butter and pour the stew into small waiting bowls, removing the bay leaf. If desired, add parsley or celery leaves, a shake of paprika or a grind of black pepper, and accompanying with crackers or toast.

POKE

Leftover poke bowls can be salvaged without risk to your mental or physical health. Remove the fish, chop a little onion and garlic and cook it in neutral oil until tender, 3–5 min. Add rice to the pan and stir-fry. Once it's browned and crisp in places, make a well in the middle, add a little more oil, and add the fish. Quickly press and fry, scrape it all up and into a bowl. This is poke-fried rice, and it is good. Add sesame seeds, and any thinly sliced nori if you have, then a squeeze of lemon or a few drops of rice vinegar, and eat.

SABLE, SMOKED

SABLE CHICORY SALAD *(30 min)*

¼ cup sliced onion, 3 tbsp red or white wine vinegar, salt, ½ cup crème fraîche or sour cream, lemon juice to taste, 1 tsp horseradish, freshly ground black pepper, 2–3 cups bite-size pieces chicory, olive oil, 1 cup wedged vinegared beets or thinly slices of peeled orange or grapefruit, ¼–½ cup smoked sable.

In a bowl, combine the onion, vinegar, and a pinch of salt and let sit 10 min. Meanwhile, mix the crème fraîche or sour cream, a little lemon juice, horseradish, a tiny pinch of salt, and a little black pepper. Taste for salt and adjust. Add a few drops of water if needed to make it the consistency of pancake batter. In a bowl, dress the chicory with a little lemon juice, a sprinkle of salt, and a drizzle of olive oil. Mix through with your hands, then spread on a plate or in a shallow bowl. Scatter the beets, or orange, or grapefruit and onion (drained of their liquid) over. Flake the fish into large pieces and scatter throughout as well. Drizzle with as much horseradish-crème fraîche as you like, and top with more black pepper. This is good with any smoked fish.

SALMON, COOKED

Leftover cooked salmon can be used in any of the recipes for *Fish, cooked (p. 273)*.

SALMON PÂTÉ

Leftover salmon pâté can be stretched. Start with 2 tbsp of cream cheese or crème fraîche or some other very fresh farmer cheese, then mix in about an equal amount of pâté, then taste and proceed. If you have any herbs, they can be chopped and mixed in, too.

SALT COD, COOKED

Leftover cooked salt cod should be mixed with potatoes that have been boiled and riced. Add pounded garlic, and lots of olive oil and you have made brandade. This is hearty and satisfying, and there's no further technique required. Brandade can either be broiled in a hot oven to get crisp on top and scooped onto bread, or it can be formed into croquettes (cylinders or little balls or pancakes) and fried.

Or, use leftover cooked salt cod in the recipe for Portuguese Eggs (p. 274), or Teaism Soup (p. 275).

SARDINES, COOKED

SARDINE CROQUETTES (*1–2 hr, but mostly waiting*)
1–2 cloves garlic, salt, 2 cups boned and flaked cooked sardines, 2–3 cups mashed or riced boiled potato, 2 tbsp pureed Calabrian chiles, ¾–1 cup combined olive oil and heavy cream, olive oil, flour, 1 egg (beaten with a little water), bread crumbs, oil for frying.

Pound the garlic to a paste with a little salt. In a large bowl, mix the garlic, sardines, potatoes, pureed chiles, and olive oil-cream mixture. If needed, add more olive oil to make them hold together. Taste for salt and adjust. Refrigerate, covered, for 1 hr. Form into little balls or into little torpedoes about 2 inches long. Set up three shallow dishes: one with the flour, one with the beaten egg, one with the bread crumbs. Bread the croquettes by dipping in flour, egg, then bread crumbs. In a heavy-bottomed pot or deep sauté pan, heat 2 inches of oil to 360°–375°F. Working in batches, fry the croquettes and drain on paper towels. Serve hot. This can also be made with canned sardines.

Leftover cooked sardines are also delicious instead of mackerel in Mackerel Salad with Salsa Verde (p. 398).

SARDINES, CANNED

SARDINE PASTA (*20 min*)
2 tbsp olive oil, ½ onion (sliced), 1 clove garlic (sliced), ½–1 can sardines, chile flakes (optional), salt, 1 lb spaghetti, 1 bunch parsley (leaves picked and roughly chopped, stems reserved; *see Parsley, stems, p. 69*), 1 cup toasted bread crumbs (see p. 176).

Heat a pan big enough to hold the pasta. Add the olive oil, onions, garlic, and a small pinch of salt, and cook until barely tender, about 5 min. Add the sardines and their oil and let them fry in the pan, breaking them lightly with your spoon. Add a sprinkle of chile flakes (if using). Once the sardines are toasty and seem part of the sauce, remove from the heat. In a large pot of boiling water salted to taste like pleasant seawater, cook the pasta. Reserve ½ cup pasta water, then remove the pasta with tongs directly into the sardine pan. Set the pan back over the heat. Add ¼ cup of the pasta water and mix the sardines and onion through the pasta. Add more water by the splash if it seems too dry. When the noodles and the sauce are well combined, stir in half the parsley and ½ cup of the bread crumbs. Sprinkle the rest of both on top just before eating.

A variation is to use fennel fronds or bronze fennel instead of or in addition to parsley.

I once ate exclusively sardines on crackers during a seven-day drive across the country.

SARDINES ON CRACKERS (*10 min*)
Canned sardines, rye crackers, salted butter or sliced avocado or both, salt, a sprinkle of an especially beloved chile flake (Guntur Sannam, Marash, or Aleppo) or a few drops of hot sauce.

If you mind the tiny bones, fillet the sardines (though the bones are reported to increase longevity). Spread the crackers copiously with butter or avocado (or both), lightly salting if you choose avocado. Lay the sardines on top, then lightly salt again. Add the chile flakes or hot sauce and eat.

SCALLOPS, COOKED

As soon as you plan to make this for dinner, roughly chop the leftover scallops and leave them, covered, at room temperature for 30 min or so. The more slowly they heat up, the better they'll be in the chowder.

SCALLOP CHOWDER (*30 min*)
2 tbsp unsalted butter, 2 slices bacon (optional; chopped or sliced), 1 clove garlic (peeled), ½ cup chopped celery, ½ cup chopped onion, salt, 4 cups clam juice, ¼ cup white wine, parsley stems, a few sprigs of thyme, a little rosemary,

1 bay leaf (all tied with twine), ½ lb yellow potatoes (peeled or unpeeled, chopped), 2 cups fresh or frozen corn (optional), 4–6 cooked scallops (at room temperature), 1 cup heavy cream, 2 tbsp combined chopped chives and parsley, freshly ground black pepper.

Heat a saucepan. Add the butter. If using bacon, add it and cook until crisp. Remove some bacon fat if you want. Add the garlic, celery, onion, and a small pinch of salt and cook until everything but the garlic is completely tender. Add the clam juice, wine, 1 cup water, herb bundle, and potatoes. Bring to a boil, then reduce to a simmer. Skim off any scum that rises. Cook until the potatoes are completely tender, about 20 min. Add the corn (if using) and simmer for 1 min. Add the scallops and cream. Remove the garlic or leave it as a surprise. Taste for salt and adjust. Add the chives-parsley and black pepper and serve hot.

This is for when you have only 2–3 leftover cooked scallops but want to feed more than one person.

SLIGHTLY SCALLOP-Y SPAGHETTI (*20 min*)
A few cooked scallops, olive oil, 1–3 cloves garlic (chopped), 3 anchovy fillets, 1 tbsp drained capers, 1 cup finely chopped parsley, salt, ½ lb spaghetti, lemon juice. *Optional garnish:* toasted bread crumbs (see p. 176) or panko toasted in butter.

Bring the scallops to room temperature. Heat a pan large enough to hold the spaghetti once cooked. Add enough oil to cover the bottom. Add the garlic and a pinch of salt and cook over low heat until fragrant. Add the anchovies and capers and cook, stirring, until the anchovies begin to break apart and melt, about 1 min. Add the parsley and remove from the heat. Chop the scallops finely—they're being treated as a seasoning. Add to the pan with the parsley. In a large pot of boiling water salted to taste like pleasant seawater, cook the pasta. When the spaghetti is just cooked, reserve ½ cup pasta water, and scoop the pasta into the pan, mixing well, adding pasta water as needed. Squeeze with lemon juice. If desired, garnish with bread crumbs or panko.

SHELLS

Jacques Cousteau wrote that the sea, once it cast its spell, held one in its net of wonder forever. Children know this innately. They should be given abalone shells and conch shells and nautilus and murex and quahogs and limpets and cowries and cockles and whelks and periwinkles and scallops, and all other seashells. They can keep them as reminders as they grow up.

SHRIMP, COOKED

SHRIMP SALAD (*15 min*)
1 tbsp finely chopped scallions or spring onions, ¼ tsp salt plus to taste, 2 tsp lemon juice or white wine vinegar, 6–8 cooked peeled shrimp, ½–1 stalk celery (depending how much you like celery), ¼ cup Greek yogurt, 1 tbsp mayonnaise, 1 tbsp chopped fresh herbs (optional; parsley, celery leaf, fennel fronds, tarragon), freshly ground black pepper (optional).

In a little bowl, combine the scallions or spring onions, salt, and the lemon juice or vinegar. Let sit for 10 min. Meanwhile, chop the shrimp into bite-size pieces. Chop the celery. Combine the shrimp, celery, yogurt, mayonnaise, herbs (if using), and black pepper (if using) to taste. Add the drained, marinated onion. Taste for salt and acid and adjust. Good on lettuce or in a toasted, buttered hot dog or other soft bun. (Adapted from A Couple Cooks website)

PICKLED SHRIMP (*overnight, but mostly waiting*)
6–8 peeled cooked shrimp, ¼ cup lemon juice, 2 tbsp white wine vinegar, 1 clove garlic (thinly sliced lengthwise), 2 scallions or spring onions (quartered crosswise and thinly sliced lengthwise), ½ lemon (quartered and thinly sliced), ½ tsp fennel seeds, ½ tsp coriander seeds, 3–4 dried chiles de árbol (broken once or left whole), ½ tsp salt plus to taste, ½ cup olive oil.

If you want to serve the shrimp to a (small) crowd, slice them in half horizontally. Otherwise leave them whole. In a large bowl, mix the lemon juice, vinegar, garlic, scallions or spring onions, lemon slices, fennel seeds, coriander seeds, chiles, and salt. Add the shrimp and mix well. Leave at room temperature for 15 min, then add the oil, mix well and refrigerate overnight. Bring to room temperature for 10–15 min before serving. Good eaten as is, or on saltines.

SHRIMP FRIED RICE *(5 min)*

Add cooked shrimp to Fried Rice (p. 205) when the rice has gotten nicely fried. A good variation is to add 2 lightly salted beaten eggs when you add the shrimp, mixing over high heat until the eggs are set.

THE MOST DELICIOUS WARM SHRIMP SALAD SANDWICH *(10 min)*

5 cooked shrimp, 2 slices white sandwich bread or a sandwich roll, ¼ cup Rémoulade Sauce (p. 396).

Heat the oven to 400°F. Reheat the shrimp briefly, about 5 min. Toast the bread or roll at the same time. Quickly chop the shrimp into big pieces. Mix with the rémoulade sauce and layer on the toast or put in a roll.

Or, substitute cooked shrimp for fried fish in Fish in Saor (p. 277). Or for tempura in Scallion Omelet Crepe (p. 90) or for scallops in Scallop Chowder (p. 287).

SHRIMP SHELLS

Place shrimp shells in a pot, cover with water by several inches, add a bay leaf, an onion skin or onion top, a few peppercorns, ¼ cup white wine, and a few parsley stems. Bring this to a boil, then reduce to a simmer, and cook until it tastes like shrimp, about 1 hr, adding water if needed. Now you have shrimp stock. Strain and use or freeze.

Or, if you are feeling even more ingenious, make:

SHRIMP SHELL AND POTATO CHIP FURIKAKE *(1 hr)*

½ cup shrimp shells, ½ cup crumbled potato chips, 1 sheet nori (torn into pieces), 2 tbsp toasted sesame seeds, 1 tsp salt or to taste.

Heat the oven to 250°F. Spread the shells on a baking sheet and bake until dry, about 35–45 min. Cool. In a spice or coffee grinder, one at a time, grind the shells, the potato chips, and nori to slightly rough crumbles. Sir in the sesame seeds and salt. Sprinkle on anything, especially rice, soup, and eggs. (From *Mastering the Art of Japanese Home Cooking* by Masaharu Morimoto)

SHRIMP AND GRITS

Chop any shrimp and mix into grits until smooth, then shape into balls, and make Fried Grits (p. 229).

SQUID, COOKED

SQUID TOMATO PASTA *(1–2 hr)*

One 28 oz can whole peeled tomatoes or equivalent fresh, 5 tbsp olive oil, 3 cloves garlic (sliced), ½ tsp salt plus to taste, a sprinkle of chile flakes, ½–1 cup cooked squid, 1 onion (peeled and halved), 1 lb pasta, a handful of chopped parsley.

In a blender, puree the tomatoes and their juice to fairly smooth. Heat a heavy-bottomed pot or saucepan large enough to hold the pasta when cooked. Add the olive oil, garlic, salt, and chile flakes. Cook over medium-low heat, stirring, until the garlic can be easily broken with a wooden spoon. Add the tomato puree, squid, and halved onion. Bring to a simmer and then cook, stirring occasionally, until the squid is very tender, 1–2 hr. Taste for salt and adjust. In a large pot of boiling water salted to taste like pleasant seawater, cook the pasta. Drain, mix with the sauce, top with parsley, and eat.

As unlikely as this sounds, this pasta can be made just as well with leftover fried squid. Its breading can be removed or left intact to melt into a lush, thick sauce. Or, to use canned squid instead of leftover cooked, use only 1 cup of tomato puree and cook the squid and tomato until just warmed and combined.

Leftover fried squid can also be chopped and added to fried rice, or used instead of fritto misto in a Fritto Misto Hoagie (p. 279).

SWORDFISH, COOKED

Leftover swordfish is perhaps the best fish for Pasta with Fish and Tomatoes (p. 421).

TROUT, SMOKED

Smoked trout stays good for a long time, but when you have only a small amount, it can be stretched by turning it into a dip.

HOT TROUT DIP (*10–15 min*)
¼ cup flaked smoked trout, 2 tbsp room-temperature cream cheese, 1 tsp mayonnaise, 1 tbsp finely minced spring onion or scallion, 1–2 tbsp freshly grated Parmesan cheese, freshly ground black pepper. *Optional garnish:* thinly sliced scallion greens or chopped parsley.

Heat the oven to 350°F. In a small baking dish, combine the trout, cream cheese, mayonnaise, spring onion or scallion, Parmesan, and black pepper to taste. Bake until hot and just bubbling and beginning to brown, 10–12 min. If desired, garnish with scallions or parsley. Serve with crackers or little toasts or crisp vegetables for dipping.

TUNA

Leftover cooked tuna makes wonderful composed salads and Pan Bagnat (p. 151), but that is well known and not much more true of tuna than any other fin fish. Mostly, leftover tuna has a gazillion traditional applications because it has been a cornerstone of cuisines. But tuna populations have suffered and may contain mercury. And elegant and lovable salads and sandwiches and pastas and tarts and more can be made with the many fish whose eating is less perilous to their survival or ours.

UNAGI (EEL)

YAKI ONIGIRI (*30 min*)
¼ cup mirin, 2½ tbsp sugar, 1½ tbsp sake, ¼ cup soy sauce, 1–3 pieces unagi sushi (eel and rice separated, eel finely chopped), 1½–2 cups freshly cooked Japanese short-grain rice.

In a small pot, combine the mirin, sugar, and sake and bring to a boil, stirring. Add the soy sauce and simmer for 10 min. Remove the sauce from the heat. Add any leftover sushi rice to the warm freshly cooked rice. To make onigiri, make a pancake of rice in one hand, add a small scoop of chopped eel, then cover with rice, continuing until you've used all the eel and rice. In a hot cast-iron skillet, griddle until crisp on both sides, then brush with sauce and serve, with more sauce for dipping if you want. (From Just One Cookbook website)

HOW TO STAND
ON YOUR FEET

Meat and tofu

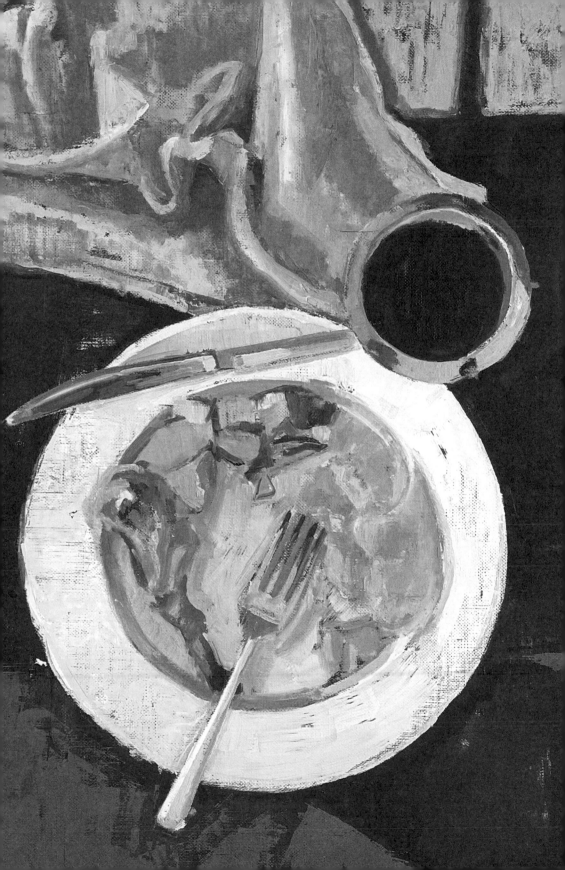

'Tis not the meat, but 'tis the appetite
Makes eating a delight.

—*Sir John Suckling, "Sonnet II"*

The older I get the more I feel a Buddhist urge to tread lightly. For now, I continue to cook and eat meat, if less than I once did, from animals about whose lives I know enough to recite an agricultural elegy. I face contradictions each time, the only resolution I find being gratitude—cold comfort for the animal's soul, perhaps, but some solace to mine.

Luckily, a cook who practices gratitude through resourcefulness—simmering lesser known cuts with herbs and wine, saving and transforming leftovers and making stock from bones and soup from stock spends less and eats better than a wasteful one. And all of the saving and transforming is old culinary doctrine, which shields it from sanctimony.

From a culinary perspective, there are two types of leftover meat, and no more. The first is quick-cooked: meat that has been cooked quickly and with direct heat. It can be grilled or fried or stir-fried or sautéed, and it can be chicken or pork or beef or goat or lamb, or, or, or . . . It is a *type*, and what can be done with it once leftover is determined by it being that type. Once quick-cooking meat has been (quickly) cooked, it shouldn't be cooked further because it will toughen. It can be sliced for sandwiches, or cubed or finely chopped or dressed. It can be *briefly* warmed—as in fried rice. But it shouldn't be simmered in a sauce because it will turn to leather.

The second type is slow-cooked: meat that has been cooked slowly and with indirect heat, like in braising liquid or smoke or a low and slow roast or a quiet poach. Slow-cooking cuts are those recently retired from active duty as a leg or a shoulder or neck, and are tough in the pot (as in life) until the collagen woven throughout is converted and becomes rich and silky and forgiving. This type is entirely happy to be simmered even longer and turned into a pasta sauce or stew or chili and so on.

More minute distinctions exist—leftover chicken thighs make good chicken ragu and leftover lamb shoulder lamb ragu, and you might choose mushrooms and marjoram for the first and tomato and wine for the second. But that is all commentary. The question of whether a meat's next use is sandwich or salad, or sauce or stew is already resolved.

It works to my advantage that I am ecumenical about animals' various parts. Not every dish can be made with every part, but there *is* something good to make with every knuckle and oxtail and liver. An exception to my ecumenicism is animals' feet—for which I have special affection. They are the same material as the rest of the animal, but have more collagen and make better soup. My considerable appreciation of feet isn't inherited—my mother never cooked animals' feet. It comes from my frugality and love of golden broth for congee and glossy sauce for pork. And so my son grows into childhood with a cultural appreciation of all the good that can be made from an animal's feet. Chicken feet bobbing in a pot means chicken soup with rice, and pig's feet mean dumplings. I didn't instill this appreciation in him out of morality. But I can't help but recognize the moral quality of the result. If we each bowed sometimes, in sight of our children, before ingredients as humble as animals' feet, it might teach useful lessons about how to treat our fellow beings.

I've included leftover tofu in this chapter because it takes the place of meat in some of my cooking. It is not a natural inclusion, and the clumsiness further evidences my own unease with which materials in our world should and should not be considered (hu)man's meat.

Here are some adaptable meat preparations that lend themselves to next day meals:

BRAISED MEAT
Salt, 3 lb meat from a shoulder or other tough cut, 2 tbsp olive oil, up to 1 cup vegetable scraps (from making mirepoix or sofrito) or chopped mirepoix, ½ tsp spices (optional; fennel seed, cumin seeds, coriander seeds), 8 cups warm stock or water, 2 cups wine (or beer, cider, the liquid from a tomato can, or a combination), bouquet garni (parsley stems, thyme, and a bay leaf).

Salt the meat very heavily, up to three times as heavily as you want. Refrigerate overnight (or if there's no time, leave at room temperature for a few hr). Heat the oven to 300°F. Heat a large Dutch oven over medium heat. Add the oil and brown the meat on all sides. Remove it to a plate. Add the vegetable scraps or mirepoix and stir well to release browned bits. Add the spices (if using) and stir. Add the stock or water, wine, and bouquet garni and bring to a near boil, just so you know everything's gotten hot. Return the meat to the pot, cover, transfer to the oven, and braise until the meat is spoon tender, 3–4 hr. Remove the meat, strain the liquid, and taste. If it's very salty, add water until it tastes good, then freeze and use as the basis of a stew, taking the time to write an appealing and appropriate label, like "Best stew to be!" If you have time, refrigerate the meat overnight, then remove and save the fat. Serve braised meat sliced or torn.

ADOBO MEAT

2 lb tougher cuts of meat (legs or thighs or shoulders), ½ cup soy sauce, ¼ cup distilled white vinegar, 2–3 bay leaves, 3 tbsp vegetable or olive oil, 5 cloves garlic (peeled and sliced or smashed), 1 tsp sugar, 1–2 tsp black peppercorns.

In a bowl, combine the meat, soy sauce, vinegar, and bay leaves. Marinate overnight in the refrigerator. Remove from the marinade, reserving the marinade. Heat a heavy-bottomed pot with a lid. Add the oil and meat and brown skin-side up. Add 2–3 cups water (depending how much sauce you like), the garlic, sugar, and peppercorns. Add a drizzle of the marinade and the bay leaves. Cover and braise over medium-low heat until spoon tender, 45 min–1½ hr. Eat with rice and as much of the sauce as you want, saving any extra as a future lunchtime rice drizzle.

LAZIEST STEAM ROAST

Salt, 3 lb shoulder meat or other tougher roast, 2 tbsp olive oil, 3 cloves garlic (minced), grated zest 1 lemon, ¼ cup chopped rosemary (or a combination of rosemary and sage).

Salt the meat very heavily, up to three times as heavily as you want, drizzle with olive oil, then rub with the garlic, lemon zest, and chopped rosemary. Refrigerate overnight (or if there's no time, leave at room temperature for 1 hr). Heat the oven to 425°F. Wrap tightly in parchment paper and then foil. Cook in a roasting pan in the oven for 20 min, reduce the heat to 300°F, and cook until spoon tender, 4–5 hr. Remove, reserving all the juices and return to the oven to brown or set over a hot grill. Use the juices as sauce or in a hundred other ways. *See Drippings (p. 315).*

DUCK CONFIT

4 skin-on bone-in duck legs, 3 tbsp salt, 3–4 cups duck fat, a few sprigs of thyme, 1 bay leaf, 2–3 cloves garlic (smashed), a little ground juniper (optional).

Cut cleanly through the skin all the way around the ankle of each duck leg. Salt the duck well on both sides. Cover and refrigerate overnight. When you're ready to cook, heat the oven to 200°F. Remove the duck legs from the refrigerator, rinse off the salt, and dry them. Make small pricks in the duck skin with a very sharp knife or pin to help fat render. In a heavy-bottomed pot or pan large enough to fit the duck in a single layer, melt the duck fat on the stove. Add the thyme, bay leaf, garlic, and ground juniper (if using), then carefully add the duck legs, skin-side up. The skin may not be covered with fat, which is fine, since more fat will render out. Cover the pot and place in the oven. Cook until the meat is spoon tender, 2–3 hr. Remove from the oven, carefully remove the legs and place, skin-side up, in a storage container. Strain the fat and use it to re-cover the duck if not using immediately. It will stay good, covered with fat, for a month or more. To reheat, warm to room temperature, remove the duck from the fat. Then either heat in a 400°F oven, skin-side up, until crisp, or, in a heavy ovenproof pan, render skin-side down, then flip and slide into a 350°F oven to warm throughout.

CHICKEN CONFIT

4 skin-on bone-in chicken leg quaters, 3 tbsp salt, 3–4 cups olive oil or duck fat, 1 bay leaf, a few sprigs of thyme, 2–3 cloves garlic (smashed).

Cut cleanly through the skin all the way around the ankle of each chicken leg. Salt the chicken well on both sides. Cover and refrigerate overnight. When you're ready to cook, heat the oven to 200°F. Remove the chicken legs from the refrigerator, rinse off the salt, and dry them. In a Dutch oven large enough to fit the chicken in a single layer, heat the olive oil or melt the fat on the stove. Add the bay leaf, thyme, and garlic, then carefully add the chicken legs, skin-side up. Cover the pot and place in the oven. Cook until the meat is spoon tender, 1–2 hr. Remove from the oven, carefully remove the legs and place, skin-side up, in a storage container. Strain the fat and use it to re-cover the chicken if not using immediately. The legs will stay good, covered with fat, for a month or more. To reheat, warm to room temperature, remove the chicken from the fat. Then either heat in a 400°F oven, skin-side up, until crisp, or, in a heavy ovenproof pan, render skin-side down, then flip and slide into a 350°F oven to warm throughout.

CHICKEN LIVER TOSCANO

1 lb chicken livers (connective tissue removed with a knife), salt, good olive oil, ½ cup dry sherry or white wine, 2 cups minced onion, 3 cloves garlic (minced), 3 tbsp drained capers, 9 anchovy fillets, 2 tbsp chopped rosemary, 2 tbsp chopped sage, ½ cup dry vermouth, 4 tbsp butter (cut in pieces).

Season the livers with salt. Heat a skillet with just enough olive oil to lightly coat. Working in batches, brown the livers, cooking them to medium-rare and moving them to a plate. Deglaze the pan with the sherry or wine between batches, pouring any liquid and drippings over the cooked livers. Wipe out the pan and add ¼ cup olive oil over medium heat. Add the onion and garlic and cook until completely tender and slightly caramelized, 10–15 min. Add the capers and cook until they seem to toast, about 5 min. Add the anchovies and cook until they begin to melt and everything looks sticky. Add the herbs and vermouth and stir to deglaze over high heat. Cool to room temperature. In a blender, combine the livers and any accumulated juices. Add the butter and puree until fairly smooth. Add the onion-anchovy mixture and pulse to a texture you like. I like it a bit nubby and textured. Very good on toast or in baguette sandwiches, or on radishes or on leftover fried chicken.

LARB

Larb is not a flexible dish on the order of braised meat or confit, which can become a dozen things on subsequent days. It is, however, one of my favorite things to make and eat. It's also remarkably good at using up bits of leftover cooked meat on second days and beyond.

1½ cups finely minced or ground cooked meat (or fish or tofu), ⅔ cup thinly sliced shallots (separated into rings), ½ tsp salt, 1 tbsp chile flakes or sliced fresh Thai chiles, ¼ cup lime juice plus to taste, 4–5 tbsp fish sauce plus to taste, 2 tsp sugar plus to taste, 2–3 cups chopped fresh mint and cilantro, ¼ cup roasted rice powder (see p. 208) or sesame seeds.

In a bowl, mix all the ingredients. Taste for salt, spice, acid, and sweetness and adjust as needed.

MEAT AND TOFU

ADOBO MEAT

ADOBO FRIED RICE (*10 min*)

1–2 tbsp oil, 4–5 cloves garlic (finely chopped), ¼ tsp salt plus to taste, 1–2 cups shredded adobo meat (mixed with leftover sauce), 2–3 cups cooked leftover rice, 2–3 thinly sliced scallions.

Heat a large pan. Add the oil, garlic, and salt, and cook until the garlic just begins to turn golden. Add the meat and leftover sauce and bring to a simmer. Add the rice and stir-fry, trying to heat the grains, but not worrying about crispness. Taste for salt and adjust. Add the scallions. Eat. If you add a fried egg, this is called adsilog.

BACON, COOKED

There's an old chestnut that there's no such thing as leftover bacon. I understand this as the metonymic claim it is. But that shouldn't overshadow how much good can be done with a little bit of the apocryphal leftover. It is salty and fatty and flavorful and amenable to being recooked a number of times in a number of arrangements. One slice can transform fried rice, boost the flavor of soup, add salty richness to pasta sauce.

Store any leftover bacon with another ingredient. Slice and store it with leftover cooked rice, and when it comes time to fry the rice, the grains are already oiled and seasoned. Or store bacon with the last bit of leftover scrambled egg and you're two pieces of toast away from a breakfast sandwich. Store bacon with leftover cooked greens and be a pot of boiling water away from a bowl of pasta. If you do not want to store bacon in company, slice or chop it and store it in a small container toward the front of the fridge. Retrieve it the next time you cook, regardless of what you're making. Its destiny—in a pot of beans, in soup you're warming or soup you're starting, in mac and cheese, in mirepoix, in dumplings—will reveal itself.

In my house if there are three or four slices of leftover bacon, it means a bacon sandwich. Toast two slices of white bread. Set a cast-iron skillet over low heat, warm the bacon until just warm and crisp, butter the bread, add the bacon, and eat. Two variations I condone are adding marmalade to one side (inspired by Gabrielle Hamilton at Prune, New York City) or adding a handful of arugula leaves.

BACON FAT

Bacon fat can be used instead of any other fat for cooking, provided it's well strained and refrigerated. There are reasons so many recipes from older days rely on bacon fat: Its smoke point is high and it is profuse on the pig. A good use is:

BACON FAT CORN BREAD *(40 min)*
3 tbsp bacon fat, 1¾ cups fine or medium grind cornmeal, 1 tsp baking powder, ½ tsp baking soda, ½ tsp salt, 2 eggs (beaten), 2 tbsp sugar, 1 cup heavy cream, ½ cup yogurt or buttermilk.

Heat the oven to 375°F. In a 10-inch cast-iron skillet or other heavy oven-proof skillet, add the bacon fat and place in the oven. Meanwhile, in a large bowl, combine the cornmeal, baking powder, baking soda, and salt. In a second bowl, whisk together the eggs, sugar, cream, and yogurt or buttermilk. Retrieve the skillet from the oven, swirl the fat to coat the bottom and sides, and pour it into the egg mixture, whisking or mixing it in. Add the bacon fat-egg mixture to the cornmeal and mix through until just barely smooth, not worrying about a few lumps. Scrape into the waiting skillet, return to the oven, and bake until a skewer emerges clean and the edges are toasty and brown, 19–24 min.

BARBECUED MEAT

MORIMOTO FRIED RICE *(5 min)*
¼ cup chopped barbecued meat, 1 tbsp cooking oil (if the meat is very lean), ½–1 shallot (chopped; or ¼ onion or 3 scallions, chopped), salt, 1 clove garlic (finely minced), ¾–1 cup cooked short-grain rice, ½ tsp sugar, 1 tsp rice vinegar, 1 egg (optional), furikake or toasted sesame seeds.

If the meat is fatty, place in a cold skillet. If the meat is lean, heat the oil first, then add the meat. Render for 30 sec or so. Add the shallot and a sprinkle of salt and cook until beginning to soften, about 1 min. Stir in the garlic, then add the rice and sugar and cook over medium-high heat, stirring occasionally, frying the rice. When slightly crisp, add the vinegar and stir until evaporated. If including the egg, in a bowl, beat it with a little salt, pour it into the pan, and mix through, scrambling lightly as you turn and mix. Remove from the heat, top with furikake or sesame seeds, and eat.

BARBECUE SANDWICH (25 min)

2 tsp vinegar-based hot sauce, 1 tbsp chicken stock or water, 1 tsp barbecue sauce (optional), 1 cup shredded barbecued meat, salt, vinegar, sugar. *For serving:* 1 buttered sandwich roll or bun, coleslaw, sliced dill pickles.

In a small saucepan, combine the hot sauce, stock or water, barbecue sauce (if using), and meat. Warm through over the lowest possible heat. Taste for salt, acid, spiciness, and sweetness and adjust with salt, hot sauce, vinegar, and sugar. Serve on a buttered roll or bun topped with coleslaw and pickles.

A variation is to add warm baked beans.

BEEF, SLOW-COOKED

COMPOSED SALAD OF HERBS, MEAT, AND SMALL POTATOES (30 min)

½ lb little new potatoes, salt, ¼ cup white wine vinegar or rice vinegar, ½ tsp Dijon mustard, ½–1 cup thinly sliced bulbed spring onions (or Vidalias, red onions, or scallions), 2 cups combined chopped soft herbs (chives, dill, chervil, celery leaves, parsley), olive oil, 1–2 cups cubed slow-cooked beef (removed from any liquid).

In a saucepan, combine the potatoes with very salty water. Bring to a boil, then reduce to a bare simmer and cook until tender, about 20–30 min. Let sit to cool in the water. In a medium bowl, combine the vinegar, mustard, and a little pinch of salt. Mix in the onions and let sit 10 min. Halve the potatoes and combine them with the mustard-onion mixture. Add 1 cup of the herbs, drizzle with some olive oil and mix, not minding if the potatoes get a bit smashed. Spread the beef onto a plate. Spoon the dressed potatoes over the beef and top it all with the remaining 1 cup herbs. This is also good with a few cold, roasted Vinegared Beets (p. 18). A delicious addition is cubes of the braising liquid that, cold, will be the consistency of Jell-O.

SUMMER VEGETABLES AND SLOW-COOKED BEEF (1 hr 15 min)

3 tbsp olive oil, 2 cups zucchini pieces (¾–1 inch), ½ small onion (finely chopped), 1 stalk celery (finely chopped), 1 red bell pepper (very thinly sliced), 2 cloves garlic (finely chopped), ½ tsp salt plus to taste, 1 tbsp tomato paste,

½ cup white wine, 1½ cups braising liquid (or a combination of braising liquid and stock or water), 2 cups chopped slow-cooked beef, 1 cup cubed boiled potatoes, ½ cup chopped parsley leaves, 1 tbsp chopped thyme (or rosemary or a combination), ½ cup toasted bread crumbs (see p. 176).

Heat the oven to 425°F. Heat a large ovenproof sauté pan or Dutch oven. Add the olive oil. Add the zucchini and cook until softened, about 8 min. Halfway through, add the onion, celery, bell pepper, garlic, and salt. When everything has softened together, add the tomato paste and cook until all the vegetables are melty, another 8–10 min. Add the wine and braising liquid and cook at a low bubble until reduced by half. Add the meat, potatoes, parsley, and thyme and mix through. Transfer to the oven and bake, uncovered, until the meat and vegetables have begun to brown, about 10–15 min. Scatter the mixture heavily with bread crumbs and return to the oven and bake until the bread crumbs are quite crisp, another 10–15 min.

A winter variation of this is to use only meat and potatoes, or only meat, and substitute 2 cups onion for the summer vegetables, then proceed as above.

TACOS *(15 min)*
1–2 cups chopped or shredded slow-cooked beef (without liquid), corn or flour tortillas, hot sauce or pickled chiles, shredded cabbage. *Garnishes:* chopped cilantro, minced onion or scallion, lime wedges, sliced avocado (optional).

In a small pot, warm the beef with a few drizzles of water (or water and hot sauce or any braising liquid that you still have). Heat the tortillas directly over the burners. Serve meat, tortillas, and garnishes.

SUGO *(45 min)*
Marcella's Tomato Sauce (p. 394), chile flakes (optional), ¼–1 cup shredded slow-cooked meat, salt, cooked short pasta or polenta for serving, Parmesan or Pecorino Romano cheese.

In a large pot, combine the tomato sauce, a sprinkle of chile flakes (if using), and meat. Warm together. Taste for salt and adjust. Mix with cooked pasta or ladle over polenta and add copious amounts of cheese.

Or use slow-cooked beef in Arancini (p. 240), instead of or in addition to the cheese. And any amount of slow-cooked beef is good in basically any soup. Try adding it to Minestrone (p. 210), or Bean and Salami Soup (p. 213), or Enchilada Stew (p. 355), or Nacho Soup (p. 360).

BEEF BONES

Use to make Meat Stock (p. 246).

BEEF FAT

Beef and pork fat do not melt as quickly when you want them to as when you don't. Slow is their speed. Melt fat on the stovetop or in an oven (200°–225°F) or in a slow cooker. As long as it is slow, and as long as you strain the melted fat well, you will succeed.

Cube fat before melting or the outsides of large pieces will caramelize before their insides have warmed. Freeze fat before you cube it—this seems counterintuitive given that you're headed for a melt, but it makes cubing neater. I learned from a Southerner to put ½ inch of water at the bottom of my fat-rendering pot. The ½ inch is bound to evaporate in the time it takes the fat to render, and in the meantime it prevents burning and sticking before the real melting has begun. Strain rendered fat well, until you see no solids suspended in it. Keep rendered fat in the refrigerator, no matter what they say about how all of us used to store our fat in dark jars in dark corners. Now we have refrigerators and if we use them we can avoid rancid fat.

Beef fat, aka tallow, has a high smoke point, which makes it ideal for deep-frying.

FRENCH FRIES OR ONION RINGS *(1 hr 30 min)*
For French fries: cut russet potatoes into fries, soak them in water for 1 hr, drain and dry them, and then fry them in batches in oil at 325°F for 5 min, then, after draining again, at 365°F until crisped and brown, removing to a paper towel–lined bowl and salting immediately. For onion rings: make the Tempura Batter (p. 139), and then fry once at 365°F. If you have the patience to strain the tallow until translucent, it may be usable again.

BOLOGNA

Use the end of a package of bologna in the Pizzeria Salad (p. 54).

BRATWURST, COOKED

Bratwurst is an incredibly adaptable sausage. Use any cooked leftovers in any recipe for leftover *Hot dogs (p. 324)* or *Sausage, cooked (p. 340)*.

BULGOGI

BULGOGI SOUP *(30 min)*
1 tbsp cooking oil, 4 cloves garlic (chopped), 4–5 scallions (sliced, whites and greens kept separate), 2 cups sliced mushrooms, ½ cup chopped kimchi plus for serving, 2 cups sliced cabbage, 2–3 cups bulgogi, 5 cups Garlic Peel Stock (p. 44) or water or dashi, 1½ cups cooked rice, 8 oz block tofu (cubed), 1 tbsp gochujang, 1 tbsp soy sauce plus to taste, 1 tbsp mirin.

Heat a soup pot. Add the oil, garlic, and scallion whites and cook until just softened, about 2 min. Add the mushrooms and cook over medium-high heat until just tender, another 3–4 min. Add the kimchi, cabbage, bulgogi, and stock. Bring to a boil, then reduce to a simmer and cook until the cabbage is tender, 10–12 min. Add the rice, tofu, gochujang, soy sauce, and mirin. Simmer until everything is warm and combined, another 5 min. Taste for salt and adjust with soy sauce. Eat.

Or use leftover bulgogi in Fried Rice (p. 205), Tacos (p. 306), or Melty Beef Panino (p. 339).

CHICKEN, COOKED

It is fine if you don't have parsley root or parsnip! Simply proceed without.

AMAZING CHICKEN RAGU *(30 min)*
½ cup–2 cups dried mushrooms (depending how much you like mushrooms!), 6 tbsp butter, a drizzle of olive oil, ⅓ cup finely chopped onion, ¼ cup finely

chopped carrot, ⅓–½ chopped parsley root or parsnip, ½ tsp salt plus to taste, 2 tbsp finely chopped fresh herbs (any combination of rosemary, thyme, sage, marjoram), 1 bay leaf, ¼–½ cooked chicken (torn into pieces), ½–¾ cup heavy cream.

In a heatproof bowl, soak the dried mushrooms in 4 cups hot water for 20 min. Reserving the soaking liquid, scoop out the mushrooms and finely chop. Strain the soaking liquid of any grit and set aside. In a heavy-bottomed sauté pan, melt 3 tbsp of the butter in the olive oil. When it's stopped foaming, add the onion, carrot, parsley root or parsnip, and salt. Cook over medium heat, stirring often, until they've begun to soften, 2–5 min. Add the chopped herbs and mushrooms and mix through. Once it sizzles a bit, and is just considering browning, add ½ cup mushroom soaking liquid and the bay leaf. Cook until combined, 2–3 min, and taste. Taste for salt and adjust. Continue cooking until nothing tastes raw, adding more mushroom liquid if needed to keep things just slightly swimmy, up to 2 cups total. Add the chicken, remaining 3 tbsp butter, and cream. Increase the heat and cook, stirring often, until the cream is half gone. When it all tastes good, eat alone or on rice or with pasta or on polenta or grits.

BETTER CHICKEN FINGERS (*20 min*)
Cooked chicken torn into large pieces, all-purpose flour, salt, egg(s), panko, white or black sesame seeds, oil for shallow-frying (grapeseed, peanut, or vegetable oil).

Set up three shallow dishes for dredging: one for flour and a little salt, one for beaten egg, and one for panko and sesame seeds. Working in batches, dip the chicken pieces in flour, then egg, then panko mixture, setting them on a wire rack as you work. In a heavy-bottomed pot, heat ½ inch of oil to 350°–375°F. Fry in batches, flipping when you can see the golden brown creep up from the bottom side. Drain on a rack and eat.

At Quinnie's, a restaurant in Hudson, New York, chicken salad is served in a sandwich of schmaltz-rubbed white toast with a piece of crisp fried chicken skin inside. It is still worthy without the schmaltz and skin.

QUINNIE'S CHICKEN SALAD (*10 min*)
1 tbsp finely chopped scallions, ¼ tsp salt plus to taste, 1 tsp apple cider (or white wine vinegar or lemon juice), 2 cups roughly chopped cooked chicken,

¼ cup medium-chopped or sliced celery, 2 tbsp mayonnaise, 1 cup roughly chopped fresh herbs (dill, celery leaves, parsley leaves).

In a bowl, combine the scallions with the salt and vinegar and let sit for 5 min. Add the chicken, celery, mayonnaise, and herbs. Mix well, and eat.

TECHINA CHICKEN SALAD *(5 min)*

½ cup chopped cooked chicken, 2–3 tbsp Techina (p. 393). *Optional for serving:* sunflower sprouts or shredded iceberg, pita or other toasted bread.

In a bowl, smash the chicken well with the techina. Very good on toasted bread with sprouts.

LOUIS'S CONGEE-ISH HEALING CHICKEN SOUP WITH RICE *(1–1½ hr)*

12 cups homemade chicken stock with its fat, cilantro stems (from 1 bunch), 2-inch piece fresh ginger (sliced or smashed), 1 clove garlic, 1 star anise, 1 cup short-grain or jasmine rice, salt, ¼–1 cup shredded cooked chicken. *Sauces for serving:* soy sauce, Francis Lam's Ginger-Scallion Sauce (p. 398), chili oil.

In a saucepan, combine the stock, cilantro stems, ginger, garlic, and star anise. Bring to a boil and then simmer until it's reduced by about one-quarter, 20–30 min. Scoop out the cilantro, ginger, garlic, and star anise. Add the rice to the stock and simmer until fully cooked and has begun to burst, another 30 min–1 hr. Season with salt to taste. This is not a clear soup. It's a thick, soothing porridge. Add the chicken for the last few moments of cooking. Dollop and drizzle with any of the sauces and eat!

TORTILLA SOUP *(15–20 min)*

4 cups chicken stock, 2 cloves garlic (chopped), salt, ¼ cup pureed chipotle in adobo or tomato puree, ¼ tsp ground cumin, ½–1 cup shredded or sliced into strips cooked chicken, 2 cups freshly fried tortillas or other tortilla chips, ½ bunch cilantro (including stems, chopped), 1 avocado (sliced). *For serving:* lime wedges, hot sauce.

In a small pot, warm the stock over medium heat. Pound the garlic to a fine paste with a small pinch of salt and mix with the pureed chipotle or tomato puree and cumin. Whisk the garlic-adobo combination into the warm stock.

Bring to a boil, reduce to a simmer, and cook at a low simmer for 10 min. Add the chicken and tortilla chips. Taste for salt and adjust. Add the cilantro and avocado. Serve with lime wedges and hot sauce.

AD HOC CHICKEN TIKKA MASALA *(40 min)*
4 tomatoes (fresh or canned), 1 tbsp oil, 1–2 tbsp chopped green chiles, 1 tsp finely chopped fresh ginger, 1 tsp finely chopped garlic, ½ cup finely chopped onion, 1 tsp salt, 1 tsp garam masala, ½ tsp Kashmiri or cayenne pepper, ½ tsp ground turmeric, ¼ tsp hing (asafoetida), 1 tsp kasuri methi (fenugreek leaves), 3 tbsp heavy cream (or crème fraîche or sour cream), 1–2 cups shredded or chopped cooked chicken, rice for serving.

In a blender, puree the tomatoes to smooth. Heat a sauté pan over medium heat. Add the oil, green chiles, ginger, garlic, onion, and salt. Cook, stirring often, until beginning to soften, 3–5 min. Add the tomato puree and let simmer for about 2 min. Add the garam masala, pepper, turmeric, hing, and kasuri methi and simmer until the tomato has begun to caramelize, another 2–3 min. Add the cream, then the chicken. Stir through at the lowest heat for 2–3 min. Taste for salt and adjust. If possible, let rest for 15 min to meld then eat over rice.

CHICKEN, OVERCOOKED

Overcooked chicken can still make perfectly good Quinnie's Chicken Salad (p. 309), where much of the flavor comes from the herbs, celery, and mayonnaise. Or use it for Larb (p. 301).

CHICKEN CURRY

CHICKEN BIRYANI *(1 hr)*
1 cup basmati rice, 2 tbsp neutral oil (peanut or grapeseed) or ghee, 1 onion (sliced lengthwise into very thin half-moons), 1 heaping tsp salt plus to taste, 1¾ cups liquid (which can include the sauce from chicken curry, water, stock, coconut milk, or a combination), 1 tsp biryani masala (store-bought or homemade; recipe follows), ¼ tsp ground turmeric, 1–2 cups roughly torn chicken curry, 1 cup chopped cilantro, yogurt or raita for serving.

Soak the basmati rice in water for 30 min, then drain. Heat a small-medium pot. Add the oil or ghee, onion, and salt and cook until just tender, 5–10 min. Add the drained rice, liquid, biryani masala, and turmeric. Bring to a boil, then reduce to a simmer, cover, and cook until the rice is almost cooked through, about 15 min. Add the chicken masala and cilantro, quickly mixing through. Cover and continue cooking over lowest heat for another 5–7 min. Taste for salt and adjust. Very good drizzled with yogurt or raita.

Biryani Masala: In a coffee grinder or spice grinder, grind together 1 bay leaf, ½ star anise, 4 cardamom pods, 1 tbsp coriander seeds, ½ tsp cumin seeds, ½ tsp black peppercorns, ½ tsp fennel seeds, a few whole cloves, and a sprinkle of cinnamon.

CHICKEN CURRY STEW *(20–25 min)*
1 can coconut milk (well shaken), 1 cup chicken broth or water, 1 tbsp fish sauce, 1-inch piece fresh ginger (peeled and sliced), 1 clove garlic, 1 cup chicken curry. *For serving:* hot rice (or leftover rice added to the soup), 1 tbsp lemon or lime juice.

In a soup pot, combine the coconut milk, broth or water, fish sauce, ginger, and garlic. Bring to a boil, reduce to a simmer, then cook for 15 min. Strain and return to the pot. Stir in the curry or masala, heat to warm, taste, and adjust seasoning. Eat with rice or any way you like, adding lemon or lime juice just before eating. This works with other curries, too.

CHICKEN CUTLETS, FRIED

CHICKEN KATSUDON *(15 min)*
1–2 fried chicken cutlets, ¼ onion (thinly sliced), ½ cup dashi, 1 tbsp sake, 1 tbsp mirin, 1 tsp sugar, soy sauce (optional), salt, 2 eggs (beaten). *For serving:* 2 tbsp thinly sliced scallions, hot rice.

Heat the oven to 400°F and recrisp the chicken, 5–10 min. Meanwhile, in a medium saucepan, combine the onion, dashi, sake, mirin, and sugar. Bring to a boil, add a few drops of soy sauce (if using), then season with salt to taste. Cook over medium heat until the onion is wilted, about 5 min. Slice the cutlets into thick slices and place into the katsudon mixture. Add the beaten eggs and shake the pan so the eggs cook. Cook until the eggs are just set, moving as needed, 30 sec–1½ min. Garnish with scallions and eat on rice. (From Just One Cookbook website)

See also Fried chicken (p. 317).

CHICKEN FAT

SOUTHERN DUMPLINGS *(45–50 min)*
1½ cups all-purpose flour, 1 tsp salt, 1 tbsp baking powder, 3–4 tbsp chicken fat, ⅔ cup whole milk, 2 tbsp chopped fresh dill or parsley, 4 cups broth.

Render the chicken fat following the instructions for rendering beef fat (p. 307). In a bowl, combine the flour, salt, and baking powder. Add the fat and work it in well by hand. Add milk and dill or parsley and mix to combine. In a medium pot, bring the broth to a low simmer. Drop in little spoonfuls of batter, trying to keep them separate, and cook 35–45 min at a very low simmer, stirring and basting as needed. Eat in broth, carefully adding anything else you want, like leftover chicken or vegetables, for the last few min. (Adapted from Danny Amend)

Chicken fat can also be spread on toasted sandwich bread!

CHICKEN LIVER PÂTÉ

At midnight after my brother's wedding, someone suggested spreading Chicken Liver Toscano (p. 300), which I had made for the party, on cold fried chicken. If you have both, this is worth trying. Leftover pâté also makes a lovely pasta sauce for one. Warm it lightly in a pan with butter and a drizzle of white wine just when the pasta is finished cooking. Add the cooked pasta to the pâté pan, adding a little pasta water if needed for mixing and saucing, then shower it all with grated Parmesan and eat. Or make:

GRILLED PÂTÉ TEA SANDWICHES *(5 min)*
2 slices sandwich bread (Pullman bread or pain de mie), room-temperature butter, 3–4 tbsp chicken liver pâté.

Cut each slice of bread into quarters. Butter the bread on both sides, then spread one side with pâté and close it into a sandwich. Heat a griddle or cast-iron skillet over medium heat. Griddle the sandwiches as you would a grilled cheese, and eat. Best with champagne and candlelight.

CHICKEN SKIN

Fry in a dry pan or in a drizzle of olive oil, starting while the pan is cold, over low heat, until the fat is completely rendered, and the skin is shatteringly crisp. Salt lightly, then break into pieces and eat on rice or in soup or in a sandwich made with Quinnie's Chicken Salad (p. 309).

CHILI

STUFFED BAKED POTATO (*1 hr 15 min*)
1–2 russet potatoes (well scrubbed), ½–1 cup chili, butter, salt, grated cheddar cheese, thinly sliced scallions, sour cream.

Heat the oven to 400°F. Prick the potato(es) with a fork and bake until it gives, 45 min–1 hr. Meanwhile, in a small pot, heat the chili, adding a few drizzles of water to keep it from sticking. Split the potato(es), mash in butter and salt to taste, then smash in cheese. Cover with the chili, then garnish with scallions and sour cream. Especially good after skiing or sledding.

Or warm the chili and use it to make Sloppy Joes (p. 320).

CORNED BEEF

KIMCHI CORNED BEEF HASH (*20–25 min*)
3 tbsp neutral oil (peanut or grapeseed), 1 medium onion or 1 leek (chopped; clean the chopped leek well), salt, 3 cloves garlic (chopped), 1 cup kimchi (chopped), 1 tbsp gochugaru or other chile flakes, 1 tbsp soy sauce, 2 tbsp butter, 2 cups chopped potato (boiled in very salty water and drained), ½–1 cup chopped corned beef, 1–2 scallions (finely sliced), fried eggs for serving (optional), toasted sesame seeds.

Heat a heavy-bottomed pan over medium heat. Add the oil, onion or leek, and a pinch of salt, and cook, stirring occasionally, until softened, about 5 min. Add the garlic and cook for another 30 sec. Add the kimchi, gochugaru, and soy sauce. Cook over high heat until the kimchi has softened and is starting to fry, 3–4 min. Add the butter. Once it's melted, add the potatoes and corn beef and smash into a cake, let fry, then flip in large sections, trying to get things sizzling and caramelized. Taste for salt and adjust. Add the scallions, then scoop into bowls. Top each with fried eggs (if using) and sprinkle with sesame seeds.

A variation is to cook eggs directly in the mixture, either by cracking them into slight wells you make in the hash, then salting each and covering them until just cooked, or by placing the egg-topped hash in a 375°F oven until the eggs are cooked to your liking. (Adapted from Seonkyoung Longest website)

DRIPPINGS

The drippings from roasting meat taste of the peregrinations of the animal's life, plus the salt and herbs with which you seasoned the meat, plus the fat you cooked it in, plus the vegetables in the pan. There is much to gain or to lose, depending on what happens next. I suggest finding ¼ cup of liquid, like stock, or wine, or water, heating the pan that contains the drippings, pouring in the liquid, then avidly scraping with a wooden spoon. Pay attention to the places where the drippings are thick. Once they've released, carefully pour the liquid—which will now be darkened and slightly thickened, and perhaps have bits floating about—into a bowl. For sauce for whatever meat you cooked, pour the liquid through a fine sieve into a small pot, let cool slightly, then taste and whisk in a tbsp of butter. If you want a thicker sauce, cut a piece of butter, roll it in flour, then whisk that in. Adjust the seasoning and pour it over the meat before eating. If you want to save the concentrated flavors of the drippings for another day, a small secret treasure, pour the liquid into a jar or ice cube tray and use it, like soup bouillon, for starting soup or stew or rice.

DUCK, COOKED

DUCK TACOS (*almost instantaneous*)
Duck makes great tacos, not least because it's so rich there's no need for sour cream or cheese. Remove the meat from the bones, warm it, and warm the

tortillas. Top tortillas with duck meat, then sliced fresh chiles, chopped onion, perhaps some sliced radishes, chopped cilantro and lime served alongside.

Or substitute for chicken in the Amazing Chicken Ragu (p. 308).

DUCK CONFIT

DUCK RILLETTES *(20 min)*

Like Chinese, Indian, American Southern, Italian, Spanish, Thai, and other cuisines that treat pleasure and economy as intertwined strands of a rope, French cuisine prescribes a treatment for each leftover. Duck rillettes were invented as a terminus for leftover duck confit. To make rillettes, remove confit from bones and shred it into a bowl. Pound and mix it with enough of the fat it was cooked in to make a rough paste. Taste, adding more fat if it tastes lean. Pour a layer of melted fat over the top and refrigerate. This will stay good for ages. To eat, bring to room temperature and scoop onto toasted baguette.

Or make Duck Noodle Soup. Instead of the stock, seasonings, and noodles recommended here, you can use a package of instant ramen.

DUCK NOODLE SOUP *(20 min)*

Some duck confit, 2–4 cups chicken or duck stock, 1 star anise, 1 tbsp sliced fresh ginger, soy sauce, sugar, salt, 1 small head bok choy (well washed and sliced; or a handful of spinach, or any cooked leftover cooking greens), 3–4 oz egg or rice noodles, chili oil.

Starting from cold, in a cast-iron skillet or other heavy pan, warm the confit, skin-side down, until it's begun to crisp and sizzle, 2–3 min. Meanwhile, in a saucepan, combine the stock, star anise, ginger, and a few drops of soy sauce and simmer for 15 min. Add sugar and salt to taste. Add the bok choy and cook until tender, about 5 min. Add the noodles and cook until just done. Remove to a deep bowl and top with the duck confit, quickly shredded from the bone or as it is. Eat drizzled with chili oil.

BITTER GREENS SALAD *(15 min)*

Some duck confit, ½ bulb fennel (thinly sliced; or sliced orange, pear, apple, or persimmon or both), Garlicky Vinaigrette (p. 400) or Basic Vinaigrette (p. 376), 2–3 cups bitter greens (radicchio, chicory, frisée, or tender cabbage), salt.

Starting from cold, warm the confit, skin-side down, in a cast-iron skillet or other heavy pan until it's begun to crisp and sizzle, 2–3 min. In a bowl, lightly dress the fennel or fruit or both with some vinaigrette, then add the greens and more vinaigrette and a pinch of salt, tasting as you go. Place on a plate, then add the warmed confit.

FAT

Strain and save small amounts of fat in a little jar by the stove, and resolve to use it. It's fine to combine different species' fat. Or, if you are as lazy as I am and have leftover rice in the refrigerator, leave fat in the pan, then fry rice in it the next day. See Fried Rice (p. 205) or Pan-Fried Farro (p. 224).

FRIED CHICKEN

A VERY GOOD CHICKEN SANDWICH *(20 min)*

Salsa Verde (p. 398), 2 tbsp store-bought or homemade Mayonnaise (p. 395) or Aioli (p. 395), baguette or other sandwich roll, ¾–1 cup sliced or cubed fried chicken (including any breading).

Make the salsa verde. Make the mayonnaise or aioli if using. Toast the baguette or roll and spread the bottom with mayonnaise. Add the chicken and top with salsa verde.

A variation is to add chopped boiled egg to the salsa verde.

COLD FRIED CHICKEN SALAD *(20 min)*

1–2 heads lettuce (depending on how much salad you want; Bibb, red leaf, iceberg lettuce, or chicory), Herbed Buttermilk Dressing (recipe follows), salt, 1–2 pieces fried chicken (cut into chunks, including any breading), lemon juice, lemon wedges (optional), freshly ground black pepper (optional).

In a bowl, dress the lettuce with the buttermilk dressing and a sprinkle of salt. In its own bowl, lightly dress the chicken, adding a squeeze of lemon, then nestle amid the lettuce. Serve with a lemon wedge and black pepper, if you like.

A variation is to add a handful of boiled potatoes, lightly dressed. Or sliced radishes. Or cooked or raw corn.

Herbed Buttermilk Dressing: 1 tsp minced shallot (or scallion or sweet onion), 1 tsp white or red wine vinegar, ⅛ tsp salt plus to taste, 1 small clove garlic, 3 tbsp buttermilk (or buttermilk substitute, see p. 138), 2 tbsp whole-milk Greek yogurt, ½ tsp sugar, 1 tbsp olive oil, 1 tbsp chopped mixed herbs (parsley, chives, chervil, or tarragon). In a bowl, soak the shallot in the vinegar with the salt for 10 min. Drain. Meanwhile, pound the garlic to a paste with a little salt and add to a small bowl. Whisk in the buttermilk, yogurt, garlic, sugar, olive oil, and herbs. Whisk in the shallot. Taste for salt and adjust.

GOAT, COOKED

Chivo guisado should be made from goats fed on wild oregano in Monte Cristi province, in the northwest of the Dominican Republic. Using leftover cooked goat is a definitive downgrade. But even in this diminished version, the intelligence of the concept remains.

A VERY FAKE CHIVO GUISADO *(25–30 min)*
2 tbsp neutral oil (peanut or grapeseed), ½ onion (finely chopped), 1–2 cloves garlic (finely chopped), ½ Scotch bonnet pepper (or 1–2 jalapeños or other appealing amount of chiles you like; finely chopped), ½ tsp salt plus to taste, 3–4 canned whole tomatoes (chopped), grated zest and juice of 1 lime, 1 tsp sugar, ½ tsp ground oregano, 2–3 cups chopped or shredded cooked goat meat, 1–3 tbsp chopped cilantro, cooked rice for serving.

Heat a heavy-bottomed sauté pan. Add the oil, onion, garlic, Scotch bonnet or chile(s), and salt, and cook until beginning to soften, about 5 min. Add the tomatoes, lime zest, lime juice, sugar, oregano, and 1 cup water. Cook at a simmer until it's stew-like, about 15 min. Add the meat and cook until the meat and stew have united and the tomato has disappeared into the overall whole. Taste for salt and adjust. Stir in the cilantro. Serve with rice.

Leftover goat can also be used in the recipes for *Beef, slow-cooked (p. 305)*.

GOAT CURRY

Add a little water and some coconut milk to a small amount of curry, bring it to a simmer, cook it until it's all combined into a thinner, soupier version of itself, and then eat it on rice. Small amounts of goat curry are also the best filling for Goat Patties.

GOAT PATTIES (*25 min plus making the dough*)
Basic Cream Cheese Dough (p. 350), ½ tsp ground turmeric, ½ cup goat curry, 1 egg, whisked (optional).

Make the dough, adding the turmeric to the flour before mixing. Roll out, cut into 4- to 5-inch rounds, and fill each with a spoonful of goat curry. Moisten the inside rim of the dough, fold in half, and crimp with a fork. Heat the oven to 375°F. Lay the patties on a baking sheet. Prick each with the tines of a fork. Brush with egg if using. Bake until golden and cooked, 10–15 min.

GOOSE, COOKED

Cooked goose is a good metaphor and a good addition to Fried Rice (p. 205) or ramen.

GREEN OR RED THAI CURRY

The most practical thing to do with leftover Thai curry, especially if you happen to have stored it away with leftover rice, is to put it in a pot, where it will be unappealing and clumpy, add a cup or two of water, bring it to simmer, cook it until the rice has loosened up, and then add a few shakes of fish sauce or a spoonful or two of Nam Pla Prik (p. 397). (Add this cautiously, if you're new to the game.) Add any leftover roasted squash, or cooked grains, or raw noodles, or a handful of peanuts, any of which will contribute without much altering the flavor, which is the indelible genius of Thai curries (and stews and soups).

GROUND BEEF, COOKED

PICADILLO *(30 min)*

1 tbsp olive oil, 1 onion (chopped), ¼ tsp salt plus to taste, 1 clove garlic (chopped), 1 tsp chopped fresh chile or ½ tsp chile flakes, ¼ tsp ground cinnamon, 1 cup cooked ground beef, 3 peeled tomatoes (finely chopped or pureed) or 1–1½ cups tomato puree, 1 tbsp red wine vinegar, ½ tsp dried oregano, 1 bay leaf, 1 potato (peeled and diced), a grating of nutmeg, ¼ cup pitted olives, ¼ cup raisins (optional).

Heat an 8–9-inch heavy-bottomed skillet. Add the olive oil, onion, and salt and cook until softened, about 5 min, adding the garlic, chile, and cinnamon halfway through. Add the beef, tomatoes, vinegar, oregano, bay leaf, and potato and cook over medium heat, stirring occasionally, until the potatoes are tender, 12–15 min. Stir in the nutmeg, olives, and raisins (if using). Taste for salt and adjust. This is good in tortillas, or on rice, or in empanadas made with Basic Cream Cheese Dough (p. 350).

SLOPPY JOES *(10–15 min)*

1 tbsp olive or vegetable oil, ¼ cup chopped onion, salt, ½ tsp ground chile powder, 1 clove garlic (minced), 2 peeled tomatoes (fresh or canned, chopped), 1 tsp wine vinegar or distilled white vinegar, ½ cup cooked ground beef, 1–2 buns, butter, The Best Coleslaw (p. 23), hot sauce. *Optional toppings:* grated cheese, sliced pickles.

Heat a small pot. Add the oil, onion, and salt and cook until softened, 5–10 min, adding the chile powder and garlic halfway through. Add the tomatoes, vinegar, meat, and a few sprinkles of water and cook until combined, another 10 min. Warm and butter the buns. Top with meat mixture, slaw, hot sauce, and any optional toppings.

GUANCIALE ENDS

PASTA ALL'AMATRICIANA *(30 min)*

A little guanciale (cut into ¼-inch pieces), 1 medium onion (chopped), 1 cup chopped tomatoes (fresh or canned), salt, ½ lb pasta, 1 tbsp butter, freshly grated Pecorino Romano cheese.

In a cold sauté pan over medium-high heat, warm the guanciale until the fat has rendered and the guanciale is cooked, about 10 min. Remove the guanciale to a bowl and pour out the fat, leaving about 1 tbsp in the pan. Heat over medium heat, then add the onion and stir, cooking, until tender, about 10 min. Add the tomatoes and cook until they break down, another 5–10 min. In a pot of boiling water salted to taste like pleasant seawater, cook the pasta. Reserve ¼ cup pasta water just before draining. Add the pasta to the pan with the tomato and onions, then add the butter, guanciale, and reserved pasta water. Cook over medium heat, stirring, until it all seems coated, 1–2 min. Add a few tbsp cheese, stir through, and serve topped with a lot more cheese. (Adapted from *The Blue Apron Cookbook*)

PASTA ALLA GRICIA (*20 min*)
A little guanciale (cut into ¼-inch pieces), 1 medium onion (chopped), salt, ½ lb pasta, 1 tbsp butter, freshly grated Pecorino Romano cheese.

In a cold sauté pan over medium-high heat, warm the guanciale until the fat has rendered and the guanciale is cooked, about 10 min. Remove the guanciale to a bowl and pour out the fat, leaving about 1 tbsp in the pan. Heat over medium heat, then add the onion and stir, cooking, until tender, about 10 min. In a pot of boiling water salted to taste like pleasant seawater, cook the pasta. Reserve ¼ cup pasta water just before draining. Add the pasta to the pan with the onion, then add the butter, guanciale, and reserved pasta water. Cook over medium heat, stirring, until it all seems coated, 1–2 min. Add a few tbsp cheese, stir through, and serve topped with a lot more cheese. (Adapted from *The Blue Apron Cookbook*)

HAM

Deli ham acquires a strange sheen when it sits in the fridge more than a few days. To avoid this, griddle yours and then eat it in a breakfast sandwich instead of bacon. Or make Croquetas de Jamón.

CROQUETAS DE JAMÓN (*overnight, but mostly waiting*)
8 tbsp (1 stick) butter, ½ onion (finely chopped), ½ cup finely chopped ham, a grate of nutmeg, salt, 1 cup all-purpose flour plus for dredging, 2 cups milk, 2 eggs (whisked), bread crumbs, grapeseed or peanut oil for deep-frying.

Heat a medium pot. Add the butter, onion, ham, nutmeg, and a small pinch of salt and cook over low heat until the onion is softened and ham is fried, 5–10 min. Add the flour and stir through, then slowly add the milk, whisking as you pour it in, bringing it to a boil, then whisking over low heat until fully thickened, about 15 min. Remove from the heat. Line a medium baking dish with parchment and smooth the mixture onto it. Cover and refrigerate until very firm, 2–3 hr. Set up three shallow dishes: one for flour, one for beaten eggs, and one for the bread crumbs. Scooping up about 1½–2 tbsp of the ham mixture at a time, form croquettes (cylinders or little balls), then dip in the flour, then eggs, then the crumbs. In a deep pot, heat 3–4 inches of oil to 350°–375°F. Working in batches, fry until golden brown and crisp, about 3–4 min. Enjoy!

Or use leftover ham in the Pizzeria Salad (p. 54). Or add to Fried Rice (p. 205) or Egg Fried Rice (p. 154).

HAM BONE

HAM BONE BROTH (*3–4 hr, but mostly waiting*)
1–2 ham bones, 1 carrot, ½ onion (or tops of some leeks or some onion skins), 1 stalk celery, 1 bay leaf, a few sprigs of thyme, parsley stems, a few peppercorns, 1 star anise (optional).

In a pot, combine the ingredients and add water to cover by 2 inches. Bring to a boil, then reduce to a simmer and cook until it tastes like subtle but delicious broth, 3–4 hr. Add water if needed. Use as you would any broth, keeping in mind the light sweetness and smokiness.

HAMBURGER PATTIES, COOKED

LEFTOVER BURGER BOLOGNESE (*2 hr*)
½–1 can peeled whole tomatoes, 3 tbsp any kind of fat, ½ cup chopped white or yellow onion (shallots or scallions), ¼ cup chopped carrot, 1 stalk celery (chopped), salt, 1 clove garlic (chopped), 2 tbsp chopped rosemary (or sage or a combination), 2 cooked burgers (finely chopped).

Reserving the liquid, drain the tomatoes and chop. Heat a medium pot. Add the fat, onion, carrot, celery, and a pinch of salt and cook for 5 min. Add the garlic and cook over low heat, stirring, until totally melted, 10–15 min, adding the herbs about halfway through. Add the burger pieces, breaking them up further as you do. Add the tomatoes and cook until it's all melded, 1–2 hr, adding up to 1 cup reserved tomato liquid if needed to keep things from burning. Taste for salt and adjust. Good on pasta or polenta with lots of freshly grated Parmesan.

LUNCH NOODLES (*10 min*)

4 oz rice vermicelli or mung bean noodles, boiling water, 2–3 tbsp peanut or vegetable oil, ½ onion or very large shallot (sliced lengthwise into the thinnest possible half-moons), 2 tbsp thinly sliced scallion, 1 habanero or jalapeño chile (sliced or chopped), 2 cloves garlic (minced), ½-inch piece fresh ginger (minced), ½ tsp salt plus to taste, ½ tsp gochujang or other fermented chili-bean sauce, 1–2 tbsp water (or rice wine or sake), 1 cooked burger (finely chopped), a handful of chopped herbs (optional; cilantro or mint or a combination).

In a heatproof bowl, cover the noodles with boiling water and soak for 5 min. Meanwhile, heat a large heavy-bottomed skillet. Add the oil, onion or shallot, scallion, chile, garlic, ginger, and salt, stirring well. Cook until just beginning to wilt, about 1 min. Add the gochujang and cook another min. When everything has softened, add the water. Sizzle until almost gone, another min, then add the drained noodles. Stir through, getting everything mixed. Add the burger pieces, mix through well, cook another min or 2. Taste for salt and adjust. Serve topped with herbs (if using).

HAMBURGER OMELET (*15–20 min*)

2 eggs, 1 tsp fish sauce, ⅓ cup chopped cilantro or mint, 2 tsp chopped fresh jalapeño or pickled chiles, 2 tbsp olive oil, 2 tbsp chopped scallion (or spring onions or shallots), ½ clove garlic (chopped), salt, ½ cooked burger (finely chopped), ¼–½ cup grated cheddar cheese, lime juice or lime zest (optional), sriracha or other chili-garlic sauce (optional).

In a bowl, beat the eggs with the fish sauce, herbs, and chiles. Heat a skillet. Add 1 tbsp of the olive oil, the scallion, garlic, and a tiny pinch of salt and cook until beginning to get tender, 5–10 min. Add the burger pieces and mix through to warm. Add the remaining 1 tbsp olive oil, increase the heat slightly, and add the egg mixture. Spread and pull away from sides several times. When nearly set, add a sprinkle of cheese, and roll or fold the omelet. If desired, eat with lime juice or zest or sriracha. I also like this with mayonnaise. Try the same technique with leftover larb.

Or finely chop leftover cooked burgers and use instead of ground beef in Picadillo (p. 320).

HOT DOGS

HOT DOG ONIGIRI *(25–30 min)*
1 cooked hot dog, Teriyaki Sauce (recipe follows), 2 cups cooked sticky rice, sesame seeds.

Cut the hot dog crosswise into thirds, then cut each segment into matchsticks. In a small pot, combine ½ cup of the teriyaki sauce and the hot dog and bring to a simmer. Make rice balls by forming a few spoonfuls of sticky rice into small pancakes, then folding rice around the hot dog mixture into any shape you like. Dip or roll in sesame seeds and serve with more teriyaki sauce for dipping.

A variation is to cut sheets of nori into strips and wrap each rice ball in a strip. Another is to add a dab of umeboshi paste to each one.

Teriyaki Sauce: ½ cup soy sauce, ½ cup sake, ½ cup mirin, a scant ¼ cup sugar. In a saucepan, combine all the ingredients and simmer for 15 min until thickened. (From Just One Cookbook website)

HOT DOG SALAD *(20 min)*
⅔–1 cup unpeeled cucumber matchsticks (about ½ English cucumber, 1 Kirby, or 2 Persians), ¼ tsp salt, ½ tsp sugar, 1 cooked hot dog, 1 tbsp peanut or similar oil (optional), 1 tsp fish sauce plus to taste, 1 small shallot or bulbed spring onion (cut into thin rings), lime juice, 1 fresh chile (habanero, Thai bird's eye, or jalapeño; thinly sliced), 1 cup chopped herbs (cilantro, mint, basil, or any combination), chopped roasted peanuts.

In a bowl, toss the cucumber matchsticks with the salt and sugar and let sit for 10 min. Cut the hot dog into matchsticks to match the cucumber. For crispy hot dog bits, heat a small skillet over medium heat. Add the oil and hot dog matchsticks and cook until browned on all sides. If you prefer, leave the hot dog unfried. To the bowl of cucumbers, add the fish sauce, shallot or spring onion, juice of ½ lime, and chile and mix through. Add the hot dog pieces and mix again. Taste and adjust the fish sauce and lime juice. Stir in the herbs. Taste again for any final adjustments. Top with peanuts! Eat the salad by itself, or wrapped in large pieces of lettuce, or on rice!

FRANKS AND BEANS *(10 min)*
Cooked hot dogs, beans.

Slice the hot dogs on the diagonal and warm them up in a pot of beans. A variation is to add a few drops of molasses and a tsp of brown sugar while it all heats, which will make it seem New England-y.

GERMAN POTATOES WITH HOT DOGS *(30 min)*
2 tbsp finely chopped shallot or spring onion, 2 tbsp white wine vinegar or white wine, 1 tsp Dijon mustard, salt, 1–2 cooked hot dogs, 2–4 large red or Yukon Gold potatoes (cut into chunks), 1 bay leaf, 2 slices bacon (sliced or chopped), ¼ cup chopped parsley.

In a small bowl, combine the shallot or spring onion, vinegar or wine, mustard, and add a tiny pinch of salt and let sit. Slice the hot dogs on the diagonal into pieces ½–1 inch thick. In a pot of boiling water seasoned with salt to taste like a delicious soup, cook the potatoes with a bay leaf until tender, about 20 min. Reserving the cooking water, drain the potatoes and transfer them to a bowl. Heat a skillet. Add the bacon and cook to render the fat, then remove to the bowl with the potatoes, including as much of the fat as you want. Add the sliced hot dog to the skillet and sear, then transfer to the bowl. Add the shallots to the potatoes and pork, and mix well. Top with chopped parsley.

BRAISED CABBAGE WITH HOT DOGS *(45 min–1 hr)*
3 tbsp olive oil, 1 onion (sliced lengthwise into very thin half-moons), ½ tsp salt plus to taste, ¾ cup combined white wine and water, 3–4 cups cored and thinly sliced cabbage, ½–1 cup sauerkraut, 1–2 cooked hot dogs (sliced on the diagonal), freshly ground black pepper.

Heat a saucepan over medium-low heat. Add the oil, onion, and salt and cook, about 10 min. Add the wine-water mixture, cabbage, and sauerkraut. Cook, partially covered and stirring occasionally, until the cabbage is cooked through, 30 min or so. Add the hot dogs and let brown slightly if you want. Taste for salt and adjust. Add black pepper. Good as is or topped with chopped parsley. A little spoonful of strong mustard, alongside, can be good, too.

HOT DOG BANH MI *(1½ hr, but mostly waiting)*
Vietnamese Sandwich Pickles (recipe follows), 1 roll (banh mi roll, 4–6-inch length of pillowy baguette, or po'boy roll), Maggi seasoning (or Bragg Liquid), mayonnaise, 1 cooked hot dog (sliced lengthwise into 3–4 slices), 4–6 diagonally-cut slices unpeeled cucumber, ½–1 jalapeño (sliced), ½–1 cup whole leaves of cilantro.

Make the sandwich pickles at least 1 hr before making the sandwich. When ready to make the sandwich, heat the oven to 400°F. Place the roll in the oven for 5 min, until warm. Remove from the oven, cut mostly in half, leaving the roll connected on one side, and scoop out some of the bread, saving it for bread crumbs, then return it to the oven to get crusty for another couple of min. When warmed and crusty, remove from the oven, sprinkle liberally with Maggi, then spread both sides with mayonnaise, making sure an even layer coats the whole inside. Lay the hot dog slices on the bottom, then top with pickles, their brine squeezed back into the jar. Top with the cucumber, then blanket heavily with jalapeño and cilantro. Add a little more Maggi if you like. Close tightly and enjoy! (Adapted from Munchies: Food by VICE website)

Vietnamese Sandwich Pickles: 3 cups daikon radish matchsticks, 3 cups carrot matchsticks, ¾ cup sugar, 1 tbsp salt, 1 cup distilled white vinegar. In a large bowl, combine the vegetables, ¼ cup of the sugar, and the salt. Let sit 15–20 min until liquid-y and you can bend a piece of vegetable. Drain (reserving the brine if you like to use for another pickle), rinse, then drain again. In a bowl, combine the vegetables, remaining ½ cup sugar, the vinegar, and 1 cup water. Cover and refrigerate for at least 1 hr and up to a few days.

Or slice or chop leftover cooked hot dogs and add them to Minestrone (p. 210). Or Arroz con Gandules (p. 399) or Coleslaw Soup (p. 379).

KEBAB MEAT

Slice the kebab meat across the grain thinly for this.

KEBAB, EGG, AND TECHINA SANDWICH *(15 min)*
1 pita with a pocket or other flatbread, 1 soft-cooked egg (see Boiled Eggs, p. 139), salt, 1–3 tbsp Techina (p. 393), ⅓–½ cup sliced kebab meat, 2 tsp pickle (amba, achar, torshi, or giardiniera), chopped cilantro (or dill or both), sliced radishes or cucumber.

Warm the pita or flatbread over a flame or in a toaster oven. Slice the egg into thick slices, then salt each lightly. Open the pita pocket or spread the flatbread. Coat one side with the techina, then add the sliced egg and salt lightly. Add the sliced meat, then coat the other side with pickle. If using a single flatbread, either spread the pickle over the techina, or dollop lightly over the meat. Stuff the remaining space with herbs and vegetables, salt again, and eat!

KEFTE

SIMPLE SANDWICH *(5–10 min)*
2–4 kefte, 1 pita or other flatbread, Techina (p. 393) or labneh, any pickles, a big handful of herbs (cilantro, dill, and mint), s'chug (optional).

Heat the oven to 400°F. On a baking sheet, place the leftover kefte and warm for 5 min. Warm the pita or flatbread over a flame or next to the kefte. If using pita, split it. Spread the techina over one side. Add the kefte. Sprinkle with pickles. Add herbs, then add s'chug (if using). Eat!
   Kefte is also good in the Kebab, Egg, and Techina Sandwich recipe above.

KEFTE SALAD *(5–10 min)*
2–4 kefte, salt, 2 cups mixed lettuces and herbs (parsley, cilantro, sorel, field lettuce, mâche), olive oil, lemon juice, ¼ cup labneh, ¼ cup toasted pistachios. *Optional additions:* croutons (see p. 176), leftover beet salad, leftover grape leaves, hummus.

Heat the oven to 400°F. Warm the kefte on a baking sheet until warm to the touch, about 5 min. In a bowl, lightly salt the lettuces and herbs, drizzle with olive oil and a few drops of lemon juice. Mix through with your hands. Spread the labneh onto a plate or in a shallow bowl. Sprinkle with the pistachios. Add the kefte, then top with the salad. Add any additions to be mixed in as you eat.

The ratio of kefte to potato doesn't matter in this next recipe. If you need to feed four on two leftover kefte, increase the number of potatoes. You can leave kefte whole or cut them up dispersing the meat further.

BAKED KEFTE AND POTATOES *(25 min)*
Salt, 1–2 cups roughly chopped waxy potato (about 1 medium), ½ clove garlic, 2 tbsp Techina (p. 393), 1–3 kefte, roughly chopped parsley (or cilantro or both), s'chug or other hot sauce, lemon juice (optional).

Heat the oven to 375°F. In a pot of boiling water salted to taste like pleasant seawater, boil the potatoes about 10–15 min. Reserving some of the cooking water, drain the potatoes. Pound the garlic to a paste with a little salt and place in a bowl. Add the techina, 2 tbsp of the potato cooking water and whisk together. Halve the kefte on the diagonal and add to the bowl along with the potatoes and mix well to coat. Spoon in a single layer into a small baking dish and bake until slightly roasty, 10–15 min. Remove from the oven and top with ample herbs and heavy dollops of s'chug or any other hot sauce. Squeeze with lemon (if using). (Inspired by *The Palestinian Table* by Reem Kassis)
 A variation is to add a tiny bit (about ½ tsp) of finely chopped preserved lemon to the techina before baking. Another is to shower the whole thing with toasted pine nuts or pistachios.

KIBBEH, COOKED

Leftover cooked kibbeh can be crumbled and used in Leftover Burger Bolognese (p. 322). Or it can be crumbled and used as the middle layer in baked kibbeh, or in Sahnieh.

SAHNIEH *(15 min)*
Butter or oil for the baking dish, 3–6 cooked kibbeh (crumbled), ¼ tsp ground cinnamon, 2–3 tbsp toasted pine nuts, 1 cup kibbeh nayeh (raw kibbeh meat, seasoned), 2 tbsp butter (cubed).

Heat the oven to 375°F. Butter or oil a small baking dish. In a bowl, mix together the crumbled cooked kibbeh, cinnamon, and pine nuts. Spread ½ cup of the raw kibbeh nayeh into the prepared dish and flatten it. Spread the cooked kibbeh mixture over that and cover with a layer of the remaining ½ cup kibbeh nayeh. Top with the butter cubes and bake until the top is just cooked, about 15 min. Good with pita or other flatbread, hummus, techina, s'chug, etc. (Adapted from Maureen Abood website)

LAMB, COOKED

SIMPLEST SOOTHING LAMB AND RICE SOUP *(20–30 min)*
4 tbsp (½ stick) butter, 1 small clove garlic (minced), 1 leek (cut into diagonal half-moons and well washed), 1 carrot (diced), 1½ tsp salt, 1 tbsp finely chopped parsley, 2 tbsp white wine, 3 cups stock (Lamb Stock, p. 330, chicken stock, vegetable stock, or a combination of stock and water), 1 cup bite-size chunks cooked lamb, 1 cup leftover cooked rice (especially good with saffron rice but any kind is fine). *Optional for serving:* olive oil or freshly grated Parmesan or Pecorino Romano cheese.

Heat a heavy-bottomed pot. Add the butter, garlic, leek, carrot, and salt and cook, stirring often, until the leeks are very melty and carrots tender, 10–12 min. Add the parsley. Add the wine and cook until the alcohol has evaporated, about 1 min. Add the stock, stir together, and bring to a simmer. Taste to make sure everything tastes united. Add the lamb and stir through. Cook for about 1 min. Add the rice, cook for another min, then taste for salt and adjust. When all is warm, it's done. If desired, serve with a drizzle of olive oil or some cheese or both.

Or add any leftover slow-cooked lamb to the Kottu Roti (p. 194). Or use in any recipe for *Beef, slow-cooked (p. 305)*.

LAMB CHOPS, COOKED

SPICY LAMB SALAD *(10 min)*
½ cup diced unpeeled cucumber, ¼ tsp salt, ½ tsp rice vinegar, 1 cup cold thinly sliced cooked lamb (against the grain), 1 tbsp Sichuan or similar chili crisp,

1 heaping tsp chopped roasted peanuts, 1 tsp toasted sesame seeds, 1 tsp toasted sesame oil. *For serving:* cilantro, rice, flatbread, or lettuce cups.

In a bowl, combine the cucumber, salt, and vinegar and let sit while preparing the remaining ingredients. In another bowl, combine the lamb and chili crisp. Add the lamb, peanuts, and sesame seeds to the cucumbers. Add the sesame oil and mix to combine. Top with cilantro. Eat on rice or with flatbread or in lettuce cups!

PISTACHIO MINT LAMB SALAD *(10 min)*
¼ tsp minced garlic, ¼ tsp salt, 1 tbsp chopped pistachios, 1 tsp finely chopped mint, 3 tbsp finely chopped parsley, ½ tsp grated lemon or lime zest, ½–1 tsp lemon or lime juice plus to taste, 2 tbsp olive oil, 1 cup julienned cold cooked lamb. *For serving:* flatbread (such as pita or roti) or lettuce cups, whole-milk Greek or regular yogurt.

In a bowl, combine the garlic, salt, pistachios, mint, parsley, lemon or lime zest, lemon or lime juice, and the olive oil and mix well. Stir in the lamb. Taste for salt and acid and adjust. To serve on flatbread, spread with yogurt, top with the lamb salad, and roll. If using lettuce cups, add the lamb salad then yogurt.

LAMB BONES

LAMB STOCK *(3 hr)*
A few lamb bones, 1 clove garlic or a small handful of garlic peels, 1 bay leaf, a few parsley stems, a carrot peel or piece of carrot, an onion peel or leek top (or piece of onion or leek).

In a stock pot, combine the ingredients and add water to cover by a few inches. Bring to a boil, reduce to a simmer, cook until it tastes like very subtle soup, about 3 hr. Strain.

LARB

If you are using leftover sticky rice, this will be extra crispy and exciting, like big pieces of crisp popped rice pancake.

SORT OF NAAM KHAO/LARB FRIED RICE *(5–10 min)*
2 tbsp canola or peanut oil, 1–1½ cups cooked rice or cooked sticky rice, fish sauce or salt, ½–1 cup larb, fresh herbs (mint, basil, and cilantro), wedge of lime for squeezing, sliced fresh or pickled chiles.

Heat a skillet over medium-high heat. Add the oil and rice and fry without moving it until it pops and browns, 3–5 min. Break it up and let it crisp a bit all over, letting each section fry a bit. Add a few drops of fish sauce or salt and the larb and toss through a few times. Top with herbs, lime juice, and chiles. Eat hot! Also good topped with a fried egg.

LARB LETTUCE WRAPS *(5 min)*
Larb, Boston or Little Gem leaves, lime juice, fish sauce, chopped roasted peanuts and/or fried shallots (see p. 7).

Bring larb to room temperature. Lay out the lettuce leaves and top each with a big spoonful of larb. Squeeze with extra lime juice and add a drop of fish sauce. Add a sprinkle of peanuts and/or shallots and eat.

LARDONS

Leftover lardons are leftover cooked bacon. They can be added to Fried Rice (p. 205) or be chopped and stirred into leftover grits. Or they can be warmed until they just begin to sizzle then scattered on a salad. Top this with a fried or poached egg. Lardons can also be added, at the beginning, to a pasta sauce. And they can be added to a pot of beans or minestrone or ribollita or to any broth or stock for flavor.

MAPO TOFU FRIED RICE *(5–10 min)*

1–2 slices bacon (optional; chopped or sliced), up to 2 tbsp neutral oil (peanut or grapeseed), 1–2 cups cooked rice, 1–2 tbsp Sichuan chili oil or chili crisp, ½–1 cup mapo tofu, 1–2 eggs (beaten with salt), 1 tbsp sliced scallions.

Heat a large heavy-bottomed pan. Add the bacon, if using, and cook to crisp. Add as much oil as needed to make about 2 tbsp fat total, then add the rice, and cook it over medium-high heat until the rice has begun to crisp. Stir in the chili oil. Add the mapo tofu and cook until the liquid is gone, 30 sec–1 min. Add the eggs, scramble through, turning off the heat to finish the cooking to keep the eggs from overcooking, continuing to stir. Taste for salt and adjust. Add the scallions and eat.

MAPO TOFU SOUP *(5–10 min)*

1 cup broth or water, ½–1 cup mapo tofu, salt, thinly sliced scallion or thinly sliced cilantro or cilantro stems.

In a small pot, bring the broth or water and mapo tofu to a boil. Once it's boiling, taste for salt and adjust. Eat topped with scallion or herbs.

MAPO TOFU NOODLES *(10–15 min)*

4 oz dried or frozen noodles (udon, Chinese egg noodles, or wide rice noodles), ½–1 cup mapo tofu, Sichuan chili crisp (optional), salt, thinly sliced scallion or thinly sliced cilantro or cilantro stems.

Cook the noodles according to their package directions, then drain. In a large heavy-bottomed skillet or sauté pan, heat the mapo tofu, then add the noodles along with whatever water clings to them. Stir well to combine, adding chili crisp if you like. Taste for salt and adjust. Top with scallions or herbs and eat.

MEATLOAF

MEATLOAF PIZZA *(10 min)*

Meatloaf, cheese pizza, fresh basil, freshly grated Parmesan cheese.

Bring the meatloaf to room temperature. Heat the oven to 400°F. Slice the meatloaf into slices ½ inch thick, then break into large bite-size pieces. Scatter over the pizza as amply as you like. Bake until warm, 5–10 min. Scatter with basil and Parmesan and eat.

Leftover cooked meatloaf can also be substituted for leftover hamburgers. Or it can be thickly sliced then sizzled to golden brown on its cut sides in a hot pan along with leftover cooked broccoli. Eat over mashed potatoes for a classic Early Bird Special.

MEATBALLS, COOKED

BEST MEATBALL SUB *(variable)*
3–6 meatballs (halved if large), Marcella's Tomato Sauce (p. 394) or other beloved tomato-basil sauce, baguette (or other crusty bun or focaccia), olive oil, fresh ricotta or sliced fresh mozzarella, salt, roughly torn basil leaves (optional).

In a pot, warm the meatballs in the sauce. Toast the bread until the outside is just crusty and the inside is soft, tearing some crumb out if needed for a mostly crusty experience. (Save the crumb for bread crumbs, see p. 176.) Drizzle the bread with olive oil. Spoon in the meatballs, draining off most of the sauce, then spoon some sauce over. Top with cheese, then lightly salt. Add basil (if using). Drizzle olive oil on the top half of the bread. Close the sub and eat.

Leftover meatballs can also be heated in tomato sauce and then eaten, alongside a glob of ricotta for a consummate lunch-for-one.

MOUSSAKA

If you do not want to warm and eat it again, substitute leftover moussaka for for lasagna in Cheesy Lasagna Stew (p. 357) or use in a Frittata (p. 140).

PANCETTA ENDS

Pancetta ends should be used to improve stock or beans. Place one in the pot with the rest of the ingredients, and fish it out or strain at the end. Taste, and if it still has flavor, consider shredding and including in a stew or pasta sauce or fried rice. Or use interchangeably with *Guanciale ends (p. 320)*, but don't tell a Roman unless you intend to anger them.

PÂTÉ EN CROÛTE

When facing an aging pâté, remember that there's enough fat and salt in a pâté to preserve it for a long time. And the pastry coffin of a pâté en croûte, full of helpful fat and salt itself, works to extend its life further. Considering the many preservative materials and techniques that have been employed, you might simply get a plate, cut a slice, add a dab of mustard and have a pickle and settle down for a snack. Or take the pâté out of its crust and make a sandwich. Taste the crust, and if you like it, toast it in pieces in the toaster oven and eat them as a snack with afternoon coffee or tea.

PEPPERONI

Pepperoni is too often relegated to a single use. Chop or julienne it, sizzle it in a pan, and add it to a tomato sauce, along with some chile flakes. Or use it in Pizzeria Salad (p. 54). Or use it in the Bean and Salami Soup (p. 213).

PIG'S EAR

SPICY PIG EAR SALAD (*10 min*)
1 cup sliced cooked pig's ear, 1–2 tsp Sichuan chili crisp, ½ tsp black vinegar, ½ tsp soy sauce, ¼ tsp sugar, 1 tsp toasted sesame seeds, 1 scallion (thinly sliced), 1 handful chopped cilantro.

Mix all the ingredients well. Good with rice and beer.

PIGS' FEET, COOKED

These are wonderful in the Composed Salad of Herbs, Meat, and Small Potatoes (p. 305). Pull the meat from the bones and proceed.

PIGS' FEET, RAW

TROTTER BROTH *(2–4 hr)*

Use pigs' feet in Meat Stock (p. 246), taking care to clean them well. Trotter broth has so much collagen in it, it will gel at room temperature, making it a perfect base for soup dumpling filling, needing only scallion, ginger, and a little Shaoxing wine lightly mixed with the pork and cubes of gelled trotter broth.

PORK, SLOW-COOKED

MEAT AND TOFU

Slow-cooked pork is among the most versatile leftovers. It's only a question of what you want to eat. Mix into tomato sauce and add chopped parsley for a pasta or polenta sauce. Or add to congee or ramen. Or use as the filling for arancini. Or add to minestrone, or warm with beans, or with beans and greens. Or make a:

WARM PORK SANDWICH *(10–15 min)*

1 sandwich roll (or piece of baguette or 2 slices rustic bread), butter or mayonnaise, ½ cup slow-cooked pork, hot sauce (optional), 2 tbsp coleslaw (or other crunchy/pickle-y vegetable such as sauerkraut, kimchi, or curtido), thinly sliced pickles (optional), sliced Swiss or cheddar cheese.

Toast the roll, then butter the cut sides or spread with mayonnaise. In a small saucepan, warm the pork with a sprinkle of water or hot sauce (if using) or both, stirring often to keep it from sticking. When it's warm, mound in the middle of the pan, top with cheese, remove the pan from the heat, and cover to melt the cheese slightly. Spoon meat and cheese into the roll, top with slaw and pickles if desired, and eat!

FRENCH WINTER VEGETABLE SOUP *(45 min)*

¼ cup olive oil, 2 tsp salt, 1 bouquet garni (sprigs of thyme, parsley stems, rosemary, sage, bay leaf), 1 onion (diced), 2 potatoes (diced), 2 leeks (sliced and well washed), 3 carrots (peeled and chopped), 2 turnips (peeled and chopped), 1 stalk celery (sliced), 1 fennel bulb (chopped, stalks reserved for flavoring beans), 2 cloves garlic (smashed), 1 cup slow-cooked pork. *For serving:* olive oil, freshly grated Parmesan cheese, freshly ground black pepper.

In a pot, combine 6 cups water, the olive oil, salt, and bouquet garni. Bring to a boil. Add all the vegetables, including the garlic, reduce to a simmer, and cook until the vegetables are totally tender, 30–35 min. Stir in the pork. Once it's all warm, serve, drizzling amply with olive oil, topping with cheese and black pepper. Also very good with chopped parsley or with Parsley Oil (p. 68). (Adapted from *A New Way to Cook* by Sally Schneider)

MAPO TOFU MASHUP *(20 min)*

1 block soft tofu, 2 tbsp pork fat or neutral oil, 1 large onion (chopped), ¼ tsp salt plus to taste, 4 cloves garlic (chopped), 1 tbsp finely chopped fresh ginger, 3 tbsp gochujang, 1 tbsp Sichuan peppercorns (roughly pounded), pinch of chile flakes or snipped dried red chiles, 1 tbsp soy sauce, any amount up to 2 cups slow-cooked pork, 1 bunch cooking greens (stemmed and chopped) or leftover cooked greens (optional), cooked rice for serving, thinly sliced scallions (optional).

Cube the tofu. Heat a large pan over medium. Add the fat or oil, onion, and salt and cook until tender, 5–10 min. Add the garlic and ginger and cook until softened, another min. Stir in the gochujang, Sichuan peppercorns, chile, and soy sauce. Add the pork and just enough water or other liquid to come up halfway. Bring to a simmer. If using cooking greens, add and cook until tender, 5–10 min, adding liquid if needed. Add the tofu. Taste for salt and adjust. Serve over rice and top with scallions (if using).

Or use leftover slow-cooked pork in A Congee-esque Soup (p. 239). Or add to cooking or leftover cooked greens, or to beans and warm them together, or, or, or . . .

PORK CHOPS OR TENDERLOIN, COOKED

Thinly slice leftover cooked chops or tenderloin and make a sandwich of them, with Aioli (p. 395) and a big handful of arugula or leftover cooked greens. Or thinly slice them, top them with thinly sliced cheese, and make a melty toasty pork and cheese croque monsieur. Or use them in place of beef in Melty Beef Panino (p. 339), or finely chop and use in Larb (p. 301). Leftover chops or loin can also be used instead of braised beef in the Composed Salad of Herbs, Meat, and Small Potatoes (p. 305) or instead of ham in the Croquetas de Jamón (p. 321).

PORK FAT

The best fried chicken I've ever made was such for two reasons, neither of which had to do with a recipe. The chicken was an old breed of chicken called Barred Rock. It is a slow-growing chicken, and the one I fried, with a small breast and muscular legs, tasted of grass and sun. Just as vitally, I cooked it in rendered pork fat, also known as lard, so that we could taste this old breed of chicken fried the way it used to be fried. Those two factors—the breed and the lard—changed everything. I probably dredged the chicken in a flour mixture. I don't remember. I remember that we chewed in near astonishment, understanding for the first time what it was that was so transcendent about fried chicken.

PORK PÂTÉ

Pork pâté is delicious on toast or in baguette sandwiches, and a slathering will improve any banh mi.

PROSCIUTTO

Lest you find yourself wondering what to do with the last little bit of proscuitto!

PROSCIUTTO PANINO *(15 min)*

2 slices rustic bread, olive oil or butter, a little prosciutto, sliced fontina or other good melting cheese, a few leaves of arugula.

Heat a heavy-bottomed pan or a cast-iron skillet and have another heavy pan nearby. Lightly drizzle both sides of the bread with olive oil or spread with butter. On one slice, layer the prosciutto, fontina, and arugula and cover with the second slice. Place in the hot pan, then weight down with the second pan, adding additional weight if needed. Cook slowly, over low heat, flipping when the first side is quite crisped and browned, 4–5 min per side. Eat.

PROSCIUTTO, END

A prosciutto end can be used, like pancetta ends and Parmesan rinds, to improve beans or stock.

QUAIL

Years ago, when I would have Sunday dinner with a chef named Cal Peternell and his family in Canyon, California, there were often two or three leftover quail brought home from Chez Panisse, where we both cooked. They were stuffed with herby bread crumbs or a delicate pâté of their own livers, salted and marinated in Muscat de Beaumes-de-Venise, and raw or cooked to rare. I cooked or warmed the quails briefly over the fire or in a hot stove when I was there, smoking a joint and forgetting what I was doing until I smelled quail skin about to burn. We made two or three feed six to eight people by cutting each, sizzling hot, down the middle, or into four little quarters, so everyone had a hot stuffed quail bit to nibble on while having their first glass of rosé. I still think one or two bites of grilled quail is enough, and a promising way to start an evening.

RABBIT, COOKED

It is a culinary cliché that any white meat of a biped or quadruped "tastes like chicken." In this case it is true. Anything that can be made with leftover chicken can be made with leftover rabbit.

RILLETTES

Store your jar of rillettes toward the front of the refrigerator, then let them sit on the counter while you toast bread to spread them on. You can repeat this twice weekly and a single jar will support your habit for several months. Rillettes are also good on cold radishes or potato chips. Or they can be added to congee, or used to make a pasta sauce: place in a sauté pan over low heat to melt the fat, then let the meat get a bit crisp, then remove the meat to a plate. Cook a mirepoix (see p. 6) in the fat, then add broth and cream, let it reduce, add the meat back in, and mix with cooked pasta.

ROAST BEEF

MELTY BEEF PANINO (*10 min*)
2 tbsp mayonnaise, 1 tsp prepared horseradish, 2 slices rustic bread (or piece of baguette split as for a sandwich or a similar sandwich roll), 1 clove garlic, olive oil, a little roast beef, ¼ cup grated or sliced melting cheese (Swiss, Havarti, or cheddar), freshly ground black pepper, a handful of arugula or peppercress (optional).

In a small bowl, combine the mayonnaise and horseradish. Toast the bread, then rub the cut sides with the clove of garlic and drizzle with oil. Spread the horseradish mayonnaise over one piece of toast, as heavily as you like. Lay the beef on the other piece, top with cheese, then add black pepper. Add arugula or cress (if using.) Close. In a heated cast-iron skillet, press with a second pan, weighted, on top, until flattened and the cheese has melted.

SALAMI

Salami is incredibly versatile. If you find yourself with some leftover, you have a number of options: 1) Use it in the recipe for Ribollita (p. 178) or Minestrone (p. 210) or Bean and Salami Soup (p. 213). 2) Heat a pan, add a couple table-spoons of olive oil, add sliced onions or shallots and a pinch of salt, cook until softened, 5–10 min. Add a spoonful of tomato paste. Add salami and cook until you have a caramelized topping for risotto or polenta or congee or grits. Spoon over your starch of choice. 3) Use it in Pizzeria Salad (p. 54). 4) Put it on pizza. 5) Add ends to a pot of beans (p. 203).

SAUSAGE, BREAKFAST, COOKED

Leftover breakfast sausages can be sliced lengthwise and heated in a hot, heavy-bottomed pan, cut-side down, which will recrisp them. They can then be layered with soft scrambled eggs, melted cheese, and hot sauce into a breakfast or lunch sandwich. If you're feeling bold, turn reheated breakfast sausages into a merguez-style sandwich. Combine harissa with mayonnaise. Layer caramel-ized or fried onions on the bottom of a sandwich roll or one of two slices of toasted sandwich bread. Spread the top side with spicy mayonnaise. Add the sausages, then a handful of cilantro leaves or iceberg lettuce. Imagine away the taste of sage and maple, and enjoy.

SAUSAGE, COOKED

A cold sausage never looks promising. Start by heating the cold sausage. This can be done in a covered pan over low heat, or in the oven at 350°F. If you're in a rush, butterfly it and heat it cut-side down. While the sausage is warming, find frozen baguette, or another type of roll. Then rummage around for the rest of a sausage sandwich, especially for leftover grilled peppers, or caramel-ized onions, or cooked greens, or sauerkraut. Once the pieces are all in hand, assemble and eat.

Or make ragu.

SAUSAGE RAGU (*15 min*)

Marcella's Tomato Sauce (p. 394) or one 28 oz can whole peeled tomatoes (drained and pureed with a little olive oil or melted butter), ½ onion (optional), 3 tbsp butter (optional), salt, 1–2 sprigs rosemary, a piece of Parmesan or Pecorino Romano rind, chile flakes (optional), 1–2 sprigs rosemary, ¼–½ cup finely chopped cooked sausage, in the casing or removed. *For serving:* cooked short pasta or polenta, freshly grated Parmesan or Pecorino Romano cheese, torn basil or roughly chopped parsley.

Make Marcella's Tomato Sauce and fish out the onion halves. Finely chop one half—this will be messy work, so use a sharp knife and don't worry about uniformity—and save the second half for Greens with Buttery Onions—and Maybe Cherry Tomatoes (p. 66). If not making the Marcella sauce, chop the raw onion medium-fine and cook it in the butter, adding a sprinkle of salt as soon as you add the onion, until it is totally tender, 10–12 min, adding a sprinkle of water if it starts to brown. In a small pot, combine the Marcella sauce and onion (or tomato puree and cooked onion), cheese rind, a sprinkle of chile flakes (if using), rosemary, and sausage and simmer for 10–15 min until it seems integrated. Eat with short pasta or ladled over polenta, garnished with grated cheese and basil or parsley.

Or use cooked sausage—along with some thinly sliced red onion, or anchovies and sliced pickled chiles—to top leftover pizza. Or, if a recipe calls for ground meat and you have cooked sausage instead, consider a substitution. You may need to add extra lime juice or herbs or chile to mask any interloping flavors. Or use leftover cooked sausage in Corn Bread Dressing (p. 186), or in Bean and Salami Soup (p. 213) or in the Pizza Sausage Bake (p. 365).

SAUSAGE, PATTIES OR BULK

This next would be a hot sausage po'boy if it were made with Patton's Hot Sausage, which is available by mail from New Orleans. Patton's is traditionally beef, and it is extraordinary. The following version is made with other sausage. It can therefore approach, but never be, a hot sausage po'boy.

ALMOST A HOT SAUSAGE PO'BOY (*10 min*)
¼ lb or so sausage (patties or bulk), cayenne pepper, butter, a piece of soft baguette (or hoagie roll or similar or white bread), American cheese (optional), mayonnaise, ½ cup shredded iceberg lettuce.

If using bulk sausage, put in a bowl and add a lot, a lot of cayenne pepper. If using patties, shake cayenne on top. Press the bulk sausage into patties at most ¼ inch thick or thinner yet. Heat a heavy-bottomed skillet, add a pat of butter, and cook the sausage patties until warmed through and sizzly, 2–3 min per side. Move the sausage patties out of the way and press the cut side of the bread into the pan to get some butter and sausage grease. Toast the bread until just warm, 2–3 min. If using cheese, place ½ slice over each hot patty. Remove the bread from the toaster oven, coat both sides well with mayonnaise. Add the sausage patties, then iceberg lettuce. Close and eat. It is reasonable to add sliced pickles and sliced tomatoes. You can also make this with leftover cooked patties, first sliced horizontally, so the patties are as thin as possible.

SHEPHERD'S PIE

CRISPY CHEESY SHEPHERD'S PIE HASH (*20 min*)
3–4 tbsp butter, 1–2 cups shepherd's pie, salt, freshly ground black pepper, ½ cup grated cheddar cheese.

Heat a heavy-bottomed pan. Add the butter. Scoop the shepherd's pie into the hot butter and spread out, so the mashed potato fries. Add as much black pepper as you want. Mix and fry until the bottom is crisp in places. Top with cheddar, hash through, and eat. This is ugly and delicious.

STEAK

Any steak makes a good sandwich, as long as it's thinly sliced. Let it come to room temperature on its own and you won't need to heat it and risk overcooking. Follow the recipe for a Melty Beef Panino, or toast and butter bread, find pickles, cheese, and anything else you like in steak sandwiches, and sandwich it all. Or use leftover steak to make:

FAUX PHO *(45 min)*

1 tsp coriander seeds, 2 star anise, 2 whole cloves, 1 cinnamon stick, 2–3 scallions (cut into a few pieces each), 4 cups beef or chicken broth, ½ bunch cilantro or 1 bunch cilantro stems, a 1-inch piece of fresh ginger (sliced), 2–3 tsp fish sauce, 4–8 oz flat rice noodles, 4 oz or so sliced cooked steak. *Garnishes:* ¼–½ cup fresh bean sprouts, ½ cup fresh herb leaves (Thai basil, basil, mint, and cilantro), 2–4 lime wedges, 1 red or green chile (sliced), sriracha sauce.

In a medium pot, toast the coriander seeds, star anise, cloves, cinnamon, and scallions until just beginning to color, 30 sec–1 min. Add the broth, 1 cup water, the cilantro and ginger, and simmer 30 min. Strain into another pot and season with fish sauce. Cook the rice noodles according to the package directions and divide into bowls. Top with the sliced steak and pour the broth over. Serve with the garnishes. (Adapted from *The Pho Cookbook* by Andrea Nguyen)

Steak can also be thinly sliced and used in the recipe for Larb (p. 301).

STEAK TARTARE

If the tartare is very loose, add fresh or toasted bread crumbs to bind it until it can be easily shaped.

SVITZERRINA *(15 min)*

4 oz or so steak tartare, 1 tbsp olive oil, 1 tbsp butter, 1 sprig rosemary. *Optional additions:* 1 tbsp compound butter (Parsley Butter, p. 69, Caper Butter, p. 431, or any other).

Form leftover tartare into a patty, like a hamburger. Heat a grill or cast-iron skillet to medium-high heat. Add the olive oil and butter, and when the butter stops foaming, add the patty. Place the rosemary sprig nearby and spoon butter over it. Cook for 3–4 min per side, depending on your taste (3 and 3 would be rare, 4 and 4 medium). Rest for 3 min off the heat. Top with the rosemary and compound butter (if using) and eat! Very good with potatoes or bread and a salad.

TOFU, FRIED

I have various tedious theories about what makes crisp batter so delicious once it's melting into soup. In the interest of space: I recommend trying it. Slice or chop leftover fried tofu. Heat or make miso soup. Add the tofu, stir through, add chopped scallions, and eat. This is even better if you have udon noodles. If you do, cook the udon in the dashi before you add the miso, then proceed as above. This is also good with rice noodles, or soba, or spaghetti. To use leftover fried tofu in fried rice, cube it and add it toward the end, with just enough time to warm.

TURKEY, COOKED

For one month a year there are as many recipes published for what to do with leftover turkey as for all leftovers the rest of the year. I have no novel additions. But most publications are likely to, each November. Thankfully, leftover turkey is nearly as versatile as leftover chicken. See *Chicken, cooked (p. 308)* and use interchangeably.

TURKEY STOCK *(2–4 hr)*
1 turkey carcass, ½ carrot, 1 bay leaf, 1 star anise, 1 clove garlic, a few pepper-corns, a few fennel seeds or a few pieces fennel scraps or tops, 1–2 onion skins or leek tops, 1 stalk celery (if you have).

In a stockpot, add the carcass with water to cover. Bring to a boil. Skim all the foam that rises. Reduce to a simmer and add the remaining ingredients. Cook at a simmer for 2–4 hr, tasting starting at 2 hr. It's done when it tastes like subtle soup.

TURKEY, SLICED

There are worse things than a dill pickle rolled up in a slice of turkey, with or without a piece of presliced Swiss cheese between turkey and pickle, with mustard for dipping. There are better things, too. But there are worse.

VEGAN OR VEGETARIAN CRUMBLES

MEATLESS PASTA SAUCE ALLA MARCELLA *(15 min)*

3 tbsp olive oil, ½ cup minced onion and carrot combined, ¼ tsp salt plus to taste, 1 clove garlic (minced), 1 cup vegan or vegetarian crumbles, chile flakes, 2 cups Marcella's Tomato Sauce (p. 394).

Heat a pot. Add the olive oil, onion-carrot combination, and salt and cook until softened, stirring occasionally, 5–10 min. Add the garlic and cook for another 30 sec. Add the vegan or vegetarian crumbles and a tiny pinch of chile flakes and stir through, increasing the heat and breaking the crumbles up into small pieces. Cook, stirring occasionally, for 5–7 min to slightly brown. Stir in the tomato sauce and cook over medium-low heat until hot and all combined, 5–10 min. Taste for salt and adjust. Good on pasta or polenta or as Sloppy Joes.

SPICED CHICKPEAS AND RICE *(30 min)*

3–4 tbsp olive oil, ½ cup minced onion and carrot combined, ¼ tsp salt plus to taste, 1 clove garlic (smashed), a scrape of ground cinnamon, 1 bay leaf, 2 tbsp pine nuts, 1 cup vegan or vegetarian crumbles (frozen or thawed), 1 cup leftover cooked chickpeas, 2–3 cups cooked rice.

Heat a pot. Add the olive oil, onion-carrot combination, and salt and cook, stirring occasionally, until softened, 5–10 min. Add the garlic, cinnamon, and bay leaf and cook for another 30 sec. Add the pine nuts and cook, stirring, until lightly golden, about 3 min. Add the crumbles and stir through, increasing heat and breaking the crumbles up into small pieces. Cook, stirring occasionally, for 5–7 min to slightly brown. Stir in the chickpeas and rice. Taste for salt and adjust. Remove from the heat, cover, and let sit 10 min then eat.

HOW TO SPEND YOUR RICHES
Dough and noodles

Riches are for spending.

—*Francis Bacon*

Sandwiches may have been invented when an Earl of Sandwich wanted to keep gambling, but in the earl's kitchens the cooks had long been relying on bread and its crusts to turn trimmings into irreproachable meals for their families.

Dumplings, pupusas, burritos, sandwiches, sauced pastas, and so on are all ingenious variations on a fundament of economical cooking—using inexpensive and expandable starch, whether corn or wheat or rice or plantain or yuca or taro, or, or, or . . . to transform small amounts of proteins and vegetables into filling meals.

It feels noble to make the most of one's resources—turning roast pork into pork noodles and then into noodle soup and so on. But it is also gratifying to know that when one does, one is limited to several good things.

One choice is to rely on the functionality of the egg. Eggs turn anything into a meal. Frittatas especially love starch and fat, which are the cornerstones of all stuffed and sauced doughs. The world's best frittata, the tortilla española, is olive-oil-stewed potatoes, onions, and eggs. But pasta frittatas and chopped knish frittatas aren't far behind and stand on similar footings. Savory bread puddings follow the same principle: an egg, and in this case a bit of milk or stock, coaxing bits of leftover starch into a coalition.

Dishes like chilaquiles and migas and fatoot samneh are another choice, adapting the same alliances to different ends: Instead of baking starch into egg, they demand frying the broken-up starch and adding eggs. Fried noodles operate on a similar design—with or without eggs, and with or without bits of crisp vegetable or herbs or meat or tofu or pickles, and so on.

All stuffed starches and noodles willingly slump toward stew. It may be hard to stomach the idea of lasagna stew or enchilada stew or pizza stew. But all are good if you give the starch time to break down into rich absorbing creaminess, just as you do when making any starchy soup, like congee, ribollita, pappa al pomodoro, rasam, or panade. In all cases, more time, more fat, and an open mind produce of leftover starches hearty and warming if homely stews. To complete the cycle, what's left of a stew can, with the addition of sourdough starter or bread crumbs and eggs and cheese, or mashed potatoes, or flour and water, or all of the above, be turned into little savory pancakes and fried.

Here are some dough recipes. They can be filled with just about anything:

PIEROGI DOUGH

2 cups (240 g) all-purpose flour, ½ tsp salt, 1 egg (beaten), ½ cup sour cream, 4 tbsp (½ stick) room-temperature butter.

In a bowl, mix the flour and salt, then mix in the egg. Work in the sour cream and butter by hand, then knead to uniform and just a bit less sticky, but still moist. Wrap well and refrigerate at least 30 min and up to 2 days. Roll the dough to ⅛ inch thick and cut into 2-inch rounds. Fill each with 1½ tsp filling, fold over, and seal with a fork. Cook in a pot of boiling water in batches until they float. Serve with melted butter. (From King Arthur Baking website)

BASIC CREAM CHEESE DOUGH

4 oz (8 tbsp) cold cream cheese (cut into pieces), 6 tbsp cold butter (cut into pieces), 1 cup (120 g) all-purpose flour, ½ tsp salt.

In a food processor, combine all the ingredients and pulse until it begins to form a ball. Gather in a ball, pat into a disc, wrap and refrigerate for 1 hr. Use for empanadas or pinwheels or pot pie or rugelach or seriously just about anything. (From the Epicurious website)

SAMOSA DOUGH

2 cups (240 g) all-purpose flour, 1 tsp ajwain seeds, ¼ tsp salt, 4 tbsp plus 1 tsp oil (peanut, grapeseed, or vegetable).

In a bowl, mix the flour, ajwain, and salt. Add the oil, mixing it in well by hand into coarse crumbs. Add ¼–½ cup water, little by little to form a stiff dough, which will probably only take just over ¼ cup. Cover with a damp cloth and set aside for 30–40 min before using.

AREPAS

AREPAS CHILAQUILES (*10 min*)

1 tbsp oil (olive or vegetable oil) or ghee, 1 egg, 1 cup Salvadoran salsa roja or homemade Quick Salsa Roja (recipe follows), 1–2 arepas (cut into strips ½ inch wide), salt. *Toppings:* pickled onions, pickled chiles, queso fresco or sour cream (optional), roughly chopped cilantro (optional).

Heat a small skillet. Add the oil or ghee over medium-high heat, then fry the egg until the white is set and the yolk is as you like it. Remove from the pan and set aside. In the same skillet, heat the salsa until just bubbling. Add the arepa strips and cook over medium heat until they're soft and yielding and their cheese is melty. Taste for salt and adjust. Tip onto a plate, add the egg, top with the toppings, and eat!

Quick Salsa Roja: In a blender, puree 1 cup whole peeled tomatoes, 2 tbsp red onion, 1 clove garlic, ¼ tsp salt, and ¼ tsp cumin.

BAO OR MANTOU (STEAMED BUNS)

Bao or mantou buns can be frozen and resteamed. Freeze in a single layer as you would fresh berries, then move to an airtight container or bag. Press the air out of the bag and return to the freezer. To reheat, steam from frozen over boiling water for 6–8 min.

BLINTZES

Blintzes can be reheated, covered at 350°F until warm, 5–10 min. If you are not in the mood to eat blintzes again, unwrap them. Remove the filling to mix into Basic Muffin Batter (p. 103) or pancake batter (pp. 138–39). The crepes can be wiped off, warmed in melted butter, dusted with sugar, squeezed with lemon, and eaten.

DOUGH AND NOODLES

BOUREKAS

Like any other savory filled pastry or bread, leftover bourekas are good with eggs. A version of this dish exists in nearly every culture. Chop or crumble bourekas. Heat a skillet, then add a tbsp of oil or butter, then the boureka pieces. Whisk eggs with a little salt before adding them to the pan. Lightly scramble until they're just set. Herbs or yogurt or pickled chiles or hot sauce are good accompaniments.

Or substitute bourekas for tamales in the Tamales à la Mexicana (p. 370) or for the knishes in the recipe for Knish Tortilla Española (p. 356).

BURRITOS

These ingredients are based on 1 cup burrito filling with rice; if you have more, scale it accordingly. If the burrito didn't include rice, find ½–2 cups leftover cooked rice.

BURRITO FRIED RICE *(10 min)*
1 cup burrito filling with rice, peanut or vegetable oil for frying, ½ onion (chopped), 1 clove garlic (minced), 2–3 tbsp chopped chiles, salt, lemon or lime juice.

Scrape the burrito filling into a bowl. Wipe or scrape any remaining wet ingredients off the tortilla. Cut whatever of the tortilla you can get fairly clean into squares. If there's any rice on the tortilla, it will become a tiny projectile when it hits the oil. In a small pot, heat ½ inch of oil to 350°–365°F. Add the tortilla squares and fry until just crisp, removing them to drain on paper towel. In a skillet, heat another tbsp or so of oil, add the onion, garlic, chiles, and a sprinkle of salt and cook until the onion has softened somewhat, 3–5 min. Add the burrito filling and stir through quickly. Don't worry how many different things are in it. Keep the heat high and scrape the bottom. As soon as it's all warm, tip into a bowl, top with fried tortilla squares, and squeeze with lemon or lime juice, and eat.

CHILAQUILES

Chop and use leftover chilaquiles in Huevos Rancheros Fried Rice (p. 160).

CREPES

CREATIVELY FILLED CREPES *(15 min)*

Leftover crepes, fillings that are exciting: crème fraîche and salmon roe; or sliced soft-boiled eggs, chives, and white anchovies; or garlicky greens and mozzarella; or dal, chana masala, or aloo gobi with cilantro chutney, or anything else that can be spread and wrapped.

Heat the oven to 250°F. Spread the crepes in a baking dish, cover, and warm until pliable, about 10 min. Fill with new filling and eat.

DOSA

DOSA UPMA *(30 min)*

Some of a dosa, 2 tbsp neutral oil (grapeseed or peanut), ½ tsp black mustard seeds, ¼ tsp urad dal, 5–7 curry leaves, ½ onion (finely chopped), ¼ tsp salt plus to taste, pinch of hing (asafoetida), ground chile powder, pinch of another masala you like (optional), chopped cilantro.

Chop the dosa. Heat a medium skillet. Add the oil, then add the mustard seeds and dal and cook to sizzling. Add the curry leaves, onion, and salt, and cook over medium heat until just beginning to soften, 1–2 min. Stir in the hing, chile powder, and masala (if using), then add the cilantro and mix well. Taste for salt and adjust. Eat hot. (Adapted from Mary's Kitchen website)

DUMPLINGS (JIAOZI, GYOZA, MOMOS, ETC.)

As long as you have enough of them and, ideally, a bit of scallion and chopped cilantro and leftover cooked greens, leftover dumplings turn even the plainest, most subtle broth into a lunchtime soup. Place 3–4 dumplings per person in a pot of broth, along with any leftover cooked greens. Warm over medium heat. Add sliced scallions and chopped cilantro just before eating.

Or, if you're inspired toward a double starch, chop leftover dumplings into pieces and fry them with rice for dumpling fried rice, making sure the dumpling wrappers have a chance to crisp along with the grains of rice. Or make:

DUMPLING RICE SALAD *(15–20 min)*

4–6 dumplings, peanut or vegetable oil, 2 tbsp soy sauce, 2 tbsp ponzu sauce, 1 tbsp sesame oil, 1 tbsp rice vinegar, salt, 1 cup thinly sliced cucumber, 1 cup shredded cabbage or romaine, ¼ cup sliced scallions, 1 cup freshly cooked short-grain rice, 2 tbsp toasted sesame seeds, fried shallots (see p. 7) or fried carrot peels (see Fried Onions but Carrots, p. 28).

Heat the oven or toaster oven to 400°F. Put the dumplings on a pan, drizzle lightly with oil, and warm 5–10 min. Meanwhile, in a small bowl, whisk together the soy sauce, ponzu, sesame oil, vinegar, and salt to taste to make the dressing. In a large bowl, combine the cucumber, cabbage or romaine, and scallions and toss with dressing to taste, keeping some dressing aside. Mix in the warm rice, divide between two bowls, top with the dumplings, drizzle with any additional dressing you want, sprinkle with any seeds or fried shallots or peels, and eat. (Adapted from Danny Amend)

EGG ROLLS

Leftover egg rolls readily recrisp in a 375°F oven. They are also delicious crumbled or chopped and added to fried rice.

EMPANADAS

Leftover empanadas can be reheated or they can be used in Chilaquiles (p. 197) or Arepas Chilaquiles (p. 351).

ENCHILADAS

Enchiladas reheat beautifully and can always simply be reheated and then
doused with hot sauce and scattered with cilantro. This is for stretching one or
two enchiladas to feed a crowd.

ENCHILADA STEW *(45 min)*
2–3 tbsp cooking oil (or annatto oil if you have it), 1 cup finely chopped cilantro
(stems are ideal for this), ½ cup finely chopped onion or scallion or shallot,
¼ cup finely chopped garlic, 1 tbsp chopped fresh chile, 2 tsp salt plus to taste,
1 bay leaf, 2 cups chopped enchiladas. *Garnish:* chopped cilantro, lime wedges.

Heat a medium pot over medium heat. Add the oil, cilantro, onion, garlic, chile,
and salt and stir through. Cook until everything has softened, about 10 min.
Reduce the heat or add a few drops of water if needed to keep things from
browning or sticking. Add the bay leaf and 4 cups water. Bring to a boil, then
reduce to a simmer. Add the enchiladas and simmer until the soup has thickened and the tortillas taste like thick slippery egg noodles, 15–30 min. Taste for
salt and adjust. Garnish with chopped cilantro and serve with lime wedges.

GALETTE, SAVORY

CHEDDAR AND SCALLION DIPPERS *(20 min)*
1 slice galette, 2 scallions (slivered), 12 thin rectangular slices cheddar cheese,
fennel pollen or freshly ground black pepper.

Heat the oven to 400°F. Slice the galette into thin batons and spread on
a baking sheet. Top each with 2–3 slivers of scallion, then cover each with
2 slices of cheese. Bake until the cheese is just beginning to melt, about 8 min.
Remove from the oven, sprinkle with fennel pollen or black pepper. Let cool,
then eat! (Adapted from Danny Amend)

GYRO

Gyros should be disassembled. Remove the meat, leaving sauce and onions
and other condiments attached. Let the flatbread dry at room temperature
and then grind to bread crumbs or toast into Dip Chips (p. 192). Thinly slice

the meat and add to Fried Rice (p. 205), or to a bean soup, like the Bean and Salami Soup (p. 213). Or use the meat in a new sandwich, warming it briefly in a pot with a sprinkle of stock or water and a dash of hot sauce, then layering with sauerkraut or kimchi and cheese, then griddling to hot.

KNISHES

KNISH TORTILLA ESPAÑOLA *(12 min)*
¼ cup olive oil, 1 onion (thinly sliced), ¾ tsp salt, 1 knish (chopped into pieces), 3 eggs (beaten).

Heat the oven to 375°F. Heat a 6–8-inch ovenproof skillet over medium-high heat. Add the oil, onion, and ½ tsp of the salt. Cook, stirring often, until the onion is softened, 5–7 min. Use a slotted spoon or tongs to transfer the onion to a bowl to cool slightly, 1–2 min, leaving the oil in the skillet. Add the chopped knish, eggs, and remaining ¼ tsp salt to the onion. Set the skillet back over medium heat. Add the egg mixture and cook, spreading the eggs to even them, until the bottom and sides just cohere. Transfer the skillet to the oven and cook until the top is just set, about 8–10 min. Remove, let cool, invert onto a plate, and eat as is. Good cold, too.

KREPLACH

If you are feeling very open-minded, leftover kreplach can be re-envisioned as wontons.

KREPLACH SOUP *(40 min)*
Kreplach, 6 cups chicken stock, 1 bunch cilantro stems, 1 star anise, sliced fresh ginger, black vinegar, chili oil.

In a pot, combine the chicken stock, with the cilantro stems, star anise, and ginger and simmer 20–30 min. Strain the broth into another pot, add the kreplach, and heat to warm through. Drizzle with black vinegar and chili oil and eat.

Kreplach can also be pan-fried, like gyoza. Heat oil in a pan with a lid. Add kreplach, reduce the heat as low as possible, then cover. Cook until they have a crisp side. Eat dipped in a sauce of equal parts black vinegar and soy sauce.

LASAGNA

CHEESY LASAGNA STEW *(30–40 min)*

3 tbsp olive oil plus for drizzling, 3 cloves garlic (sliced), ½ tsp salt plus to taste, 1 tbsp rosemary leaves (whole or chopped), 2 tbsp chopped parsley, 2 tbsp white or red wine, 2 cups tomato puree, 3 cups cubed lasagna, freshly grated Parmesan cheese (optional).

Heat a heavy-bottomed pot. Add the oil, garlic, and salt, and cook, stirring often, until just tender, about 30 sec–1 min, then add the rosemary and parsley. Add the wine and cook until the alcohol has evaporated, about 1 min. Add the tomato puree, 2 cups water, and the cubed lasagna. Bring to a near boil, reduce to a simmer, and cook until the noodles have softened and all is combined and cheesy, 20–30 min. Eat as is, or with Parmesan grated on top, or olive oil drizzled over, or both.

LASAGNA NOODLES, COOKED

I deal with any leftover lasagna noodles by cutting them roughly into large irregular pieces and thinking of them as the pasta shape maltagliati (which means "badly cut"). These can then be refrigerated and dealt with later in the week or frozen and dealt with next month. When you are ready, turn maltagliati into Pasta e Fagioli (p. 211). Maltagliati are also good in Leek and Herb Pasta (p. 55) or cooked and tossed with Basil Pesto (p. 394) or White Pesto (p. 394).

LINGUINE WITH CLAMS

CREAMY CLAM NOODLE SOUP *(10–12 min)*

1½–2 cups linguine with clams, 1 cup clam juice, ½ tsp salt plus to taste, ½ cup heavy cream, ½–1 tsp butter, freshly ground black pepper.

In a small pot, add 2 cups water. Remove the clams from their shells if they're still in them and put the empty shells in the pot. Bring to a boil until any sauce still clinging to shells has released itself into the water. Remove the shells and use for your garden or decoration. Add the clam juice, salt, and cream to the pot and boil for about 5 min, until combined and creamy. Meanwhile, take scissors and cut the linguine into approximately 2-inch lengths. They don't have to be uniform, and it's fine if you get some clams. Add the chopped up linguine and clams and the butter to the pot. Simmer for only as long as it takes the pasta and clams to heat up, about 1 min. Taste for salt and adjust. Top with pepper to eat.

LO MEIN

FRIED LO MEIN *(15 min)*
1 tbsp peanut or vegetable oil, ½ onion or large shallot (sliced lengthwise into thin half-moons), 1 green chile (sliced or chopped), 2 cloves garlic (minced), ½ tsp salt, ½–1 cup lo mein, a handful of chopped cilantro (or mint or a combination).

Heat a large heavy-bottomed skillet. Add the oil, onion or shallot, chile, garlic, and salt. Cook until the onion is beginning to get tender, 5–10 min. Add the lo mein. Cook, stirring well, to warm and fry. When slightly crisp in places, remove from the heat, top with herbs, and eat.

COLD LO MEIN SALAD *(5–10 min)*
½–1 cup lo mein, 1 tsp rice vinegar plus to taste, 1 tsp thinly sliced scallions.

Combine the ingredients. Taste for vinegar and adjust. Eat.

Or turn leftover lo mein into an undefinable but delicious lunchtime soup by warming it in broth.

MACARONI AND CHEESE

MACARONI AND CHEESE GRATIN (15–20 min)
1 cup or more macaroni and cheese, olive oil or heavy cream, arugula (half the amount of mac and cheese), butter or oil for the baking dish, dried bread crumbs.

Heat the oven to 375°F. Place the mac and cheese in a bowl. If it has a bread crumb topping, stir the topping into the cheese-pasta mixture. Add just enough olive oil or heavy cream to make it mixable. Mix in the arugula. Butter or oil a small baking dish. Spoon in the mixture and flatten the top. Top as thickly as you like with bread crumbs. Drizzle with more olive oil and bake until the top is golden and the gratin is sizzling, about 15 min. Eat.

MAFTOUL

MAFTOUL SOUP (20–25 min)
2–3 cups stock (Meat Stock, p. 246), vegetable stock, or Savory Stock/Broth, p. 247), 1 potato (optional; cubed), 1–2 cups cooked maftoul, ½ cup cooked beans (optional), chopped parsley or any other soft herbs (cilantro, chives, celery leaves), olive oil for serving.

In a small pot, combine the stock and potato (if using). Bring to a boil, then simmer until the potato is tender, 10–15 min. Add the maftoul and beans (if using). Bring to a boil, reduce to a simmer, and cook until it tastes combined, another 5–10 min. Eat hot, topped with herbs and drizzled with olive oil.

MANICOTTI

Substitute leftover manicotti for the lasagna in Cheesy Lasagna Stew (p. 357).

MATZO BALLS

Matzo balls should be warmed in broth and eaten again. It can be less broth and more matzo ball if you like, and the garnishes can be scallion-ginger sauce and chili crisp instead of fresh dill.

NACHOS

NACHO SOUP *(20 min)*

4–5 cups stock (Savory Stock/Broth, p. 247, or chicken stock), salt, 2–3 cups nachos, lime wedges, chopped cilantro. *Optional additions:* hot sauce, sliced avocado, cooked beans, julienned cabbage, thinly sliced radishes.

In a pot, taste the stock and add salt to taste. Bring to a simmer, add the nachos, simmer until the nachos have broken down and become noodle-y, about 10–15 min. Ladle into bowls, squeeze with lime, and top with cilantro. Add any optional additions and eat.

NIAN GAO

SAVORY RICE CAKE STEW *(5–10 min)*

1 cup cooked nian gao (rice cakes), 2–3 cups dashi (or chicken stock or other flavorful broth), any cooked greens. *Optional condiments:* chili oil, scallion oil, black vinegar.

In a pot, combine everything and warm, occasionally stirring to help the rice cakes separate. Eat hot! Good with chili oil or scallion oil or black vinegar or any other condiment you love.

NOODLES, ANY, COOKED

COCONUT CURRY NOODLE SOUP *(20 min)*

1 tbsp neutral oil (peanut or grapeseed), 1 clove garlic (finely chopped), 1 tbsp finely chopped fresh ginger, 3 tbsp Thai red curry paste, 4 cups chicken or fish stock, ½–⅔ cup coconut milk, 1 tbsp fish sauce plus to taste, ½–1 cup cooked noodles. *Optional garnishes:* lime juice, pickled chiles or nam pla prik, chopped cilantro, fried shallots (see p. 7).

Heat a medium pot. Add the oil, garlic, ginger, and curry paste and cook until combined, softened, and fragrant, 3–5 min. Add the stock, coconut milk, and fish sauce. Bring to a boil, then reduce to a simmer. Check for thickness, adding up to 1 cup water to thin. Taste for salt and adjust fish sauce. Add the noodles and simmer until tender. Serve in bowls with any garnishes.

PAD THAI

PAD THAI OMELET *(5 min)*

2 tbsp vegetable or peanut oil, 1 tbsp chopped garlic, 1 tbsp chopped shallot (or onion or scallion), 1 tsp chopped fresh chiles, 1–1½ cups pad Thai, ½ tsp sugar, ¼ tsp salt, 2 eggs (beaten), ¼–½ cup chopped peanuts, ½ cup chopped cilantro.

Heat a heavy-bottomed skillet. Add the oil, garlic, shallot, and chiles and cook to soften, 20–30 sec. Stir in the pad Thai and cook until it's loosened up and is moving around, 30 sec or so. Meanwhile, in a bowl, add the sugar and salt to the beaten eggs. Pour the eggs over the noodles and cook into an omelet, moving away any cooked egg to make room for uncooked. Cover as needed to get everything to cook through. If you like, break the egg and noodle into large pieces and stir-fry, or fold, or leave flat. Tip into a bowl or onto a plate, top with the peanuts and cilantro, and eat.

Pad Thai can also be stir-fried on its own. Heat a pan, add a drizzle of oil, add pad Thai, and then, once it's begun to crisp, add a big handful of chopped peanuts and a squeeze of lime juice. Add any chopped cilantro or mint or basil just before eating.

PAKORA

PAKORA KI SABZI *(30–40 min)*

3 tbsp neutral oil (peanut or grapeseed), 1 bay leaf, 2 dried red chiles, 4 whole cloves, 1 tsp cumin seeds, 1 tsp mustard seeds, ½ cup finely chopped onion, 1 tsp finely chopped green chiles, 1 tsp finely chopped fresh ginger, 1 tsp finely chopped garlic, ¾ cup fresh or canned tomatoes (finely chopped), ½ tsp salt plus to taste, ½ tsp ground turmeric, ½ tsp ground red chile powder, ½ tsp ground coriander, ½ cup whole-milk yogurt, 1 tbsp kasuri methi (fenugreek leaves), pinch of hing (asafoetida), 2 cups cooked chopped pakora, ¼ tsp garam masala.

Heat a skillet. Add the oil, bay leaf, dried chiles, cloves, cumin seeds, and mustard seeds and cook until the seeds begin to pop. Add the onion and cook over medium heat until just softened, about 5 min. Add the chopped chiles, ginger, garlic, tomatoes, and salt, and cook until the tomatoes have broken down, 5–7 min. Add the turmeric, chile powder, and coriander and cook until fragrant, 1–2 min. Add ½ cup water and cook, stirring to combine. Whisk in the yogurt, kasuri methi, and hing. Bring to a boil, whisking, then reduce to a simmer. Add another ½ cup water and simmer until just combined, 5–10 min. Add the pakoras to the sabzi and simmer until softened, 3–5 min. Add the garam masala. Taste for salt and adjust. Eat with rice or flatbread. Good with chopped cilantro on top if you have it. (Adapted from My Ginger Garlic Kitchen website)

Or make this, which is also good, with any kind of pakora.

PAKORA CHAAT (*30 min*)
3–4 cooked pakora, Tamarind Chutney (p. 397), Cilantro Chutney (p. 397), plain yogurt, 3 tbsp chopped scallion or shallot, ¼ cup finely chopped cilantro or cilantro stems, crumbled sev (or other crispy snack such as papad chips, corn chips, or other bean or corn-based snack), chaat masala.

Bring the pakora to room temperature, then cut them in half. Place them on a plate, drizzle with tamarind chutney, then cilantro chutney, then yogurt, not using all of any of the sauces but only what looks good to you. Top with scallion or shallot, cilantro, and sev or similar, finishing with a sprinkle of chaat masala. (Adapted from Cooking Curries website)

PAN CON TOMATE

Substitute leftover pan con tomate for the stale bread in Salmorejo (p. 180) or Gazpacho-ish (p. 382).

PASTA, COOKED

I eat most leftover pasta unchanged. As long as it isn't sauced with cheese or cream, I take the container out at breakfast and then, once it has had a few hours to acclimate, eat it as-is at lunch. This is not resignation but affirmation: leftover pasta is delicious.

But I also fervidly love pasta frittata. This is the other best use of leftover pasta. Before you start, read the basic instructions for a Frittata (p. 140).

PASTA FRITTATA *(12–15 min)*

3 eggs (whisked with a little salt), 2–3 cups cooked pasta, olive oil, ½ cup chopped parsley or celery leaves (optional), freshly grated Parmesan cheese for serving.

Heat the oven to 375°F. Cook the egg/pasta/herb mixture in olive oil in an ovenproof skillet as directed in the frittata recipe. Transfer to the oven and bake for 10–15 min. Shower with Parmesan when out of the oven.

PASTA, RAW

One of the best things to do with a tiny bit of pasta is to cook it directly in soup, any soup. Bring the soup to a boil, add the pasta, and cook until done. Add chopped parsley and freshly ground black pepper before eating.

If you have the very ends of the bags of various different bags of pasta, make Pasta Mista. Follow the instructions for making Chickpea Pasta (p. 218). Cook all the ends together in well-salted water until half the shapes are done. Some will remain undercooked. Reserve 1 cup pasta water, then drain the pasta. Add the pasta to the chickpeas along with the pasta water and a scattering of chile flakes (if using) and cook at a simmer until some of the pasta is almost falling apart but all has cooked through. Taste for salt and adjust. Top copiously with freshly ground black pepper and Parmesan and eat.

PASTA COOKING WATER

Saving all pasta water is a step further than good economy, even for me. I counsel, rather, consulting your plan and then deciding. If you are making a pasta sauce in a nearby pan, ladle some of the water into a pan and add butter, then firmly shake the pan forward and back several times, and it will get creamy. This adds a lovely light gloss to any sauce. In a pinch, this can be a subtle sauce on its own.

If you don't have any broth on hand, pasta water can begin a soup—once a good deal of fresh water has been added. In a soup pot, cook the aromatics (onion and carrot and garlic, or fennel, or garlic and ginger, etc.), until tender. Add lentils and watered-down pasta water to cover by several inches and cook until completely tender. Amend as you like, making a tadka (see p. 308), or adding cooked greens, or topping with yogurt. Or, use leftover pasta water to boil more things. If potatoes are sitting on your counter and potato salad sounds good for tomorrow's lunch, quickly wash and quarter them, then put them in the pasta pot, turn it on, and cook until tender. If boiled eggs sound good, they will cook as happily in pasta water as in fresh water.

PIEROGIS

PAN-FRIED PIEROGIS (*10 min*)
Neutral oil (peanut or grapeseed), pierogis, butter, a little handful of finely chopped parsley (or chives, dill, or scallions), freshly ground black pepper (optional).

Heat a skillet. Add just enough oil to barely coat the bottom. Add the pierogis and cover, letting them fry on one side. Open to check on them and add a few drops of water if needed, and adjust the heat to prevent burning. Cook until browned on one side and easy to release. Top with butter, herbs, and black pepper (if using) and eat.

PIGS IN A BLANKET

With leftover pigs in blankets, you face a fork in the road. To one side, there is the decision to remove the blankets, turning your leftovers into pig(let)s. If that direction beckons, remove the pastry wrappers and use any recipe for *Hot Dogs (p. 324)*. To the other side, there is leaving them covered. In that case, the most promising thing to do is make a pigs-in-a-blanket frittata. See Frittata (p. 140).

PIZZA

Changing a pizza's topping produces a refreshing transformation. My favorite method, inspired by Zante's Pizza in San Francisco, is to top leftover pizza with a sabzi, like saag paneer or bharta.

It can also be assuring to just reheat pizza until crisp and then top it with fresh arugula and shaved Parmesan. Or, top it before heating with dots of raw spicy sausage, which will cook while the pizza heats. Pickled chiles belong on all reheated pizza because the crisp dough can withstand them. My technique for the reheating itself comes from *Cook's Illustrated*. Place cold slices on a baking sheet. Cover with foil. Bake at 275°F until gooey and recrisped, 25–30 min.

Or substitute pizza for lasagna in the Cheesy Lasagna Stew (p. 357).

PIZZA CRUSTS

PIZZA SAUSAGE BAKE *(1 hr 45 min)*

6 cups cubed pizza crusts, 6 tbsp butter plus for the baking dish, 2 cups chopped onion, 1 cup chopped celery, ½ cup chopped fennel, 1½ tsp salt, scant 1 cup chopped fresh herbs (any combination of sage, thyme, fennel fronds, rosemary, parsley), 1 cup chopped fresh or canned tomato, 2 eggs (beaten), 1 lb raw bulk sausage (broken up into pieces), 1–1½ cups stock or water, freshly grated Parmesan cheese, lemon wedges.

Heat the oven to 400°F. On a baking sheet, toast the crusts until crisp, about 10 min. Remove from the oven and reduce the oven temperature to 350°F. Butter a medium baking dish. In a saucepan, melt the 6 tbsp butter. Add the onion, celery, fennel, and salt. Cook over medium heat until it can all be broken with a wooden spoon, about 10 min. Remove from the heat. Add the herbs and mix through. Add the tomato and mix through. Add the crusts, eggs, and sausage. Spread the mixture a few inches deep in the baking dish. Add stock or water until completely moistened. Press down the top and bake until completely cooked through and integrated, deeply melted together and browned and crisp on top. Serve topped with Parmesan or squeezed with lemon. Eat with a lettuce salad.

Leftovers make delicious little fried cakes. Mix 1 cup leftover pizza bake with 2 tbsp bread crumbs and form into cakes. Sprinkle with salt and shallow-fry in olive oil until golden and crisp on both sides.

DOUGH AND NOODLES

POT PIE

If you don't want pot pie again, remove the leftover pie's top, scoop out the filling, put it in a pot, add some water and heavy cream and maybe chopped potatoes or frozen corn, and heat it up. Now it's chowder. Add a sprinkle of white wine for acidity, or stock if it's still too much like a filling and too little like a stew. If you do not want to compost the pie top, heat an oven to 400°F, line a baking sheet with parchment and toast the pie top until it's warm and crisp, then break it into pieces and dip it into the chowder.

PUPUSAS

Substitute for arepas in the Arepas Chilaquiles (p. 351). The dishes are distinct, but both make good chilaquiles.

QUESADILLAS

BEAN AND QUESADILLA SOUP *(25 min)*
2 cups refried beans or other cooked beans, any amount slow-cooked meat (pork shoulder or chicken thighs), any amount roast vegetables or cooked greens, 1–4 quesadillas (sliced into ribbons), salt, cilantro, pickled chiles. *Optional for serving:* sour cream, yogurt, or grated cheese.

In a pot, warm the beans and any meat and/or vegetables with enough water to achieve it the consistency of stew. Add the quesadilla ribbons and simmer until they are tender and slippery, 10–15 min. Taste for salt and adjust. Add cilantro and pickled chiles to taste. Eat topped with sour cream or yogurt or grated cheese if you like.

Or use leftover quesadillas to make Chilaquiles (p. 197).

QUICHE

There are at least three ways to deal with leftover quiche: 1) Eat it again as quiche, warm or cold. 2) Substitute quiche for knishes in Knish Tortilla Española (p. 356). 3) Treat quiche like blintzes, scraping out the filling, whisking it into pancake batter, and snacking on the crust, or freezing it to become future bread crumbs.

RICE NOODLES

While cold pasta can be wooed out of rigidity by a half hour at room temperature, cold rice noodles need a committed softening. A basic formula is to heat a smidge of curry paste, then add water or broth, then the noodles and stir them over low heat to rehydrate them. Add enough coconut milk to make it all stew-y, shake in some fish sauce, and continue stirring until it's all bubbling. Top with chopped cilantro and chopped toasted peanuts.

Or substitute rice noodles for rice in Fried Rice (p. 205).

SAMOSAS

SAMOSA CHAAT *(1 hr)*
1–2 cups cooked chickpeas, 2 cardamom pods, 1 bay leaf, 1 cinnamon stick, salt, ½ clove garlic (chopped), ½ tsp chopped fresh ginger, 1 tbsp peanut or vegetable oil, ¼ cup grated onion, 2 whole peeled tomatoes (chopped), ¼ tsp ground Kashmiri chile or cayenne, ¼ tsp ground cumin, ½ tbsp ghee, ½ inch fresh ginger (julienned), a tiny scrape garam masala, 1 tsp kasuri methi (fenugreek leaves). *For serving:* whole-milk yogurt, 1–2 samosas (broken into pieces), chopped onion, chopped cilantro, Cilantro Chutney (p. 397), Tamarind Chutney (p. 397), ½ tbsp crushed kasuri methi (fenugreek leaves), chaat masala.

In a small pot, combine the chickpeas, cardamom, bay leaf, cinnamon stick, and a little water and cook for 20 min, adding water if needed to keep it from burning or sticking. Add salt to taste. Pound the garlic and ginger to a paste with a little salt. In a saucepan, heat the oil. Add the onion and the ginger-garlic paste, and cook for a few sec. Add the tomatoes, ground chile or cayenne, and cumin and cook, until softened, about 20 min. Add the chickpeas with their spices and cook until well combined, another 15 min. Meanwhile, in small skillet, heat the ghee and fry the ginger in it to flavor the ghee. Scoop out the ginger, then add the garam masala and methi to the ghee. Stir this flavored ghee into the chickpea curry. To serve: Spoon the chickpea curry into bowls. Top with yogurt, then 1–2 samosas, onion, cilantro, chutneys, methi, and chaat masala. Eat! (Adapted from Cook with Manali website)

The best way to approach leftover sandwiches is to deconstruct them. If you are in the mood for another sandwich, choose fresh bread. Heat any meat but deli meat in a small pot with a drizzle of broth or water and vinegar, then make a new sandwich.

Or, if you aren't in the mood for a sandwich, substitute non-deli meat for the hamburger in Leftover Burger Bolognese (p. 322), or in Sugo (p. 306). Cube and freeze the bread from the first sandwich for Ribollita (p. 178), or Stuffing (p. 181).

If it is a deli meat sandwich, remove all the fillings and deposit them in a new sandwich. Or make:

CHEESY SAVORY BREAD PUDDING *(2–3 hr, but mostly waiting)*
3 tbsp butter or olive oil, 2–3 cups combined sliced celery and leek or onion, salt, 1 tsp chopped thyme or rosemary, 1 bay leaf, 8 cups cubed sandwiches, 2 eggs, 4 cups combined liquid (chicken stock and milk or cream), butter for the baking dish, 1½–2 cups chopped leftover soft cheeses.

Heat a pot. Add the butter or olive oil, the celery-leek mixture, and a small pinch of salt and cook until tender, 5–10 min. Stir in the thyme or rosemary and the bay leaf and remove from the heat. Add the chopped sandwiches to the vegetables and mix through. In a bowl, whisk the eggs with the liquid and pour over the sandwiches, pressing down to make sure everything is soaking. Let sit 30 min–1 hr, until it's swollen with custard and soft. Meanwhile, heat the oven to 350°F. Butter a 9 × 12-inch or 9 × 13-inch baking dish. Add the bread pudding, nestling soft cheese bits throughout. Bake until slightly risen and browned on top, pressing down to ensure all the liquid is absorbed, 45 min–1 hr. Enjoy!

If your sandwich is Grilled cheese, make:

RE-GRILLED CHEESIER SANDWICH *(5–10 min)*
Freshly grated Parmesan cheese, room-temperature butter, grilled cheese sandwich.

Spread the Parmesan on a plate. Heavily butter whatever is left of the sandwich on both sides, then press each side into the Parmesan until both sides are heavily coated. Heat a small skillet over medium. Fry the sandwich, pressing it down with a heavy spatula, until browned and crisp. Repeat on the second side, and eat. This is good with any kind of leftover sandwich, up to a few days old. Or use grilled cheese remnants in the Cheesy Savory Bread Pudding (recipe above).

Peanut butter and jelly sandwiches can be frozen and used in a Twizzard (p. 478), or they can be chopped and stored and used as part of a Bread Pudding (p. 182). They're also good re-griddled. Spread the outside of a leftover peanut butter and jelly sandwich with butter or mayonnaise. Heat a griddle, then crisp it on both sides until crisp and golden brown. Cut into little triangles or squares and eat.

If the sandwich is of the tuna salad (or similar) type, I generally recommend scooping the salad out of the leftover sandwiches. It can be eaten or re-sandwiched. Depending on the sogginess of the bread, it can be frozen and then added to the next batch of ribollita—for which there are various recipes (p. 178 and p. 179)—or turned into savory French toast the next day, or put in the compost. Or try:

CRISPY SANDWICH *(5 min)*
Copious quantities of mayonnaise, 1 old tuna sandwich, 1 tbsp butter, detached optimism.

Heat a cast-iron skillet or griddle. Meanwhile, spread one side of the sandwich with mayonnaise. Add the butter to the pan, then place the sandwich, mayonnaise-side down, into the pan. Turn the heat to medium-low and cook for 1 min, covered. Uncover, spread the mayonnaise on the side facing up, then flip and re-cover, cooking for another min. Flip once more, pressing down, and cook for 10–20 sec. Remove to a plate. Let cool for a moment before eating. Add cheese before griddling for a tuna melt.

SOUP DUMPLINGS

These can be delicately, oh so delicately resteamed—once, anyway. A microwave helps, if you are well acquainted with yours. Otherwise use a stovetop steamer.

SPAGHETTI, COOKED

SESAME NOODLES *(10 min)*

1¾ tbsp soy sauce, 1 tbsp sesame oil, 1 tbsp Chinese rice vinegar, 1 tbsp tahini, ½ tbsp creamy peanut butter, 1 tsp sugar, 1 tsp sambal oelek, ½ tsp finely minced fresh ginger, 8 oz cooked spaghetti, ½ cucumber (peeled and sliced into matchsticks), 2 tbsp roasted peanuts.

In a bowl, whisk together the soy sauce, sesame oil, vinegar, tahini, peanut butter, sugar, sambal, and ginger. Add as much of the sauce as you like to your leftover spaghetti and toss to combine. Top with the cucumber and peanuts to taste.

SPRING ROLLS

Leftover spring rolls can be deep-fried in a neutral oil (peanut or grapeseed), and thus given new life!

TACOS

A taco will remain a taco in your mind until it has been disassembled. Once it has been, its tortilla can become chips, or turned into a quesadilla, and its meat and vegetables added to fried rice, or to soup, or made into a sandwich. Alternatively, thinly slice tacos as they are and crisp and stew them with a little broth and perhaps some leftover meat, then scramble in or fry eggs and top. Any sauces you ate with the tacos will complement the results.

Or use leftover tacos in Burrito Fried Rice (p. 352), making sure to have rice cooked before you begin. Or use them to make Enchilada Stew (p. 355).

TAMALES

TAMALES À LA MEXICANA *(10 min)*

2 tamales, 2–3 tbsp neutral oil (peanut or grapeseed), ¼ cup finely chopped onion, ¼ cup finely chopped fresh or canned tomato, ¼ tsp salt plus to taste, ½–1 jalapeño (finely chopped). *Optional for serving:* grated Cotija or other cheese and/or chopped cilantro.

Chop the tamales into large pieces. Heat a medium pan. Add the oil, onion, tomatoes, and salt and cook until the onion has softened, about 5 min. Add the jalapeño and sauté 30 sec. Stir in the tamales, and cook until the tamales are beginning to brown. Remove from the heat. Taste for salt and adjust. If desired, serve topped with cheese and/or cilantro and eat.

DOUGH AND NOODLES

HOW TO APPREHEND A SALAD

Salads

You cannot see the lettuce and the dressing without suspecting a salad.

—*Arthur Conan Doyle*,
The Exploits of Brigadier Gerard

Much as you treat eggs boiled and peeled yesterday as halfway to Egg Salad Fried Rice (p. 381) or Gado Gado (p. 417) or Better Ramen or Other Lunchtime Soup (p. 150), consider lettuce's overnight steep in vinegar and salt halfway to the rest of its cooking. The drooping leaves will seem more dignified and things will start looking brighter. Partially cooked salad will, of course, need further cooking to be eaten. The cooking can take several forms. 1) You can finely slice salad and add it to a savory pancake batter, where whatever remains of lettuce's crispness offers subtle contrast to the tender pancake. 2) You can chop and combine it with cooked yolks and spoon the nubby mixture into deviled eggs. 3) You can puree salad with more vinegar into a verdant herby start for a vinaigrette. 4) In some cases you can further bake it with béchamel and cheese into a gratin. 5) You may find occasion for turning it into soup. Though there is brief joy to be found in the soggy crispness of leftover Caesar eaten directly from the refrigerator, the one thing leftover lettuce salad rarely makes a good version of is another lettuce salad.

Leftover Middle Eastern salads, on the other hand, acidic and herby and salty and piquant and somewhere between salad and dip, are welcome leftovers, still in salad form. Muhammara and baba ghanoush can be swiped onto garlicky toast, or expanded into something more voluminous by the addition of yogurt or tahini. Plenty of other salads, including Sichuan cucumber and Thai larb and Nigerian abacha and Japanese goma-e, also hold up well to the passage of time. Really, the only leftover salads that don't are the ones European Americans think of when they hear the word "salad."

Here are three good vinaigrettes. They are of no use to leftover lettuce salads, but good on fresh lettuce:

BASIC VINAIGRETTE

1 shallot (minced), ¼ tsp salt plus to taste, 1 tsp Dijon mustard, juice of ½ lemon, 1 tbsp red wine vinegar, 1 clove garlic, ⅓–½ cup olive oil.

In a bowl, combine the shallot, salt, mustard, lemon juice, and vinegar. Smash the garlic and add to the bowl. Let sit for 5 min. Whisk in the olive oil, without worrying about emulsifying. Taste on a lettuce leaf for salt and acid and adjust.

ANCHOVY-GARLIC VINAIGRETTE

1 clove garlic (chopped), ⅛ tsp salt plus to taste, 4 anchovy fillets (chopped), ¼ tsp Dijon mustard, 1 tsp lemon juice, 4 tsp wine vinegar, ⅓–½ cup olive oil.

Pound the garlic to a paste with the salt. Pound in the anchovies. In a bowl, combine the paste with the mustard, lemon juice, and vinegar. Let sit for 5 min. Whisk in the olive oil without worrying about emulsifying. Taste on a lettuce leaf for salt and acid and adjust.

CREAMY VINAIGRETTE

1 clove garlic (chopped), ¼ tsp salt plus to taste, 1 tsp red wine vinegar, 1 cup crème fraîche or Greek yogurt, 1 tsp heavy cream (or buttermilk), a squeeze of lemon, 1 tbsp olive oil (optional).

Pound the garlic to a paste with the salt. In a bowl, combine with the vinegar and let sit for 5 min. Add the crème fraîche or yogurt, cream, and lemon juice. Taste for salt and acid and adjust. Add a little water if needed to thin. Add olive oil if you miss its flavor.

BABA GHANOUSH

BABA GHANOUSH MAYONNAISE (*2 min*)

In a bowl, mix 2–3 tbsp baba ghanoush and 1 tbsp mayonnaise. This is good for general dipping, mixing, or sandwich spreading. It is also a reasonable replacement for plain mayonnaise in a salad like chicken or tuna, or especially tofu, for which you just smash tofu. A small handful of sprouts is a good addition.

BABA GHANOUSH PIZZA (*10–15 min*)

½ clove garlic, salt, 3 tbsp baba ghanoush, ¼ cup chopped parsley, ½ tsp capers or chopped olives, olive oil, a long piece of baguette or Italian bread (halved as for a sandwich) or several slices rustic peasant bread, fresh mozzarella cheese (torn or shredded).

Heat the oven to 400°F. Pound the garlic to a paste with a little salt. In a bowl, combine the garlic paste with the baba ghanoush, parsley, capers or olives, and enough olive oil to make it an easily spoonable paste, up to a tbsp. Spread the mixture thickly on the bread. Top with the mozzarella. Bake until bubbling and melted, 7–10 min. Also good with freshly grated Parmesan added.

A variation is to add a sprinkle of chile flakes to the baba ghanoush mixture.

The principle for this next is the Lebanese dish makdous, in which little eggplants are stuffed with garlic and walnuts and peppers or chile and soaked in olive oil. Here it's all smashed together.

WHIPPED MAKDOUS (*10–15 min*)

Walnuts, baba ghanoush, salt, red wine vinegar, ½ clove garlic (optional), chile flakes (optional), olive oil (optional).

Pound or puree enough walnuts to make half as much walnut paste as you have baba ghanoush. In a blender or a bowl, combine the baba ghanoush and walnut paste and blend. Season with salt to taste. Add a drop of vinegar. If you think it needs more garlic (than was in the original baba ghanoush), pound the garlic to a paste with a little salt and stir into the mixture. If desired, add a sprinkle of chile flakes and a drizzle of olive oil. The mixture should be slightly piquant, garlicky, rich, and delicious. Taste for salt, vinegar, and olive oil and adjust. Eat as a dip on pita or grilled or toasted bread or crackers. Good in a sandwich, too.

SAVORY BREAD PUDDING *(35–40 min)*
Olive oil, 1 cup bread salad, chicken or vegetable stock.

Heat the oven to 350°F. Lightly oil a small baking dish. Add the bread salad, pressing it down lightly into a layer 1½–2 inches thick. Add enough stock to just seep above the surface when you press down against it with a spatula. Place into the oven and bake until the liquid has evaporated, any vegetables have caramelized, and the bread seems cooked, 35–45 min. Broil briefly just before eating. Good with freshly grated Parmesan cheese or a dollop of ricotta on top.

PANCOTTO *(1½ hr)*
1 cup bread salad, 4 tbsp olive oil, 1 clove garlic (chopped or sliced), a sprinkling of hardy fresh herbs (a sprig of rosemary, a few sprigs of thyme, 1–2 sage leaves), salt, 1 piece cheese rind (Parmesan, Pecorino Romano, or other hard cheese), ¼ cup cooked and seasoned beans, chile flakes (optional). *Optional garnishes:* grated Parmesan cheese and/or chopped parsley and/or Parsley Oil (p. 68).

Pick any raw onions out of the bread salad, without being overly finicky, and set them aside. Heat a heavy-bottomed pot. Add 2 tbsp of the olive oil, the picked-out onions, garlic, herbs, and a little pinch of salt and cook over medium heat until just softened, about 30 sec. Add the bread salad, 3 cups water, and the cheese rind and cook at a low simmer until the bread has totally absorbed the liquid and broken down into a creamy stew-y mess. Add the beans, a sprinkling of chile flakes (if using), and the remaining 2 tbsp olive oil and continue to cook for another 15 min. Taste for salt and adjust. Serve with any garnishes you choose. This is also a wonderful place to add leftover cooked or raw greens (kale, chard, turnip, or radish greens, or the finely chopped stems of any). Add them early in the process to ensure they get completely tender.

CAESAR CORNMEAL PANCAKES *(10 min)*

½–¾ cup Caesar salad (drained and roughly chopped), ½ cup Cornmeal Pancake Batter (p. 138), freshly ground black pepper, ghee or olive oil, freshly grated Parmesan cheese.

In a bowl, combine the Caesar salad with the pancake batter and season with black pepper. Heat a skillet. Add the ghee or olive oil and cook into small pancakes, flipping once you see small bubbles. Serve topped with Parmesan.

EGGS PIERRE DE LUNE-NOSRAT *(15 min)*

6–8 Boiled Eggs (p. 139), ½ clove garlic, salt, 2 anchovy fillets (chopped), ⅓ cup grated Parmesan cheese, 3 tbsp olive oil, juice of ½ lemon or 1 tbsp white wine vinegar, ½–¾ cup Caesar salad (drained and finely sliced), freshly ground black pepper.

Peel and halve the eggs. Remove the yolks to a bowl and set the whites aside. Pound the garlic to a paste with a little salt. In a bowl, combine the anchovies to the garlic and pound together, then add both to the yolks, along with the Parmesan, olive oil, lemon juice or vinegar, and ¼ tsp salt. Mix well. Taste for salt and adjust. Mix in the Caesar salad and season with black pepper. Fill the egg whites and eat!

This can be done with the lettuce from other salads as well. These can be made several hours in advance.

COLESLAW

COLESLAW SOUP *(1 hr)*

1 bay leaf, one 12–16 oz kielbasa (cut in 4 pieces), 8 tbsp (1 stick) butter, 3 cups combined chopped or sliced leek and onion (or just one of them), 1 tsp salt plus to taste, 1–2 cloves garlic (minced), 2 cups chopped potatoes, 2–4 cups coleslaw, about 2 cups stale sourdough bread chunks (crusts removed), freshly ground black pepper.

In a small pot, combine 7–8 cups water, the bay leaf, and kielbasa. Bring to a boil, reduce to a simmer, and cook at a simmer until the kielbasa is swollen, about 25 min. Remove the kielbasa and save the cooking water. Heat a medium pot. Add the butter, the leek-onion mixture, and salt and cook until tender, 10–12 min, adding the garlic about halfway through. Stir in the potatoes, then add the coleslaw, along with any liquid in the container, and the reserved kielbasa cooking water. Bring to a simmer, then add the bread and cook at a simmer until the bread is melted into the soup and it all tastes unified and delicious, 45 min–1 hr. Cut the kielbasa into thick slices and add to the soup. Taste for salt and adjust. Top with black pepper. (Adapted from Gabrielle Hamilton in the *New York Times Magazine*)

A SURPRISINGLY DELICIOUS GRATIN *(1 hr)*

3 cups coleslaw, 1 cup Béchamel (p. 395), ¼–½ cup grated melting cheese (cheddar, Gruyère, mozzarella, or any combination), ¼ tsp salt plus to taste.

Heat the oven to 350°F. Drain the coleslaw (reserve the liquid for drizzling over rice, unless it's just a little). In a medium gratin or baking dish, combine the coleslaw, béchamel, cheese, and salt and mix well. Taste for salt and adjust. It should be highly seasoned. Cover with foil and bake until the cabbage and anything else in the coleslaw is totally tender, about 25 min. Uncover and cook until it's bubbling and toasty and caramelized around the edges, about 20 min. Eat hot.

Coleslaw also improves almost every sandwich. Add your leftovers to grilled cheese or pulled pork, or fried chicken, or fried tofu.

The liquid at the bottom of leftover coleslaw is an ideal combination of tartness and creaminess and sweetness. It is lovely on steaming rice. Make or warm a pot of rice, put it in bowls, and pour the coleslaw liquid over, not minding if a little coleslaw comes along for the ride.

CROUTONS FROM SALAD

CROUTON SOUP *(2½–3 hr)*

¼ cup olive oil plus for drizzling, ¼ cup sliced celery, ¼ cup sliced onion, ¼ cup combined chopped parsley and rosemary, ½ tsp chile flakes, 1 tsp salt, 2–3 cups croutons, 2 cups whole peeled tomatoes (chopped, with their juice), 4 cups home-cooked chickpeas with their liquid (or 3 cups drained canned chickpeas and 1 cup water), 1–2 cups chopped cooked or raw stemmed greens.

Heat a medium pot. Add the olive oil, celery, onion, herbs, chile flakes, and salt. Cook until softened, 10–15 min. Stir in the croutons. Stir in the tomatoes and cook until they've begun to break down, another 5 min. Add the chickpeas and cooking liquid (or water) plus 3 cups water, and bring to a boil, then reduce to a simmer. Cook until completely broken down and combined, 1–2 hr. Add the greens and cook until tender, about 15 min. Drizzle heavily with olive oil and eat.

EGG SALAD

Quantities for this next will change depending on the size tortilla you use. If you use smaller flour or corn tortillas, use less of each ingredient, or use all of the ingredients and make 2 quesadillas.

EGG SALAD QUESADILLA *(10 min)*

1 tsp very finely chopped spring onion or scallion, lemon juice, salt, 1 large flour tortilla, ¼–⅓ cup grated or thinly sliced cheddar cheese, 2 tbsp egg salad, 3 tbsp roughly chopped mixed herbs (cilantro, basil, parsley, mint, arugula), ¼ tsp chaat masala.

In a small bowl, mix the spring onion or scallion with some lemon juice and a tiny pinch of salt and let sit for 5 min (this will shrink in volume by half during soaking). Cut the tortilla in half. Heat a heavy-bottomed pan over medium heat, then reduce the heat to medium-low. Add one half of the tortilla, sprinkle with half the cheese, dot with the egg salad, as evenly as possible. Add the herbs, drained onion or scallion (use the soaking liquid for a salad dressing), then the chaat masala. Add the remaining cheese and the second tortilla half. Cover and cook until the cheese is melted, about 2 min. Flip, cover, and cook until the cheese begins to seep out. Remove to a plate, cut, let cool 30 sec or so, and eat.

EGG SALAD FRIED RICE *(5 min)*

2–3 tbsp neutral cooking oil (peanut or grapeseed), 3 tbsp sliced or chopped onion or scallion, 1 tbsp finely chopped garlic, 1 cup leftover cold cooked rice, salt, anything else you want in your fried rice, 1–3 tbsp egg salad.

Heat a wide pan or wok. Add the oil, onion or scallion, and garlic, frying for 5 seconds, then adding the rice. Spread the rice over the surface of the pan and salt to taste. When it seems like every grain has had a moment to fry, scoop the rice all together, add anything you want and the egg salad and stir it through.

FATTOUSH

Leftover fattoush can be substituted for Caesar salad in Caesar Cornmeal Pancakes (p. 379).

GREEK SALAD

Remove the cheese from the Greek salad. Set it aside to use in a sandwich or another salad. Store it in a small clean container and label it. With the rest, make:

GAZPACHO-ISH (*10 min*)
2 cups leftover Greek salad, ¼ cup olive oil, ¼ cup crustless bread (optional; soaked in water and drained), sherry vinegar, ¼ cup chopped peeled cucumber (optional), salt.

In a blender, combine the salad, olive oil, the bread if using, and a few drops of sherry vinegar, stopping when it's frothy and smooth. If you have a cucumber, it'll make it even frothier, but you won't miss it. Taste for salt and vinegar and adjust. Chill and drink.

KALE SALAD

KALE-FRIED GRAINS (*10 min*)
1 tbsp olive oil, ½ cup chopped onion, 1 clove garlic (thinly sliced), ½ tsp salt plus to taste, ½ tsp ground turmeric, 1 tbsp chopped pickled jalapeño or fresh chile, 1½–2 cups cooked grains (rice, farro, barley, etc.), ½–1 cup kale salad (with whatever else is in it), 1–3 tbsp chopped pine nuts or walnuts (if not already in the salad).

Heat a cast-iron or other skillet or wok over medium-high heat. Add the olive oil, onion, garlic, and salt and cook until beginning to soften, about 5 min. Stir in the turmeric and chiles. Add the cooked grains and spread thoroughly, as though you mean to fry each grain. Cook until beginning to crisp. Once the grains are thoroughly fried, add the kale salad and stir through well, continuing to scrape. Taste for salt and adjust. If you're adding nuts, mix through.

KOY PA

Include leftover koy pa in Fried Rice (p. 000).

LETTUCE SALAD

GREENEST MOST DELICIOUS SAUCE BASE *(5 min)*
½ cup wilted lettuce salad, 1 cup chopped crunchy vegetables (celery, peeled cucumber, lettuce hearts, or a combination), 1 packed cup chopped herbs (basil, cilantro, dill, chervil, sorrel, arugula), 1 clove garlic (chopped), 2 tbsp sherry vinegar, ⅓ cup olive oil, 1 tsp salt plus to taste.

Combine the ingredients in a blender. Blend until very, very smooth and airy. You now have a sauce base.

To make a green, green dressing, combine the base with a handful of spring onions soaked in lemon juice with salt for 10 min, and enough olive oil to make it vinaigrette-swimmy. Or for a creamy sauce, add a dollop to homemade or store-bought mayonnaise or crème fraîche. Or for a pasta sauce, add grated cheese.

Or substitute leftover lettuce salad for Greek salad in the Gazpacho-ish (p. 382), adjusting the salt and vinegar as needed.

MUHAMMARA

Muhammara can be expanded in a number of ways. Mix it with yogurt for a new salad/dip. Add it to pureed tomatoes for pasta sauce. Or, add pounded chopped walnuts and chopped parsley and marjoram for a red pesto-ish pasta sauce.

NIÇOISE SALAD

Leftover composed salads—of which Niçoise is one—should be taken apart. Boiled green beans can go in their little container, eggs in theirs, potatoes in theirs, etc. Approach each of the constituent pieces on its own—look under *Eggs, boiled (p. 149)* for the egg, and *Lettuce salad (p. 383)* for what to do with the lettuce. Or combine remaining green beans and potatoes, drizzle heavily with dressing or olive oil, drape anchovies over top, add any leftover eggs, quartered, and eat. Or, keep potatoes for tomorrow and layer olives, beans, eggs, anchovies, and tuna together in a sandwich.

PASTA SALAD

As unlikely as it sounds, pasta salad makes an acceptable pasta frittata. Follow the directions in Pasta Frittata (p. 363), making any adjustments you like, adding cheese when you add the pasta, or grating with Parmesan when it's out of the oven. A big handful of fresh herbs, such as roughly chopped celery or parsley or basil leaves, is a good addition.

POTATO SALAD

There is no reason not to just eat potato salad again, especially once it's been perked up with a squeeze of lemon and a drizzle of olive oil and maybe some fresh herbs. Or try:

CRISP POTATO CROQUETTES (*1 hr, but mostly waiting*)
¼ cup finely chopped cucumber, salt, 1–2 cups potato salad, 4 scallions (chopped), Maggi Seasoning, ½ cup all-purpose or rice flour, 1 egg (beaten), panko, neutral oil for frying.

In a small bowl, combine the cucumber with a pinch of salt and let sit for 10 min, then press out the liquid. Meanwhile, in another bowl, mash the potato salad with a potato masher or fork. Add the cucumber and scallions, then a few drops of Maggi. Taste and adjust. It should be very highly seasoned. Form into 1½–2 tbsp balls, patties, or cylinders. Set up three shallow dishes: one with flour, one with beaten egg, one with panko. Dip the croquettes into

the flour, then the egg, then the panko. Refrigerate for 30 min to firm up. In a
deep pot, heat several inches of oil to 350°–365°F. Working in batches, fry the
croquettes turning as needed, until golden, about 6 min per batch. Remove to
paper towels to cool and eat. (Adapted from A Couple Cooks website)

Or make roasted potatoes.

ROASTED POTATOES *(20 min)*
Potato salad, olive oil, salt.

Heat the oven to 400°F. Rinse the potato salad in a colander, letting some
of the mayonnaise stay but getting off most. Place a baking sheet in the oven
to heat. Remove, drizzle lightly with olive oil, then spread out the washed
potato salad and drizzle with more olive oil. Roast to browned and crisped,
stirring and flipping if/as needed. Sprinkle it with salt and eat. Also good with
chopped scallions or parsley or gremolata sprinkled over the top. (Adapted
from the Epicurious website)

RÉMOULADE (SALAD)

Leftover rémoulade salad is delicious as a salad dressing. Place it in a bowl,
draining off some of the liquid. Add several big handfuls of arugula or finely
sliced fennel or a combination. Lightly salt, drizzle with olive oil, then toss
through with your hands, adding a drizzle of the reserved liquid if it's dry.
Excess liquid should be used like *Coleslaw liquid (p. 380)*.

RICE SALAD

RICE SALAD SALAD *(30 min, but mostly waiting)*
Up to 1 cup rice salad, a large handful of lettuces, salt, Basic Vinaigrette
(p. 376) or a squeeze of lemon juice and olive oil, a dollop of something strong
tasting and likable (taramasalata, hummus, techina, Greek yogurt), something
substantial (boiled egg, stuffed grape leaf, pâté-covered toast, or leftover oily
grilled vegetables).

Let the rice salad sit on the counter to come to room temperature. Dress the lettuces with a little salt and vinaigrette, then mix in the rice salad. Place in a bowl, dollop with taramasalata etc., add the egg etc., and eat.

SEAFOOD SALAD

SEAFOOD TOSTADA (*10 min*)
Oil for frying, 1 stale corn tortilla, ¼ avocado, salt, ¼ cup seafood salad, lime juice, hot sauce (optional), chopped cilantro, thinly sliced scallions, thinly sliced pickled or fresh chiles (optional).

In a pan big enough to hold the tortilla, heat ¼ inch of oil to about 365°F. Fry the tortilla until golden and crisp, 10–20 sec, then remove to paper towels or a cooling rack. Slice the avocado and lay it in shingles on the tostada, salting each slice lightly. Spoon the seafood salad over the avocado, then squeeze on a bit of lime juice. Top with hot sauce (if using), then the cilantro and scallions. If desired, top with chiles. Eat.

SEAWEED SALAD

Use in a Rice Bowl (p. 281) or for soba salad. Or eat on a bowl of hot freshly cooked rice, top with toasted sesame seeds, add any other sauce you like, and eat.

TABBOULEH

TABBOULEH SANDWICH (*10 min*)
1 pocket pita, 3–4 tbsp alfalfa sprouts, olive oil, salt, 1 slice bacon (cooked to crisp and crumbled), ¼ cup tabbouleh, 2 tbsp chopped cucumber, 1–2 tbsp chopped tomatoes, ¼ avocado (chopped or sliced).

Warm the pita in a toaster oven or a 400°F oven, then slit off the top to make a big pocket. In a small bowl, toss the alfalfa sprouts lightly with olive oil and a little salt. Add the bacon, tabbouleh, cucumber, tomatoes, avocado and lightly salt. Lightly drizzle with olive oil. Add the mixture to the pita, and eat.

TACO SALAD

Substitute taco salad for the burrito in Burrito Fried Rice (p. 352).

TOMATO SALAD

ANOTHER GAZPACHO-ISH *(5 min)*
2 cups tomato salad, 1½ cups any combination of chopped crunchy vegetables (red bell pepper, peeled cucumber, celery, crunchy lettuce hearts), scant 1 tsp salt, 1 clove garlic (chopped), 2 tsp sherry vinegar, 6 tbsp olive oil.

In a blender, combine all the ingredients. Blend until very, very smooth and airy. Chill and drink as is, or garnish with little croutons, chopped egg, chopped cucumber, olive oil, or any combination.

TUNA SALAD

ONIGIRI *(25 min)*
Short-grain rice, rice vinegar, sugar, sheets of nori, tuna salad.

Cook the rice. Whisk a little sugar into rice vinegar. When it's still warm, drizzle a little bit of vinegar onto the rice. Cut nori sheets in thirds. Dampen your hands. Make a little pancake of rice, add a spoonful of tuna salad, then close rice around it, in a triangle if you can manage it, or in a ball if you can't. Fold a strip of nori around it. Make as many onigiri as you have ingredients for, and eat them.

A lazy and equally delicious version of this is to simply put the hot white seasoned rice in a bowl, add the tuna salad to a little well in its middle, scatter sliced nori on top, and add some toasted sesame seeds to the whole thing. Or make a:

TUNA MELT (*10 min*)

1 slice whole-grain or rye bread, 2 tbsp tuna salad, 1–2 tsp chopped or sliced pickled chiles, mayonnaise or butter, 2–3 tbsp grated cheddar cheese (or the equivalent thinly sliced), chopped combined cilantro and basil (or just one of them).

Heat the oven to 400°F. Lightly toast the bread for 2–3 min. Meanwhile, in a small bowl, stir together the tuna salad and chiles. Spread the toast with mayonnaise or butter, then spread with the tuna-chile mixture. Blanket with cheese and return to the oven until the cheese is totally melted, about 4 min. Top with herbs, let cool 1–2 min, and eat.

HOW TO SAVE YOUR SOUL

Sauces and dips

Saucepan in hand, I refuse to be snowed.

—*Robert Farrar Capon*, The Supper of the Lamb

A little sauce can be extended—by adding more olive oil or cream or water or, or, or—or it can be mixed into a greater amount of something else, like olive oil or butter or vinegar or fish sauce or mayonnaise. Or a little bit of sauce can be stirred into a cooked vegetable or cooked rice or cooked noodles. It can, as many things can, also be added to soup. And it can always be drizzled onto hot buttered toast.

Exercise restraint when saucing in the first place. It is easiest for us recipe writers to write recipes using whole measurements, with 1 cup of one thing and 1 tbsp of another. That doesn't mean that the resulting amount is the ideal one for what you're making. As you drizzle and dollop, keep in mind that you were not prescribed the full amount of sauce. Taste what you're saucing and stop when you like it. Then scrape the remainder into a little glass jar. If you have the energy, label the jar so you can tell by sight whether it is parsley oil, or pesto, or s'chug. If you worry it will go bad, remember that olive oil is a universal balm. Add a pour to what's left and your sauce will live another day.

Here are the sauces I make often, whose souls I recommend for unquestionable salvation:

TECHINA
For ½ cup techina, combine ¼ cup tahini, ¼ cup water, ½ clove garlic (finely minced), 1 tsp lemon juice, and ½ tsp salt in a blender. Blend to smooth.

OLIVE TAPENADE
1 cup jarred olives (drained, pitted, and chopped), 1 clove garlic (finely minced), 1 tbsp capers (drained and chopped), ¼ cup finely chopped parsley leaves, ¼ cup olive oil, grated zest of ½ lemon (optional), 1–2 anchovy fillets (optional; finely chopped), 1 drop red wine vinegar (optional).

Mix all together well, taste for salt and oil and adjust.

MARCELLA'S TOMATO SAUCE

One 28 oz can or jar whole peeled tomatoes (with liquid), 5 tbsp butter, 1 onion (peeled and halved).

In a pot, combine everything, smashing up the tomatoes as you do. Simmer for 45 min–1 hr. Remove the onion halves. See *Onion from Marcella's Tomato Sauce (p. 66)*. Puree the sauce if you want it smooth.

MY ALFREDO SAUCE

1½ cups heavy cream, 8 tbsp (1 stick) butter, 1 clove garlic (peeled), 2 cups freshly grated Parmesan cheese.

In a saucepan, combine the cream, butter, and garlic clove and simmer for 2–3 min. Remove from the heat, remove the garlic (which can be reused), and whisk in the cheese.

BASIL PESTO

1 clove garlic, ¼ tsp salt, 3–4 cups basil leaves (about 1 bunch basil, save the hard stems for water or tea), ¼ cup lightly toasted nuts (pine nuts, walnuts, or pecans), ½ cup freshly grated Parmesan cheese, ½ cup olive oil.

Chop or pound the garlic to a paste with the salt. In a blender, combine with the basil, nuts, and cheese. Then add the olive oil and pulse to blend, using a wooden spoon or blender insert to get a thick, uniform paste with as little blending as possible.

The same ratios and principles can be applied to most herbs. Replace half the basil with parsley for basil-parsley pesto. Replace most with carrot tops and have basil–carrot top pesto.

WHITE PESTO: A SORT OF SALSA DI NOCI

¾ cup walnuts, 1 clove garlic (chopped), ¼ tsp salt plus to taste, 3 tbsp chopped marjoram, 3 tbsp chopped parsley, ⅔ cup olive oil, ½ cup freshly grated Parmesan or Pecorino Romano cheese.

Heat the oven to 400°F. Toast the walnuts on a tray until fragrant and lightly browned, about 10 min. In a large mortar, pound the garlic to a paste with the salt. Pound in the walnuts. Mix in the herbs and olive oil with a spoon, scraping the sides of the mortar. Add the cheese. Taste for salt and adjust.

AILLADE

½–⅔ cup nuts (pistachios, hazelnuts, almonds, or walnuts), 2 cloves garlic (chopped), ¼ tsp salt plus to taste, grated zest of 1 lemon or orange, ½ cup olive oil, lemon or orange juice.

Heat an oven to 400°F. Toast the nuts on a tray until fragrant and lightly browned, then roughly chop. In a mortar, pound the garlic with the salt into a paste. Add the toasted nuts to the garlic paste, pounding and scraping the sides of the mortar as needed. Add the grated zest, olive oil, and a squeeze of citrus juice. Taste for salt and adjust. If needed, you can add a few drops of water or more olive oil for a sauce that is dollop-able and slightly swimmy.

BÉCHAMEL

1 cup whole milk, 1 tbsp butter, 1 tbsp all-purpose flour, a sprinkle of salt, 2–4 tbsp freshly grated Parmesan cheese (optional).

Bring milk to room temperature. In a small pot, melt the butter, stir in the flour, and whisk over low heat until combined. Slowly add the warmed milk to the flour-butter mixture, whisking constantly. Whisk until it's boiling, then reduce to the lowest possible heat and cook until it no longer tastes floury, 20–25 min. Add a sprinkle of salt, then taste and adjust. Add the cheese (if using).

MAYONNAISE

1 egg yolk (at room temperature), a tiny smidgeon Dijon mustard, lemon juice or water as needed, 1 cup olive oil, ⅛ tsp salt plus to taste.

Use a damp kitchen towel to make a ring into which you can set a medium bowl. Add the yolk, mustard, and 1–2 drops lemon juice or water and whisk well. Begin to add the olive oil, drop by drop, waiting to add a stream until you can see that an emulsion has formed. Quicken the pace of the olive oil addition, adding a few more drops of lemon juice or water if it gets too thick. Whisk in all the oil, add the salt, whisk through, let sit for 5 min, then taste for salt and adjust.

AIOLI

1 clove garlic, ⅛ tsp salt plus to taste, 1 cup Mayonnaise (recipe above, made without salt) or store-bought mayonnaise.

Pound the garlic to a paste with the salt. In a bowl, whisk half the garlic paste into the mayonnaise, let sit for 5 min, then taste, adding up to the full amount of garlic paste, and more salt as needed.

SPICY MAYONNAISE

¼ cup Mayonnaise (p. 395) or store-bought mayonnaise, 1–4 tsp of hot sauce (sambal oelek, sriracha, or other chili-garlic sauce), or chipotles in adobo or other chiles.

Mix well.

TARTAR SAUCE

¾–1 cup Mayonnaise (p. 395) or store-bought mayonnaise, ⅓ cup chopped drained cornichons, 2–3 tbsp chopped drained capers, 3 tbsp chopped parsley leaves, 1–2 tbsp lemon juice, ⅛ tsp salt plus to taste. *Optional additions:* 1 boiled egg (finely chopped), 1–2 drops hot sauce.

Combine, taste for salt and adjust. Dip in fried things and eat!

RÉMOULADE SAUCE

1 cup Mayonnaise (p. 395) or store-bought mayonnaise, ⅔ cup chopped celery leaves or parsley, 1 tbsp chopped drained capers, 1 tsp lemon juice, 1 tsp white wine vinegar or rice vinegar, ½ tsp Dijon mustard, ½ tsp salt plus to taste, freshly ground black pepper to taste.

Mix. Taste for salt and black pepper and adjust.

SAUCE GRIBICHE

1 hard-boiled egg (yolk and white separated), ¼ tsp salt plus to taste, 1 tsp Dijon mustard, ⅓ cup olive oil, 2 tsp vinegar plus to taste, 1 tsp finely chopped cornichons, 1 tsp drained capers (chopped if very big), ¼ cup chopped herbs (parsley, chervil, tarragon, celery leaves), freshly ground black pepper.

In a bowl, smash the egg yolk and salt, then add the mustard. Add the olive oil, combining with gusto. When well combined, add the vinegar and mix. Add the egg white, cornichons, capers, and herbs and mix lightly. Season with black pepper to taste. Taste for salt and vinegar, and adjust.

CILANTRO CHUTNEY

1 bunch cilantro (soft stems included, chopped), 1 green chile (chopped), 1 tbsp lemon or lime juice plus to taste, ¼ tsp sugar, ¼ tsp salt plus to taste, ¼ tsp ground cumin, ½–¾ tsp chaat masala, 1–2 tbsp water if needed to blend.

This is easiest in a spice or coffee grinder. Blend everything until smooth, using only as much water as you need to get it to blend. Taste for salt and acid and adjust. If it tastes like it's still missing something, add a tiny bit more chaat masala.

CILANTRO COCONUT CHUTNEY

1 cup unsweetened shredded coconut, 1 cup chopped cilantro (stems included), ½ tbsp chopped fresh ginger, 1–2 green chiles (chopped), ¼ tsp salt plus to taste. *For the tadka:* 2 tsp vegetable oil or ghee, ½ tsp mustard seeds, pinch of hing (asafoetida), 5–6 curry leaves.

In a blender, combine the coconut, cilantro, ginger, chiles, and salt and blend to smooth, adding the amount water you need to get a texture you like, ¾–1 cup. *Make the tadka:* In a skillet, heat the oil or ghee. Add the mustard seeds, hing, and curry leaves. Once it's all sizzled, pour it over the chutney. (Adapted from *Cook with Manali* website)

TAMARIND CHUTNEY

1 tbsp tamarind concentrate, 5 tbsp sugar, ¼–½ tsp salt, ¼ tsp cayenne pepper, ¼ tsp ground cumin, ⅛ tsp hing (asafoetida).

In a small saucepan, bring 1 cup water to a boil. Whisk in the tamarind and sugar until totally dissolved. Add the salt, cayenne, cumin, and hing and simmer until thickened, about 20 min.

NAM PLA PRIK

Thai bird's eye chiles (sliced), fish sauce.

In a jar, add the sliced chiles and cover with fish sauce, refilling it as desired. This lasts forever.

NUOC CHAM

1 clove garlic (finely minced), 1 Thai bird's eye chile (sliced), 2 tbsp sugar plus to taste, ½–1 lime, ¼ cup fish sauce.

In a bowl or in a mortar, combine the garlic and chili (pound if in a mortar). Add the sugar and lime juice (to taste) and let sit for 5 min. Stir in the fish sauce and ¼ cup water. Taste for sugar and lime juice and adjust.

DUMPLING DIPPING SAUCE
Black vinegar, soy sauce, julienned fresh ginger.

Combine equal quantities of black vinegar and soy sauce, then add a lot of fresh ginger. Dip away. Lasts in the fridge eternally.

SALSA VERDE
1 shallot (finely chopped), salt, red or white wine vinegar, 1 bunch parsley, ½ clove garlic, 1 anchovy fillet (finely chopped), 1 tsp capers (drained and chopped), ½ cup olive oil.

In a small bowl, combine the shallot and ½ tsp salt and enough vinegar to cover. Let sit for 10 min. Pick the parsley leaves from the stems, saving the stems to use in stock or beans. Finely chop the leaves. Pound the garlic to a paste with ¼ tsp salt. Drain the shallot of its vinegar, reserving it for a future vinaigrette. Mix the shallot, pounded garlic, anchovy, capers, and olive oil. Taste for salt and adjust.

FRANCIS LAM'S GINGER-SCALLION SAUCE
1 small bunch scallions (minced), 1½-inch piece fresh ginger (peeled and grated or finely chopped), ½ tsp salt plus to taste, ½ cup peanut oil.

In a large heatproof bowl, combine the scallions, ginger, and salt. In a small saucepan, heat the oil until it just begins to smoke. Pour the hot oil over the scallions and ginger. Let cool, then store, refrigerated, for use for all-purpose dipping and drizzling, especially on tofu, chicken, eggs, rice, noodles, etc.

S'CHUG
2 cups cilantro leaves, 1½ cups parsley leaves, 2 green chiles (serrano, chopped), ½ tsp ground cumin, ¼ tsp ground coriander, ⅛ tsp sugar, ¼ tsp salt plus to taste, 2 cloves garlic (chopped), 3 tbsp olive oil, 2 tbsp water.

In a food processor, combine all of the ingredients and pulse to a thick paste. Taste for salt and adjust. (Adapted from Yotam Ottolenghi in the *Guardian*)

ACHIOTE OIL

ARROZ CON GANDULES *(30–40 min)*
¼ cup achiote oil, ½ cup Puerto Rican Sofrito (p. 7), 1½ tbsp salt, 3 cups rice, the amount of broth needed to cook the rice (see ratios on p. 205), 4–8 oz any kind of smoked meat (ham hock, bacon, hot dog, smoked turkey leg), one 15 oz can gandules or pigeon peas (drained).

Heat a large pot over medium heat. Add the achiote oil, sofrito, and salt and cook over medium heat until the sofrito has softened, 5–10 min. Add the rice, broth, and smoked meat and bring to a boil. Reduce to a simmer, cover, and cook until the rice is done, which varies depending on your rice. Add the gandules or peas, then cover and let sit off the heat for 10 min to steam. Eat. (If you don't have gandules, this can be arroz sin gandules!)

AILLADE

AILLADE MAYONNAISE *(2 min)*
1 tbsp aillade, ¼ cup mayonnaise.

Stir together. This is good on halved boiled eggs and on sandwiches, especially BLTs and their relatives.

AILLADE PESTO *(10 min)*
1 bunch parsley, ½ tsp salt plus to taste, ½ cup freshly grated Parmesan cheese, 2–4 tbsp aillade, up to ½ cup olive oil.

Pick the parsley leaves from the stems, saving the stems to use in stock or beans. Finely chop the leaves. In a mortar or blender, combine with the salt. Add the Parmesan and aillade, then drizzle in the olive oil, mixing until it's a spoonable paste. Taste for salt and cheese and adjust to your taste. Use as you would any pesto.

BOILED GREEN BEANS WITH AILLADE *(15 min)*
Salt, 1 lb thin green beans, ¼ cup aillade.

In a pot of boiling very salty water, cook the green beans until tender. Reserve ¼ cup cooking water before draining. In a bowl, combine the aillade with the reserved cooking water. Add the warm green beans and toss well. A scattering of quickly pickled onions and/or chopped olives can be a nice addition.

AIOLI, LEFTOVER OR BROKEN

AIOLI PASTA (*20 min*)
Salt, 1 lb pasta, 2 cups broken aioli, 1 cup chopped toasted walnuts, ½ cup chopped parsley leaves, ½ cup toasted bread crumbs (optional; see p. 176).

In a large pot of boiling water salted to taste like pleasant seawater, cook the pasta. Reserve ¼ cup pasta water just before draining. In a bowl, toss the pasta with the broken aioli, walnuts, and parsley. If needed to loosen the sauce, add the reserved pasta water by the sprinkle (you may need none at all). Top each bowl with toasted bread crumbs (if using).

GARLICKY VINAIGRETTE (*10 min*)
½ shallot or 2 scallions or a little onion (minced), ¼ tsp salt plus to taste, 2 tbsp lemon juice or white wine vinegar plus to taste, ¼–⅓ cup whole or broken aioli.

In a small bowl, combine the shallot or scallions or onion, salt, and lemon juice and let sit for 10 min. Whisk in the aioli, adding a sprinkle of water if needed, then taste. Taste for acid and adjust.

FAST CAESAR (*10 min*)
1 clove garlic (chopped), ⅛ tsp salt plus to taste, 2 anchovy fillets, ¼–½ cup whole or broken aioli, ¼–½ cup freshly grated Parmesan cheese, 1 tsp lemon juice plus to taste.

In a mortar, pound the garlic to a paste with the salt. Add the anchovies and pound in. Add the aioli, whisking or pounding, then add the Parmesan. Mix well, add lemon juice, taste, and adjust. Add a drizzle of water if needed to thin.

Any amount of leftover aioli, whether 1 tsp or ¼ cup, in any condition, can be spooned directly into soup or any beans while they are warming on the stove.

Or, scoop leftovers into soup or beans already in your bowl. The aioli will lightly thicken the broth and improve it.

ALFREDO

HAPPY BREAD *(10 min)*
1 tsp garlic, salt, ½ baguette (or similar bread, cut as for a long sandwich), softened butter, 1–2 tbsp or more Alfredo sauce, freshly grated Parmesan cheese, grated lemon zest.

Heat the oven to 425°F. Pound the garlic to a paste with a little salt. Spread the cut side of the bread with butter, then with the garlic paste, then Alfredo sauce. Top with Parmesan, as lightly or heavily as you like. Bake until just browning and bubbling, about 8 min. Sprinkle with lemon zest and eat.

ALFREDO QUESADILLA *(5 min)*
2 corn or Sonoran-style flour tortillas, 1 tbsp Alfredo sauce, 2 tbsp grated cheddar cheese. *Optional additions:* cooked shredded chicken (or ground beef or chorizo or tofu), sliced avocado, chopped cilantro, hot sauce.

Heat a skillet. Spread 1 tortilla with the Alfredo sauce. Top with grated cheddar and any optional additions. Top with the second tortilla and griddle, flipping once, until hot and bubbling.

MORE ALFREDO *(20 min)*
Anywhere from a leftover spoonful to ¼ cup leftover Alfredo sauce can be put in a pot and whisked with more of what made it. In a small pot, warm the leftover Alfredo sauce with a tbsp of butter. Add a drizzle of cream if you have. Whisk and taste. If you want to add Parmesan cheese, do, or leave it as is. Cook pasta in water salted to taste like pleasant seawater, reserving ¼ cup pasta water before draining. Tip the thinned Alfredo sauce into the pasta, adding reserved pasta water if needed, and top it all with copious amounts of grated Parmesan. Lemon zest can also be nice.

SAUCES AND DIPS

ANCHOVY BUTTER

Use leftover anchovy butter in the Braised Lettuce on Toast (p. 82) or smear onto hot grilled shrimp or lamb chops.

ANCHOVY VINAIGRETTE

If the vinaigrette is very liquid, scoop out and use mostly the solids. The rest can become another vinaigrette tomorrow.

ANCHOVY MAYONNAISE (*5 min*)

1 tbsp anchovy vinaigrette, ¼–⅓ cup mayonnaise, ½–1 tsp drained capers (chopped), chopped cooked egg (optional).

In a bowl, stir together the anchovy vinaigrette, mayonnaise, and capers. Stir in the egg (if using). This is delicious in tuna sandwiches, on ham sandwiches, and on hot dogs! If you add chopped boiled egg, it will have become a salty, savory gribiche-like sauce, wonderful for spooning over fried fish or meat or tofu or boiled or roasted asparagus or potatoes or broccoli.

FISH RANCH (*5 min*)

½ clove garlic, ⅛ tsp salt plus to taste, 1 tbsp anchovy vinaigrette, 1 tsp red wine vinegar, 1 cup crème fraîche or sour cream, 1 tsp heavy cream or yogurt, a squeeze of lemon, up to ¼ tsp finely chopped herbs (parsley, dill, or chervil).

Pound the garlic to a paste with the salt. In a bowl, combine the garlic and the vinaigrette, vinegar, crème fraîche or sour cream, heavy cream or yogurt, lemon juice, and herbs (if using). Taste on a leaf for salt and lemon and adjust. Delicious on escarole and other chicories or iceberg.

BAGNA CAUDA

BAGNA CAUDA CAESAR (*5 min*)

¼ cup bagna cauda at room temperature, 1 tbsp lemon juice, 1 egg yolk (raw or cooked), ½ tsp Dijon mustard, 1–2 tbsp freshly grated Parmesan cheese, water or olive oil.

In a bowl, whisk everything together, adding water or olive oil as needed. Taste on a lettuce leaf and adjust.

Bagna cauda is also good whisked into mayonnaise for anchovy mayonnaise, which is delicious on grilled shrimp and on sandwiches.

BARBECUE SAUCE

BBQ SAUCE YOGURT DIP *(2 min)*
1 tsp barbecue sauce, 2 tbsp plain yogurt, salt (optional).

Combine and taste, adding salt if needed. Good dipping sauce for fries.

BÉCHAMEL

Use leftover béchamel in the Cheesy Cauliflower (p. 31), Greens Gratin (p. 46), Swiss Chard Stem Gratin (p. 89), or Cheese Soufflé (p. 145). Or, warm up any leftover béchamel you have, add a handful of grated cheese, then mix it with pasta.

BEURRE BLANC

HOT BOILED NEW POTATOES WITH BEURRE BLANC *(30–40 min)*
1–2 lb small potatoes, 1 bay leaf, 1 clove garlic or a garlic peel, salt, ½–1 cup beurre blanc.

In a pot that fits them snuggly, add the potatoes. Add water to cover by 1 inch. Add the bay leaf and garlic. Salt the water to taste like a salty sea. Bring to a boil, then reduce to a bare simmer and cook until the potatoes are perfectly tender, 20–30 min. Drain and top immediately with the beurre blanc, smashing a little if you want.

Any amount of leftover beurre blanc can also be used like compound butter dolloped on top of a soup, or spooned over grilled meat or fish, or spread in a sandwich. Make sure that whatever you're adding it to is warm.

BLUE CHEESE DRESSING

Add a spoonful of whole-milk yogurt and a small spoonful of mayonnaise to whatever blue cheese dressing you have left and you have more dressing. Leftover blue cheese dressing also makes a wonderful addition to lunchtime sandwiches. Or it can be used on hamburgers.

BOLOGNESE

I find it useful to occasionally sing a song of *pasta, pizza, polenta, risotto*, because anything that was once a pasta sauce can also be a pizza topping, a polenta topping, or a risotto topping (or a topping for grits, or congee, or any other mush). If there isn't quite enough Bolognese sauce left for any of those, make or open a jar of tomato sauce, add whatever amount of Bolognese there is, and proceed with . . . pasta, pizza, polenta, or risotto.

Leftover Bolognese also makes good Sloppy Joes (p. 320).

BUFFALO SAUCE

Leftover Buffalo sauce can be used to Buffalo any chicken wings or vegetable florets you have. Deep-fry or roast the chicken wings or vegetable, then coat with Buffalo sauce, and broil it very briefly until crisp. Or, mix Buffalo sauce into mayonnaise for Buffalo mayonnaise.

CHIMICHURRI

Chimichurri is a piquant and delicious Argentinian condiment for meat—which you likely know if you have some left over. It stays good for days but quickly gets muddy looking, a function of the erosive action of vinegar. Avoid this by combining leftover chimichurri with another sauce, like mayonnaise or sour cream—with some avocado whisked in for a Green Goddess-y feel—or with room-temperature butter for chimichurri butter.

CILANTRO CHUTNEY

Save and drizzle any leftover cilantro chutney onto rice or add to the base of any sabzi you're making or to scrambled eggs. Or drizzle over cooked eggs.

CLAM DIP

CLAM DIP RANCH *(5 min)*
2 tbsp clam dip, grated zest of ½ lemon, a sprinkle of salt, 2 tsp olive oil.

Mix well and dress crisp greens!

DAIKON OROSHI

TEMPURA DIPPING SAUCE *(5–10 min)*
⅔ cup dashi, 4 tbsp soy sauce, 4 tbsp mirin.

Combine. Just before using as a dipping sauce, add the oroshi, stirring it through as you dip.

An Izakaya dish called saikoro steak calls for cooking steak in garlicky oil with a little sake, and topping it with fried garlic, ponzu sauce, and grated daikon. Any variation of this, whether steak, or a burger, or grilled mackerel, is another good daikon oroshi destination.

GRAVY

GRAVY DIP FOR SANDWICHES *(5–10 min)*
In a pot, combine the gravy with an equal amount of meat stock or Savory Stock/Broth (p. 247) and a sprig of thyme and simmer, whisking, until combined. Add a tiny sprinkle of salt. Taste. Add a drop of sherry or red wine or red wine vinegar and dip your sandwich in it.

GREMOLATA

GREMOLATA BUTTER *(2 min)*

1–4 tbsp gremolata, 2–6 tbsp room-temperature butter.

Mix the gremolata into the butter. Put a pat on cooked vegetables, or pasta or rice or polenta or cooked meat or fish or tofu, and so on.

A variation is to add olive oil to leftover gremolata until it's swimmy. Another variation is to add chopped toasted nuts. Both are great for all-purpose dolloping.

Gremolata is also great stirred into hot beans or rice. And it is essential in Chip-Crusted Pork Chops (p. 466).

GUACAMOLE, EVEN BROWNING

AVOCADO SOUP *(5 min)*

¼ cup guacamole, 1 cup water, 1 tbsp cream or whole milk, a dollop of sour cream (optional), salt.

In a blender, puree all the ingredients until very very smooth. Taste for salt and adjust. Warm slowly over low heat if you want it warm. Good with or without the sour cream stirred in. Also good cold.

GUACAMOLE SOUR CREAM DIP *(1 min)*

¼ cup guacamole, ⅓ cup sour cream.

Mix well. A good dip for celery or carrots or tortilla chips.

Or whisk whatever's left, no matter how discouraging, into tortilla soup for the last 15 min of cooking.

HERB BUTTER

Even the smallest amount of herb butter is an eternal general improver. Spread it on toast then top with an olive oil–fried egg. Or warm leftover rice with herb butter. Or include it in the total amount of butter in scones. Or mix it into pasta with pesto for added richness. Or mix it into pasta without pesto. Or spread it on top of pancakes. Or spoon it onto oatmeal or any other porridge. Or add it to hot boiled potatoes. Or add it to baked potatoes. Or put a dab or pat on fried chicken or a pork chop or grilled fish or steak or tofu or vegetables.

HERB OIL

HERB MAYONNAISE *(5 min)*

There is no faster way to make herb mayonnaise than to mix mayonnaise into the bowl containing the herby remains of herb oil. You can mix at any ratio you like. This is also a good opportunity to add a smattering of chopped capers.

MORE HERB OIL *(5 min)*

There's no reason not to just add more herbs and olive oil and use it again. If you want it to taste different than it did yesterday, add the grated zest of a lemon, or chopped olives, or a different herb, well chopped.

Or turn leftover herb oil into pesto. Add a handful of chopped or pounded nuts, a little garlic pounded to a paste with salt, and freshly grated Parmesan or Pecorino Romano. Add olive oil as needed for a pesto-ish texture. Good on pasta and anywhere else pesto is good.

Or use whatever herb oil you have as part or all of the oil in the recipe for Basic Vinaigrette (p. 376).

HOISIN

HOISIN BROTH *(5 min)*

This is a cheap trick, but it works. Combine 3 tbsp hoisin sauce with about 6 cups water (to your taste). Bring to a simmer and use as a broth for a lunch-time soup of leftover rice, egg, and scallion, or a base for store-bought egg noodles or udon, or any other noodle soup.

HOLLANDAISE

HOLLANDAISE BUTTER (*5 min*)

Smash hollandaise sauce with an equal amount of room-temperature butter and use as an improved, lemony butter for toast, scones, or muffins; or on pasta, rice, or vegetables, or to top soup or cooked meat, and so on.

HUMMUS

HUMMUS SOUP (*15 min*)

¼ cup hummus, 2 cups cooked chickpeas (drained), ¼ cup olive oil, ground cinnamon, salt.

In a blender, combine the hummus, 1 cup water, and 1 cup of the chickpeas and puree to fairly smooth. Pour into a pot and heat to a simmer. Add the olive oil and remaining 1 cup chickpeas. Simmer 10 min. Stir in a scrape of cinnamon. Season with salt to taste. This can be made thicker by pureeing more cooked chickpeas with the hummus, or by adding cooked leftover squash, or some cooked saffron rice. It is delicious topped with crisp croutons and/or squeezed with lemon juice.

A variation is to add ½ bunch cooking greens sautéed in olive oil until tender with one stalk of thinly sliced or chopped celery.

BRATTLEBORO COOP NOODLES (*20 min*)

Salt, ½ lb long pasta (spaghetti, ramen, soba, or Chinese soup noodles), ¼ cup hummus, 1 tbsp soy sauce, 2 tsp sesame oil, ½ tsp or more any beloved chili sauce (sriracha or Sichuan chili crisp), 1 clove garlic (finely minced or pounded to a paste), ½–1 cup julienned carrot or cucumber (optional), ¼–½ cup dry-roasted peanuts, a small handful of thinly sliced scallions (or chopped cilantro, including stems, or both), a scattering of toasted sesame seeds (optional).

In a large pot of boiling water salted to taste like pleasant seawater, cook the pasta. Reserve a little pasta water just before draining. Meanwhile, in a large bowl, whisk together the hummus, soy, sesame oil, chili sauce, and garlic. Scoop the hot cooked pasta directly into the bowl and mix well, adding the carrot or cucumber (if using). Add a pour of pasta water as needed to make it saucy. Top with peanuts, scallions, and sesame seeds (if using).

JERK MARINADE

JERK RICE AND PEAS *(30–40 min)*
1–3 tbsp jerk marinade, unsweetened coconut milk (in the proper ratio for the type of rice you have; see p. 205), ½ tsp salt, one 15 oz can pigeon peas (drained), 1 cup rice.

In a large measuring cup, combine the marinade and coconut milk until you have the total amount of liquid your rice requires. In a heavy saucepan over medium-high heat, stir to combine. Add the salt, pigeon peas, and rice to the liquid, bring to a boil, then cover and reduce to a simmer. Cook according to the package directions, allowing variation because of the peas' extra moisture. Let it continue cooking until the rice is swollen and tender and the liquid is absorbed. Remove from the heat, cover, and let sit for 10 min. Eat. Delicious topped with yogurt!

MARINADE

Bring any leftover fish or meat marinade to a boil, then use it to baste the main ingredient or as a sauce. Make sure to taste the marinade after it has boiled, and make adjustments if that will improve it. Vegetable or tofu marinades can just be saved and reused.

MAYONNAISE

A LITTLE MAYO AND NOT MUCH ELSE VINAIGRETTE *(5 min)*
½ clove garlic, salt, 1 slice preserved lemon, 1 tsp red or white wine vinegar, 3 tbsp mayonnaise, olive oil.

Pound the garlic with a little salt and place in a bowl. Squeeze the preserved lemon over, then discard the membranes, finely chop the peel, and add it to the bowl along with the vinegar. Mix well. Stir in the mayonnaise and 1 tbsp water, then add a long drizzle of olive oil. Taste for salt and oil and adjust. Very good on frisée or chicories.

The last little bit of mayonnaise, spread on the outside, also makes some of the best grilled cheese.

SAUCES AND DIPS

NAM PLA PRIK

Nam pla prik should be refrigerated and then dabbed on rice until it's gone.

NUOC MAM

Leftover nuoc mam is wonderful drizzled over hot rice, especially topped with avocado and toasted sesame seeds, or avocado and fish like mackerel or sardines or salmon.

OIL, USED

I strain fry oil through a fine sieve and store it in the fridge. I can't say for certain that it's an entirely salutary practice. Despite some reservations, I do it.

I strain and reuse oil from confit-ing meat or fish or vegetables, as well, also through a fine-mesh sieve (lined with cheesecloth if I have any). If labeled with its purpose, in clear letters on tape, it can be used to confit another batch of the same ingredient. This must be refrigerated.

If used oil is rancid, run your car on it or look for a local biodiesel collector.

OLIVE OIL

Pour any last little bit of leftover olive oil into an existing vinaigrette, or put it in a tiny cup and leave it by the stove, or drizzle it over any leftover pasta or vegetables or rice or soup you're about to store away.

OLIVE TAPENADE

OLIVE MAYONNAISE (*5 min*)
1 cup mayonnaise, ¼ cup tapenade, a drizzle of olive oil, a few drops of red wine vinegar, a scrape of grated lemon zest (optional).

Combine. So good on sandwiches. If you want it more olive-y, add more tapenade. If you make this inside an empty tapenade jar, you will get every last bit of the tapenade into your sauce!

I loved eating these next as a snack when I was a child.

OLIVE TOASTS *(15 min)*
Thinly sliced baguette, olive oil, tapenade, thin slivers of roasted pepper (optional; 1 sliver per toast), thinly sliced fresh mozzarella cheese, flaky salt.

Heat the oven to 400°F. Drizzle the bread with olive oil and toast. Top with the tapenade, then the roasted pepper (if using), then the mozzarella. Warm until the mozzarella is just melted, another few minutes. Add a few grains of flaky salt. Eat hot.

DOLLOPIER TAPENADE *(2 min)*
Olive oil, 1–2 tbsp tapenade, salt.

Add olive oil to your tapenade, until it's spoonable. Season with salt to taste. This is great for spooning over cooked vegetables or over sliced tomatoes and mozzarella.

OLIVE BUTTER *(5 min)*
4–6 tbsp salted or unsalted room-temperature butter, 1–2 tbsp tapenade, a scrape of grated orange zest (optional), 1 tbsp finely chopped parsley (optional).

In a bowl, combine everything together well with a wooden spoon. Use on grilled fish or vegetables, meat, or vegetables, or refrigerate or freeze, and use as needed.

TAPENADE-STUFFED SUMMER VEGETABLES *(20 min–1 hr)*
3 medium tomatoes or zucchini, olive oil, salt, 1–2 tbsp tapenade, 1 tbsp finely chopped parsley, 3–4 tbsp toasted bread crumbs (see p. 176) or smashed croutons (see p. 176), freshly grated Parmesan cheese.

Heat the oven to 400°F. Slice vegetables in half lengthwise, drizzle with olive oil and lightly salt. Arrange them on a sheet pan cut side up and roast until the insides are soft enough to be scooped out, 10–30 min, depending on the vegetable. Meanwhile, in a bowl, combine the tapenade, parsley, and bread crumbs and mix well. Add a little salt and olive oil. Add the scooped out vegetable middles to the bread crumb mixture and mix well. Taste for salt and adjust. It should be highly seasoned. Remove the scooped vegetable from the oven, stuff them with the mixture, replace on the sheet pan, top with Parmesan, and roast until browned and toasty, another 15–30 min.

This next is really more template than recipe and can be made with chopped olives instead of tapenade, or with pesto, or pepper spread, or tomato spread, or any other paste you find on your refrigerator door.

OLIVE AND NUT AND HERB RICE *(5 min)*

2 cups hot rice (freshly cooked or leftover rewarmed), 2–3 tbsp tapenade, ¼ cup chopped parsley (or dill or a combination of any herbs you have lying around), 2 tbsp toasted pine nuts or toasted chopped walnuts, salt, olive oil (optional).

In a bowl, stir together the rice, tapenade, and parsley. Add the pine nuts or walnuts and mix through. Season with salt to taste. Add a drizzle of olive oil for extra deliciousness if you want, just before eating.

OLIVE VINAIGRETTE *(5 min)*

1 tbsp tapenade, ½ tsp Dijon mustard, 1 tbsp red wine vinegar, 3–4 tbsp mildest possible olive oil, ½ tsp mayonnaise, salt.

In a bowl, whisk everything together, erring on the side of less olive oil and less salt until you taste it on a lettuce leaf. Taste for salt and adjust. Good with romaine and escarole.

And probably the best thing to do with a tiny bit of leftover tapenade is to dollop it on hot bean or vegetable soup. Soup diffuses the strong rich bite of olive and garlic, making everything more exciting. Another good, fast strategy is to add leftover tapenade to any tomato-based pasta sauce, perhaps adding some olive oil–packed tuna at the end, as well.

ONION DIP

CAFE MUTTON POTATO CHIP AND ONION DIP OMELET *(5–10 min)*

3 eggs, salt, ghee (or clarified butter or olive oil), ¼ cup onion dip, a handful of plain potato chips.

In a bowl, whisk the eggs with a tiny pinch of salt. In a small skillet (nonstick or cast-iron if you have one), warm the ghee. Add the eggs, nudging and moving them until just set—see Omelet (p. 140) for detailed instructions. Remove from the heat, add the onion dip to the middle of the omelet, then add the chips, lightly broken. Fold over, slide onto a plate, and eat. (From Shaina Loew-Banayan at Cafe Mutton, Hudson, New York)

Or substitute onion dip for clam dip in Clam Dip Ranch (p. 405).

PARSLEY OIL

A wonderful thing about leftover parsley oil is that it can become any other parsley sauce. Add lemon zest to make it parsley-lemon oil, or walnuts to make it pesto, or olives to make it tapenade. Add it to room-temperature butter and it becomes parsley butter. Parsley oil can also be substituted for parsley. Let parsley oil come to room temperature before using because it is uptight directly from the fridge.

PESTO

A thin layer of oil poured over the surface of the pesto before you store it away helps it stay green, as does pressing whatever you're using to cover it directly onto the sauce's surface. It will still change color. This doesn't signal that the sauce has gone bad, but that the basil phenols have been exposed to oxygen and are reacting. By the time it's tossed with pasta or potatoes or baked into pastry, it won't be noticeable.

LEMONY PESTO POTATO SALAD *(20 min)*

Salt, 1½ cups roughly cubed potatoes, grated zest of 1 lemon, ¼ cup chopped toasted nuts, 1 tbsp olive oil plus to taste, 2 tbsp pesto, 1 tbsp crème fraîche or sour cream.

SAUCES AND DIPS

In a small pot of boiling water salted to taste like pleasant seawater, cook the potatoes until they can be easily pierced by a fork and taste good. Drain, transfer to a bowl, and immediately add the lemon zest, toasted nuts, olive oil, pesto, and crème fraîche or sour cream and mix well, not overworrying about the pieces getting shaggy. Taste for salt and oil and adjust. Good warm or cold.

SNACKY PINWHEELS (*2 hr, but mostly waiting*)
Basic Cream Cheese Dough (p. 350), ½ clove garlic, salt, 1–3 tbsp pesto, 1 cup freshly grated Parmesan cheese, 1 tbsp olive oil, 1 egg (beaten).

Make the cream cheese dough and refrigerate for 1 hr to chill. Heat the oven to 350°F. Line a baking sheet with parchment paper. Pound the garlic with a little salt and add to a small bowl. Add the pesto (more if you want these more pesto-y, less if you want them subtle), Parmesan, and olive oil. Roll out the dough to a rough rectangle ⅛ inch thick. Spread the pesto mixture over the entire surface, leaving a 1-inch border. Starting on a short side, roll into a log (this will give you the broadest pinwheel). Cut the log crosswise into discs ⅓–½ inch wide. Lay spiral-side up on the lined baking sheet. Brush with the beaten egg. Bake until browned and cooked through, 28–30 min. Eat warm or at room temperature, ideally with white wine or sherry.

PESTO SCONES (*25–30 min*)
2 cups (240 g) all-purpose flour, ½ tsp salt, 1 tbsp baking powder, 6 tbsp (3 oz/85 g) cold butter (cut into pieces), 1 cup (113 g) grated cheese (any combination of sharp cheddar or similar), ¼–½ cup pesto, 2 eggs (beaten), ⅓ cup milk (or cream, sour cream, or ricotta cheese).

Heat the oven to 375°F. Place parchment paper on a baking sheet. In a bowl, combine the flour, salt, and baking powder. Mix in the butter with your fingers until tiny pieces emerge. Add the cheese and pesto and mix through. In a bowl, whisk together the eggs and milk. Add to the flour mixture and mix until just combined. Flour a surface well. Pat into a 10 × 2-inch rectangle, then cut into 10 scones. Set on the baking sheet and bake until puffed and golden brown around the edges, 20–23 min. (Adapted from King Arthur Baking website)

PISTOU

Pistou and olive tapenade aren't the same but leftovers of both can be used the same ways. *See Olive tapenade (p. 410).*

PONZU

Any amount of leftover ponzu is enough. Even just a tbsp drizzled on rice will make it citrusy and exciting.

PUTTANESCA

Puttanesca is strongly flavored enough that a little goes a long way. Stir any small amount into plain tomato sauce. Also good on a tuna sandwich, made with olive oil–packed tuna, and a little handful of arugula.

QUESO

QUESO MAC AND CHEESE *(20 min)*
4 tbsp butter, ½ cup half-and-half or heavy cream, 2 cups queso sauce, salt, 1 lb short pasta.

In an ovenproof skillet, combine the butter, half-and-half or cream, and queso sauce and warm. In a large pot of boiling water salted to taste like pleasant seawater, cook the pasta. Drain the pasta and add to the sauce, mix through, taste for salt and adjust. Add freshly ground black pepper if you like. If you like a browned top, put under a broiler to sizzle for a moment.

RAITA

Pour leftover raita directly over hot cooked rice, especially basmati. This makes a version of a dish called "curd rice," and it's delicious.

SAUCES AND DIPS

Raita also makes a good chicken or lamb marinade. Strain out any vegetables and eat them over rice. Add some salt and olive oil to the raita, then marinate whatever you want overnight. Brush the marinade off before grilling.

RÉMOULADE

Use leftover rémoulade sauce in The Most Delicious Warm Shrimp Salad Sandwich (p. 290), or serve it with fried fish.

ROMESCO

Romesco is an ideal sauce for any seafood, even if it's just a bit, slathered on after cooking. It's also wonderful stirred into mayonnaise for a sandwich condiment. Or, thin it with more olive oil and use it as an all-purpose drizzle. Or, mix into toasted bread crumbs as a wonderful meat or fish or vegetable sprinkle.

SALSA, TOMATO

This is surprisingly good, and an incredibly fast and cheap way to start a red rice or bean dish.

SALSA SOFRITO *(10 min)*
2–3 tbsp neutral cooking oil (peanut or grapeseed), ½ cup tomato salsa, ¼ tsp salt or to taste.

Heat a small pot. Add the oil, salsa, and salt. Cook until the tomatoes have caramelized and the oil and tomato are fairly separated, 10–12 min. Taste for salt and adjust. This is also good as a topping for plain hot rice.

SALSA SOFRITO BEANS *(25 min)*
2–3 tbsp neutral cooking oil (peanut or grapeseed), ⅓ cup finely chopped onion, 1 tbsp chopped garlic, ¼ tsp salt plus to taste, ⅛–¼ tsp ground cumin,

⅛–¼ tsp dried oregano, ¼ cup tomato salsa, one 15 oz can black or pinto beans (drained and rinsed).

Heat a saucepan. Add the oil, onion, garlic, and salt, and cook until it's begun to soften, 2–3 min. Add the cumin, oregano, and salsa. Cook until the tomatoes have caramelized and the oil and tomato are fairly separated, 10–12 min. Stir in the beans and cook until they are warm, adding a little pour of water or broth if needed to keep from smashing then taste for salt and adjust. Good on rice, or with tortillas, or on their own.

SALSA VERDE

Use leftover salsa verde interchangeably with Parsley Oil (p. 68). Or spoon it over any leftover boiled egg or any rice or any soup or anything you plan to put in a sandwich tomorrow.

SATAY SAUCE

GADO GADO *(30 min)*
1 package firm or extra-firm tofu, 3 tbsp neutral oil, 2–3 Boiled Eggs (p. 139), 1–2 vegetables that can be quickly boiled (optional), wedges or spears of raw vegetables (cabbage, cucumbers, bell peppers, in any combination), ½ cup satay sauce, fried shallots (homemade, see p. 7, or store-bought).

Cut the tofu into ½-inch-thick slices and dry with a cloth. Heat a large shallow pan. Add the oil and fry the tofu, in batches if needed, until completely golden on each side. If a piece is sticking and hard to turn, it's just not fried yet. Leave it until it releases fairly easily, adjusting heat as needed to avoid burning. Cook the boiled eggs to your preference, then peel and halve them. While the eggs are cooking, boil vegetables in water salted to taste like pleasant seawater, then let them cool. Arrange the raw and boiled vegetables, the eggs, and the tofu on a plate. Spoon the satay sauce into a small bowl and scatter the fried shallots over the satay and anywhere else. Dip and eat and dip and eat. (Adapted from Hetty McKinnon in *The New York Times Magazine*)

SAUCE, ANY

There is a universal sauce experience that is unmoored from any one cuisine or dish. It is having eaten the main ingredient out of a sauce and facing the decision to keep or discard what's left. It may be mapo tofu's red fermented bean chili slurry, or the vinegary dregs of a now cucumber-less cucumber salad, or lamb vindaloo without the lamb. In all of these instances I take the same prudent step. I warm up leftover rice and add whatever sauce I've salvaged. There is no name for the meal this produces. It is only enough for me, but I unfailingly enjoy it. A fried egg is never out of place on such a concoction.

SAUCE GRIBICHE

GRIBICHE MAYONNAISE (*2 min*)
1–4 tbsp sauce gribiche, ¼–½ cup mayonnaise.

Mix together well and use as you would tartar sauce or rémoulade, for fried things, or on any sandwich, or on vegetables.

SHAWARMA SAUCE

SHAWARMA SAUCE DRESSING (*5–10 min*)
1 tbsp finely minced scallions or onions, vinegar, ¼ cup shawarma sauce, 1 tbsp lemon juice, ⅓ cup olive oil, salt.

In a small bowl, combine the scallions or onions with vinegar to cover and let soak for 10 min. Drain and add to a bowl. Whisk in the shawarma sauce, lemon juice, olive oil, and salt to taste. Use to dress lettuce like iceberg, butter, or Little Gem.

SWEET AND SOUR SAUCE

NUOC MAM (*5 min*)
1 packet sweet and sour sauce, juice of 2 limes, ½ cup water, 5–6 tbsp fish sauce, 2 cloves garlic (minced), 2–3 Thai bird's eye chiles (minced).

Mix all together, taste for fish sauce, lime, and spice and adjust. Good for general dipping.

TABASCO

When you have a bottle containing only a tiny bit of Tabasco, use it up. Add a few drops to mayonnaise for spicy mayonnaise—which you can then put in a small clear jar labeled "spicy mayonnaise." Or make an Oyster Omelet (p. 283), which has a sauce of Tabasco and powdered sugar. Or put a few drops into Salsa Verde (p. 398), which will make that Italian condiment more worldly.

TAHINI

It takes only a few spoonfuls of tahini to make hummus. Combine with a can of drained chickpeas, pounded garlic, lemon juice, and water and blend.

If tahini separates, reblend it to smooth with an immersion blender. If it's too stodgy to move, microwave briefly to warm, then blend.

TAMARIND CHUTNEY

I have used leftover tamarind chutney instead of soaked and strained tamarind to make sambar. I have also used it in other recipes that called for soaked and strained tamarind. Everything I've made with it has been delicious. I'm sorry, I'm sorry. It's a hack, but I love it.

TARAMASALATA

WORLD'S BEST OMELET* *(5 min)*
2–3 eggs (beaten), salt, 1 tbsp olive oil or ghee, 3 tbsp taramasalata.

Whisk the eggs with a tiny pinch of salt. In a small skillet (nonstick or cast iron), warm the olive oil or ghee. Add the eggs, nudging and moving them until just set. (See Omelet p. 140.) Remove from the heat, add the tarama-salata, fold, and eat in a shallow bowl to protect from inevitable drips.

*Or maybe second-best omelet: See Tzatziki Omelet (p. 422).

TARTAR SAUCE

Substitute tartar sauce for rémoulade sauce in The Most Delicious Warm Shrimp Salad Sandwich (p. 290). Or, add 1 chopped boiled egg, 1 tsp finely chopped cornichons, 1 tsp finely chopped capers (optional), a handful of chopped herbs (parsley, chervil, tarragon, celery leaves), ¼ tsp salt plus to taste, freshly ground black pepper, and have a version of Gribiche sauce.

TERIYAKI SAUCE

Teriyaki sauce is a delicious addition to Egg Fried Rice (p. 154). Drizzle in a few tsp at the very end. It is also good with Yaki Onigiri (p. 292) or Hot Dog Onigiri (p. 324). Or use it to make yakitori: Soak bamboo skewers in water for 30 min to prevent burning. Skewer small pieces of chicken or vegetable or tofu interspersed with inch-long pieces of scallion. Grill and then brush with sauce midway through cooking.

TOMATO PASTE

The very little bit left at the end of a tube is only an obstacle when a new tube arrives. I advise what I advise for Tabasco: Use it up. Add a dab to the beginning of a pan of frying rice. Add some to a batch of tomato sauce. Add it to tapenade. Or start a vinaigrette: Squeeze whatever is left in the tube into a bowl, add a drizzle of vinegar and a smashed garlic clove, let it sit for a while, then whisk in olive oil and dress lettuces with it. Or make any bean soup, adding the tomato paste at the start, when you cook the aromatics.

TOMATO SAUCE

SHAKSHUKA *(20–30 min)*

¼ cup olive oil, ½ medium onion (sliced lengthwise into medium-thin half-moons), ½–1 red or yellow bell pepper (sliced into strips), salt, 3 cloves garlic (sliced), 1–2 cups tomato sauce, 4–5 eggs, 1 cup chopped cilantro, pita or bread for serving.

Heat the oven to 400°F. Heat a medium-large ovenproof skillet. Add the olive oil, onion, bell pepper, and 1 tsp salt and cook until the vegetables have begun to soften, about 5 min. Add the garlic and cook until everything is soft, another 3–5 min. Add the tomato sauce, stir well, and bring to a simmer. Crack the eggs into ramekins or teacups, then tip each into the sauce. Salt the eggs lightly. Put the pan into the oven, uncovered, until the whites are set and the yolks are as you like them, 5–10 min. Remove, top with cilantro, and eat with pita or bread.

PASTA WITH FISH AND TOMATOES *(15 min)*

¼ cup olive oil, 2 cloves garlic (sliced), ½ tsp chile flakes plus to taste, 1 cup tomato sauce, 1 tbsp drained capers (optional), 1–2 cans olive oil–packed tuna or 4–8 oz fresh tuna (or swordfish or halibut), salt, 1 lb short pasta (ziti).

Heat a large pan. Add the olive oil, garlic, chile flakes, and a pinch of salt and cook until the garlic has just softened, 30 sec–1 min. Add the tomato sauce and capers (if using) and bring to a simmer. Cut or flake the fish into bite-size pieces and salt it lightly, if fresh, then add to the simmering sauce and remove from the heat. Let cook in the residual heat of the sauce, stirring occasionally, for 5 min. Check for doneness, and if any pieces aren't cooked through, set the pan back over low heat and simmer for 1 min or so, until they are. Taste for salt and adjust. In a large pot of boiling water salted to taste like pleasant seawater, cook the pasta. Reserve ½ cup pasta water just before draining. Add the cooked pasta to the sauce along with a little pasta water if needed to get everything moving. Mix and eat.

RED RICE *(30–40 min)*

¼–½ cup tomato sauce, stock or broth as needed for your rice (see a list of rice-to-liquid ratios on p. 205), 1 tbsp neutral oil (peanut or grapeseed), ½ onion (finely chopped), 1 bay leaf, ½ tsp salt plus to taste, 1 cup rice, 1 tbsp butter, freshly ground black pepper.

In a large measuring cup, combine the tomato sauce and add enough stock to come up to the total amount you need for your rice. Heat a small pot. Add the oil, the onion, bay leaf, and salt and cook until the onion is just beginning to soften, 2–3 min. Add the rice and stir to toast until opaque, 1–2 min. Add the tomato-stock mixture and butter, bring to a boil, then reduce to a low simmer, cover, and cook according to the type of rice. Remove from the heat, fluff with a fork, let sit covered 5 min, then eat. Garnish with black pepper before eating.

Or poach eggs in plain leftover tomato sauce. Or warm a leftover meatball or two in it. Or warm greens in it and eat for lunch. Or substitute leftover tomato sauce for chopped tomatoes in Ribollita (p. 178), or Fast Ribollita (p. 179), or Pappa al Pomodoro (p. 180) or Minestrone (p. 210) or Inauthentic Tomato Dal (p. 231).

TOUM

Even a tiny bit of leftover toum makes a marinade. Add lemon juice and olive or neutral oil and marinate away.

TZATZIKI

TZATZIKI OMELET *(5 min)*
2–3 eggs (beaten), salt, 1 tbsp olive oil or ghee, 3 tbsp tzatziki.

Whisk the eggs with a tiny pinch of salt. For detailed omelet instructions, see the basic Omelet (p. 140). When your omelet is just set, add the tzatziki, fold, and eat in a shallow bowl to protect from inevitable drips.

VELOUTÉ SAUCE

Is it probable that you have oysters sitting around waiting to be called on when you find yourself with leftover velouté? We are already in a rather marginal case, but . . .

OYSTERS ROCKEFELLER *(25 min)*

1 dozen oysters, ½ cup velouté sauce, ½ cup mixed herbs (tarragon, celery leaf, parsley, savory, chervil), salt, 2 tbsp fresh bread crumbs (p. 176).

Wash and shuck the oysters. Set the oven to broil. In a blender, combine the velouté and herbs and blend until smooth. Season with salt to taste; it should be lightly seasoned. Top each oyster with a little spoonful of velouté, then top lightly with bread crumbs. Broil until browned, 4–6 min. Eat.

VINAIGRETTE

If you have a splash of vinaigrette and old bread, you have bread salad; if you have vinaigrette and rice you have rice salad; if you have vinaigrette and roasted beets you have beet salad. Alice B. Toklas contended that if you had an onion and vinaigrette—plus mustard and a cup of heavy cream—you had a "winter salad." I doubt this, but I'm open to being proven wrong.

Every last spoonful of vinaigrette should be kept. When the time comes to make a salad, whether of bread or beet or onion or lettuce, add to it—why not a bit of mustard, some lemon-soaked shallots, and olive oil? Or a pounded-up anchovy and some red wine vinegar? This can go on as long as you like. If the vinaigrette starts to taste rancid, guiltlessly start again, knowing you've squeezed as much life from yours as you could. My only firm recommendation is against prematurely discarding it, because it is a most purposeful improver as long as it is allowed to loiter.

WASABI PASTE

If you find yourself with a little wasabi paste, put a dab on hot rice at lunch-time, and then add smoked or canned fish or tofu, furikake and sesame seeds, and some sliced nori. This makes a very fast and very good lunch.

HOW TO KEEP A FAMILY TREE
Pickles, etc.

Salt is born of the purest parents: the sun and the sea.

—*Pythagoras*

Every cuisine has a pickle. And any part of any pickle—whether one olive or one teaspoon of brine—should be marshaled to the service of transforming and improving leftovers.

Olives and capers provide one blueprint. With a smattering of either, the last of the leftover tomato sauce pivots toward puttanesca. Mixed through cooked vegetables, even a teaspoon of chopped olives or capers bestows a bright, saline tang. One of the most practical applications of a bit of either is to cast it against a plain backdrop. Suspend the last spoonful of chopped olives in butter or olive oil, or stir them into rice, or smash them onto a piece of toast, and you will have turned the mere residue of salty savor into another meal. Olive tapenade has been a condiment since the days of Cato the Elder. It is ancient and it is magical. Tapenade can go on pasta, in sandwiches, on toast, with or without fresh cheese. Or it can be spooned onto beans, smeared over boiled eggs, drizzled over meat, or, or, or . . .

Beyond recommending that you refrain from discarding them, I recommend carefully choosing the pickles and cured things you buy. There are terrible versions of any, but more important, there are exceptional ones—lovely, deep-violet, shriveled and oily Greek olives, deeply salty pickled Sichuan mustard greens, tart lime achar. All have a deeper impact than their size and portability would suggest, and it must be an impact you like. If the brine in a jar of olives you chose indiscriminately doesn't taste good to you, discard it. Then choose the next jar carefully and use it wisely and down to the salty end.

ACHAR LIQUID

Any amount of achar is the best enhancement I've ever encountered to a boring soup. Scrape whatever you have into a pot with the beleagured chicken noodle or winter vegetable, and it will come immediately to life. Or make:

PICKLE RICE *(30–40 min)*
1 cup basmati rice, 2 tbsp achar juice (with or without pickle), about 1⅔ cups water or coconut milk or a combination, pinch of salt. *Optional garnishes:* chopped mint or cilantro, yogurt for drizzling, chopped peanuts or pine nuts.

Soak the basmati for at least 30 min. Drain. In a 2-cup measuring cup, combine the achar and enough water or coconut milk or a combination to come up to 1¾ cups. In a medium-size pot, add the liquid, the rice, and salt. Bring to a boil, cover, reduce to a simmer, and cook until the rice is tender and the liquid is absorbed, about 20 min. Remove from the heat and let sit for 10 min. Fluff with a fork and eat with all or some or none of the garnishes. It's also a good idea to add a sprinkle of achar juice to fried rice once it's become fried and crisp.

ACHAR SANDWICH IMPROVER *(2 min)*
Achar juice, mayonnaise (or cream cheese or Greek yogurt).

In a bowl, combine, starting with a ratio of 1 tsp achar juice to 2 tbsp mayonnaise, adjusting as you like. Especially good in grilled cheese.

ANCHOVY FILLETS

ANCHOVY BUTTER *(5 min)*
½ clove garlic, ⅛ tsp salt, up to 10 anchovy fillets (chopped), 8 tbsp (1 stick) salted or unsalted room-temperature butter.

Pound the garlic to a paste with the salt and place in a bowl. Add the anchovies and butter and mix everything together well! Especially delicious slathered on whole grilled or sautéed shrimp, on radishes, on grilled or roasted meat, and on grilled or toasted bread.

ANCHOVY PAN CON TOMATE *(10 min)*
1–2 anchovy fillets, olive oil you like the taste of, slices of rustic baguette or similar bread, 1 clove garlic, 1 overripe tomato.

Pound the anchovies to a paste. Add a drizzle of olive oil. Toast or grill the slices of baguette. Rub each slice of toast with the garlic, then lightly smear with a tiny bit of anchovy paste, rub with overripe tomato, then drizzle heavily with olive oil.

Or use the last few anchovies in Onion-Anchovy Pasta (p. 27) or Fast Caesar (p. 400).

ANCHOVY OIL

Traditionally tonnato sauce is served with cold meat. This one is delicious over chicken or pork, whether roasted or fried. It is also very good for dipping slices of hot dog, sausage, or potato chips into. It also makes a good salad dressing, once thinned with a bit of water.

Adapt this recipe to the amount of anchovy oil you have, using equal amounts of anchovy oil and mayonnaise.

A VICTORIOUS TONNATO SAUCE *(5 min)*
⅓ cup anchovy oil, ⅓ cup mayonnaise, 2 tsp drained capers, juice of ½ lemon, 1 tbsp olive oil.

In a blender, puree everything.

CREAMY DRESSING *(5 min)*
Any amount anchovy oil, an almost equal amount of mayonnaise, an almost equal amount of sour cream (or Greek yogurt or crème fraîche), an amount of pounded garlic that seems slightly aggressive, 1–3 anchovy fillets, salt to taste, a little lemon juice or red wine vinegar.

In a blender, puree everything. Think of it as fishy ranch dressing and use it to dress crisp or bitter lettuces, or as a dip.

ANCHOVY PASTE

Use last bits of anchovy paste in small amounts in any of the recipes above. Then once the paste is gone, buy a tin or jar of good anchovies, which are more versatile and better tasting.

BOTTARGA, GRATED

Bottarga lasts for a geologic period of time, and should ideally be grated just before being used. But if you find yourself, at the end of the night, with a little bit of it grated, combine it with room-temperature butter, mix well, then store in labeled wax paper for mixing into pasta or ramen or rice.

CAPERS

CAPER BUTTER *(3 min)*
1–2 tbsp capers (roughly chopped), 4 tbsp (½ stick) room-temperature butter.

Combine well. Delicious on toast topped with scrambled or poached or boiled egg. Also delicious on grilled or fried meat or fish or vegetables. If you want it more caper-y, add more capers to the butter.

A variation is to add a tbsp of finely chopped parsley or dill or both. Another variation is to add 1 tbsp finely chopped anchovy. Another variation is to add a scrape of garlic you've pounded to a paste with salt. Another variation yet is to add a few drops of the caper juice.

Or use the last few capers in the Best Grain or Bean Salad (p. 206), Olive Tapenade (p. 393), Tartar Sauce (p. 396), Sauce Gribiche (p. 396), or Salsa Verde (p. 398).

CAPER BRINE

Mix a few drops of caper brine into a Bloody Mary. If you like dirty martinis, caper brine is another way to dirty yours.

CHILE BRINE

PIZZERIA SALAD DRESSING *(5 min)*
1 tbsp red wine vinegar, ¼ cup olive oil, 2 tsp finely minced onion or scallion, ½ tsp dried oregano, chile brine, salt.

In a jar, mix the vinegar, olive oil, onion or scallion, oregano, and chile brine to taste. Taste and season with salt. Good, and quite spicy, on Pizzeria Salad (p. 54) or on iceberg or other crisp lettuce.

Chile brine is also a perfect ingredient for making more pickled chiles. Strain it of seeds, bring it to a boil, taste for salt, sugar, and vinegar and pour over sliced fresh chiles. Or pour it over sliced onions to make spicy onion pickles. Or do the same with any other vegetable you want to turn into a spicy vinegar pickle.

Or pour leftover brine into a little bottle and serve with pulled pork, fried shrimp, fried rice, and anything else that needs a vinegary bite. Or, maybe simplest, put tiny teaspoons of seedy brine on salted halved boiled eggs for a perfect amount of acid and spice.

CHOW-CHOW (PICCALILLI)

Use leftover chow-chow instead of cornichons in Tartar Sauce (p. 396).

CORNICHONS

Tartar Sauce (p. 396), Sauce Gribiche (p. 396), and Rémoulade Sauce (p. 396) all benefit from the addition of a few extra cornichons. If you have no tartar or gribiche sauce, and no designs on making them, mix cornichons into mayonnaise, add a drop of vinegar or lemon juice, and spread it on your next sandwich.

Use leftover cornichon brine as you do *Pickle brine (p. 438)*.

CURTIDO

Use curtido in place of sauerkraut in any of the recipes for leftover Sauerkraut (p. 440). They are not the same, but can be used interchangeably in leftovers recipes.

GIARDINIERA

GIARDINIERA CHICKEN SALAD *(5–10 min)*
1 cup diced or shredded cooked chicken, 3 tbsp drained giardiniera, ½ tbsp giardiniera brine, 1 tsp mayonnaise, 2 tbsp chopped fresh herbs (basil or parsley), salt if needed.

Combine! Taste for salt and adjust. Good on all bread, but especially dark brown bread, I think.

GIARDINIERA "PIMIENTO CHEESE" *(10 min)*
Up to ½ cup drained giardiniera, 4 oz room-temperature cream cheese, ¼ tsp salt plus to taste, 1–2 tsp grated onion, 2–3 oz grated cheddar cheese (about 1 cup), 2 tsp pickled giardiniera brine or pickled chile brine, 1 tbsp mayonnaise.

By hand or in a food processor, combine the giardiniera, cream cheese, salt, onion, cheddar, and brine. Pulse. Add the mayonnaise. Pulse again. Taste for salt and adjust. Good on crackers, chips, toast, or sandwiches.

I have also used leftover giardiniera instead of chopped garlic to sauté greens. It is unpardonably lazy but I still do it.

GIARDINIERA GREENS *(variable but short)*
¼ cup giardiniera (plus some brine), 1 bunch cooking greens (including cabbage), olive oil, salt.

Chop the giardiniera roughly. Stem and chop or otherwise prepare the greens. Heat a pan. Add the olive oil, giardiniera, and greens and cook, adding some brine from the jar of giardiniera (or water), if needed. Taste for salt, which it might not need, and add if it does. Cook until completely tender and slightly fried and delicious.

KATSUOBUSHI, USED

FURIKAKE (*20 min*)
Up to 1 cup used katsuobushi, a few pieces used kombu, 1 tsp soy sauce, 1 tsp sugar, ¼ tsp salt, 2 tbsp sesame seeds, 2 sheets toasted nori (halved then julienned).

Finely chop the katsuobushi and kombu. In a dry pot, combine and cook over medium-low heat until the katsuobushi is dry and separated. Add the soy sauce, sugar, and salt and cook over medium heat until the liquid has evaporated and the katsuobushi is dry and crispy. Transfer to a tray or plate to cool. Once completely cooled, add the sesame seeds and nori. Store in an airtight container or freeze. (Adapted from Just One Cookbook website)

KIMCHI

KIMCHI PANCAKES (*10 min*)
1 cup kimchi, any pancake batter (pp. 138–39), 2–3 tbsp kimchi brine, 1–2 tsp gochujang, 1–2 scallions (cut on the diagonal into 1-inch-long pieces), peanut or grapeseed oil for frying.

Thinly slice the kimchi. In a bowl, combine the batter ingredients. Add the kimchi, kimchi brine, gochujang, and scallions to the batter. In a deep pot, heat 2 inches of oil to 350°–375°F. Add ¼–⅓ cup of the pancake mixture at a time and fry in batches until crisp, 2–3 min per side.

Put the kimchi brine in a measuring cup and add enough ice water to come to 1½ cups. In a bowl, combine the all-purpose flour, rice flour, egg, and liquid. (Adapted from Korean Bapsang website)

KIMCHI FRIED RICE *(20 min)*

2 tbsp neutral oil, 2 tbsp finely chopped onion, ¼ tsp chile flakes, 2–2½ cups cooked rice, 1 tbsp gochujang, ¾ cup kimchi (thinly sliced), 3–4 tbsp kimchi brine, 1 tsp soy sauce, 1 tsp sesame oil, 1 tsp sesame seeds, fried eggs for serving.

Heat a skillet. Add the oil and onion and cook until beginning to soften, about 5 min. Stir in the chile flakes, add the rice, and fry, pressing the grains against the pan, and moving unfried rice into open spots when you can. Add the gochujang, kimchi, kimchi brine, soy sauce, and sesame oil and cook 1–2 min over high heat. Add the sesame seeds. Eat topped with fried eggs.

KIMCHI DUMPLINGS *(20 min)*

1 clove garlic, 1 tsp minced fresh ginger, 1 tsp salt, 8 oz ground pork, 8 oz firm tofu, ½ cup finely chopped kimchi, ½ cup finely chopped bean sprouts, 3 scallions (very finely minced), 2–3 tbsp gochujang, 1 tbsp sesame oil, 1 tbsp soy sauce, one 14 oz package round dumpling wrappers.

Pound the garlic and ginger to a taste with the salt and place in a bowl. Add the pork, tofu, kimchi, bean sprouts, scallions, gochujang, sesame oil, and soy sauce and mix well. Place a heaping teaspoon of the mixture in the middle of a dumpling wrapper. Fold the wrapper over to make a half-moon and seal the edges. Set up a steamer or bring a large pot of water to a boil. Steam for 10 min or boil for 2 min. Dip in the sauce of your choice! (Adapted from Korean Bapsang website)

SIMPLEST HEALING KIMCHI BROTH *(5–7 min)*

6 cups dashi, ¼ cup kimchi brine, ½ cup thinly sliced kimchi, 1–2 handfuls bean sprouts, 1 tsp gochugaru or other chile flakes, 1–2 tbsp gochujang, 1½ tbsp soy sauce, 1 tsp minced garlic, 1 scallion (finely chopped).

In a pot, combine the dashi, kimchi brine, kimchi, bean sprouts, gochugaru, gochujang, soy sauce, and garlic and bring to a simmer. Simmer for 3–5 min, add the scallion, and eat! If you'd like, add tofu or rice noodles for something more filling. (Adapted from Korean Bapsang website)

KIMCHI JJIGAE *(30–40 min)*

2 tbsp neutral oil or butter, about 8 oz pork belly or pork shoulder (cut into ½-inch pieces), 1 cup old kimchi (thinly sliced), 1 clove garlic (minced),

1–2 tbsp gochugaru, ½ cup kimchi brine, soy sauce (optional), ½ block tofu (cubed or sliced), 2–3 scallions (chopped).

Heat a small pot. Add the oil or butter and pork and lightly brown, about 5 min. Stir in the kimchi, garlic, and gochugaru and cook for about 2 min. Add the kimchi brine and 2–3 cups water. Bring to a boil, then reduce to a simmer and cook about 15 min. Taste and adjust seasoning with soy sauce (if using). Add the tofu and scallions and simmer for 5 min. Good over hot white rice.

KIMCHI BRINE

Use kimchi brine in Kimchi Pancakes (p. 434), Simplest Healing Kimchi Broth (p. 435), or Kimchi Jjigae (p. 435). Or use it in place of sauerkraut juice in Sauerkraut Michelada (p. 441). Or drink it straight or with seltzer.

OLIVES

The thing to do with just a few olives is to pit and chop them without planning further. Once they're chopped, and you see whether it's a tbsp or a half cup's worth, you can make decisions. Mix chopped olives into room-temperature butter, perhaps with a sprinkle of leftover chopped parsley or some lemon zest to make olive butter, which can anoint steak or toast or stew or scrambled eggs. Or add olives to some olive oil and use as an olive-y drizzle over a salad or a main dish, or scatter them over the main course, or sprinkle them into the pan with the roasting chicken, or the roasting potatoes, or add them to the simmering sauce on the stove. Or add them to a pan of sautéing cooking greens when you add the greens so the olives get fried and sizzly. Or make:

OLIVE TUNA SALAD (*10–15 min*)
3 tbsp finely minced scallions or 2 tbsp finely chopped red or white onion, red wine vinegar, 1 can olive oil–packed tuna (undrained), 1–3 tbsp chopped olives, 1 clove garlic (finely minced), grated zest of 1 lemon, 1 tbsp finely chopped drained capers, a few drops of caper brine (optional), 2 tbsp chopped parsley,

lemon juice or a few more drops wine vinegar, a sprinkle of red chile flakes (optional), salt, olive oil (optional).

In a bowl, combine the scallions or onions with vinegar to just cover and let soak for 10 min. Drain. In a bowl, flake the tuna well along with some of its oil. Add the drained olives, garlic, lemon zest, capers, a few drops of caper brine (if using), parsley, a squeeze of lemon juice, and chile flakes (if using). Taste for salt and olive oil and adjust. This should be very rich and savory. Eat on a sandwich or toast or crackers!

Or for something more elaborate, make:

PISSALADIÈRE *(1–1½ hr)*
¼ cup olive oil plus for brushing, 1½ lb yellow onions (sliced lengthwise into very thin half-moons), ¼ tsp salt plus to taste, 5–6 sprigs thyme, one 14 oz package frozen store-bought puff pastry (thawed), 10 good anchovy fillets (sliced lengthwise), ¼–½ cup olives (pitted and roughly chopped).

Heat a large deep sauté pan or pot. Add the oil, onions, and salt and cook, sitting occasionally and covering and uncovering as needed, until caramelized and golden brown, 30–45 min. Remove from the heat and stir in the thyme. Heat the oven to 375°F. Lay the puff pastry on a baking sheet. Brush lightly with olive oil. Scatter with the onions, then arrange the anchovies and olives in any pattern that appeals to you. Bake until golden brown, 20–25 min.

OLIVE BRINE

There are those, among whom I count my younger self, who will not drink a martini unless it is spiked with olive brine. In those days, I also only drank vodka martinis—which I liked best with no vermouth, with olive brine, and icy cold. I'm twenty years older now. I only drink gin martinis, with only barely less vermouth than gin—mine are almost yellow—and I won't let olive brine near them. I still allow a very occasional olive, having at some point begun to prefer the yellow of a lemon twist. Nonetheless, I respect my younger self's opinion that olive brine was a good martini ingredient.

PICKLES

ANYTHING AND PICKLE SANDWICH *(5 min)*
White sandwich bread, butter (optional), ½ cup chopped pickles, 1 cup chopped protein (cooked meat, fish, eggs, or tofu), 1 tbsp chopped fresh dill, a scrape of hot mustard powder or Dijon, 1–2 tbsp crème fraîche (or sour cream, Greek yogurt, or heavy cream), a big squeeze lemon juice, salt, freshly ground black pepper, a few drops of Tabasco.

Toast the bread and butter it. In a bowl, combine the pickles, protein, dill, mustard powder or Dijon, crème fraîche, lemon juice, salt to taste, a lot of black pepper, and any Tabasco. Make into a sandwich and eat. This is also good on crackers.

Or include leftover pickles in Tartar Sauce (p. 396) or Sauce Gribiche (p. 396).

PICKLE BRINE

PICKLE-BRINED ROAST CHICKEN *(6–24 hr)*
One 24 oz jar pickle brine, 1 whole chicken (2–3 lb) or 2–3 lb chicken drumsticks and thighs, 2 tbsp oil, 3 tbsp butter.

In a large bowl, or other container big enough to hold the chicken, combine the pickle brine with enough water to just submerge the meat, using a weight, if needed. Leave 6–12 hr for drumsticks and thighs, 6–24 hr for a whole chicken. Remove from the brine and pat dry. Heat the oven to 400°F. Heat an ovenproof cast-iron pan. Add oil. Brown the chicken on all sides. Transfer to the oven and roast for 15 min, then reduce the oven temperature to 365°F. Add the butter to the pan. Baste every 15 min until done, about 45 min for a small chicken and up to 1 hr 15 min for a big one, or 30–40 min for drumsticks and thighs.

QUICKLED VEGETABLES *(10 min)*
Whatever vegetable you're pickling (onion, carrot, cauliflower, etc.), pickle brine, salt, and sugar to taste.

Cut vegetables into small, picklelish pieces. In a saucepan, bring the pickle brine to a boil. Taste and adjust with water and salt. Season with sugar to taste. It should be balanced and strong. Place the vegetables in a jar or heat-proof bowl. Pour the boiling pickle brine over the top. Let sit to cool. These can be stored for several weeks. Quickled vegetables are very good at turning stale bread and vinaigrette into bread salad, and turning yesterday's potatoes into potato salad, or any leftover vegetable into a revived dish today.

Or add leftover pickle brine to a Bloody Mary or a Gibson. Or make a pickle soda by adding pickle juice to seltzer. Or make a Pickletini by combining gin, dry vermouth, and a few drops of pickle juice to a shaker, and shaking.

PICKLED BEETS

CITRUS AVOCADO SALAD *(15 min)*
½ small red onion (thinly sliced), 2 tsp red wine vinegar, ¼ tsp salt, 1 avocado (thinly sliced), 1 small citrus fruit (a mandarin or clementine, divided into segments) or a few segments of a larger citrus (a grapefruit, navel orange, or Cara Cara orange), flaky salt, a few slices pickled beets (wedged or sliced), olive oil, smoky chile flakes (optional; Guntur Sannam, Aleppo, or Marash).

In a small bowl, marinate the onion in the vinegar and salt for 10 min. Meanwhile, lay the sliced avocado on a plate. Place the pieces of citrus among the avocado. Salt all lightly with flaky salt. Drain the onions, reserving the vinegar for Basic Vinaigrette (p. 376) or any other use. Sprinkle the onions over the other ingredients, then spoon the beets around and among it all. Drizzle heavily with olive oil and finish with chile flakes (if using). Also good with a few sprigs of cilantro or chervil placed here and there.

PRESERVED LEMON

Even the last browned, squashed bit of last year's preserved lemon should be used. Scrape off any mold. Puree it in a food processor, then add yogurt for a lovely bright sauce, or olive oil for a vinaigrette, or use it as a fish or chicken or tofu marinade, or add a spoonful to broth to make it lemony.

Use preserved lemon brine that has been emptied of lemons in place of vinegar in any vinaigrette like Basic Vinaigrette (p. 376), omitting the salt because preserved lemon brine is salty.

SAUERKRAUT

At a restaurant called Kitty's, in Hudson, New York, egg sandwiches are served topped with sauerkraut at no extra charge. This small luxury makes the experience feel especially considered. I recommend adding the end of a jar of sauerkraut to egg breakfast sandwiches, along with a judicious layer of mayonnaise. Or make:

CAMINO SAUERKRAUT SALAD *(1 hr, but mostly waiting)*
1 cup very thinly sliced cabbage, salt, 1 tbsp neutral oil (peanut or grapeseed), 1 tsp any color mustard seeds, 1 small clove garlic (sliced), 1 cup well-drained sauerkraut.

In a bowl, season the cabbage lightly with salt. Mix well and set aside for 45 min or so. Meanwhile, heat a small pan. Add the oil and mustard seeds and cook until they just begin to pop, keeping the heat on low and covering it if they threaten to escape. Remove the pan from the heat and add the garlic, stirring and swirling to keep it from burning, then pour the seasoned oil over the waiting cabbage. Add the sauerkraut and mix well. Taste for salt and adjust. Eat. Very good with sausages.

SAUERKRAUT QUESADILLA *(5 min)*
2 corn tortillas, ½ cup grated cheddar or similar cheese, 1 tbsp sauerkraut, 1 tbsp roughly chopped fresh herbs (cilantro, basil, mint, dill, parsley), roughly chopped boiled egg or freshly scrambled egg (optional). *Optional for serving:* hot sauce, sliced avocado.

Heat a heavy-bottomed pan over low heat. Add a tortilla, then top with half the cheese, the sauerkraut, herbs, egg (if using), lightly salting the egg. Add the remaining cheese and the second tortilla. Cover and let cook 1–2 min. Uncover and if the cheese is melted, flip; if not, re-cover and cook until it has, then flip. Cook on the second side until the cheeses sizzle into the pan. Remove. If desired, serve with hot sauce.

SAUERKRAUT BRINE

CAMINO SAUERKRAUT BEET SOUP *(2–3 hr, but mostly chilling)*
3 tbsp olive oil, 2 cups combined chopped onion and fennel (or celery), ½ tsp salt plus to taste, 3 cloves garlic (thinly sliced), 1–2 cups very thinly sliced cabbage, 2 cups finely chopped peeled roasted beets, 1½ cups sauerkraut, ¼ cup sauerkraut brine. *For garnish:* Greek yogurt (or crème fraîche or sour cream), chopped fresh herbs (parsley, dill, celery leaf, or a combination), freshly ground black pepper.

Heat a medium pot. Add the olive oil, onion-fennel mixture, and salt, and cook until the vegetables have begun to soften, about 5 min. Add the garlic and cabbage and cook until they've wilted and softened, another 3–5 min. Add the beets, sauerkraut, and sauerkraut brine. Add water to cover, enough to leave this swimmy. Bring to a boil, then reduce to a simmer and cook until it all seems unified, about 5 min. Chill the soup to cold. Eat garnished with Greek yogurt, herbs, and black pepper. Good with garlic-rubbed toast!

SAUERKRAUT MICHELADA *(1 min)*
¼–⅓ cup sauerkraut brine, beer.

Combine brine with a can of beer. Enjoy!

TSUKEMONO

Tsukemono are one of my favorite additions to rice. Warm a big bowl of rice. Lay a few slices of cured salmon or leftover or canned fish or avocado on top. Add toasted nori, then pickles, then sprinkle toasted sesame seeds or furikake over it all.

VEGETABLES À LA GRECQUE BRINE

The liquid from vegetables à la grecque can be used for another batch of vegetables à la grecque. Slice 1 to 4 different vegetables. Bring the liquid to a boil and cook each vegetable on its own until just tender and easy to pierce with a sharp knife. Remove with a handheld sieve to a tray to cool. Store layered in a jar in their liquid. The liquid is also great for making Fish in Saor (p. 277).

ZHA CAI

Any zha cai, like any tsukemono, make a delicacy of a bowl of rice.

HOW TO FIND REASON

Drinks

If all be true that I do think, There are five reasons
we should drink: Good wine, a friend, or being dry,
Or lest we should be by and by, Or any other reason why.

—*Henry Aldrich*

In *Simple French Food*, Richard Olney has a recipe for *Soupe à la Bourguignonne* (Red Wine Soup) made of pork fat, butter, onions, flour, water, bread, herbs, and almost an entire bottle of red wine. There's another for a "typical Bordelais tourain": of fat, onions, salt, tomatoes, sugar, boiling water, stale bread, and dry white wine. "A native," Olney writes, "may first eat his sopped bread crust, empty out his (red) wine glass into the soup, and drink the rest from the soup plate, a performance known as *faire chabrol*. I've never made either soup but I like how appreciative they are of the things I like best: humble ingredients, wine, and making a festive to do.

The most straightforward way to use leftover wine is to cook *in* it. Wine and broth is an unparalleled combination for braising tougher cuts of meat (see Braised Meat, p. 298). If you have a lot of leftover wine, it's also reasonable to cook in wine alone, with occasional pours of broth or water to keep the flavor balanced. Boeuf à la Mode (p. 458) is of this lineage, as are coq au vin and coq au vin blanc and coq au vin jaune—the last slow-cooked in the golden wine of Jura, which leaves the bird tasting as if it woke up drunk. I make a version called Chicken in Leftover Wine (p. 457), which combines them all.

What sort of wine is best for cooking what? Father Robert Farrar Capon, whom I listen to on cooking but obey absolutely on drinking, wrote the most useful rule: "White for lighter meats, red for heavier, but don't make a fetish of it." *Can wine be too good for cooking?* Olney says yes. "One may respectfully find a place in the kitchen for a great wine only if heat never comes into contact with it." *Can wine be too bad?* Olney says if you wouldn't drink it, don't cook with it. The writer Daniel Gritzer says that a wine that starts out heavy and overly sweet stays that way in the finished dish, but that a wine that was *once* good makes a good finished dish. When a bottle of wine has been open too long, its alcohol oxidizes. Its alcohol is also what disappears in cooking. I add once-good wine to any braise or stew with impunity.

It can also help to remember that every liquid has been used for cooking at some point. There are soups of tea, and sauces of rum, and desserts made of anything that has quenched our thirst.

AMARETTO

AMARETTO CREPES *(1 hr, but mostly waiting)*
3 tbsp butter (melted and cooled for a few min) plus for cooking, 1 tbsp amaretto, 1 cup milk, 2 eggs (lightly beaten), 1 cup (120 g) all-purpose flour, ½ tsp salt, 1 tbsp sugar.

Whisk the melted butter, amaretto, milk, eggs, flour, salt, and sugar until completely smooth and the consistency of heavy cream. Refrigerate, covered, 45 min–1 hr. Heat a small skillet. Add butter and cook crepes, one at a time, using a scant ¼ cup of batter per crepe. It may take a few to get it all right. Cover as you cook these. Delicious dusted with powdered sugar, or with whipped cream or with cream whipped with a tiny bit of additional amaretto, or any other way.

APPLE CIDER

APPLE CIDER POUND CAKE *(1 hr)*
Butter and flour for the loaf pan, ½ cup (60 g) all-purpose flour, 1 tsp baking powder, ¼ tsp salt, ½ tsp ground cinnamon, 7 tbsp (3½ oz/100 g) melted butter, 1 cup (200 g) sugar, 3 tbsp sour cream or whole-milk yogurt, 3 large eggs, ½ cup apple cider or juice, 1 tsp vanilla extract.

Heat the oven to 350°F. Butter a 9 × 5-inch loaf pan, then lightly flour it, tapping out the excess. In a medium bowl, whisk together the flour, baking powder, salt, and cinnamon. In a second bowl, combine the melted butter, sugar, and sour cream or yogurt. Whisk in the eggs, apple cider or juice, and vanilla. Add the dry ingredients to the wet ingredients, stirring to combine. Pour into the prepared pan and bake until a skewer emerges almost clean, 35–40 min. (Adapted from Crazy for Crust website)

APPLE CIDER GLAZE FOR CAKE *(5 min)*
⅓ cup apple cider or juice, 2 tbsp sugar.

In a small saucepan, bring the cider or juice and sugar to a boil. Simmer a moment or two until glossy and syrupy, then remove from the heat. Glaze pound cake with it, or use it as syrup on pancakes!

DRINKS

This next is best to do directly in a pan where you've just cooked pork chops or another meat that has left some lovely browned bits to scrape up.

APPLE CIDER PAN GRAVY *(10 min)*

½ cup broth, ½ cup apple cider, ¼ cup heavy cream, salt.

In a skillet that has just had meat cooked in it with browned bits for deglazing, add the broth and cider or juice and bring to a boil. Let cook about 5 min. Add the cream and cook to a thin gravy. Add salt to taste and gravy-ify.

APPLE CIDER VINAIGRETTE *(12 min)*

1 shallot (finely minced), ¼ tsp salt plus to taste, 2 tbsp apple cider or juice, 1 tsp smooth or grainy Dijon mustard, ⅓–½ cup olive oil.

In a small bowl, combine the shallot, salt, cider or juice, and mustard and let sit 10 min. Whisk in the olive oil. Taste on a leaf for salt and adjust.

A little bit of apple cider can also be used in Braised Meat (p. 298).

BEER

Beer is commonly used in batters, but I use any leftover beer, whether flat or fizzed, for up to 2 cups of liquid in Braised Meat (p. 298).

BLOODY MARY MIX

BLOODY MARY MICHELADA *(5 min)*

Ground chile powder, salt, 1 lime (halved), a few tbsp Bloody Mary mix, hot sauce (optional), 1 can or bottle light beer.

Combine chile powder and salt on a plate. Rub the rim of a tall glass with a lime half, then place it rim-side down on the plate to line the rim with chile salt. Pour a few tbsp Bloody Mary mix into the glass. Squeeze in the juice of the remaining lime half and add hot sauce (if using). Fill with ice, then add beer. Finish with any lime juice. Stir and drink.

SIMPLEST CARNITAS (*6 hr to overnight*)
3 lb boneless pork shoulder, salt, 2 tbsp neutral oil, 1½ cups Coca-Cola,
4–6 bay leaves, 4 cloves garlic (smashed and peeled). *For serving:* corn tortillas,
salsa(s) of choice, sliced radishes, sliced cabbage, cilantro, chopped onion.

Cut the pork into 2–3-inch chunks and salt them heavily—at least twice as
heavily as feels right. Cover and refrigerate for at least 3 hr and up to overnight. Heat a heavy Dutch oven. Add the oil, then brown the pork, in batches
if needed, over medium heat, to deep caramel. Remove the pork to a plate
once browned. Add the Coke, scraping up all the browned bits from the pot.
Return the pork to the pot and add additional broth or water as needed to
cover the meat by about three quarters. Add the bay leaves and garlic. Bring
to a boil, then reduce to the lowest possible heat and cook, partially covered,
until the meat is spoon tender, 3–4 hr. Remove the pork from the liquid and
shred. Return pork to a heavy skillet to caramelize. If desired, add some of its
braising liquid once it has. Reserve the remaining braising liquid for a future
soup or braise. Eat as tacos, topped with salsas, vegetables, cilantro, and onion.

Or use Coca-Cola, regardless of flatness or age, for up to 2 cups of the liquid in
Braised Meat (p. 298).

COFFEE

LEFTOVER COFFEE BROWNIES (*1 hr*)
Butter for the baking pan, 4 eggs, 8 tbsp (4 oz/113 g) melted butter, 1½ cups
(300 g) sugar, ¼ cup brewed coffee, 1 tbsp vanilla extract, 1 tsp salt, ¾ cup
unsweetened cocoa powder, 1 cup (120 g) all-purpose flour, 1 cup bittersweet
chocolate chips (70% cacao), powdered sugar (optional).

Heat the oven to 350°F. Butter a 9 × 9-inch or 8 × 8-inch baking pan. In a
large bowl, whisk the eggs, melted butter, sugar, coffee, vanilla, and salt. Sift
in the cocoa powder and add the flour, whisk to combine. Stir in the chips.
Pour the batter into the prepared pan and bake until just set, 35–45 min. Let
cool to room temperature before serving. If desired, dust with powdered sugar.
(Adapted from Billy Parisi's website)

DRINKS

Are you really going to make an entire mousse to avoid tossing a little coffee? It's as good a reason as any. This contains raw eggs.

MAIDA HEATTER'S CHOCOLATE MOUSSE (*overnight, but mostly waiting*)
8 oz semisweet chocolate (or bittersweet or unsweetened, depending on your palate; chopped), 2–4 tbsp brewed coffee, 8 eggs (separated), ⅓ cup (65 g) granulated sugar, 1 tsp vanilla extract, tiny pinch of salt.

Place the chopped chocolate in the top of a small double boiler. Set over low heat and bring the water to a low simmer. Add the coffee and cook over low heat, whisking occasionally, until the chocolate is almost melted. Remove from the heat and continue to stir until smooth. Let cool slightly. In a stand mixer fitted with the whisk, beat the egg yolks at high speed until they are pale, thick, and lemon-colored, about 5 min. Gradually add the sugar and continue to beat until very thick, another 5 min. Reduce the speed to low and add the vanilla and cooled chocolate, scraping to combine. Transfer to a medium bowl. Wash the whisk and mixer bowl, then beat the egg whites with the salt until just past soft peaks. In two or three additions, gently fold half the egg whites into the chocolate, then fold the chocolate mixture into the remaining whites. Refrigerate the mousse overnight, then eat.

VIETNAMESE COFFEE ICE POPS (*6 hr to overnight*)
2 cups brewed coffee, ⅔ cup sweetened condensed milk.

Combine, freeze in ice pop molds, and eat for a sweet energy boost. (Adapted from DavidLebovitz.com)

DAIQUIRI MIX

Leftover daiquiri mix can be turned into ice pops. Combine with an equal amount of unsweetened juice or coconut milk, pour into molds, and freeze.

EGGNOG

Substitute eggnog for cream in Bread Pudding (p. 182), decreasing the quantity of sugar, as well, so you don't suffer sugar shock.

FRUIT JUICE

Any fruit juice can be frozen into ice cubes. Use juice cubes to improve a fruity cocktail or a can of seltzer. A single ice cube tray can host an array of different juice cubes. If you have several, blend quickly in a blender to have immediate sorbet/shaved ice/granita.

GREEN TEA LEAVES, USED

FAKE BUT GOOD LAPHET DRESSING *(several days, but mostly waiting)*
¾–1 cup used green tea leaves, 1 clove garlic (chopped), ½-inch piece fresh ginger (chopped), ¼ tsp salt, 3 tbsp peanut or sunflower oil, 1 tsp distilled white vinegar or lemon juice.

Leave the tea leaves to dry on a tray for several days. In a food processor, combine the dried tea, garlic, ginger, and salt and blend. Slowly add the oil and vinegar or lemon juice. Use as tea leaf dressing (Salad with Tea Leaf Dressing, recipe follows).

SALAD WITH TEA LEAF DRESSING *(10 min if the dressing is already made)*
2–3 cups finely julienned romaine lettuce, 2 tbsp Fake but Good Laphet Dressing (recipe above), 1 tbsp fried garlic slices, 1 tbsp fried yellow split peas, 1 tbsp chopped toasted peanuts, 1 tbsp toasted sunflower seeds, 1 tbsp toasted sesame seeds, salt, a wedge of lemon or lime for squeezing, 1 diced tomato (optional).

In a bowl, toss together the lettuce, dressing, fried garlic slices, fried split peas, peanuts, sunflower seeds, and sesame seeds. Taste for dressing and salt and adjust. Add a squeeze of lemon or lime and top with tomato (if using).

DRINKS

HOT CHOCOLATE

Once refrigerated, hot chocolate becomes chocolate milk, and should be drunk as such. Or, freeze leftover hot chocolate for frozen hot chocolate or hot chocolate ice pops, both delightful contradictions. Or make:

HOT CHOCOLATE WHIPPED CREAM (*10 min*)
½–1 cup heavy cream, 1 tsp powdered sugar, 2–3 tbsp hot chocolate (cold).

In a cold bowl or a stand mixer, whip the cream with the powdered sugar to soft peaks. Whip in the leftover hot chocolate. Voilà. This is good on ice cream or on fresh hot chocolate or on coffee or on its own.

ICED TEA

TEA-BRINED CHICKEN OR RIBS (*overnight, mostly waiting*)
4 cups iced tea (sweetened or unsweetened), ¼ cup salt, 2–3 sprigs rosemary, 6 cloves garlic (peeled and smashed), 1 lemon (zested and thinly sliced), 3–4 lb whole chicken or rack ribs.

In a pot, bowl, or container large enough to fit the meat, mix together the tea, salt, rosemary, garlic, lemon zest, and lemon slices. Add the meat, cover, and refrigerate for 24 hr. Remove and cook. For the chicken, roast it whole following the recipe for Pickle-Brined Roast Chicken (p. 438) or cut it into serving pieces and roast or grill. For the ribs, first braise or slow roast them, and then grill.

A variation is to use tea-brined chicken in your favorite recipe for fried chicken. Or make:

ARNOLD PALMER (*3 min*)
1 cup sweetened iced tea, 2 cups lemonade.

Combine and drink on ice. This is endlessly variable.

SPIRITED ARNOLD PALMER (*3 min*)
⅔ cup iced tea, ¾–1 cup sparkling water or seltzer, 1 shot limoncello.

Combine and drink on ice.

MARBLED TEA EGGS *(24 hr, but mostly waiting)*

8 eggs, 2 cups iced tea, 2 tsp minced fresh ginger, 2 scallions (chopped), ½ cup soy sauce, ½ tsp Chinese 5-spice powder, 3 star anise, 1 cinnamon stick.

In a saucepan, cover the eggs with water. Bring to a boil, then turn off the heat, cover, and leave for 7 min. Drain, crack gently all over but do not peel and place the eggs in a 1-quart canning jar or similar. Add the iced tea, ginger, scallions, soy sauce, 5-spice powder, star anise, and cinnamon to the empty saucepan. Bring to a simmer, then remove from the heat. Pour the hot liquid over the eggs, adding water if needed to cover. Refrigerate in the liquid and eat a day or up to a week later. Use any remaining liquid for another batch, or in Braised Meat (p. 298). (Adapted from Yan Can Cook website)

MILKY ICED TEA *(5 min)*

1½ cups iced tea, 3 tbsp heavy cream or more to taste, maple syrup to taste.

Combine, shake well, and drink on ice. Good with a mint sprig.

KVASS

OKROSHKA WITH KVASS *(2 hr)*

2 cups kvass (chilled), 2 cups water or kefir (chilled), 2 large potatoes (peeled, cooked, and finely cubed), 4 hard-boiled eggs (cubed), 1 long cucumber (finely chopped), 5–6 radishes (finely chopped), ½ tsp salt plus to taste, 1 cup sour cream, 2 scallions (thinly sliced), 1 bunch dill (chopped), ¼ cup chopped parsley (optional).

Combine all of the ingredients and mix well. Chill for at least 2 hr. Taste for salt and adjust.

LASSI

Small amounts of leftover lassi make a perfect beginning for another cool, yogurt-based drink. Pour it into the blender. Add yogurt and anything else you want, and blend. Chill before drinking, or drink on ice.

DRINKS

LEMONADE

Combine leftover lemonade with sweetened or unsweetened iced tea and drink. Or combine with coconut milk, or juice, and freeze in ice pop molds.

MATÉ

There may be no caffeinated beverage more delicious than cold leftover maté, sweetened with maple syrup, combined with at least as much whole milk, well-shaken and poured over ice. Plan to be focused or at least awake for the 4–5 hr after drinking.

MULLED WINE

If for some reason you don't want to just reheat mulled wine and drink it, put it in a pot along with dried figs. Heat just to a boil, then let them sit off the heat until plump. Eat over yogurt or ice cream.

SAKE

FISH NO NITSUKE (*30 min*)
¼ cup sake, 1 tbsp mirin or seasoned rice vinegar, 1 tbsp sugar, ¼ tsp salt, 1–2 tsp julienned or chopped fresh ginger, 1–2 scallions (optional; white and light-green only, slivered lengthwise), ½ lb white fish (cod, halibut, haddock, or similar, in two or more portions).

In a pot big enough to fit the fish in a single layer, combine ¼ cup water, the sake, mirin or rice vinegar, sugar, and salt and bring to a simmer. Add the ginger and scallions (if using) and cook on the lowest possible simmer. Add the fish and then something that can sit directly on the fish to keep it submerged: like an otoshibuta (drop lid) or a gratin or other dish that fits inside the pot. Cook until just opaque, 6–7 min for 1-inch-thick fillets, checking earlier if you feel anxious. Remove the fish to a plate, then simmer the sauce until slightly thickened, 30 sec–1 min. Eat on hot rice.

SMOOTHIE, ANY

Any smoothie that isn't being drunk should be frozen into ice pops. If you don't have enough smoothie to fill even one ice pop mold, use an ice cube tray.

TEA

Put it in the fridge and drink with the milk of your choice and maple syrup on ice.

TEA LEAVES, USED

Use in Fake but Good Laphet Dressing (p. 453).

WINE

CHICKEN IN LEFTOVER WINE *(2 hr)*
Salt, 5 bone-in, skin-on chicken thighs, 2 tbsp olive oil, ½ cup chopped onion (scallion, or leek, or a combination), ½ cup chopped carrot, 1 cup chopped fennel, a few cloves garlic (smashed), bouquet garni (thyme, bay, parsley stems, rosemary, or any combination), 3–4 slices bacon (sliced or chopped), 1½ cups wine, ½–1 lb mushrooms (optional; stemmed and chopped), a handful of chopped parsley or celery leaves (optional).

Salt the chicken very well and leave at room temperature for 15 min, or in the refrigerator overnight. Add 1 tbsp of the olive oil to an unheated Dutch oven. Turn on the burner. Working in batches, add the chicken skin-side down and cook until the skin browns and crisps, 5–10 min, removing the pieces to a plate as they brown. When all the chicken is out, add the onion, carrot, and fennel, stirring well to scrape up the browned bits. Cook over medium heat until the vegetables soften, 5–10 min. Add the garlic, bouquet garni, bacon, and wine. Continue to scrape any browned bits. Bring to a boil, then reduce to a simmer. Meanwhile, heat the oven to 325°F. Once the wine is simmering, return the chicken to the pan, nestling it in, skin-side up. Cook, uncovered, in the oven, until the meat is spoon tender, 40 min–1 hr. Meanwhile, if you're including mushrooms, heat a pan over medium-high heat. Add the remaining

1 tbsp of olive oil and mushrooms and cook, stirring occasionally, until browned and cooked through, 5–10 min. Season with salt to taste. When the chicken is done, add the mushrooms to the pot and stir through. Just before serving, put the entire pot under the broiler to crisp the skin. Shower with herbs (if using), just before eating.

BOEUF À LA MODE WITH GREMOLATA *(5 hr to overnight, but mostly waiting)*
Salt, 3–4 lb piece braising meat (chuck roast), ½ tsp ground nutmeg, ½ tsp ground allspice, 2 tbsp olive oil, ½ cup chopped onion, ½ cup chopped carrot, ½ cup chopped celery, 1 tbsp tomato paste, 2 bay leaves, 2–3 cloves garlic (peeled), 1 bouquet garni (a few sprigs of thyme, a handful of parsley stems), ½ cup dried mushrooms (optional; porcini or shiitake), 3–4 cups wine, 1 pig's foot (optional; or beef or veal knuckle), 2 to 4 cups meat stock (or vegetable stock or dashi), Gremolata (p. 116).

Salt the beef heavily (about three times as heavily as you think you should), then rub more or less evenly with the nutmeg and allspice. Cover and leave at room temperature for 1 hr or refrigerate overnight. Bring to room temperature before cooking. Heat the oven to 300°F. Heat a heavy Dutch oven over medium heat. Add the olive oil and meat and brown on all sides, 10–12 min. Remove to a plate. Add the onion, carrot, celery, and tomato paste to the pot, scraping the bottom with a wooden spoon. When the browned bits have come up, add the bay leaves, garlic, bouquet garni, mushrooms (if using), and wine. Bring to a boil over high heat and cook until reduced by half. Add the browned beef and pig's foot (if using). Add enough stock to come halfway up the roast's sides. Cover and place in the oven. Cook until totally tender, 3–4 hr. Make the gremolata. Remove the roast, strain the broth, then skim the fat the best you can. Taste the broth. If it is acidic, add a little more beef stock. Taste for salt and adjust. If the roast was tied, remove any twine and return the meat to the sauce until ready to serve. Just before eating, warm the roast in its broth, then remove to a cutting board and slice thickly. Serve on a platter, with a little broth poured over and more available at the table, and gremolata heavily sprinkled over everything.

WINE VINEGAR *(1–3 months, but mostly waiting)*
1 bottle wine, ½ tsp hydrogen peroxide (if the wine contains sulfites), 1 cup unchlorinated water, ½ cup raw cider vinegar (unfiltered and unpasteurized) or a vinegar mother.

Put the wine into a big sterilized jar, adding the hydrogen peroxide if the wine has sulfites. Stir in the water with a spoon. Add the raw vinegar or mother and stir well. Cover the jar with a piece of cheesecloth and secure with a rubber band and place somewhere at room temperature. Stir twice a day for 3 days, then re-cover with the cheesecloth and leave for a month. Taste, and if you like it, put it in bottles and refrigerate. If you don't like it yet, leave it, tasting once a week until you do. If you want to keep making vinegar, you can bottle half of yours and replace it with the same amount of wine and do it all again. (Adapted from *Homebrewed Vinegar* by Kirsten Shockey)

A little bit of wine can also be substituted for vinegar in vinaigrette.

DRINKS

HOW TO HAVE
SOMETHING TO EAT
Snacks

Bring salad or sausage or scrapple
A berry or even a beet.
Bring an oyster, an egg, or an apple,
As long as it's something to eat.

—*Ogden Nash*

My most useful observation on leftover snacks is: Take it apart and it will look more promising. It is best to refrain from storing the gussied up vegetables called *crudités* together, because that imprints them in your mind as a neglected appetizer. (The exception is carrots and celery. Add half an onion to them, and they're mirepoix. Chop carrots and celery together now, and then chop a bit of onion and cook it all in olive oil, then freeze it for when you need it.) Store leftover olives in their own container, where they will quietly suggest Olive Tapenade (p. 393). Do the same with the radishes, because alone, they will inspire tacos or tortilla soup.

I apply the same principle to snacks that come home uneaten in lunchboxes. Ants on a log are easier to repurpose when the ants have been removed to their container, and the peanut butter or cream cheese to its own, for tomorrow's sandwich. Even cracker sandwiches can be disassembled if you have the verve. I only sometimes do.

It is worth noting that store-bought snacks that might seem silly to save—broken chips at the bottom of a bag or a bowl, sweet cereal left in a box—can be employed for the virtues that make them fun in the first place. They are crunchy and salty (or sweet) and they last a long time. Potato chip crumbs and smashed cereal bits and similar that are past their prime for snacking find their utility as crunchy bits of seasoning for future snacks . . .

ANTS ON A LOG

Disassemble and deal with each bit on its own: 1) Eat or return the raisins to their box. 2) Put the peanut butter or cream cheese in a little container (labeled) to use on a sandwich the next day. 3) Rinse off the celery and use it in a mirepoix (see p. 6).

BOBA TEA PEARLS

Tapioca balls from bubble tea can be used again, in another cup of boba tea. They are fine at room temperature in a simple syrup (p. 103) or can be stored in simple syrup in the fridge for several days to a week.

CEREAL

BOTTOM OF THE BOX OF CEREAL BARS *(10 min)*
Butter for the pan, about 7 oz marshmallows, 2 tbsp butter, 1 tsp salt, 4 cups mixed cereal.

Butter a small to medium baking pan. In a saucepan, combine the marshmallows, butter, and salt and melt. Add the cereal, mix through, pour into the prepared pan, and cool. Cut or tear into bars. This can also be made with a combination of cereal ends and crushed pretzel remains! (Adapted from *Life with the Crust Off* website)

The ends of any wholesome honey or nutty cereal can also be used in Granola Cookies (p. 487).

CHEETOS

FRIED RICE CHEETO SALAD *(15 min)*
1 tbsp olive oil, ¼ cup thinly sliced onion, ¼ tsp salt plus to taste, ½–1 cup leftover cooked rice, a handful of Cheetos, 1 Boiled Egg (p. 139, quartered or sliced) or scrambled egg, a big handful of salad greens. *For serving*: raita, yogurt, or spicy mayonnaise.

Heat a skillet over medium heat. Add the oil, onion and salt and cook until just beginning to soften, 2–3 min. Add the rice, spread out in the pan to fry, letting the grains get fried and crisp. Add the Cheetos and mix through. Add the egg, then remove from the heat. Put the salad greens in a bowl. Spoon the fried rice on top. Drizzle with raita or yogurt or spicy mayonnaise and eat.

CHIPS

The end of a bag of chips can be used as salt. They can be used as a variation on furikake, or added to the Shrimp Shell and Potato Chip Furikake (p. 290). Or make:

CHIP-CRUSTED PORK CHOPS (*3 hr 45 min, but mostly waiting*)
Salt, 2 bone-in pork chops (about 1 lb each), 2 tbsp Gremolata (p. 116), 2¼–2½ cups smashed potato or corn chips, 2 tbsp mayonnaise, ½ tbsp Dijon mustard, 1 tbsp olive oil or other neutral oil.

Salt the chops very well and leave them, covered, in the refrigerator or at room temperature for 3 hr. In a shallow bowl, combine the gremolata and chips. Heat the oven to 375°F. In a small bowl, combine the mayonnaise and mustard and smear it over the chops. Roll in the chip-gremolata combination. Heat a heavy-bottomed ovenproof skillet over medium heat. Add the oil and brown the chops on all sides, about 10 min total. Place the skillet in the oven and cook to the doneness you like. How long it takes will vary with the thickness of your chops, but likely between 20–30 min. Once it's cooked, broil briefly if needed to complete golden browning. Let rest 5–10 min, slice, and serve.

CHIP COOKIES (*30 min*)
2 sticks (8 oz/225 g) room-temperature butter, ½ cup (100 g) sugar, ½ tsp vanilla extract, a scant ½ tsp salt, 2 cups (240 g) all-purpose flour, ½ cup smashed potato or corn chips.

Heat the oven to 350°F. Line two baking sheets with parchment paper. In a bowl, with an electric mixer, cream the butter and ¼ cup (50 g) of the sugar until fully combined and fluffy. Beat in the vanilla and salt. Add the flour and mix until combined. Add the chips and mix until just integrated. Roll into little balls the size of an unshelled walnut. Roll each in the remaining ¼ cup (50 g) sugar. Flatten slightly and bake, at least 1 inch apart, 12–15 min. Cool on a rack. (Adapted from Smitten Kitchen website)

DORITOS

DORILOCOS SALAD *(15 min)*
¾ cup shredded cabbage or jicama, ¼ cup salted peanuts, a squeeze of lime juice, a scrape of chile powder (Miguelito powder, achar masala, or other chile powder), hot sauce, ¼ cup Doritos, a ladleful warm beans (optional).

In a bowl, toss together the cabbage or jicama, the peanuts, lime juice, chili powder, and hot sauce to taste, and let sit for 10 min. Add the Doritos, mix through, then add the beans, if using, and eat!

Or, combine the very end of a bag of Doritos with lime zest to make a delicious seasoning salt! Sprinkle on cooked eggs, or rice, or noodles, or congee, or oatmeal.

ENERGY BARS

I don't think these start out particularly good. The bright side is that they don't end up much worse than they started. If you're hungry enough to need an energy bar, you're hungry enough to eat an old one. Save them for those occasions by wrapping leftovers well in wax paper and leaving them in whatever backpack you're wearing; they will await you there, basically eternally.

FRITOS

Use in place of Cheetos in Fried Rice Cheeto Salad (p. 465) or in place of Doritos in Dorilocos Salad (recipe above).

POPCORN

Stale popcorn can be recrisped. Spread it onto a baking sheet and bake at 250°F until it seems dry and crisp, about 5 min.

Or make:

POPCORN OAT WAFERS *(20 min)*
2 cups stale popcorn, ½ cup rolled oats, ½ tsp ground cinnamon, ¼ tsp salt, ¼ tsp baking powder, ¼ cup olive or vegetable oil, 3 tbsp maple syrup.

Heat the oven to 325°F. Line a sheet pan with parchment paper. In a food processor, combine the popcorn, oats, cinnamon, salt, and baking powder. Add the oil and maple syrup and pulse to combine for 45 sec or so, then scrape down the bowl and process again until the mixture has the appearance and texture of wet sand. Pour onto the lined pan. Divide it into 12 little piles, which will seem sandy, and not cookie like. With damp hands, flatten each pile into rounds ⅛ inch thick, having faith that eventually they'll come together . . . just not yet. Bake until they are just barely starting to brown around the edges, 8–10 min. Carefully remove the sheet pan from the oven and let them cool completely on the sheet. They won't cohere into wafers until then. Then remove one by one and eat, or store in an airtight container. (Adapted from Kitchn website)

POPCORN TREATS *(2 hr, but mostly waiting)*
Butter for the pan, 3 tbsp butter, 10 oz marshmallows, 6 cups stale popcorn. *Additional flavoring:* a drizzle of maple syrup, honey, or any other flavoring you like.

Butter a 9 × 13-inch pan. In a large pot or pan, melt the butter over low heat. Add the marshmallows and stir until completely melted. Remove from the heat. Add the popcorn and any additional flavoring. Mix to combine. Pour and press into the prepared pan. Cool completely, cut into squares, and eat. These can also be rolled into balls.

SAVORY POPCORN CRUMBLE *(40 min)*
2 cups stale popcorn, ½ cup rolled oats, ¼ cup sesame seeds, ¼ cup olive oil, salt.

In a food processor, pulse the popcorn and oats to a crumble. Heat the oven to 350°F. In a bowl, combine the popcorn-oats mixture with the sesame seeds, olive oil, and salt to taste. Spread it on a baking sheet. Bake, stirring occasionally, until crisp, about 30 min. Good on oatmeal or porridge or sprinkled over cooked vegetables or a salad or anywhere else you might use a savory granola.

Or make popcorn-flavored whipped cream to put on top of ice cream or pecan pie. In a pot, combine the heavy cream and popcorn, and bring to a boil. Remove from the heat and let sit while it cools. Strain and refrigerate until well chilled, then whip!

There are also people who add stale popcorn to scrambled eggs. I'm not one of them . . . yet.

PORK RINDS

I rarely find myself with leftover pork rinds because they are one of my three favorite snacks—alongside potato chips and corn nuts. But if you have some, try this salad, inspired by a chicharrón I once ate at Cosme, in New York City.

PORK RIND SALAD (*15 min*)
1 clove garlic, salt, 2 tsp lime juice plus to taste, ½ very thinly sliced kohlrabi (or fennel), 4 cups mixed soft fresh herb leaves (any combination of parsley, basil, cilantro, celery leaf, arugula, sorrel, purslane, tarragon, or frisée), 2 tsp olive oil plus to taste, up to 1 cup pork rinds.

Pound the garlic to a paste with a little salt and transfer to a bowl. Add the lime juice and let sit for 10 min. Add the kohlrabi and mix through. Mix in the herbs and olive oil. Taste for salt and adjust. When it is all well-seasoned, add the pork rinds, another squeeze of lime juice, and olive oil if needed, and eat! Try this salad with other fried fat, like salmon or chicken skin.

PRETZELS

Stale dry pretzels can be ground and used as bread crumbs. Pretzel dust makes a perfect lunchtime finishing salt for rice and beans. And staling soft pretzels can be turned into:

PRETZEL CROSTINI *(10–15 min)*

Pretzels, olive oil, any additional spices you want (za'atar or chaat masala, or five spice powder, etc.).

Heat the oven to 375°F. Slice leftover pretzels into ¼–½-inch–thick slices. On a sheet pan, lay in a single layer and drizzle heavily with olive oil. Toast until crisp, 10–15 min. Sprinkle with any additional spices. Let cool slightly and eat.

HOW TO TAKE
YOUR MEDICINE

Sweets

Sugar is important, whether as food or as a medicine.

—*Jean Anthelme Brillat-Savarin,*
The Physiology of Taste

I agree with M. F. K. Fisher that "probably one of the best ends to a supper is nothing at all." Except for a sip of Scotch or amaro or grappa or another half-glass of red wine, when everyone else has moved on to their cake. Or some good dark chocolate, broken into uneven pieces. Or a half of a golden russet apple in fall or a fig or piece of canary melon in summer . . .

But I know I'm basically alone. I bake desserts for those who find dinners incomplete without them. And I like coming up with solutions for what's left—because in my house, there *is* such a thing as leftover pie and cake and cookies. And each will become a Twizzard or trifle or pudding or cluster or crunch. I don't wonder whether what I make will be beautiful and arresting because it won't. It will slump, be soaked in liqueur, be dolloped with freshly whipped cream, and by the time it emerges from my kitchen again, it will be homely and doubly loved.

Here are my most variable uses for leftover sweets, plus butter cookies and brownies, which are essential:

TIPSY TRIFLE
¾ cup heavy cream, 2 tbsp fresh ricotta cheese, 2 cups cubed cake (no frosting or filling), ½ cup best possible dessert wine (Muscat de Beaumes-de-Venise, or Sauternes, or something similar).

In a chilled bowl, whip the cream and ricotta to just past soft peaks. In a glass bowl, make layers in this order: one-third of the cake cubes, one-third amount of the wine drizzled over the cake, one-third of the whipped cream. Repeat this layering a second time. Make a final layer with the remaining cake and final drizzle of wine. Reserve the rest of the cream. Cover and refrigerate or place in the freezer for 3 hr. Serve cold, top with the reserved whipped cream.

CAKE CRUMB MUFFINS

Butter for the muffin tin, ⅔ cup cake crumbs (no frosting or filling), 4 tbsp (2 oz/56 g) room-temperature butter, ⅓ cup brown sugar, Basic Muffin Batter (p. 103).

Heat the oven to 350°F. Butter a muffin tin. In a bowl, combine the crumbs, butter, and brown sugar by hand to make a crumble. Make the muffin batter and fill the muffin cups halfway with batter. Top generously with the cake crumble. Bake until risen and set, 20–25 min. Cool 5 min in the tin before moving to a cooling rack.

This is admittedly insane, but it delights:

CANDY ICE CUBES

Jelly beans, Sour Patch Kids, etc.

Place 1 piece of candy in each ice cube mold of a tray. Fill the remaining space with water. Freeze. Use when you are in the mood to be very very nice, or at least thought of that way.

A GREAT POST-HALLOWEEN TREAT

Butter for the baking pan, 1 cup brown sugar, 8 tbsp (4 oz/113 g) salted or unsalted melted butter, 2 eggs, 2 tsp vanilla extract, 1¾ cups (210 g) all-purpose flour, 2 tsp baking powder, ½ tsp salt, 1–2 cups chopped or crushed candy bar (any kind).

Heat the oven to 350°F. Butter a 9 × 13-inch baking pan. In a bowl, whisk together the brown sugar and melted butter. Whisk in the eggs and vanilla. In a second bowl, combine the flour, baking powder, and salt. Gradually add the flour mixture to the butter mixture. When combined, add the candy and stir through. Scrape the batter into the prepared pan and bake until a skewer emerges clean, 30–35 min.

TOM HUNT'S CHOCOLATE SITUATION

4 oz darkest possible baking chocolate, 8 tbsp (4 oz/113 g) salted butter (cut into pieces), ¼ cup maple syrup, 1 tbsp whiskey, 2 cups chopped or broken stale or hard cookies, softened butter for the loaf pan.

Break or chop the chocolate into small pieces. In in a double boiler or small metal bowl set over simmering water, combine with the butter, maple syrup, and whiskey. Stir well until everything melts together. Stir in the cookies. Butter a loaf pan. Pour in the chocolate mixture, refrigerate, and cut into pieces to eat once it's firm enough, 3½–4 hr. Keep in the refrigerator.

COOKIE PUDDING

5–6 stale or hard cookies, 1 cup heavy cream, 1 tbsp powdered sugar, ½ cup yogurt, grated zest of 1 lemon.

Roughly smash the cookies. In a chilled bowl, whip the cream with the powdered sugar to very soft peaks. Add the yogurt and whip to slightly stiffer but still soft peaks. Mix in the lemon zest and smashed cookies. Divide among four glasses. Top each with a leftover cookie bit if you have. Cover and refrigerate for 2 hr or until serving.

COOKIE CLUSTERS

1–1½ cups broken or crushed stale cookies, 8 oz bittersweet chocolate (in pieces).

Place the cookies in a large bowl. Line a baking sheet with parchment paper. In a double boiler or a small bowl set over a pot of simmering water, melt the chocolate, then cool to 90°F. Pour the chocolate over the cookie pieces and stir to coat all. Spoon clusters onto the baking sheet. Refrigerate until set, 2–3 hr.

SUMMER TRIFLE

1 cup heavy cream, powdered sugar, 2 cups crumbled cookies (plain, sugar cookies, biscotti, wafers, sandies), 2 cups fresh berries.

In a bowl, with an electric mixer, beat the cream and a sprinkle of powdered sugar to just barely stiff peaks. In individual glasses or a serving bowl, layer the whipped cream, then cookies, then berries. Repeat, then eat!

ANY FRUIT CRUMBLE COFFEE CAKE

Butter for the pan, 2 cups (240 g) all-purpose flour, ½ cup (100 g) sugar, 1 tbsp baking powder, ½ tsp salt, 5 tbsp plus 1 tsp (76 g) room-temperature butter, ¾ cup milk, 1 egg (beaten), up to 2 cups any fruit crumble (with or without the crumble topping). *For the topping:* ½ cup brown sugar, 2 tbsp all-purpose flour, 2 tbsp butter, ½ cup chopped toasted nuts (walnuts, pecans, pistachios) or staling galette or pie crumbs, or nut dust.

Heat the oven to 375°F. Butter an 8 × 8-inch baking pan. In a bowl, with an electric mixer, combine the flour, sugar, baking powder, and salt. Add the butter and combine. Add the milk and egg and mix to just combine. It doesn't have to be smooth. Spoon into the prepared pan. Add the leftover fruit crumble and swirl through the batter. Make the toping: In a bowl, mix the brown sugar, flour, butter, and nuts by hand. Sprinkle over the batter, then bake until a skewer emerges mostly clean, about 20 min. Cut into squares while still warm. Good for breakfast or a snack. (Adapted from The Spruce Eats website)

ANY PASTRY SOUR CREAM COFFEE CAKE

Butter and flour for the pan, 1 cup (200 g) sugar, 8 tbsp (4 oz/113 g) room-temperature butter, 2 eggs, 2 cups (240 g) all-purpose flour, 1 tsp baking powder, ¼ tsp baking soda, ½ tsp salt, 1 cup sour cream or whole-milk yogurt, 1½–2 cups crumbled stale pastry.

Heat the oven to 350°F. Butter and flour a 9½-inch tube pan or a 9 × 9 inch pan, tapping out all the excess flour. In a stand mixer, beat together the sugar, butter, and eggs until fluffy. In another bowl, mix the flour, baking powder, baking soda, and salt. Add the flour mixture to the butter and egg mixture in three additions, alternating with the sour cream or milk, beginning and ending with the flour and beating between additions. Spread half of the mixture in the pan. Sprinkle with half the crumbled pastry. Repeat with the remaining batter and pastry. Bake until a skewer comes out clean or almost clean, 30–40 min. Remove from the oven and let sit 10 min before loosening the edges and then turning it out of the pan.

A variation is to scatter the cake with chopped toasted nuts and drizzle with warm honey just before serving. (Adapted from King Arthur Baking website)

LEFTOVER PASTRY BREAD PUDDING

Butter for the baking dish, 2 eggs, 3 cups heavy cream or half-and-half, ⅔ cup sugar, 2 tbsp melted butter, ¼ tsp ground cinnamon, 2 cups cubed leftover pastries (or a combination of pastry and stale bread).

Butter a medium-size baking dish. In a bowl, whisk together the eggs, cream or half-and-half, sugar, melted butter, and cinnamon. Add the pastries or pastries-bread combo to the prepared baking dish, then pour the custard on top. Let sit 4 hr until the custard is totally absorbed. Don't be shy about pressing it down. Heat the oven to 350°F. Bake uncovered until slightly risen and browned on top, 40–50 min.

TWIZZARDS

8 scoops vanilla ice cream, 1 slice pie (or galette or similar, crumbled).

Put a stand mixer bowl in the freezer for 10 min if you have room. If you don't just skip ahead. Add the ice cream to the bowl. Mix on low with the paddle attachment until smooth, about 1 min. Add the chopped or crumbled pie. Eat with a spoon! If it's an apple pie, a few drops of apple cider can be a nice addition. (Adapted from The BakerMama website)

BUTTER COOKIES

2¼ cups (270 g) all-purpose flour, ½ tsp baking powder, ¼ tsp salt, 12 tbsp (6 oz/170 g) unsalted room-temperature butter, ¾ cup (150 g) sugar, 1 egg (at room temperature), 2 tsp vanilla extract, ¼–½ tsp almond extract (optional).

In a bowl, whisk together the flour, baking powder, and salt. In a stand mixer fitted with the paddle, beat the butter and sugar until completely smooth and creamy, about 2 min. Add the egg, vanilla, and almond extract (if using) and beat until combined, about 1 min. Scrape down the sides and up the bottom of the bowl and beat again as needed to combine. Add the flour mixture to the wet ingredients and mix on low until combined. The dough will be soft. Divide evenly in half. Place each half on a piece of lightly floured parchment paper. With a floured rolling pin, roll the dough out to about ¼ inch thick. Use more flour if the dough seems sticky. Lightly dust one of the rolled-out doughs with flour and place a piece of parchment on top. (This prevents sticking.) Repeat with the second piece of dough. Cover both with plastic wrap or aluminum foil, then refrigerate for at least 1–2 hr and up to 2 days. When you're ready to bake, heat the oven to 350°F. Take out one of the sheets of dough and use a cookie cutter to cut out the cookies. Gather the scraps and reroll, and continue cutting out cookies until all the dough is used. Repeat with the second piece of dough. Arrange the cookies on baking sheets 3 inches apart. Bake for 11–12 min, rotating the sheets front to back halfway through. Allow the cookies to cool on the baking sheet for 5 min, then transfer to a wire rack to cool completely before eating or decorating. (From Sally's Baking Addiction website)

AMY'S BROWNIES

Butter for the pan, 4 oz unsweetened chocolate, 2 sticks (8 oz/225 g) butter, 3 eggs, 1–2 cups (200–400 g) sugar, 2 tsp vanilla extract, 1 cup (120 g) all-purpose flour, chocolate chips (or chocolate wafers or nuts or candy).

Heat the oven to 350°F. Butter a 9 × 13-inch baking pan. Melt the chocolate and 2 sticks butter In a double boiler or a small bowl set over simmering water, melt the chocolate and 2 sticks of butter. Remove from the heat and allow to cool for 5 min. Beat in 1 egg at a time. Add the sugar and vanilla and beat until combined. Add the flour. Spread the batter in the prepared pan and top with chocolate chips or anything else you like. Bake until a skewer emerges mostly clean, 25–30 min. Start checking them after 20 min.

SWEETS

AMARETTI

BITTER GREENS CRUNCH (*10 min*)
2–4 amaretti, 2 tbsp butter, 1 clove garlic, (peeled), 1 sprig rosemary, ½–¾ cup chopped walnuts or whole pine nuts, salt.

Smash the amaretti to the size of chopped walnuts. In a small pan, melt the butter. Add the garlic and rosemary and let sputter for a moment. Add the nuts and amaretti. Stir to toast, adding a pinch of salt. Tip out of the pan once toasted and cool on a plate. Discard (or include) the garlic and rosemary. Delicious sprinkled over a bitter greens or fennel salad or cooked bitter greens.

   Variations are to add a little handful of chopped drained olives, and/or a small spoonful of drained capers.

These can also be used in the Cookie Pudding (p. 477) or Cookie Clusters (p. 477).

APPLE PIE, GALETTE, CROSTATA, OR SIMILAR

Use in Twizzards (p. 478) or instead of the cake in the Cake Crumb Muffins (p. 476).

BAKLAVA OR BAKLAVA FILLING

BAKLAVA RICE PUDDING (*50 min*)
Make rice pudding according to any recipe you like. If using crumbled baklava pastry, retoast it in a 400°F oven for 5 min. If just using baklava filling, proceed with it cold. Spoon either on top of servings of rice pudding.

BEIGNETS

Beignets are donuts, and can certainly be used in the Lemony Donut Pudding (p. 484). They are among the few ingredients in this book I have a hard time envisioning ever being left over. But that is only me.

SWEETS

BISCOTTI

Any single leftover biscotti is wonderful soaked in vin santo and eaten with whipped cream, or used in the Cookie Pudding (p. 477) or in Tom Hunt's Chocolate Situation (p. 476). They can also simply be pulsed to crumbs in a food processor and used to line sweet galettes, like the No One's the Wiser Fruit Galette (p. 102).

BIRTHDAY CAKE

Leftover birthday cake tastes better directly out of the freezer than any other cake, except perhaps wedding cake. Once you have eaten the bites you want, use the cake, frosting removed, to make Cake Crumb Muffins (p. 476) or Tipsy Trifle (p. 475).

BLACKBERRY PIE, GALETTE, CROSTATA, OR SIMILAR

Use in Twizzards (p. 478) or instead of cake in Cake Crumb Muffins (p. 476).

BREAD PUDDING

Drizzle with a little cream or milk and reheat. Or slice and turn into French toast.

BROWNIES

Pulse leftover brownies to crumbs, combine with melted butter, and use as the base for a no-bake cheesecake, or scatter over vanilla ice cream and top it all with whipped cream, or combine with broken meringues, whipped cream, and raspberries for a chocolate Eton mess.

CANDY

Either use in Candy Ice Cubes (p. 476) or add to any chocolate chip or oatmeal cookie recipe, mixing them in when you mix in the chips or oatmeal or raisins, etc.

CANDY CANE

Broken candy canes are great scattered over Amy's Brownies (p. 479). Mix smashed-up candy cane pieces with the chocolate chips or wafers, then scatter over the batter and bake.

CHEESECAKE

CHEESECAKE MILKSHAKE *(5 min)*
1 cup crumbled cheesecake (crust removed and snacked on), 1 cup ice cream, ½ cup whole milk.

Blend well and eat with a spoon.

CHERRY PIE, GALETTE, CROSTATA, OR SIMILAR

Use in Twizzards (p. 478) or instead of cake in Cake Crumb Muffins (p. 476).

CHOCOLATE BAR

HOT CHOCOLATE *(5–10 min)*
Chocolate, whole milk, sugar (optional).

In a small saucepan, melt the chocolate, then add the milk, whisking until smooth, not letting it boil. Taste and add sugar if needed.

Leftover chocolate bars can also be chopped and used in place of chocolate chips in Amy's Brownies (p. 479) or in any chocolate chip cookies.

SWEETS

COOKIES

Stale cookies can be used in Cookie Clusters (p. 477), Cookie Pudding (p. 477), or in a Twizzard (p. 478).

COOKIE DOUGH

Even the longest-frozen cookie dough reliably produces cookies when cut into rounds and baked at 350°F.

CREPES

Leftover crepes can be brought back to life. In a skillet, melt butter, add a cold crepe, leaving it in quarters if that's how it was, or rolled if that's how it seems most comfortable. Sprinkle injudiciously with sugar, and let fry and caramelize until it smells delicious, then eat.

CUPCAKES

Use in the Tipsy Trifle (p. 475) or Cake Crumb Muffins (p. 476).

DANISH

Use in the Any Pastry Sour Cream Coffee Cake (p. 478) or in the Leftover Pastry Bread Pudding (p. 478).

DONUTS (APPLE CIDER, VANILLA, PLAIN)

It's fine to combine any of the listed types.

LEMONY DONUT PUDDING (*1 hr*)
Butter for the baking dish, 2 eggs, ¼ cup sugar, grated zest of 1 lemon, ¼ tsp ground cardamom, ¼ tsp ground cinnamon, 2 tbsp melted butter, 1½ cups whole milk, 4 cups quartered donuts.

Heat the oven to 350°F. Butter a small to medium baking dish. In a bowl, whisk together the eggs, sugar, lemon zest, cardamom, and cinnamon. Add the melted butter and milk and stir to combine. Spread the donuts in the prepared baking dish and pour the custard mixture over them, pressing down and smashing as needed. Let sit for 10–15 min to absorb. Bake until browned and golden and slightly risen, 40–45 min (depending on how pudding-y or firm you like it). Let cool for 15 min before eating. Good with whipped cream.

DONUT EGG AND CHEESE (*5 min*)
1 donut, 1½ tbsp butter, 1 egg, salt, 1 tbsp grated cheddar.

Carefully slice the donut in half horizontally as you would a bagel. (If it's so old you're worried it's going to crumble, sprinkle it lightly with water first.) In a small skillet, melt ½ tbsp of the butter. Reduce the heat as much as possible and cook the donut, cut-side down, in the butter until the cut side is nicely browned and crisped, 30 sec–1 min. Meanwhile, in a bowl, whisk the egg with a tiny sprinkle of salt and the cheddar. In a second skillet, melt the remaining 1 tbsp of the butter and scramble the egg and cheese to the texture you like. Remove the donut to a plate, cut-side up. Top with the egg and eat—you may need a fork and knife. Good with hot sauce.

DONUTS, CHOCOLATE

Substitute chocolate donuts for the apple cider or plain ones in the Lemony Donut Pudding (p. 484), but omit the lemon zest.

FROSTING

CANDY DOTS (*a few days of waiting*)
Leftover frosting readily becomes the penny candy that is just dots of . . . well, icing . . . on wax paper. Put frosting into a zip-seal plastic bag, snip off one corner, squeeze into dots on wax paper and leave to harden. Divvy out as needed. You can also make them different colors by adding food coloring or a touch of beet juice or turmeric or blueberry juice before piping and dotting.

FRUITCAKE

Two strange facts entwine in the case of fruitcake. 1) There is always some left. And 2) It never goes bad. I recommend slicing what *is* left very thinly and then toasting and buttering it heavily, and sandwiching in things with strong flavors, like Gorgonzola cheese and fig jam, or marmalade and cooked bacon, or thick slices of good brie, and then eating it as a snack with a few sips of mid-afternoon sherry, or a cup of very strong tea. There will still be some left, of course, but you will run out in time for the next fruitcake.

FUDGE

Stale fudge makes the best hot chocolate.

FUDGY HOT CHOCOLATE *(5–7 min)*
In a small pot, add a 1–2-inch cube of fudge per 1 cup of milk and whisk over medium heat until melted. Heaven.

GINGERBREAD

GINGERBREAD CRUMBS *(5–15 min)*
Heat staling gingerbread in a 250°F oven until hard, if needed. In a food processor, pulse to crumbs, then freeze. Add to your next graham cracker or cookie crust.

GRAHAM CRACKERS

Stale graham crackers can be recrisped. Heat the oven to 225°F. Spread the graham crackers in a single layer on a baking sheet and slow-bake until the graham crackers are crisp again. Or make a:

GRAHAM CRACKER CRUST *(20 min)*
1¾ cups stale graham cracker crumbs, 2 tbsp powdered sugar, 6 tbsp (3 oz/85 g) melted butter.

Heat the oven to 350°F. In a bowl, combine the graham cracker crumbs, powdered sugar, and melted butter. Press it into a 9-inch pie pan, letting it come up the sides. Bake until you can smell the graham crackers, 10–15 min. Remove, cool, and fill with a creamy filling, like cheesecake, chocolate pudding, or meringue. (From King Arthur Baking website)

GRANOLA

GRANOLA COOKIES *(20 min)*
8 tbsp (4 oz/113 g) room-temperature butter, scant 1 cup (185 g) sugar, 1 egg, ½–1 tsp vanilla extract, 1 cup plus 2 tbsp (135 g) all-purpose flour, ¼ tsp salt, ½ tsp baking soda, ¼ tsp ground cinnamon, ½–1 cup granola. *Optional additions:* a handful of shredded coconut or raisins, some chopped walnuts, or any combination.

Heat the oven to 375°F. Line a baking sheet with parchment paper. In a stand mixer, beat the butter and sugar until combined. Beat in the egg and vanilla. In a separate bowl, whisk together the flour, salt, baking soda, and cinnamon. Add the flour mixture to the sugar-butter mixture and whisk to combine. Stir in the granola and any add-ins by hand. Drop by the tbsp in glops at least 2 inches apart on the lined baking sheet. Bake until cooked and lightly crisped around the edges, about 10 min.

HALVAH

HALVAH BROWNIES *(30–40 min)*
Butter for the baking dish, 2 cups dark chocolate chips (70% cacao), 2 sticks (8 oz/225 g) butter (cut into pieces), 4 eggs, 1⅔ cups (335 g) sugar, 1 cup (120 g) all-purpose flour, ½ tsp salt, ½ cup tahini, ½ cup halvah (broken into little pieces).

Heat the oven to 350°F. Butter a 9 × 13-inch baking dish. In a metal bowl placed over a small pot of boiling water, melt the chocolate and butter. Remove from the heat and stir until shiny, then cool to room temperature. In a large bowl, whisk the eggs and sugar until pale and creamy, 3–5 min. Gently fold the chocolate mixture into the egg, then gently fold in the flour and salt. Pour the batter into the prepared baking dish. Dollop the tahini onto the batter in 10–12 places, swirling through, then dot with halvah, pushing it in a little. Bake until just set on the border and still a little wobbly in the middle, 18–20 min. Cut and eat warm or at room temperature. (Adapted from Yotam Ottolenghi's website)

ICE CREAM, MELTED

Melted ice cream can be refrozen and then used in milkshakes.

JELL-O

It's worth remembering that you can rewarm Jell-O in a double boiler and then reset it. If you forgot to add a layer of pretzels and whipped cream the first time, you have a second chance.

KNAFEH

Knafeh reheats well, in a hot oven or on the stovetop, uncovered. It can be reheated a few times. Leftovers are also delicious used in the Summer Trifle (p. 477).

MARSHMALLOWS

Hard marshmallows can be resoftened. They just need consistent heat applied briefly. Put them in a silicone bag and seal tightly and pour boiling water over them and they should soften up. Alternatively, you can put the bag in a bowl of very hot water for 2 min or so. Or you can use them in Bottom of the Box of Cereal Bars (p. 465) or Popcorn Treats (p. 468). If you end up with melty and sticky marshmallows, on the other hand, scrape them out of the bag and into a bowl. Then use as above.

MARZIPAN

Hard marzipan can be resoftened. Place it in a double boiler and knead it as it warms or microwave in 10–30-sec intervals until it's soft and pliant.

MERINGUES, CRUMBLED

Use crumbled meringes in the Summer Trifle (p. 477).

MILKSHAKE, MELTED

Refreeze a melted milkshake and then blend with an immersion blender or in a stand blender until it's a milkshake again.

MOUSSE

Mousse improves—becomes denser and fuller flavored—over a few days. If you don't think you'll finish it, freeze it in ice pop molds. Or make:

CLAIRE ROULIN'S MOUSSE BROWNIES *(30 min)*
Butter for the pan, 2 oz dark chocolate (melted), 8 tbsp (4 oz/113 g) melted butter plus for pan, 2 cups mousse, 1 cup sugar (200 g), 1½ cups flour (180 g).

Heat the oven to 350°F. Butter an 8 × 8-inch brownie pan. In a bowl, gently stir together all the ingredients. Pour the batter into the prepared pan. Bake until just set, about 25 min. Slice while still warm.

MUFFINS

Use leftover muffins in the Any Pastry Sour Cream Coffee Cake (p. 478) or Leftover Pastry Bread Pudding (p. 478), or, if it doesn't seem too involuted, make Cake Crumb Muffins (p. 476).

OREOS, STALE

Let's be honest. Oreos are good stale.

PANDORO OR PANETTONE

NUTELLA SANDWICHES *(5 min)*
Pandoro, butter, Nutella.

Slice the pandoro into ¼-inch-thick slices. Butter one side of each. Spread Nutella on the unbuttered side of one slice of pandoro. Heat a griddle or cast-iron skillet over medium heat. Place the Nutella-slice onto the griddle, butter-side down, then cover with the second slice of bread, butter-side up. Griddle until the bottom is lightly toasted and brown and then flip, cooking the second side to brown. Continue with any remaining sandwiches. Eat warm. The same thing can be done with day-old glazed yeast donuts, or any others lightly sweet yeasted bread or bun.

Or use in French Toast (p. 181) or Bread Pudding (p. 182).

PASTRY

If your pastries are flabby and saggy but you are sanguine about recrisping them and eating them again, put them on a wire rack set in a sheet pan in a 275°–300°F oven until they feel crisp! Just a few min should do it.

Otherwise, any stale or staling pastry can be used in the Any Pastry Sour Cream Coffee Cake (p. 478) or the Leftover Pastry Bread Pudding (p. 478).

PIE DOUGH

CINNAMON SUGAR TWISTS *(25 min)*
Pie dough scraps, melted butter or heavy cream, cinnamon sugar.

Heat the oven to 375°F. Combine the dough scrapes into a long ribbon. Paint with melted butter or heavy cream, then sprinkle with cinnamon sugar. Braid two pieces into a twist and cook until crisp, about 20 min. A very good treat.

POUND CAKE

Use staling pound cake in the Tipsy Trifle (p. 475) or Cake Crumb Muffins (p. 476).

RICE KRISPIES TREATS

I have tried to stale these. I left one uncovered at room temperature for days, and another uncovered in the refrigerator. I could not stale them. They went from chewy to crispy, but remained utterly delicious.

RICE PUDDING

KLATKAGERS/DANISH PANCAKES *(10 min)*
1 egg, 1 tbsp sugar, 1 tsp vanilla extract, ¼ cup milk, 2 tbsp melted butter, 1 cup rice pudding, ⅓ cup all-purpose flour, butter or ghee for cooking, jam or syrup for serving.

In a bowl, whisk together the egg, sugar, vanilla, milk, melted butter, rice pudding, and flour. Cook as you would any other pancakes, by the ladle or spoonful, in batches, in melted butter or ghee. In Denmark these are served with jam, but you can serve them with whatever you like. (Adapted from Nordic Food & Living website)

RICE PUDDING MUFFINS *(25–30 min)*
Butter for the muffin tin, 1 cup rice pudding, 2 tbsp melted butter, 1 egg, 1 tsp vanilla extract, 3 tbsp sugar, 1 tsp baking powder, ½ tsp baking soda, ⅔ cup all-purpose flour. *Optional additions:* ½ cup raisins or other dried fruit, or nuts, or a combination.

Heat the oven to 350°F. Butter a muffin tin. In a bowl, mix together the pudding, melted butter, egg, vanilla, sugar, baking powder, baking soda, flour, and optional additions, letting lumps remain as they feel compelled to. Divide among the muffin cups. Bake until a skewer emerges mostly clean, 20–22 min. Let cool a few min in the muffin tin before cooling on a rack or plate.

HOW TO GIVE THANKS
Empty containers

There are hundreds of ways to kneel down and kiss the ground.

—*Rumi*

Every winter, I silently marvel at the birds outside my window, pecking at bare branches. I admire their conviction that the branches aren't bare at all.

The last stroke of scallion and ginger and oil left in a bowl will dress hot cooked noodles, if the noodles are tipped into the waiting bowl. The paste stuck to the sides of the mustard jar will join a new sauce if encouraged to, via vigorous shaking. This is just as true of a thumbnail of chili sauce or miso, which can season scrambled eggs. (This is achieved by cracking eggs directly into an "empty" jar, replacing the lid, shaking vehemently, then scrambling.) Even a sticky pan from which a sauté has been retrieved can contribute to another meal, if you leave it on the stove until it's time to warm the rice or the broth.

If it will bother you to see a messy pan on the stove, turn on its burner, add a bit of water, and swish it around today. Add a splash of fish sauce, or vegetable cooking water, or bean broth, bring it to a quick boil, pour it into a jar, and you'll have savory broth at the ready for a lunchtime soup tomorrow. Similarly, you're not making a salad *now*, but if you add vinegar and olive oil to the almost-empty mustard jar and shake it rather than rinsing it out, when you do make a salad, there a vinaigrette will be.

I used to be single and share a house with a roommate. No one minded that the refrigerator overflowed with jars scraped nearly clean, or containing murky liquids that had been hastily added and shaken—and the freezer with bags of fennel and herb stems, meat bones, farro liquid, and pickle juice. I labeled nothing. No one minded, but now someone does. I now keep scraps for stock, bean broth, and poaching or confiting liquid in one section of the freezer. (Or I try.) Though I vowed I never would, I take masking tape and label jars or bowls to be stored away, whether or not I've added vinegar and oil to make vinaigrette—though in that case I would boldly label the result "vinaigrette." It always seemed silly to me to waste tape, and it's not hard to dip a finger into a bowl or jar to confirm a suspected identity. But my husband refuses. Plus used tape can be put in a fire.

The best trick I have for ensuring that I *see* the bits that remain is to keep my kitchen inventory low. If necessity is the mother of all invention, it is also the parent of the conviction that somewhere, you must have stored *something* away to make the beans taste better, and to give the salad some crunch. This sort of saving is rewarding in the same way praying is: For a moment you are fully present in your life, clear about the value of every last bit of it.

ALMOND BUTTER, EMPTY JAR

EMPTY JAR NUT BUTTER NOODLES *(15–20 min)*

¼ cup hot water, empty almond butter jar, 1 clove garlic, ¼ tsp salt, ¼ cup fish sauce, 1½ tbsp lime juice (about 1 lime), 1 tbsp sugar, 1–2 fresh or dried chiles, 1 pound or so mung bean or rice noodles (soaked in water), salt, a handful of chopped peanuts, a big handful of chopped herbs (cilantro, basil, mint, or any combination), a big handful of julienned carrot and cucumber (or just one of them), any "nut dust" you have at the bottoms of cans/bags/containers of nuts.

Add the hot water to the empty jar and scrape all the remaining nut butter down to the bottom. Mix well into a nutty liquid, closing and shaking if helpful. Pound the garlic to a paste with the salt and add to the jar. Add the fish sauce, lime juice, sugar, and chile(s). Shake well. Cook the noodles in salted boiling water, then drain and mix with the sauce. Top with peanuts, herbs, julienned vegetables, and "nut dust." Great at any temperature.

AMBA, EMPTY JAR

AMBA RAITA OR AYRAN *(2–3 min)*

For a raita, fill an empty amba jar with yogurt about halfway, scraping and stirring the sides as you do. Close and shake well, open and pour into a bowl, scraping well. Use as you would any raita. If you want a refreshing drink (ayran), do the same thing, but once you've emptied the yogurt into a bowl, whisk in a bit more yogurt and some water. Taste, and when you like the flavor and consistency, pour over ice and drink.

BALSAMIC VINEGAR, EMPTY BOTTLE

Mostly full bottles of balsamic seem, like Tupperware lids, to exist in perpetual excess. Once a cook realizes that rice vinegar and wine vinegar can adapt themselves infinitely, while balsamic retains a sticky stubbornness, the balsamic falls into disuse. If you have a half-full bottle, boil its contents down to make a delicious, sweet syrup for ice cream. Once you've emptied a bottle, swirl boiling water around its insides. This will make a pleasantly sweet and acidic evening tea, with a little honey stirred in, and maybe some rye whiskey to mark the occasion of having used up the balsamic.

BARBECUE SAUCE, EMPTY BOTTLE

EMPTY BARBECUE BOTTLE STIR-FRY SAUCE *(3 min)*

Empty barbecue sauce bottle, 1 tbsp finely minced garlic, 1 tbsp finely minced fresh ginger, 2 tbsp sesame oil, 2 tbsp lime juice, 1 tbsp fish sauce, 1 tsp salt, 1 tsp sugar.

Combine all the ingredients in the empty bottle. Shake well and add to stir-fried noodles and/or meat and/or rice instead of soy sauce, or oyster sauce, or another stir-fry sauce.

MEAT BRAISING LIQUID *(2 min)*

Pour warm water or chicken or vegetable stock into an empty barbecue sauce bottle. Close and shake well and use as part of the braising liquid in any Southwestern or other chili-ish braise, including actual chili. For a braised meat recipe, see Braised Meat (p. 298).

BUTTER WRAPPERS

Butter wrappers make great baking pan greasers. Save yours in a stack in a container in the baking drawer, and when it's time to butter a pan, use as many as needed, rubbing what's left directly into the baking pan or onto the sheet pan. They are also wonderful container tops when the real Tupperware lids go missing. Press butter wrappers directly onto the surface of a leftover to be stored. The thin layer of fat on the wrapper will be further protective of whatever it covers. If you have grits or polenta or oatmeal that you want to keep warm and soft, wrappers can also be laid on its surface, keeping it from developing a crust.

CASHEW BUTTER, EMPTY JAR

Use to make Empty Jar Nut Butter Noodles (p. 499).

CHILI SAUCE, EMPTY BOTTLES AND JARS

EMPTY CHILI SAUCE NOODLES *(15 min)*
About a half pound/8 oz bean vermicelli or thin rice noodles, salt, lime juice (up to 1 lime), 3 tbsp fish sauce, ½ cup total chili sauce from almost-empty containers, 2 cups julienned vegetables (peeled cucumber, carrot, scallion, and/or whole kernels of corn), 1 cup chopped mixed fresh herbs (cilantro, mint, basil), ½–⅔ cup chopped roasted peanuts.

Cook the vermicelli in salted boiling water. Pour bits of lime juice and fish sauce into each nearly empty chili sauce container and shake each well, continuing until you've used about 3 tbsp of fish sauce and 1 lime's worth of juice. Combine all the loosened-up chili sauce in one of the empty sauce jars. Shake well, pour over the noodles, and toss to combine. Garnish with the vegetables, herbs, and peanuts, and eat.

FISH SAUCE, EMPTY BOTTLE

Pour fresh lime juice and a tiny sprinkle of sugar directly into an empty fish sauce bottle. Shake it well, then use it in any Thai or other Southeast Asian noodle or rice dish or soup or salad.

GOAT CHEESE, EMPTY CONTAINER

SLIGHTLY GOAT CHEESY SCRAMBLED EGGS *(5 min)*
2–3 eggs, empty goat cheese container, salt, butter.

Crack eggs directly into the empty goat cheese container and beat well with a fork, scraping up any goat cheese that remains. Salt lightly. In a skillet, melt butter, add the eggs, scramble to your liking, and eat. This can also be done with an empty feta or other farmer-style cheese container.

GOCHUJANG, EMPTY JAR

Use in Empty Chili Sauce Noodles (recipe above).

EMPTY CONTAINERS

HONEY, EMPTY JAR

HONEY-GARLIC VINAIGRETTE (*15 min*)
½ clove garlic (finely chopped), 1–2 tbsp lemon juice, ½ tsp mustard, ¼ tsp salt plus to taste, 5 tbsp olive oil, empty honey jar.

Combine everything in the honey jar and shake well. Let sit 10 min before tasting. Taste on a lettuce leaf for salt and adjust.

HOT SAUCE, EMPTY BOTTLE

Use in Empty Chili Sauce Noodles (p. 501).

ITALIAN DRESSING, EMPTY BOTTLE

BOTTOMLESS VINAIGRETTE (*5 min each time*)
1 cup olive oil, ⅓ cup red or white wine vinegar, 1 tsp sugar, 1 tbsp dried oregano, salt and freshly ground black pepper to taste, empty Italian dressing bottle.

Add all the ingredients to the empty bottle and shake! And then do it again, and again! Good on Pizzeria Salad (p. 54).

JAM, EMPTY JAR

Pour a little milk or nut milk or yogurt into the nearly empty jam jar and shake it. Use the liquid as a smoothie base.

Or make tea in your empty jam jar, or add a shot of your booze of choice, shake, and pour over ice. Or make:

JAM-HONEY SYRUP (*5 min*)
Boil a little water and pour it into an empty jam jar. Scrape well and then shake to remove all the bits of jam. In a pot, combine with a few spoonfuls of honey. Bring to a quick boil, then as soon as it's syrupy, use it for drizzling over biscuits or pancakes or in tea.

KETCHUP, EMPTY BOTTLE

The only thing better than fish sauce in fried rice is fish sauce that has first been poured into an empty ketchup bottle, shaken, and *then* added to fried rice. The sweetness of the ketchup is a perfect counterpoint to fish sauce's salt and umami. If you have an empty ketchup bottle and enough fish sauce, add the latter to the former and label it "for fried rice."

MAPLE SYRUP, EMPTY BOTTLE

SWEET WATER (*1 min*)
Fill the empty bottle, which is caked with maple sugar crystals, with water. Shake very well, then shake some more, then drink on ice. Delicious. If you use a bit less water, you can also use the well-shaken liquid as a substitute for sugar.

MAYONNAISE, EMPTY JAR

Use an empty mayonnaise jar for the Almost Empty Container White Sauce (p. 506).

MISO PASTE, EMPTY JAR

MISO BUTTER (*3 min*)
Place a few tbsp of room-temperature butter in the empty miso paste jar and smash it all around to get it miso-y. Eat wherever you eat butter.

Or use an empty miso paste jar to make a very simple savory broth by adding hot water to it, closing, shaking, and then using in soup or beans or to braise meat.

MOLASSES, EMPTY JAR

Warm ½ cup water or milk and pour into the empty jar, replace the lid and shake well. Taste, then drink as is, or use to make another warm drink, improved by the subtle complexity of the molasses.

MUSTARD, EMPTY JAR

An empty jar of mustard is a good place to make any vinaigrette. Mix the ingredients inside it and shake well.

PARCHMENT PAPER

Parchment paper can be reused. Dust off any crumbs, roll it into a tube, secure it with a rubber band or bit of tape, and use it again until something sticky sends it out of service.

PEANUT BUTTER, EMPTY JAR

Use in the recipe for Empty Jar Nut Butter Noodles (p. 499).

RANCH DRESSING, EMPTY BOTTLE

This is a good place to make a Creamy Vinaigrette (p. 376), using the bottle as the bowl. Shake rather than whisk.

SAMBAL, EMPTY CONTAINER

BETTER MAYONNAISE (*1 min*)
Scoop some mayonnaise into your empty sambal jar. Stir it around. Now it is better.

Or use in Empty Chili Sauce Noodles (p. 501).

SEASONING (SUCH AS LAWRY'S OR OLD BAY), EMPTY CAN

It is hard to overstate the deliciousness of a sauce of mayonnaise, mixed with a tiny bit of seasoning salt and lime juice. Make it directly in the empty can. This is an ideal dipping sauce for fried potatoes or potato chips.

SICHUAN CHILI CRISP, EMPTY JAR

Use in the recipe for Empty Chili Sauce Noodles (p. 501).

SRIRACHA SAUCE, EMPTY BOTTLE

Use in the Empty Chili Sauce Noodles (p. 501).

STIR-FRY, SPICY, PAN

MOST DELICIOUS SOUP IN THE WORLD (*10 min*)
Empty stir-fry pan, 4 cups miso soup, cubed tofu if you have it, any rice leftover from the stir-fry meal.

Set the empty stir-fry pan over medium-high heat. Add the miso soup and heat until you can just scrape all the stuck bits off the pan and stir them into the soup. Add any tofu and any leftover rice. Taste and adjust seasoning, now or right before you eat it. A tip: It's best to make this right after the stir-fry dinner. It makes doing dishes much easier, and produces soup for lunch the next day.

TAMARIND PASTE, EMPTY JAR

If you swirl hot water around an empty container of tamarind paste, you can get another tamarind serving out of it.

VANILLA, EMPTY BOTTLE

The very tiny bit of vanilla inevitably left in an empty bottle can usually make one more tsp extract. Pour in water, shake, and use.

VANILLA BEAN, USED

VANILLA EXTRACT (*a few months, but all waiting*)
Put the used vanilla bean(s) in a small bottle or jar. Cover it with vodka. Let it sit until it's the color of vanilla extract, then remove the bean(s). You can do this several times with the same bean.

VANILLA SUGAR (*a few weeks, but all waiting*)
Put the used vanilla bean(s) in a small jar. Cover it with sugar. Let it sit until it smells and tastes of vanilla, then remove the bean(s). Use the sugar anytime you're baking something that also calls for vanilla. You can do this several times with the same bean.

YOGURT, EMPTY CONTAINER

ALMOST EMPTY CONTAINER WHITE SAUCE (*5 min*)
1 small clove garlic, salt, ¼ cup yogurt (still in the container), 1½ tbsp mayonnaise, 1 tbsp tahini.

Pound the garlic to a paste with a little salt and add it to the yogurt container. Add the mayonnaise, tahini, and 1 tbsp water and shake it all well. Very good on shawarma or gyros or over salads or on any sandwich.

ACKNOWLEDGMENTS

Thank you to the dozens of hands and minds that helped make this book. Thank you to Heather Schroder, who supported me through a truly bad idea about biblical food and gave me free rein as it evolved into a leftovers cookbook. Thank you to Kari Stuart, who talked me through every facet of every problem, real and imagined, and continues to, weekly. Thank you, as ever, to Kara Watson at Scribner, with her seemingly limitless patience for my vicissitudes and inability to leave good enough alone.

This book would have been all text had I not met Caitlin Winner, a gloriously talented painter and human. To work with Caitlin on finding the beauty in bits of leftover food and empty jars, and watch as she ushered them onto canvas, was humbling and heart-lifting. The beauty of Caitlin's work kept me reading and re-reading these hundreds of pages on scraps. The gentle genius Alvaro Villanueva turned rather mad ideas into a reality, which, to my mind, reads clearly and easily—a feat given how unclear and complicated it was to sort out what went where and how it should look on the page. I would trust my overcomplications to Alvaro any day, confident that he could make them comprehensible.

I'm grateful for my collaboration with two wonderful people: Amanda Kingsley, whom I tasked with writing down the name of every ingredient she could find or think of, A to Z, whose work became the backbone of this book, and Morgan Marshall, who manifested themselves right into the middle of my life when I needed them the most. Amanda and Morgan, I hope when you're old you encounter humans twenty years your junior who support and collaborate and contribute the way you both did to this book. Thank you, my friends.

Piper Olf, the serene soul who sat at a desk in my studio through quarantine, tasting hundreds of leftovers creations, day in, day out, failures and successes both: thank you. I would not have been able to do all this cooking without your steady presence and honest responses. I hope you never have to eat bacon shortbread again—because of you, no one else will have to. Thank you to all my generous recipe testers: Kate Ray, Liza Agrba, Sheila Janes, Allegra Ben-Amotz, Hannah Diel, Erin Hughes, Sara Saljoughi, Laura Harrold, Rachel Wertheimer, Janel Jin, Chessa Hickox, Rebecca Cooney, Laura Krug, Stephanie Ganz, Amy Adler, Katherine Betzer, Grace Kennedy, Karla Roberts, Amiel Stanek, Danny Amend, Claire Roulin, Amy Brill, Fiona Jordan, Michele Duell, Suzannah Schneider, Anya Binsacca, Lauren Deal, Jacqueline Lawler, Lizi Breit, Laura Grego, Rachel Freeman, Martina Trommer, Jilly Tilley, Katherine A Bryant, Youngna

Park, Zachary Leener, Emily Crook-Hanna, Tim Snow, Katie Walker, Jaclyn Findlay, Rachel Kobasa, Charlotte Freeman, Ryan McLaughlin, Tessa Pitre, Anna May Seaver, Niki Kenny, Melissa Alford, Diane Lieu, Terry Honsaker, Julie Metz, Anna Harb, Marty Brown, Marion Nelson, David Klein, Caryna Camerino, Kate Jones, Leslie Engel, Jim and Carolyn Olivier, Rachel Rasmussen, G Cherichello, Chetney Marie Dudzic, Heather Borkowski, Kristin Kimball, Alicia Reyer, Bonnie Suarez, Alan Plofker, Wendy Rubin, Martha Murray, Michelle Spanedda, Abi Sessions, and Laura Pfeffer. Thank you to Rye Gentleman, for making some RULES to which this wily text could (try to) adhere.

Samin Nosrat and Roger Hodge, thank you for reading everything I write with open hearts. Thank you to Elazar Sontag, Klancy Miller, Andy Baraghani, Stephen Satterfield, and Harold McGee for your words of support.

Thank you to the brilliant and tireless copyeditors and proofreaders who found my mistakes.

My everlasting gratitude to the team at Scribner, especially Nan Graham, Stu Smith, Jaya Miceli, Abigail Novak, Brianna Yamashita, Sabrina Pyun, Ruth Lee-Mui, and most especially Katie Rizzo, production editor extraordinaire. And also most especially to Vanessa Santos, Ilana Saperstein, and Ella Stearns at MONA Creative, who put up with so much digital ineptitude and my general awkwardness and worked tirelessly to get this book into hands.

Thank you to Olivia Tincani for recipes, inspiration, and sisterhood deeper than I knew existed. Thank you to Christine Jones for believing in me. Thank you to my brother and my mother, my fellow cooks, sharers of the kitchen, companions at the irons. Thank you to all lovers of economy, all scrimpers and savers, everyone who taught me that to keep was better than to waste, and that to appreciate was the truest and only godlike materialism. Thank you to Pete, my love, my love, you whimsical and steady man. Thank you to Louis, my love, my love: though you rarely eat my food, I cook it all for you.

Thank you to all mothers everywhere, and to new cooks, trying to figure out this capricious activity called cooking. Thank you to readers for sharing this time with me.

INDEX

lemon(s) (*cont.*)
  vegetable soup, 49
  zest of, 116–17, 121
lemonade, 456
lemon balm, 57
lentil(s), 204, 231–32
  soup, 253
lettuce
  bolting or flowering, 57
  Grace Young's stir-fried iceberg,
    54
  iceberg, core of, 53
  iceberg, old, 53–54
  pizzeria salad, 54
  romaine, 81–82
  salad, 383
  salad with tea leaf dressing,
    453
  saucey blue cheese salad, 53
  wilted, 57–58
  wraps, larb, 331
limes, xvi, 121
  peel or zest of, 116–17
linguine with clams, 357–58
lo bak go, 58
lobster
  cooked, 280
  shells of, 280–81
  stock, 253, 280–81
lo mein, 358
lovage, 59
lox, 281

macadamia nuts, 122
macaronade, 249
macaroni and cheese, 359
  creamy, 144
  fondue, 157
  queso, 415
mackerel, 281
Madison, Deborah, 168
maftoul, 359
Majumdar, Simon, 165
makdous, whipped, 377
makhlouta with pita, 193
Manchego, 161

mangoes
  overripe, 122
  unripe, 122
manicotti, 359
mantou buns, 351
maple syrup, empty bottle of,
    503
mapo tofu, 332
  mashup, 336
maraschino cherry liquid, 123
marinade, 409
marjoram
  stems of, 59
  wilted, 59
marmalade, orange, 127
marshmallows, 488
marzipan, 489
mascarpone, 161
mashed potatoes, 59–61
matar paneer, 61
maté, 456
matzo
  balls, 359
  old, 189
mayonnaise, 395, 409
  aillade, 399
  anchovy, 402
  baba ghanoush, 377
  better, 504
  blue cheese, 143
  empty jar of, 503
  gribiche, 418
  herb, 407
  olive, 410–11
  parsley, 69
  spicy, 396
McDowell, Erin, 236
McGee, Harold, 125, 204
McKinnon, Hetty, 417
meat, 294–345
  barbecued, 304–5
  braised, 298–99
  braising liquid for, 500
  drippings, 315
  fat, 317
  kebab, 327